Scientists under Hitler

Scientists under Hitler

Politics and the Physics Community in the Third Reich

Alan D. Beyerchen

New Haven and London   Yale University Press

Designed by John O. C. McCrillis
and set in Baskerville type.
Printed in the United States of America by
The Vail-Ballou Press, Inc., Binghamton, N.Y.

Published in Great Britain, Europe, Africa, and
Asia (except Japan) by Yale University Press,
Ltd., London. Distributed in Australia and
New Zealand by Book & Film Services,
Artarmon, N.S.W., Australia; and in Japan by
Harper & Row, Publishers, Tokyo Office.

Library of Congress Cataloging in Publication Data
Beyerchen, Alan D   1945–
    Scientists under Hitler.

    Bibliography: p.
    Includes index.
    1. Physics—History—Germany. 2. Physicists
—Germany. 3. National socialism. I. Title.
QC9.G3B48   530'.0943'086   77-2167
ISBN 0-300-01830-4

Contents

Illustrations

Preface

It seems natural to link politics and the physics community in our age of electronic and atomic warfare. Prior to the advent of the sophisticated weapons of World War II, however, this connection was not commonly perceived. Although the importance of technology was well known, politicians tended to regard physics as an esoteric subject that had little relation to the important affairs in life. Physicists viewed politics in a similar light. Until recently historians have reflected these views, writing political history that made only cursory mention of science and producing history of science stripped of its social and political context.

This gap has been particularly conspicuous regarding the Third Reich. Historians of science have been intensely concerned with scientific developments in twentieth century Germany, but they have largely tended to avoid addressing the political environment of research during the Third Reich. Historians of Nazi Germany have been concerned with other professional groups, such as the members of the civil service, the clergy, and the army, but have seldom taken note of the members of the scientific community. This study is an effort to bridge the gap and expand our knowledge and awareness in both fields of history.

The theme of this book is how prominent scientists, particularly physicists, responded to the political environment of the Third Reich. Most of these men were leaders of their professional community; a few were renegades. I have chosen to focus on the physicists in the universities and state-supported research institutions, largely because they formed the core of that gifted group of German scientists whose atomic research eventually helped reveal the political significance of "pure" science. In addition, as the leaders of organized German science and as civil servants, the academic physicists occupied positions of responsibility and authority affecting the entire physics community. They were unable to evade political pressures.

These pressures came principally from two sources, the state and the party. It is fully documented that the policies of the state and party offices were often at odds with one another, and that competing political and ideological factions within the party further confused

matters. The image of the monolith projected by the Nazis has dis-
solved; the picture is now seen more clearly as a montage of rivalries
between mutually antagonistic bureaucratic structures.

Amid the welter of competing influences and powers, the physics
community was forced to deal primarily with two separate phenomena. The first was the government's attempt to align German academia with National Socialism, the most dramatic aspect of which
was the policy of dismissing Jews from the civil service. The second
was an unsuccessful attempt by a small band of politically active
scientists to inject racial considerations into the content and conduct
of physics as a discipline. Considering these developments, the questions which arise in the course of this study are: What was the impact of the dismissal policy upon the German physics community?
Why did the effort to produce an "Aryan physics" eventually fail?
and What was the extent to which the maintenance of professional
values constituted opposition to National Socialism?

In an effort to answer these questions, I have relied primarily on
unpublished documents, tape-recorded interviews, and correspondence with participants. A number of persons have generously made
available private papers in their possession. In this connection, I
owe thanks to Mrs. Richard Courant, Mrs. Wolfgang Finkelnburg,
Mrs. Hermann Lisco and Mrs. Arthur von Hippel (the daughters of
James Franck), Professor Walther Gerlach, Professor Samuel Goudsmit, Professor Werner Heisenberg, and Professor Theodore H. von
Laue. The staffs of various historical research institutions, such as
the Institut für Zeitgeschichte and Deutsches Museum in Munich,
the Bundesarchiv in Koblenz, the Berlin Document Center, and
the Hoover Institution on War, Revolution and Peace at Stanford
have been very helpful. In addition, I wish to express my gratitude
for the encouragement and aid of Professor Charles Weiner, for-
merly of the Center for History of Physics of the American Institute
of Physics in New York; Dr. Judith Goodstein of the California Institute of Technology Archives; Professor Armin Hermann of the
Lehrstuhl für die Geschichte der Naturwissenschaften und Technik
in Stuttgart; and Dr. Hermann Weisert of the Heidelberg Uni-
versitätsarchiv. The abbreviated titles of these and other institutions
as used in the notes are presented in the bibliography.

Materials from one research center need to be explained in more
detail. The Archive for History of Quantum Physics was originally
established at the Library of the University of California at Berkeley

as part of the Sources for History of Quantum Physics (SHQP) project. (For a discussion of the scope of this project, see Thomas Kuhn et al., *Sources for History of Quantum Physics, An Inventory and Report* [Philadelphia: American Philosophical Society, 1967]). The eighty-five microfilm reels and thousands of pages of transcribed interviews of the SHQP holdings form the core of the Archive, which also includes the Niels Bohr Scientific Correspondence (BSC) and other collections of private papers. The location of a letter in the Archive will be designated by the author and recipient, date, abbreviation SHQP or BSC, and two numbers in parentheses. The first number refers to the reel and the second to the section of the reel under which the letter is cataloged, for example, Werner Heisenberg to Niels Bohr, 14 June 1938, BSC (20,2).

I am particularly indebted to Mrs. Leslie Clark and Professor John Heilbron for their aid in the use of Archive materials. Since this study is an effort to bridge the gap between political history and history of science, it is hoped that political historians will take note of the richness of the Archive. Its thousands of documents provide insight into the lives of many prominent and perceptive men and women who by no means limit their discussions strictly to technical matters.

A number of individuals made available useful information through interviews and correspondence. Their time has been deeply appreciated. Professor P. P. Ewald, Mrs. Wolfgang Finkelnburg, Professors Paul Forman, Walther Gerlach, Werner Heisenberg, Friedrich Hund, Theodore H. von Laue, Mrs. Hermann Lisco, Professor Lothar Nordheim, Mrs. Constance Reid, and Professor Otto Scherzer have been kind enough to read and comment upon portions of an earlier version of the manuscript. Professors Forman and Hund are especially remembered for the help and heartening interest they provided.

In addition, I wish to acknowledge the support and helpful criticism of the members of the faculty of the University of California at Santa Barbara, particularly Professor Lawrence Badash and Professor Joachim Remak. From 1967, when he first suggested to me the topic of scientists in Nazi Germany, to the present, the counsel and friendship of Professor Badash has been a constant source of encouragement. To both Professors Badash and Remak I owe much of my desire to understand men and women of the past in the context of their own values. We need not accept their versions of truth, but we must grasp their standards and perceptions if we are to gain the insight which allows us to disagree with them on a basis other than polemic.

There is no adequate way to express the debt I owe to the many friends, relatives, and associates who have patiently tolerated my preoccupation with this topic over the years. Put simply, without their support this book could not have been written. I owe particular thanks to Mr. Frank Smith, whose encouragement made possible the completion of the final version of the manuscript. More than to any-one else, for reasons too numerous to list, I owe a debt of gratitude to my wife, Marila.

Financial assistance was provided during the research and writing of earlier versions of this study by a National Defense Education Act Title IV Fellowship, a National Science Foundation Graduate Fel-lowship, and the Academic Senate of the University of California, Santa Barbara. The indispensable aid of the Inter-library Loan Department of the UCSB library is also deeply appreciated.

All translations are my own unless otherwise indicated.

Cape Cod
August 1976

1. The Background

In the early years of the Third Reich, Max Planck, the dean of German physicists and president of the prestigious Kaiser Wilhelm Society, a government-supported research foundation, was involved in an incident that symbolized the problems facing scientists under Hitler. P. P. Ewald, himself a prominent physicist, recounts the story:

> . . . I think it was on the occasion of the opening of the Kaiser Wilhelm Institute of Metals in Stuttgart, and Planck as president of the Kaiser Wilhelm Gesellschaft came to the opening. And he had to give the talk, and this must have been in 1934, and we were all staring at Planck, waiting to see what he would do at the opening, because at that time it was prescribed officially that you had to open such addresses with "Heil Hitler." Well, Planck stood on the rostrum and lifted his hand half high, and let it sink again. He did it a second time. Then finally the hand came up, and he said, "Heil Hitler." . . . Looking back, it was the only thing you could do if you didn't want to jeopardize the whole Kaiser Wilhelm Gesellschaft.[1]

In retrospect it seems a small incident. Yet it epitomizes the hundreds of decisions required of physicists in the Third Reich, especially those in positions of authority or responsibility, in their efforts to keep their discipline from being politically consumed. The fundamental issue was the extent to which compromise with the regime was necessary in order to retain the greatest possible degree of professional autonomy. Like the vast majority of the professoriate, German physicists desired strongly to remain aloof from political concerns. And also like most of their colleagues, they were not truly able to do so.

The Structure and Attitudes of German Academia

Since their origin during the high and late Middle Ages, German universities—like their counterparts in other lands—have traditionally been centers of training for the middle-class professions of law, medicine, and the ministry. With the development of the modern state in the German cultural area, however, particularly in Prussia in the seventeenth and eighteenth centuries, the institutions of higher

learning also assumed responsibility for the education of the professional civil service.

The administrative bureaucracy was originally composed of aristo-
crats by birth who were in effect the king's personal aides. Beginning with the end of the eighteenth century, however, the civil
service was dominated by an educated aristocracy of merit whose
allegiance was to the state rather than to the monarchy. The new
aristocracy, and generally members of the older nobility as well, conformed to an outlook epitomized by the concept of *Bildung* (education).[2]

Bildung meant much more than advanced instruction and schooling. It also entailed the notion of character and personality formation
within a cultural environment which stressed duty, adherence to
principle, and a lofty concern for the "inner" or "spiritual" (*geistig*)
values of life. These values found their highest expression in the
concept of *Kultur* (culture). In the eighteenth century, the term had
meant the cultivation of mind and spirit, but by the nineteenth century, it had come to connote all of man's humanistic achievements
in society. It was contrasted with *Zivilisation* (civilization), which
was identified with a Western, decadent, utilitarian concern for the
material conditions of life and technological advances.[3]

The connotations of Bildung led rather easily to an air of moral
superiority among the educated (*gebildete*) elite, even toward the
titled nobility.[4] Members of this elite, which the noted scholar Fritz
Ringer has called the German "mandarins," comprised government
officials, doctors, lawyers, ministers, secondary school teachers, university professors, and any others who had received university training.[5] The government funded the universities and held the ultimate
administrative authority over them, but each school had the right to
manage its purely academic affairs. Professors ranked as higher civil
servants and derived especially great prestige from their functions as
the collective repository of the virtues of education and as the trans-
mitters of these values to the future administrators of the state. It
became a fundamental tenet of mandarin ideology, in fact, that the
state itself existed to preserve and protect the culture held in trust
by the aristocracy of education.

During the reform movement which swept through Germany in
the wake of the Napoleonic conquests, the philosophical faculty replaced medicine, law, and theology as the heart of the university.[6]
The humanistic disciplines had to face a growing challenge from the

physical sciences, however, which gained in significance and influence throughout the nineteenth century as a result of technological progress in Germany. Much of the older professoriate regarded the empirical disciplines as manifestations of Zivilisation rather than Kultur and resisted their acceptance in the universities. Nevertheless, by the end of the century, the physical sciences had become an established and dynamic element of German academic life. They brought with them an emphasis on creative research (exemplified by the creation of the Ph.D. research degree) and the importance of the research institute (each organized originally around a laboratory). Research and teaching thus became closely allied in German higher education.[7]

In addition, government and industrial institutes began to proliferate in the late nineteenth and early twentieth centuries in response to the growing need for research. The establishment of chemical laboratories led the way in this development. In 1887 the state-funded Imperial Institute of Physics and Technology (Physikalisch-Technische Reichsanstalt, or PTR) was founded in Berlin as a type of national bureau of standards. By the Weimar period, the PTR was the largest state-supported physical research laboratory in Germany.[8] The Kaiser Wilhelm Society (Kaiser Wilhelm-Gesellschaft, or KWG) was established in 1911 and by the 1920s administered an ever-growing network of research institutes.[9] Part of the KWG funding came from the government and part from private industry. Industrial laboratories for physics were also founded in this period and provided close links between physics and industry.

The purists among the academicians viewed such developments with a mixture of contempt and apprehension. They drew a sharp distinction between the all-encompassing term *Wissenschaft* (learning or scholarship) and the much narrower *Naturwissenschaft* (science).[10] Science was unmistakably regarded as an activity less worthy than pure learning.

Ringer has shown that the "orthodox" position among humanistic scholars about 1900 was based on the fear that their privileges and prestige were threatened by the advent of the industrialized mass age. They were particularly alarmed at the prospect of the "leveling" of society represented by the goals of international socialism. They were opposed to the divisiveness of party politics and energetically defended the "national cause." Many academicians also felt there was a link between the increasing prominence of the Jews in German society and the ills of interest group politics during the Weimar period.[11] The great majority of scholars viewed the Weimar government with icy reserve: they were willing to serve the German state, but not the Social Democrats. They regarded parliamentary politics as sordid and factional, but they did not realize that their own stance, which was allegedly "above politics," was just as divisive as that of the parties they abhorred.[12] The National Socialist German Workers Party of Adolf Hitler was too much a mass movement to attract them. But Nazi rhetoric that rejected the role of a mere political party was appealing. Hitler declared that his movement, too, was above politics. National Socialism promised a national uplifting instead of an international leveling of society.

Ringer omits the natural scientists in his study of academic political attitudes, but among physicists, the political consensus was also strongly nationalist. Paul Forman has demonstrated that in physics, as in the academic community at large, this outlook was not considered political at all.[13] Forman has suggested that their deep-seated conviction that science and politics were a priori incompatible prevented the physicists from perceiving the political nature of their own behavior.[14]

Although a wide range of nationalist behavior was regarded by scientists as nonpolitical, open support for the Weimar republic was not permissible. Thus the travels of Albert Einstein abroad in the early postwar years, during which the physicist served as an instrument of Weimar foreign policy, exceeded the bounds of acceptable nonpolitical activity.[15] Einstein's avowed pacifism, internationalism, and support of Zionism contributed to his status as an outsider in most German scientific circles during the 1920s.

On the other hand, open opposition to Weimar was also regarded as a transgression of the professional code. The two most prominent physicists whose right-wing behavior was frowned upon by their colleagues were the Nobel laureates Philipp Lenard and Johannes Stark. Their overt support for National Socialism was unusual among academicians and truly exceptional among physicists. Their vocal adherence to *völkisch* (national-racial) concepts—not only in politics, but in their views on the nature and practice of physics itself—marked them as renegades among their fellow scientists during both the Weimar and Nazi periods.

The strident anti-Semitism displayed by Lenard and Stark was unconventional in German academia, but a milder version was widespread. This variety was expressed mainly in professorial appointments. In 1909–10, for example, 19 percent of the instructors at German universities were of Jewish origin, while Jews accounted for only 7 percent of the full professors. Anti-Semitism was weaker in some fields than others, however, and medicine and the natural sciences had an appreciably greater representation of Jews than other disciplines.[16] Up to 1933, the extent of Jewish participation in these fields continued to increase, so that the anti-Semitic policies of the National Socialists had a highly significant impact upon academic science.

In addition to their belief that nationalist considerations transcended politics and to their practice of quiet anti-Semitism in professional appointments, the vast majority of Weimar academicians also subscribed to the rejection of a vaguely conceived "materialism." The academicians used this term as an ambiguous catchword to represent the source of all the ills of German society. Materialism meant too much commercialism, concern for money, industry, and technology. It connoted a general moral and social decadence and lack of respect for intellectual and spiritual values. Materialism fed the vulgar tastes of the masses and was responsible for their lack of national sentiments (evidenced by their votes for the Social Democratic and Communist parties).[17] It stood for the evils of Zivilisation enthroned above the virtues of Kultur.

The rejection of modern industrial society was not limited to the universities, of course. Assaults upon modernity and its attendant evils (urbanism, materialism, liberalism, socialism, parliamentarianism, rationalism, etc.) were launched by large segments of the German intelligentsia, who were marked by what Fritz Stern has termed "cultural despair." Their hostile reaction to the modern world was coupled with a romantic longing for disappearing traditional values. The usual condemnation of science was represented in the beliefs of one of the foremost of Stern's cultural pessimists, to whom science signified:

> positivism, rationalism, empiricism, mechanistic materialism, technology, skepticism, dogmatism, and specialization, in fact everything but the disinterested and devoted quest for knowledge. He loathed science both for what it was and what it did.[18]

Physical scientists and mathematicians thus found themselves in an exceedingly hostile intellectual environment in Germany. In particular, they were held accountable in academic circles for the concept of mechanistic determinism linked by many professors to an abhorrent materialism. Forman has suggested that several Weimar physicists and mathematicians were sufficiently affected by this criticism to respond to it in their own work. They quickly approved the rejection of causality involved in the new conceptions of the quantum theory generated in the mid-1920s, thus liberating themselves from the onus of determinism. Modern physics was, Forman has asserted, "primarily an effort by German physicists to adapt the content of their science to the values of their intellectual environment." [19]

THE WEIMAR CENTERS OF MODERN PHYSICS

Within Germany three intellectual centers figured particularly prominently in the generation of the new theories of modern physics between 1900 and 1930. The small university town of Göttingen was the seat of a long-standing, broad mathematical-physical tradition which was of particular importance in statistical mechanics. Berlin was the organizational center of German physics as well as the site of a university with a staff of excellent physicists. And Munich was the training ground for many of the brightest young scientists who contributed to the new ideas in physics. The manner in which National Socialism affected each of these creative centers reveals basic elements of its impact upon the physics community as a whole.

Göttingen was unusual among German universities in having a relatively high degree of interdisciplinary contact between physics and mathematics. Foremost among its mathematicians was David Hilbert. He had encouraged the Göttingen mathematical-physical tradition which stretched back into the mid-nineteenth century, but he was ill during much of the Weimar period. Although he could not perform his earlier towering role, his spirit of interdisciplinary contact continued to be felt throughout the 1920s.[20] His younger colleague Richard Courant was very active in collaboration with the physicists, and his 1924 book *Methoden der mathematischen Physik* (Methods of mathematical physics) became an influential textbook. Largely through Courant's efforts, Göttingen received funds from the Rockefeller Foundation for new and expanded physics and mathematics institutes on the Bunsenstrasse.[21]

In addition to Hilbert and Courant, there was an impressive array of mathematical talent in Weimar Göttingen. Edmund Landau in number theory, Emmy Noether in algebra, and Hermann Weyl in relativity theory and the foundations of mathematics—all were figures of renown. Emmy Noether's work toward an axiomatic treatment of algebra led Weyl to recall her as the greatest woman mathematician in history.[22]

Göttingen's physicists were able to rival its mathematicians in talent. Max Born in theoretical physics was in close contact with Copenhagen, Munich, and Berlin, and he proved to be a key figure in the development of modern physics. Among the young physicists who worked with him during the Weimar period were Werner Heisenberg, Wolfgang Pauli, Eugene Wigner, and Maria Goeppert-Mayer, all later Nobel laureates, as was Born himself.

Göttingen also possessed two distinguished professors of experimental physics. Robert Pohl gave the large general lecture courses and directed the First Physical Institute, while James Franck supervised the small laboratory classes and the Second Physical Institute. Pohl was very much concerned with the quality of basic physics instruction (his lectures were famous) and with research in optics.[23] For his work on excitation potentials before the war, Franck had shared the 1925 Nobel prize. Franck's keen intuitive insight into fundamental problems of modern physics complemented Born's tendency toward formalism.[24]

The high degree of communication and intellectual excitement in Göttingen during the twenties has made it a symbol of "the beautiful years" prior to the advent of National Socialism.[25] Even though it was far from the republican hustle of Berlin and the conservative bustle of Munich, however, Göttingen could not escape the political upheaval of the thirties. In fact, since many of its physicists and mathematicians were Jewish, Göttingen was severely affected in 1933 by the Nazi policy of dismissing "non-Aryans" from civil service positions.

An impressive collection of scientific talent had also gathered in Berlin, the city regarded by many physicists as the stronghold of German physics.[26] As professor of theoretical physics at Berlin University, Max Planck had founded quantum theory, which provided the basis for much of modern physics. There also Max von Laue, a pupil of Planck famed for his work in x-ray crystallography, held an extraordinary (ausserordentlicher) professorship in theoretical physics. Einstein was also connected with the university, although he worked to a great extent alone. In 1924, these famous men were joined by Walther Nernst, who had discovered the third law of thermodynamics. When Planck retired in 1927, one of the key figures in quantum physics, Erwin Schrödinger, was appointed as his successor. The center of the scientific life of the university was the weekly colloquium where these men—all Nobel laureates—were joined by researchers from industrial laboratories and the Imperial Institute for Physics and Technology.[27]

Berlin was also distinguished by the work conducted at the Institute of Technology (Technische Hochschule, or TH), especially in the late twenties when the Nobel laureate Gustav Hertz was the professor of experimental physics and Richard Becker held the chair for theoretical work.[28] The level of physics in the capital city was further enhanced by the research in associated fields such as physical chemistry and radiochemistry. Particularly noteworthy in this regard were the Kaiser Wilhelm Institute for Physical Chemistry and Electrochemistry headed by the Nobel prizewinner Fritz Haber and the Kaiser Wilhelm Institute for Chemistry guided by Otto Hahn and Lise Meitner. For his discovery of nuclear fission at the end of 1938, Hahn, too, received Nobel recognition.

At least as important as Berlin's scientific reputation was its role as the center of organized German science. The Berlin physicists largely dominated the policies of the German Physical Society (Deutsche Physikalische Gesellschaft), which had expanded to a national organization shortly after World War I. Along with other Berlin figures such as Haber, they played key roles in the Kaiser Wilhelm Society, the Prussian Academy of Sciences (Preussische Akademie der Wissenschaften) and the fund-dispensing Emergency Association of German Science (Notgemeinschaft der deutschen Wissenschaft).

The impact of National Socialism upon physics in Berlin was not limited to the toll of the dismissal policy, although that was serious enough. The Nazi seizure and exercise of power also had consequences for Berlin's moral and organizational leadership of German physics. Because Berlin was the cultural and intellectual nerve center of Weimar Germany as well as its political capital, those Germans who rejected Berlin's political leadership also tended to reject its cultural guidance.[29] This phenomenon appeared in all areas of Weimar intellectual life, including physics. Lenard and Stark, for example, displayed a consistent antipathy toward the Berlin leadership in science beginning with World War I. Stark's antagonism led to his attempt to reorganize German science under new leadership during the Nazi period.

Munich was a seedbed of counterrevolution and anti-Semitism in the Weimar years. The key representative of modern physics in the Bavarian capital was Arnold Sommerfeld, professor of theoretical physics at the university since 1906. Unlike Wilhelm Wien, his colleague in experimental physics, who was nearly as opposed to Berlin's leadership and modern physics as Lenard and Stark, Sommerfeld worked closely with his northern counterparts. His work on quantum theory was certainly important, but perhaps his most significant contribution to the new physics was his training of more than a generation of Germany's best theoretical physicists, including no less than four Nobel prize winners.[30] Sommerfeld's word in academic appointments carried a great deal of weight. In 1928, nearly one-third of all full professors of theoretical physics in the German-speaking world were Sommerfeld pupils.[31]

Although Sommerfeld had a number of Jewish students, the heavily Catholic university did not appoint many Jews to academic positions.[32] Thus the dismissal policy had little effect there. The impact of National Socialism upon Munich physics was felt much more strongly through politicized academic appointments. The political criteria were basically Nazi party membership and adherence to the attempt by Lenard and Stark to inject racial ideology into physics. Although these men labeled their views "deutsche Physik" (German physics) in a claim to speak for the true national spirit, they remained a small enough minority to justify the use of one of the more applicable synonyms for their movement, "Aryan physics."

THE NATIONAL SOCIALISTS COME TO POWER

Although the proponents of Aryan physics claimed to have Hitler's backing, the Führer never took a direct hand in the affairs of the physics community. In the years preceding the Nazi seizure of power, however, he did formulate basic views on education and the civil service to guide the Nazi movement. The Führer explained in *Mein Kampf* that as necessary as chemistry, physics, mathematics, and such subjects may be in a "materialisticized" (*vermaterialisierte*) era of technology, it was dangerous to devote more and more schooling to these disciplines. What Germany needed was education (Bildung), based not on the materialistic egoism fostered by the sciences, but on individual sacrifice to the community.[33] History and some other fields could aid in accomplishing this task, but they were not enough. Of utmost priority in education, Hitler declared, was the production of sound bodies. Second came character development. Least important was scholarly training, for, he asserted:

> a person less scholarly educated [gebildet], but with a good firm character full of decisiveness and will power is worth more to a people as a whole than a physically degenerated, weak-willed, cowardly pacifistic individual.[34]

Obviously, Hitler had no love for intellectuals. The historian Joachim Fest has even remarked: "Fundamentally National Socialism represented a politically organized contempt for the mind." [35]

Hitler's attitude toward the professional civil service was equally contemptuous. In a private talk with the editor of a nationalist newspaper in 1931, Hitler was asked where he would acquire the trained minds to run the administrative machinery of the state once he had seized power. Where would he get the necessary brains? *He* would be the brains, Hitler emphatically replied. Anyway, he demanded,

> do you think perhaps that, in the event of a successful revolution along the lines of my party, we would not inherit the brains in droves? Do you believe that the German middle class (sarcastically), this flower of the intelligentsia, would refuse to serve us and place their minds at our disposal? The German middle class would take its stand on the famed ground of the accomplished fact; we will do what we like with the middle class.[36]

And the Jews? Richard Breiting noted in a second conversation that there were good and capable people among them—men who had been awarded iron crosses during the war, men with great minds like Einstein. Hitler's answer was this:

> Everything they have created has been stolen from us. Everything that they know will be used against us. They should just go and foment their unrest among other peoples. We do not need them.[37]

The editor went away marveling that the Führer considered even Einstein an alien who would have to go.[38]

The deepening economic depression and its attendant unemployment and despair fed the growth of Hitler's movement. Hitler was officially appointed chancellor on January 30, 1933, and the National Socialists thereupon quickly consolidated their power.[39]

One very important factor in regard to the civil service, including

the German professoriate, was the apparent legality of the Nazi ascent to power. The technical propriety undermined opposition to
the regime and provided a basis for the hope that Hitler would
learn to behave less radically once in a position of responsibility.
The cloak of legality provided Hitler with a tremendous psychological advantage over the law-abiding middle class.[40]

One of the basic National Socialist goals was formally to legalize
anti-Semitism. The doctrine of the "racial enemy" was, of course,
one of the vital components of the Nazi movement—its role in Nazi
ideology has been aptly compared to that of the "class enemy" in
communist thought.[41] As early as 1920, in its twenty-five-point program, the party had indicated that only racial comrades (*Volksge-
nossen*) could be citizens, and that Jews were excluded from this category. Furthermore, the program stated that only citizens should hold
public office at any level.[42] During the mid-1920s the Nazis had displayed their consistency and earnestness on this point by introducing
Reichstag legislation to remove Jews from the civil service.[43]

The first clear indications to most Germans of the continuity of
Nazi anti-Semitic policies came in 1933 at the end of the second
month of power for Hitler. Hundreds of public officials had already
lost their posts because they were anti-Nazi. On March 31, however,
Jewish judges in Prussia were dismissed from office specifically because they were Jewish.[44] The following day a government-sponsored
National Boycott took place. Although officially described as "relatively peaceful," Jewish stores were placarded while brownshirts
blocked the doorways, windows were smashed, Jews were beaten up
on the street and kept from entering their offices, public libraries,
and so on. The police stood by or were simply not to be seen, but
the Nazi police "reinforcements" patrolled everywhere. The whole
operation was in the hands of the wildly anti-Semitic Nazi Julius
Streicher and was overseen by the Minister of Propaganda Joseph
Goebbels.[45]

A contemporary and widely publicized indication of Nazi goals
involved Albert Einstein. Although he was one of the world's best-
known and most respected scientists, in Germany his outspoken pacifism, internationalism, and Zionism also made him one of the most
hated. He was in America when Hitler came to power, and responded to attacks upon him in the Nazi press by declaring his refusal to return to a Nazi-governed Germany. Moreover, he held that
the world ought to be made aware of the dangers of National So-

cialism.[46] When he arrived on the Continent in late March, he avoided Germany and settled in a sea resort near Ostende, Belgium, to await developments. The Nazis reacted to his declarations and actions by seizing his property and subsequently placing a price on his head.[47]

The day his ship docked, March 28, 1933, Einstein wrote a letter of resignation to the Prussian Academy of Sciences, Germany's most exclusive and prestigious learned society.[48] He apparently wished honorably to sever all connection with the German government and to spare his friends in the Academy from having to deal with pressures to dismiss him.

But the pressures were already mounting. The Nazi-appointed Prussian minister of education, Bernhard Rust, to whom the Academy was formally responsible, demanded on March 29 that the Academy consider disciplining Einstein for his "agitation" against the new German state.[49] When Einstein's resignation was received and accepted the next day, the issue appeared to be dead. But on the evening of March 31, just hours before the National Boycott began, the minister expressed an "urgent wish" for the Academy to make a public declaration on Einstein.[50]

Max Planck, Einstein's friend and supporter, was in Sicily on vacation. Another standing secretary, the jurist Ernst Heymann, acceded to Rust's demands and drafted a press release declaring that the Academy was opposed to Einstein's "atrocity-mongering" (*Greuelhetze*) abroad and had "no reason to regret Einstein's withdrawal." [51] The statement appeared on April 1. Einstein's name also figured that day in a propaganda speech by Joseph Goebbels:

> We had allowed international Jewry to be shown a goodwill it did not at all deserve. And what was the Jews' thanks? At home they repented, while out in the world they kindled a lie and atrocity campaign which exceeds even that of the world war. The Jews in Germany can thank the refugees like Einstein for the fact that they themselves are today—completely legitimately and legally—being called to account.[52]

The scientist's outspoken opposition to National Socialism made his name a synonym for traitor in Germany as long as the Third Reich existed.

Despite the events of April 1, the Law for the Restoration of the Career Civil Service of April 7, 1933, was unexpected—even some party members were unprepared for it.[53] It was designed by the ministry of interior (at that time run by the Nazi former civil servant Wilhelm Frick) to change the fundamental composition of the state bureaucracy without destroying its effectiveness in administering the affairs of the state.[54] The provisions were simple, but devastating: certain civil servants were to be relieved of their duties in order to restore a "national" career civil service and simplify the administration. Affected were (1) those without proper qualifications who had taken office since November 9, 1918 (i.e., political appointees); (2) those whose previous political activities did not guarantee that they would at all times unreservedly serve the new state; (3) those of "non-Aryan" descent. To simplify the administration, officials could be retired even when they were still capable of service. Also, any official transferred to a new position, even one of inferior rank and pay, had either to accept his new assignment or ask for retirement.

The wording of the law left a few loopholes. It was to be temporary, with the provisions to be in effect only until September 30, 1933. In addition, there were exemptions for the non-Aryans as a concession to President Paul von Hindenburg, who insisted that war veterans be treated specially.[55] A non-Aryan official could stay in office if (1) he was in office before August 1, 1914; (2) he had fought at the front in the war; (3) his father or son had been killed in the war.

On April 11, the key question of who was non-Aryan was answered by the first supplement to the law. An official was in the non-Aryan category if he had a Jewish parent or grandparent, and these individuals were assumed to have been Jewish if they practiced the Jewish religion.[56]

Numerous supplements to the Civil Service Law further explained its application. On May 6, the third supplement explicitly emphasized that all instructors at institutions of higher learning were included as civil servants, even those not on the government payroll, such as Privatdozenten. The provision relating to "politically unreliable" persons was expanded. Anyone who had conducted himself in a communist manner was to be dismissed, whether or not he was in any way connected with the Communist party or its organs. In replacing retired or dismissed civil servants, first consideration was to be given to those who had undergone earlier suffering on the basis of their "nationalist conduct." [57] The law was supplemented several times more, and the process of reconstructing the bureaucracy was not completed until 1937.[58]

A lingering problem related to persons who were part-Jewish.

A conflict arose between the party, which wanted to treat them as Jewish, and the state (i.e., civil service), which wanted to treat them as German. The Nuremberg Laws of September 15, 1935, and the supplement of November 14, 1935, were to some extent victories for the bureaucrats.[59] A person of mixed descent was considered Jewish if at least three grandparents were Jewish or if two grandparents were Jewish and he or she was a practicing Jew or married to one. These laws affected all Jews in Germany, including university instructors. Quarter-Jewish persons were thus no longer subject to dismissal. The Nuremberg Laws made no provision, however, for exemption based on war service.[60]

The implementation of the 1933 Civil Service Law and its supplements had immediate and far-reaching consequences for the entire academic community.[61] Physics proved to be one of the most heavily affected disciplines, suffering a loss of at least 25 percent of its 1932–33 personnel, including some of the finest scientists in Germany. Göttingen, the scene of the Weimar "beautiful years," makes an especially revealing case study of the impact of the dismissal policy on the academic physics community.

2. Göttingen—1933

Since scientists seldom engaged in political activity, it was primarily the non-Aryan clause of the Civil Service Law that had the greatest effect on the physicists and mathematicians. The impact of the new law was particularly severe in Göttingen because the directors of three of the four institutes for physics and mathematics were Jewish —James Franck, Max Born, and Richard Courant. The different courses of action these men chose to follow and the common fate they suffered provide insight into the implementation of the dismissal policy throughout Germany. The responses of their colleagues and pupils also reflected widespread reactions. The result was an exodus of scientific talent unparalleled in recent history, for men like Franck, Born, and Courant were among the best in their fields in Germany, and at that time German science was among the best in the world.

PUBLIC PROTEST: JAMES FRANCK

Since German university classes met from November through February and May through July, the Civil Service Law of April 7 was announced during the middle of spring break in Göttingen. Most of the students and many of the faculty were away on vacation. The director of the Second Physical Institute, however, was still in the city and thus able immediately to consider the implications of the ordinance.

James Franck was as frequently praised for his kindness, integrity, and deep sense of principle as for his talents as a scientist. At the beginning of the war, he had dropped his research and engaged in front-line combat as a volunteer. This action was strictly out of a sense of duty, for the military manner of thinking was entirely foreign to him—the story goes that he was once put in charge of a column of men and gave the order "Stillgestanden—bitte" (Come to attention—please).[1] But if command formalities were alien to his nature, personal courage was not. Both iron crosses were among his decorations, and he received a commission as an officer even though he was Jewish.

His sense of principle became more and more outraged as events of the spring of 1933 unfolded. The front-page story in the nationalist-oriented *Göttinger Tageblatt* cheered that now unqualified political appointees would be eliminated,[2] but the nature of the National Boycott day left no doubt that the anti-Semitic provisions were a major aspect of the Civil Service Law. Franck was undoubtedly well informed of the measures enforced by the Nazis in Berlin on April 1, since many of his close friends and his daughter Elizabeth lived in that city. In addition, the newspapers on April 1 had carried the story of Einstein's resignation from the Prussian Academy of Sciences and the Academy's precipitous reply.[3] In conversations with his closest friends and co-workers, Franck became more and more determined that something must be done. Under the exemption clauses, he would be spared. But would not accepting exemption be tantamount to sanctioning the government's activities? As director of the institute, he would certainly have to discharge some of his own staff, as well as watch the dismissal of colleagues in other institutes. His resolve was strengthened by actions of the Nazi-dominated student leadership.

The students were one of the most vocal forces of National Socialist policy at the universities. On April 13, the German Students Association announced its campaign "Against the Un-German Spirit," which would climax in public book burnings on May 10. Among the pronouncements in the twelve-point declaration were: the Jew could only think Jewish, and when he wrote German he was lying; students should view Jews as aliens, and Jewish works should appear in Hebrew, or at least be designated as translations if they were printed in German; students and professors should be selected "according to their guarantee of thinking in the German spirit." [4] The student law promulgated the same day by the Prussian minister of education restored student self-government, which had been taken away under the Weimar ministry, and restricted membership in student organizations to Aryans only. Quotas for non-Aryans in the German schools soon followed.[5] Also on the thirteenth, the first dismissals under the Civil Service Law were announced at half a dozen universities.[6]

Evenings at Franck's home were consumed in intensive discussion. Many of his friends and colleagues used well-intentioned arguments to try to dissuade him from taking hasty action.[7] With his characteristic insight, however, Franck saw that a fundamental issue of principle was at stake. Over Easter weekend, he decided to resign his position in protest. It was a lonely and courageous step. His family today remembers clearly that the final decision was made "for himself and by himself and nobody else had any part in making it." [8]

On the eve of his protest, behind the closed doors of his study, a small group helped Franck formulate the text of his letter of resignation. His family recalls among the close friends and assistants present that evening: Hertha Sponer, the chief assistant in Franck's institute; Arthur von Hippel, an assistant who was the husband of Franck's daughter Dagmar; and possibly Heinrich Kuhn, an assistant who would be affected by the non-Aryan provisions of the Civil Service Law.[9]

The group worked out two documents. One was to the Nazi-appointed Prussian minister of education, and read simply:

Mr. Minister: 17 April

With these lines I ask you, Mr. Minister, to release me from my duties as full professor at the University of Göttingen and Director of the Second Physical Institute of this university.

This decision is an inner necessity for me because of the attitude of the government toward German Jewry.[10]

The other was a statement to the rector. Before the evening was out, Franck phoned the *Göttinger Zeitung,* the second of the city's newspapers, and gave it a portion of this letter. Such public protest appears quite reasonable in retrospect, but at the time it was regarded as highly unusual and was hoped to have a very great impact. "The whole affair was carefully timed," his family recalls, "so that the receipt of the letters coincided with the publication in the newspapers." [11]

The following day, the newspaper carried these lines from Franck's letter to the rector:

I have asked my superior authorities to release me from my office. I will attempt to continue my scientific work in Germany.

We Germans of Jewish descent are being treated as aliens and enemies of the Fatherland. It is demanded that our children grow up in the awareness that they will never be allowed to prove themselves as Germans.

Whoever was in the war is supposed to receive permission to serve the state further. I refuse to make use of this privilege, even though I also understand the position of those today who consider it their duty to hold out at their posts.[12]

The newspaper stressed that Franck had no intention of seeking a position abroad as long as he had the opportunity to continue experimental research in Germany. The article pointed out the honors

Franck had won, his war record, the esteem he had brought Göttingen and the economic benefits the city had enjoyed because of his reputation (increased numbers of students and Rockefeller money to expand the buildings of the institute). The writer of the article concluded:

> Professor Franck's decision is to be evaluated essentially, even exclusively, on moral grounds. We hope and wish that this step, by which Franck has shattered his life's work and meaning, has the effect of retaining for our scientific activity other researchers who, according to the lawful ordinances, will be forced to step down. Otherwise losses could be incurred which could be made good again only after a long time, or even never at all.[13]

Unfortunately, the warning went unheeded.

The sentiment of the *Göttinger Zeitung* was echoed on the same day in the evening edition of the liberal *Vossische Zeitung* in Berlin. An article in that paper also expressed hope that Franck's action might lead to a consideration of the implications of recent events for the future. The foreign press quickly picked up the story.[14]

The *Berliner Tageblatt,* however, took the view that Franck would have done better to have remained at his post at the institute if he wished to protest Nazi policies.[15] Others in Göttingen even suggested to Franck that things were really not so bad. Rudolf Hilsch, Robert Pohl's chief assistant, recalls that when Franck came to say good-bye to everyone, Hilsch admonished the professor with a piece of folk wisdom: "Es wird nichts so heiss gegessen, wie es gekocht wird" (nothing is eaten as hot as it is cooked). He was mistaken, Hilsch soon realized.[16]

Franck had at this time no thought of emigration. In this stand he was encouraged by the Berlin physics leaders Max Planck and Max von Laue.[17] When Heinrich Rubens had died in 1922, Franck had been offered the Berlin chair for physics, but he had declined in order to stay in Göttingen. Walther Nernst had been appointed instead. By 1931, plans were already afoot to try to appoint Franck again since Nernst was almost to retire. Fritz Haber indicated to Franck that he might also take over the Kaiser Wilhelm Institute for Physics when he succeeded Nernst at the university. Eventually he might direct Haber's own institute after Haber retired in 1936.[18] By late 1932, Franck was the leading candidate for the Berlin professorship. In January 1933, he was contacted by the Ministry of

Education and asked to come to Berlin for preliminary negotiations,[19] but the process was interrupted by the political upheaval. Even so, the possibility that Franck would be able to continue his scientific work in Germany in some capacity outside the civil service was still quite real—or so at least it must have seemed to him.

Immediately following the publication of Franck's letter, however, rumors began to circulate in Göttingen. It was reported that Franck and those who had participated in discussions with him had conspired to hinder the national revolution. Using the argument that the foreign press had been able to turn his protest into anti-German propaganda, forty-two instructors at the university issued a condemnation of Franck's action. The medical faculty and the agricultural institute were especially heavily represented in this group, while only one signatory was in mathematics or physics.[20] The charge was that Franck's public resignation had impeded both the domestic and foreign policy of the new government. "We are unanimously agreed," stated the signatories, "that the form of the above declaration of resignation is equivalent to an act of sabotage, and we hope that the government will therefore accelerate the realization of the necessary cleansing measures." [21]

Two days later, the Göttingen press curtly announced that on April 25 six university professors had been placed on leave by the Prussian Ministry of Education: Professors Honig (criminal law), Bondy (social psychology), Bernstein (statistics), Born, Courant, and Noether. The subtitle of the article was ominous: "More will follow." [22]

PASSIVE PROTEST: MAX BORN

Unlike Franck, Born did not wish to remain in Germany. "We decided after my 'placement on leave,' " he wrote later, "to leave Germany immediately." [23] At the beginning of May, he and his wife left with their son for the mountains of northern Italy, where they had planned to rent a place for the summer vacation. The reasons for Born's quick departure can be traced to his personality, health, and the events of the Weimar period.

The Einstein-Born correspondence reveals Born as a man sensitive to the currents of his times even as he tried to isolate himself from them. In his political views and attitude toward human relationships, he indicates, he was in agreement with his friend Einstein.[24] But his aversion to publicity and public debate was even stronger than Einstein's. His personality, which one of his assistants remembers as "noble and reserved," was largely responsible.[25] Born himself explained that he still believed in the "quiet temple of learning." [26]

In the early Weimar days, Born was willing to support Einstein openly against the anti-Semitic opponents of relativity theory, especially at the Nauheim convention of German scientists and doctors in 1920.[27] But it was against his nature to do so. And when a possibility arose in 1922 to bring his old roommate and friend Theodor von Kármán to Göttingen, he did not push the candidacy. It had not been easy to get Franck appointed the previous year. Now Born took one look at the number of Jews who were already professors in the faculty of mathematics and natural science (Courant, Edmund Landau, Felix Bernstein, Franck, and himself) and another look at the opposition (primarily the people in the agricultural institute), and decided that he could not face the fight necessary to add another Jew to the staff.[28]

In addition, Born's health was frail. He always seemed to suffer seriously from head colds and asthma in the fall.[29] The famous picture of the participants in the Solvay conference in Brussels (October 1927) reveals him, alone among many men several years his senior, wearing a heavy overcoat and muffler. During the exacting 1925–27 period, he had exhausted himself, and the resultant nervous breakdown interrupted his work for about a year in 1928–29.[30] He spent some time in a sanatorium on the shore of Lake Constance. At first, he was confined to bed, but once he was up and around, he found that the other patients—all representatives of "the good middle class"—talked about almost nothing except Hitler and their hopes concerning him, with spicy anti-Semitic asides. "That," Born has written, "drove me back into my room." [31]

He dreaded his year as dean of the faculty in 1931–32. Even before his term began, he was planning on the need for recuperation afterward. His hope was to go to the California Institute of Technology in Pasadena for the winter of 1932–33, even though he admitted that the situation in physics had changed in the last five years and he could no longer offer the Americans anything "really new." [32] The trip never materialized.

The year lived up to his darkest expectations. The worst problem was that the government, hard-pressed by the depression, tried to save funds by dismissing a percentage of the assistants. Born led a successful movement to have the natural science faculty voluntarily designate about 10 percent of each professor's income to provide livelihood for the young people. Most of the faculty agreed readily, but a minority, consisting primarily of the agricultural personnel, objected with a prolonged hatefulness the likes of which, Born wrote, he had never before seen.[33] Undoubtedly they did not relish donating part of their pay to what they apparently considered a Jewish clique in the mathematics and physics institutes.

With his strong feelings about anti-Semitism, Born had no love for the Nazis. In 1932, the theoretician Friedrich Hund and Born were riding on a train northbound out of Göttingen. The train stopped briefly in one of the smaller towns of Brunswick, an area which supported the Nazis rather early. The swastika flags were already in place on the flagpoles at the station. Hund remembers that Born nodded toward them and declared that when those flags flew over all of Germany, he would leave.[34] With this general disposition and the toll of the year of his deanship on Born's emotional and physical health, it is clear that he would hardly be up to an open fight to hold his post.

After he had recovered somewhat from the asthma attacks brought on by the tension and ferment of the weeks preceding his departure, Born informed the curator of the university that he fully shared Franck's position and wanted no special treatment. What Franck had said in his resignation was also valid for Born himself as a German Jew, even if, as the curator had seemed to imply in a letter to Born, he were to be reinstated.[35] In a letter to Einstein a week later, Born indicated that he now found himself feeling his Jewishness quite strongly, a feeling he had not been particularly aware of before. Oppression and injustice had aroused rage and resistance in him.[36]

Although Born had briefly considered remaining at his post, once he made up his mind to resign, his decision was final. He never attempted to return to Nazi Germany and fight to stay on at Göttingen. Instead he turned his back upon a homeland that no longer desired his services. He wrote to Einstein that Franck was staying in Göttingen in the impossible attempt to find something in Germany. As for himself: "I wouldn't have the nerves for it, also see no sense in it." [37]

Born began to cast about for a position abroad so that he could continue his scientific work. By July, when the English physicist F. A. Lindemann (later Lord Cherwell, Churchill's scientific adviser) came to Italy to try to win him for Oxford, Born had already

accepted a post at Cambridge.[38] He was prominent enough to be
tendered offers at a number of schools even in the middle of the
depression. For emigrants lacking his reputation, the future looked
bleak. Surveying the situation, Einstein wrote to Born: "My heart
aches when I think of the young ones." [39]

QUIET PROTEST: RICHARD COURANT

Franck had resigned publicly, and Born had emigrated silently.
But the result was in both cases essentially the same: each man to
some extent played into Nazi hands and removed himself from the
scene. Courant, however, was determined not to give up his post
without a stiff fight. He was supported by many of his friends, pupils,
and associates. His publisher, Ferdinand Springer, was especially
quick to approve Courant's intention to hold out.[40]

Two days after his name appeared in the paper, on April 28, 1933,
Courant wrote a letter to his former assistant Hellmuth Kneser. It is
a deeply revealing document, for it is apparent that Courant was
still stunned as he tried to fathom what had happened and why. In
regard to Franck's resignation, he explained:

> Franck had, before I returned from vacation, come more and
> more firmly to the conclusion that he should voluntarily resign.
> Neugebauer [Courant's chief assistant] and I, and also other
> friends, restrained him again and again, and forced him to post-
> pone doing it. One day, I believe on Easter Sunday, Franck's
> decision was made, against our initial wishes. We, that is, Born
> and I, considered for a short while whether we were morally
> bound to follow Franck. We decided instead, however, to at-
> tempt to stay and to support our establishments here with all of
> our powers.
>
> A completely perverted version of this affair was spread by
> rumors and garbled nonsense, namely that Franck's resignation
> was the result of a joint sabotage resolution, and that we had
> pushed Franck forward solely for tactical reasons. This grotesque
> version induced a relatively small group of Göttingen colleagues
> to come out with a public declaration against Franck's resigna-
> tion and with a call for a quick cleansing of the university. Our
> forced leave came the day after the publication of this declara-
> tion.
>
> I could imagine that the state of affairs I have described pre-
> cipitated the steps taken by the ministry.[41]

Members of Courant's institute remember that the possibility of a mass resignation was raised. Otto Neugebauer recalls that mass action was considered during the discussions in Franck's home by Franck, Born, Courant, and Weyl. (Weyl was not Jewish, but his wife was.) Such a dramatic move would have evoked memories of the famous "Göttingen Seven," a group of professors who had defended academic prerogatives against the state in the nineteenth century.[42] Herbert Busemann, who was not directly involved in the discussions, recollects that one reason a mass resignation did not materialize was that the principals could not agree upon a specific event as a focus for their protest.[43] This lack of decision was one of the crucial results of the Nazi tactic of legality, which cast opposition in the role of unlawfulness and moral wrong, making unity among persons such as the Göttingen professors almost impossible. And disunity in the face of Nazi determination was disastrous.

Despite Courant's impression, it seems doubtful that Franck's resignation was directly responsible for the dismissal of Born and Courant. At the most, the resignation probably triggered actions that had already been planned. Kurt Daluege (Nazi-appointed Prussian minister of police) had on March 12 already received the list of professors of Jewish ancestry which very likely formed the basis for the dismissal announcement of April 25 in Göttingen. Born, Courant, and Noether were included, but not Franck, whom the Nazis had apparently intended to leave at his post.[44]

Courant's April 28 letter to Kneser stated that he had as yet received no official written information on his status. But as an active participant in the war, he wrote, as a severely wounded front-line infantry officer, he had no reason to expect that he would be affected by the Civil Service Law. Perhaps political charges were being leveled against him, since he had briefly been a Social Democratic party city councilman in Göttingen right after the war. But his views were not really Marxist at all, and he had shortly thereafter left the party. Perhaps the charges were related to the fact that at the very end of the war he had been elected to a soldiers' council (which was modeled after those of the Russian Revolution) by his small detachment. But he had simply led his men in their assigned task of disbanding in orderly fashion.

In the past months, he continued, such matters had been dredged up to create totally perverted rumors about his past. In addition, the science faculty—especially the mathematical institute—was disliked "purely instinctively" by many groups in Göttingen. There was also jealousy that he had so conspicuously expanded the mathematical and physical institutes with foreign money. Counteracting these attitudes and tales was difficult. "There has arisen an atmosphere of rumors," he declared, "assertions which never quite reach us clearly, and which have culminated in the slogan 'Stronghold of Marxism.' " [45]

What did he intend to do? He felt he must not let himself succumb to bitterness, that he must attempt to stay as long as possible and try to continue his scientific work. He still hoped that he would be given the chance to respond to the charges against him, whatever they might be.[46]

The tempo of events accelerated swiftly, and on the very next day, April 29, Courant wrote Kneser again. The German Students Association had not only kept Landau, Hilbert's Jewish assistant Paul Bernays, and others from lecturing, it had extended its campaign to include Neugebauer, charging that he was a communist. It threatened boycott action, and Courant feared Neugebauer might relinquish the acting directorship of the institute even if the threat were withdrawn. Weyl did not seem inclined to take over, leaving only the professor of applied mathematics Gustav Herglotz. Personality conflicts and friction were also mounting within the institute itself. And the rumors continued to multiply. Now it was charged that Courant had trooped around with a red flag during the revolution, or that he had disarmed homeward-bound regiments at the end of the war, or that he had been a member of the Independent Socialist party. The entire work of the past decades—and more—seemed to be disintegrating. Courant observed sorrowfully, "I am very much afraid—quite aside from my own person—that something irreversible is happening." [47]

On May 2, Courant sent a letter to Abraham Flexner of the Institute for Advanced Study about his fears for the Göttingen institute. Neugebauer had already received his walking papers—though from the dean and not from the ministry. Perhaps, Courant inquired, it might be possible to arrange positions in America for himself and his chief assistant? In the meantime, both would try to continue their scientific work.[48]

What else could one do? Even when the official written notification arrived on May 5, it did not state formal reasons for Courant's release from office. It simply declared that he was placed on leave as of May 2 under the law of April 7, that this leave was to be observed in every university-related activity, and that, until further notice, his pay would be continued.[49]

In talking with the head of the science section of the Prussian Ministry of Education, the mathematician Theodor Vahlen, Kneser was dismayed to find Vahlen under the impression that Courant was, of all things, a Zionist.[50] Here was still another rumor. A number of Courant's former pupils attempted to help combat the hydra by writing letters to the ministry on their own, stressing that he gave no preference in his institute to Jews (another charge), that he was extremely patriotic, that he had brought financial advantages to Germany during difficult times, and so forth.[51]

Others, particularly Neugebauer and Kurt Friedrichs, who was at the Brunswick Institute of Technology, decided to submit a petition on Courant's behalf. The text stressed the financial benefits that Courant had brought to Göttingen and Germany, his esteem as a scholar, his outstanding success as a teacher, and his correctness in refusing to lower himself by publicly challenging the rumors in Göttingen: "true to the old law of the Prussian civil service, that a Prussian official is to defend himself against the accusations and rumors of outsiders not by words, but strictly by means of the propriety of his actions."[52] Among the signers were Planck, von Laue, and Schrödinger from Berlin; Sommerfeld from Munich; Heisenberg and Hund from Leipzig; former assistants and associates Emil Artin, Erich Bessel-Hagen, Franz Rellich, Helmut Hasse. There were twenty-eight names in all. The petition was turned in by mid-June. Significantly, the man who was asked to present the document to the curator was not a pure scientist or mathematician, but the Göttingen aerodynamics expert Ludwig Prandtl.[53]

Prandtl's Institute for Applied Mechanics with its famous wind tunnel was quite different from the mathematical and physical institutes on Bunsen Street. There were people in the latter institutes who deprecated the former, even though everyone was aware of the import of Prandtl's pioneering work in aerodynamics and fluid flow. Courant, for example, tells a story about Landau, who had an abiding contempt for anything even remotely applied. Prandtl once wrote a paper on grease and oil and their lubricating function in certain engineering problems. Landau was always careful to avoid such messy items, and whenever someone said something that reminded him of applied work, he would declare, "Ah, Schmieröl!" (grease!)[54]

Now, however, and for the duration of the Third Reich, the theoreticians had dire need of support from men engaged in such practical pursuits.

Even before he handed in the Courant petition, Prandtl had talked
formally with the curator about the dismissal of Göttingen scientists.[55] He had also come into conflict with National Socialists in his
institute. In a political report written on him in 1934, it was claimed
that not only did he mistreat one of his co-workers specifically because of the man's Nazi and anti-Semitic views, but he deliberately
promoted a Jew to assistant in April 1933, even though an equally
qualified National Socialist was available.[56] But the highest Nazi
leaders recognized the importance of aviation, and Prandtl was a
noted authority in the field. His position in Göttingen was a strong
one. The *Göttinger Tageblatt* had run a major article in June 1933
that commented how fortunate it was that Prandtl had not accepted
a call to Munich in 1922.[57] Eventually, the writer of the 1934 report
was forced to back down even though his charges against Prandtl
were undisputed.[58]

Even Prandtl's efforts were in vain. It was also of no avail when
Prandtl, Friedrichs, and Kneser sent a request directly to Berlin that
they be heard on Courant's behalf.[59] Although his former assistants
continued throughout the summer to try to get someone to listen to
their refutation of the rumors, Courant was tiring of the struggle.
He had at first declined offers from abroad, explaining to the curator
that he did not want to do anything which could be construed as
a political demonstration on the part of a dismissed German professor.[60] Everything was to be done quietly through channels, even the
petition. Freidrichs recollects that,

> When the petition was submitted, all of those concerned with
> it—and Courant himself—expected that Courant would stay if
> he were reinstated. In the meantime he had come to realize that
> this reinstatement was pointless, since as a Jew he would have
> to leave Germany anyway.[61]

Courant once explained his change of heart poignantly: "I saw now
that there was nothing sensible left to do but emigrate. My youngest
son did not seem able to understand why he should not be in the
Hitler Youth, too." [62]

In late August 1933, Courant accepted a post in Cambridge. In
order to avoid the Reich emigration tax, which had been originally

designed in 1931 to stem the flow of marks out of Germany during the depression, he threaded his way through mazes of paperwork in order to be regarded as working abroad "in the German interest" while "on leave." [63] In this way, he hoped to retain some portion of his money and possessions. The situation was complicated by the fact that on October 20 Courant was finally notified that he was not affected by the Civil Service Law. His leave was therefore lifted.[64] By this time, he was already packing for England, and ironically had to request hurriedly a voluntary leave in order to embark during the first week of November.[65]

Born's placement on leave was also lifted in October, at the same time he was granted leave to Cambridge.[66] It seems clear that the government policy was to place everyone potentially affected by the Civil Service Law on leave, and then sort out the exemptions later. But by that time, many of these persons had already left, like Born, or were planning to leave, like Courant. This exodus appears to have been the Nazi goal from the beginning. Thus Courant's judgment was correct, yet holding out at one's post was infinitely more difficult than he anticipated. The silent, inscrutable workings of the bureaucracy became an unbeatable foe. In the end, a public resignation was perhaps the most effective course of action after all.

The widespread acceptance of the legality of the Nazi revolution made protest within government service self-defeating. One was faced with the contradictory position of protesting the illegality of the law, a concept which might make sense in Anglo-Saxon countries but did not in Germany. The key to the whole dismissal policy was the civil service itself, particularly men like the Göttingen curator. In reading correspondence between him and Franck, Born, and Courant, one gets the very clear impression that emotionally he was on their side and wished them well. However, he maintained his professional reserve and carried out the revolution for the Nazis. "Do you believe that the German middle class . . . would refuse to serve us and place their minds at our disposal?" Hitler had asked when interviewed in 1931. He was right.

THE INSTITUTES

The loss of Franck, Born, and Courant was a disaster for Göttingen. But heavy as this toll was, it did not end there. Many more members of the institutes were relieved of their duties, while others left of their own volition. Because the role of the director was crucial, the headless institutes could produce very little work even though some of the personnel remained. And the entire dismissal process generated an oppressive sense of hopelessness. Born's assistant Lothar Nordheim remembers that it was clear that those dismissed would have to leave Germany, and that their main concern was simply how to do so: "Intermixed with this was despair about the end of freedom and the termination of the intellectual and artistic flowering in Germany during the 1920s." [67] The "beautiful years" had come to an end.

Robert Pohl, whose institute did not employ any Jews and was thus unaffected by the dismissal policy, tried to administer what was left of the Göttingen physics program. Franck never returned to his institute after resigning, and his assistants—Sponer, von Hippel, Kuhn, Kroebel, and Günther Cario—took care of the students and the laboratory work. [68]

One of the few bright spots during this time was the seminar which Franck held in his home. Nordheim recalls that the purpose of the sessions was largely "to solace ourselves with our ideas on physics and discuss our progress in finding jobs outside Germany." [69] Kroebel has written that these meetings led to closer ties among the participants, because "each individual had at that time much to give which was imponderable, but humanly significant." [70] This result was characteristic of the influence of Franck's personality.

The first of Franck's staff to leave was Eugene Rabinowitch, his personal assistant. As a newly naturalized Russian Jew, Rabinowitch quickly lost both his stipend from the Emergency Association of German Science and his citizenship. Shortly after Franck's resignation, he left for Copenhagen, where he had been invited by Bohr to work for a year. [71] He then moved to England, and in 1938 came to America. During the war he worked on the Manhattan Project, and later he emerged as one of the guiding forces of the *Bulletin of the Atomic Scientists,* a journal concerned with the relationships between science and politics and science and society.

Kuhn was also forced to leave Göttingen. He accepted an offer from Lindemann to go to Oxford, and Pohl granted his request for release from his duties as assistant in late July. [72] During the war, he contributed to the atomic bomb project in Great Britain. Von Hippel was not affected by the Civil Service Law, but as Franck's son-in-law he chose to abandon Göttingen as well. He embarked in mid-October for Istanbul, where nearly one hundred German technicians, physicians, economists, and other specialists found positions with Ataturk's newly founded university.[73] He returned to northern Europe to work at Copenhagen at the beginning of 1935, and ultimately settled in 1936 at the Massachusetts Institute of Technology. Sponer was also unaffected by the law, but her professional ties were to the Franck circle, which was now disintegrating. In addition, as a female university instructor, she clearly did not represent the Nazi image of womanhood, and her academic future in Germany appeared dismal. In 1934 she accepted a position at Oslo, and in 1936 she went to Duke University. Only Günther Cario and Werner Kroebel remained in Göttingen's Second Physical Institute.

Born's institute suffered even more than Franck's, for its staff was totally dispersed by the new law. It was charged against Born that his institute was communist infected.[74] This charge was untrue. However, the Russian physicist Georg Rumer had worked in the institute for a time, and both Walter Heitler and Nordheim, the two assistants, had recently visited the Soviet Union. Nordheim had in fact been there from autumn 1932 until January 1933. For him, it was a traumatic experience to arrive fresh from one dictatorship and find himself facing the onset of another one.[75]

Nordheim's experiences during the dismissal process were probably very typical for junior faculty members. On April 28, 1933, two days after Born and Courant found their names in the newspaper, Nordheim received a polite notice from the dean of the faculty (not from the curator or the Ministry of Education) "recommending" that he not exercise his right to teach until his case had been decided by the ministry.[76] During the summer, in addition to attending the seminar with Franck, he had been able to continue his research. He and the other theorists had no need of laboratory facilities.[77] On September 11, a curt form letter from the ministry notified him that his right to teach had been revoked. On the twentieth came word from the curator's office that his position as assistant would terminate on October 31. By early October he had left Göttingen to take up a research associateship in Paris, where Rockefeller funds supported his work with Léon Brillouin.[78] Eventually, like Sponer, he went to Duke University, and today lives in California.

Edward Teller held a position in Arnold Eucken's institute for physical chemistry in Göttingen, and had been working with Born on the latter's book on optics.[79] Although Eucken did not dismiss

him, he recommended that Teller leave the country soon. After a
year in Copenhagen on a Rockefeller fellowship, he went to work
with F. G. Donnan at the University College in London for another
year. He still remembers with particular gratitude the consideration
with which refugees were treated in Britain.[80] In 1935 he moved to
America, where both he and Nordheim were actively engaged in the
Manhattan Project.

Heitler, Born's chief assistant, also left the country in the fall of
1933. There was a standing arrangement for one of Born's post-
doctoral pupils to spend a year at the laboratory of Lennard-Jones in
Bristol. Martin Stobbe was in Bristol during the 1932–33 year, and,
since he was not Jewish, he and Heitler exchanged places for the
coming year.[81] Later Heitler moved to Dublin's new Advanced Institute with Erwin Schrödinger, and finally settled in Zurich.

During the summer semester, since Heitler and Nordheim, as non-
Aryans, were not allowed to lecture, Pohl asked the young astronomer Otto Heckmann to hold the theoretical classes. With Born's
agreement, Heckmann accepted the task.[82] Upon his return from
Bristol, Stobbe delivered the winter semester lectures. His conscience
could not be reconciled with the demands of the government, however. He resigned, destroying his academic career in Germany, and
left for America. Hermann Weyl, to whom Stobbe came in Princeton, attempted in vain to help the young man find a position. Weyl
concluded:

> Under trying circumstances he showed an unusual firmness of
> character and courage without adopting in the least a provoca-
> tive attitude, and won the esteem and admiration of all men in
> Göttingen who had preserved their independence of mind.[83]

There were very few positions available, and Stobbe had not yet had
time to make a name for himself. He shifted to England in 1936 for
a year and then found a temporary position in Oslo. With all the
uncertainty and relocations, he never managed to finish his book
on aspects of quantum mechanics. He apparently died during World
War II.[84]

Three of the members of the mathematical institute had just returned from studies in Italy, and they had no desire to remain in a
German environment so similar to Mussolini's Fascism. All three
were Jewish and although anti-Semitism was not part of Italian
Fascism then, they had gotten a taste of what life under National

Socialism would be like.[85] Two of these men, Hans Lewy and Herbert Busemann, went on a trip to Italy after Hitler came to power. There Busemann advised Lewy, who was an assistant to Courant, to leave Germany because Lewy would be unable to keep quiet. During the early part of the spring semester break Lewy left Göttingen, stopping first in Paris, where he lived on what little he had been able to save. It was there that he received notice that he had been suspended from his teaching duties. He managed to obtain a position at Brown University for the fall and arrived in Rhode Island practically penniless.[86] Later he moved on to the University of California at Berkeley.

Werner Fenchel, the third member of the trio, had spent some time in Copenhagen prior to 1933, and he was now able to secure a position in Denmark. From there he helped his friend Busemann to emigrate as well. Since Busemann's family was wealthy, Courant had prevailed upon him to work within the institute without salary. Busemann thus had no position at stake during the dismissal crisis. Although Weyl, who thought that something might still be salvaged, tried to prevail upon him to stay, Busemann left for Copenhagen in early May.[87] Although Fenchel remained in Denmark, Busemann later followed the path of so many others to America.

Paul Bernays, Hilbert's personal assistant for more than a decade, was released because he was non-Aryan, but Hilbert kept him on for a time at his own expense.[88] In 1934, Bernays found a position in Zurich. Also dismissed as non-Aryan was Paul Hertz, a titular extraordinary professor in theoretical physics who received a small salary through a bookkeeping device called the "mathematical-physical seminar," which never met but provided a few assistantships. With his wife and four children, Hertz went back to his hometown of Hamburg and continued his work on statistical mechanics. Before emigrating to America in 1938 (he died there in 1940), he managed to give a few short lecture courses in Geneva and Prague through the aid of an American committee set up to help dismissed academicians.[89]

As noted earlier, Neugebauer, who was not Jewish, was attacked as a communist. Since he refused to give evidence of his loyalty to the new government, he lasted only one day as director of the institute.[90] Undoubtedly the help of Niels Bohr's brother Harald, a mathematician, enabled him to reach Copenhagen, where he spent the next four years, eventually emigrating to America.

Neugebauer had no communist affiliation, but another assistant,

Rudolf Lüneburg, was associated with Leonhard Nelson's leftist philosophical circle. Through the aid of a friend, he left Germany to work with the American Optical Company.[91] Of the personnel suspended from the three institutes under discussion, only Neugebauer, Lüneburg, and Lüneburg's friend and fellow assistant Heinrich Heesch were so-called Aryans.

It is not clear what charges were leveled against Heesch, who was dismissed by Erhard Tornier, the Nazi functionary who temporarily directed the institute after everyone had left in the fall of 1933.[92] A 1934 report referred unfavorably to his friendship with Lüneburg and Prandtl's dismissed assistants Willy Prager and Kurt-Heinrich Hohenemser. Research funds with which he hoped to work were denied him, since the ministry declared his continuation in academia unacceptable in advance.[93] He did not return to university life until after the war was over.

Emmy Noether was both Jewish and a convinced pacifist who had sided with the Social Democrats in the early days of the Weimar republic.[94] She quickly lost her right to teach and her small salary. Weyl later indicated something of her gentle and upright character during this period when he wrote: "her courage, her frankness, her unconcern about her own fate, her conciliatory spirit, were, in the midst of all the hatred and meanness, despair and sorrow surrounding us, a moral solace." After Neugebauer had rejected the directorship of the institute, Weyl had assumed it for a short time. "I suppose," he continued,

> there could hardly have been in any other case such a pile of enthusiastic testimonials filed with the Ministerium as was sent in on her behalf. At that time we really fought; there was still hope left that the worst could be warded off. It was in vain.[95]

Even after she left Göttingen for Bryn Mawr, Noether displayed no trace of bitterness or malice. She even went back to Göttingen to work independently for a time in the summer of 1934. (She died in 1935.)[96]

Weyl himself, whose wife was Jewish, eventually chose to depart from Göttingen. At the end of the summer semester, he went to Switzerland for a rest. While there he decided to accept an offer to join Einstein at the Institute for Advanced Study. His resignation in Göttingen was effective as of the end of the year.[97]

There was hardly anyone left in Göttingen to teach the winter semester classes. Landau, who had been a civil servant since before the deadline of August 1, 1914, had not been dismissed. In contrast to nearly all those around him, he was at first very optimistic about the future of the Jews under the Nazis.[98] He had long held the Zionist view that Germans and Jews were better off as two recognizably separate races.[99] Although his classes had been disrupted at the opening of the summer semester, he began to lecture in the fall. There was an uproar among the National Socialist students, however, and the demonstrations and boycott they incited forced Landau, too, to resign.[100] He returned to Berlin, where he died in 1938.

The mathematical institute seemed empty. Only Gustav Herglotz and Courant's assistant Franz Rellich were left to carry on the Göttingen tradition. During his long illness in the 1920s, Hilbert had received a blood transfusion from Courant, so the joke went that there was only one Aryan mathematician in all of Göttingen, and in his veins flowed Jewish blood. By the end of 1933, the joke was no longer amusing.

As shown in table 1, the institutes which had contributed so much to physics and mathematics during the Weimar period had thus been largely destroyed by the end of the first year of Nazi power. Although the First Physical Institute was unscathed, the Second had lost its director and half its staff. There was nothing left of Born's theoretical physics institute. Three of the four professors of mathematics and almost all the younger faculty had left Göttingen. Other institutes connected with physics and mathematics in Göttingen had also suffered losses, such as Edward Teller's exit from Eucken's physical chemistry institute and Willy Prager's and Kurt-Heinrich Hohenemser's departure from Prandtl's aerodynamics institute. Felix Bernstein, for example, was forced out of his institute for statistics, and the world-renowned mineralogist Viktor M. Goldschmidt was also driven to emigrate.

Although the destruction took several months to complete, the major portion of the Göttingen structure of tradition and achievement had been demolished during just a few weeks in April and May. All else was aftermath: the velocity of the events of the early spring was vastly different from the pace of the frustrating summer months. Although their motives and actions were diverse, all paths taken by the Göttingen professors—whether public, passive, or quiet protest—led to the same result: emigration. The younger Jewish scholars had no option but to cast about for a position and follow the professors into exile.

There is a well-known story that Hilbert once found himself

TABLE 1

The Impact of the Dismissals

Mathematical Institute	Before	After
Administrative Director:	Richard Courant (+)	xx
Directors:	David Hilbert	David Hilbert
	Edmund Landau (+)	xx
	Gustav Herglotz	Gustav Herglotz
	Hermann Weyl	xx
Chief Assistant:	Otto Neugebauer	xx
Regular Assistant:	Hans Lewy (+)	xx
Temporary Assistants:	Franz Rellich	Franz Rellich
	Werner Weber	Werner Weber
	Heinrich Heesch	xx
	Rudolf Lüneburg	xx
Mathematical-Physical Seminar		
Temporary Assistants:	Paul Bernays (+)	xx
	Paul Hertz (+)	xx
	Wilhelm Cauer	Wilhelm Cauer
	Werner Fenchel (+)	xx
	[Herbert Busemann (+)]	xx
[Contract to teach algebra:	Emmy Noether (+)]	xx
First Physical Institute		
Director:	Robert W. Pohl	Robert W. Pohl
Chief Assistant:	Rudolf Hilsch	Rudolf Hilsch
Regular Assistant:	Gerhard Bauer	Gerhard Bauer
Temporary Assistant:	Rudolf Fleischmann	Rudolf Fleischmann

Second Physical Institute

Director: James Franck (+)
Chief Assistant: Hertha Sponer
Regular Assistants: Günther Cario
　　　　　　　　Arthur von Hippel

Temporary Assistants: Heinrich Kuhn (+)
　　　　　　　　　　Werner Kroebel

Personal Assistant to Franck: Eugene Rabinowitch (+)

Institute for Theoretical Physics

Director: Max Born (+)
Regular Assistant: Walter Heitler (+)
Temporary Assistant: Lothar Nordheim (+)
[In Bristol, England, during 1932–33: Martin Stobbe]
[Assistant in Institute for Physical Chemistry,
　working with Born 1932–33: Edward Teller (+)]

SOURCE: Based in part on the *Amtliches Namensverzeichnis und Verzeichnis der Vorlesungen für das Winter-Semester 1932/33* (Göttingen: Druck Dieterichsche Universitäts-Buchdruckerei, 1932), pp. 28–30.

+ Jewish

Second Physical Institute

Director: xx
Chief Assistant: xx
Regular Assistants: Günther Cario
　　　　　　　　xx

Temporary Assistants: xx
　　　　　　　　　Werner Kroebel

Personal Assistant to Franck: xx

Institute for Theoretical Physics

Director: xx
Regular Assistant: xx
Temporary Assistants: xx
　　　　　　　　xx
　　　　　　　　xx

seated next to the Nazi minister of education at a banquet sometime after the destruction of the Göttingen institutes. "And how is
mathematics in Göttingen now that it has been freed of the Jewish
influence?" the minister asked. Hilbert's response revealed the state
of the mathematical-physical tradition of more than half a century:
"Mathematics in Göttingen? There is really none any more." [101]

POSTSCRIPT

The question of how the authorities would fill the vacant positions
arose immediately after the dispersal of the physics and mathematics
faculty members. The directorships were particularly important, because the head of an institute determined everything from the area
of research undertaken by the staff to the journals ordered in the
field by the library. The director was also crucial in research fund
requests, which were granted in large measure on the basis of his
reputation.

The response of the bureaucracy was a legalistic approach which
compounded the damage to research in Göttingen. The university
and education ministry officials determined that Franck, Born, and
Courant were unaffected by the Civil Service Law, and that their
positions could not be filled until they legally abandoned them. This
decision had the beneficial effect of preventing the appointment of
professionally unqualified National Socialists to the permanent directorships of the institutes. But it also meant a long, unproductive
period before the posts were occupied again.

Courant's post was the first to be filled by a permanent successor.
For a time, the mathematician hesitated to relinquish his position.
He came back to Göttingen from Cambridge at Christmas in 1933
and spoke with the curator, friends, and colleagues. In February, in
the "interest of all concerned," he decided to request an extension of
his leave in order to assume a guest professorship in New York.[102]

It was a difficult decision for Courant. He wrote to a colleague in
Germany that it was not easy to bear the thought of separating himself from Germany and the institute in Göttingen where he had
spent so much of his professional life.[103] This feeling was, of course,
shared by most of the emigrés. The ousted sociologist Franz Neumann recalls, for example, that he spent the first three years in
England "in order to be close to Germany and not to lose contact
with her." [104] Among the exiles there was the strong hope that National Socialism was a temporary phenomenon or at least that its

worst evils would moderate in time. Then they could go home again.

The move to America seemed terribly final to Courant. By continuing his "on leave" status, he maintained the slightest thread of contact with Germany. He knew there was little chance that he could ever return to Göttingen permanently, but he could not give up this possibility, however small.[105]

When the English term ended in May 1934, Courant visited Germany again. Those who remained convinced him that he should allow himself to be pushed into retirement without a struggle. If he were to step down, it might help the reconstruction of the institute because some of his former pupils might then be called to Göttingen. On June 23, therefore, he declared his readiness to relinquish the directorship (he was still listed in the catalog of classes as "on leave") and to change his status to emeritus.[106] Courant stepped down from the institute directorship effective October 1, 1934, and was succeeded by Helmut Hasse, who had worked with Emmy Noether. Courant was officially retired under the Nuremberg Laws as of December 31, 1935.[107]

In contrast, Franck's characteristic insight led him to give up his post quite early, but it remained unfilled for some time. At first his resignation was simply not accepted, and he was placed on leave like the others.[108] His hopes for a position in Germany outside the state service faded quickly, however. He was not interested in industry, and, as far as can be ascertained, at no time was he offered an industrial position.[109] Yet a Kaiser Wilhelm Institute post was not in the offing. Haber, who had resigned his own directorship on April 30, 1933, wrote Franck that Planck and von Laue were working tirelessly to change the laws which had caused the resignations of Franck and himself. Planck still hoped to secure an institute directorship for Franck, but Haber was not optimistic.[110] Internal problems of the Kaiser Wilhelm Society soon destroyed all hopes, and in June 1933, Franck tentatively accepted the offer of a guest lectureship at Johns Hopkins in Baltimore for the coming winter. The position was confirmed in July.[111]

In September, Niels Bohr came down to Lübeck to meet with him, and it was arranged that Franck would go to Copenhagen after America.[112] The first of the Göttingen professors to give up his post, Franck was the last to actually leave the town, on November 27, 1933.[113] One of his assistants, Werner Kroebel, has recalled that the train platform could barely hold all the people who came to see him off.[114] It was "an impressive, unforgettable experience of a silent protest." [115]

Franck spent 1934–35 with Bohr, then worked at Johns Hopkins again from 1935 to 1938 before settling down as professor of physical chemistry at the University of Chicago. At Chicago he later became involved in the Manhattan Project, the American effort to develop the first atomic bomb. His name is particularly associated with the far-seeing committee recommendation against the use of the first atomic weapons, usually called the Franck Report.

Shortly after his departure, the ministry informed Franck that he was unaffected by the Civil Service Law, and that if he wanted to resign, he would have to give up his pension and other rights. Franck agreed on January 1, and on February 8, 1934, retroactive to the date of his agreement, his resignation was accepted.[116]

Franck's clarified status allowed the faculty to begin looking for his successor. The offer first went to Walther Bothe, a later Nobel laureate in Heidelberg. For a number of months, however, it was not clear whether Bothe would be available for the Göttingen post. Finally, he declined in order to remain in Heidelberg, where he became the director of the physics institute of the Kaiser Wilhelm Institute for Medical Research.[117] The faculty then appointed Georg Joos from Jena, who became director of the Second Physical Institute effective April 1, 1935.[118]

Born's post remained vacant quite a while longer. He had requested official leave on July 1, 1933, in order to accept the appointment in Cambridge. He had then retracted his request and submitted his resignation on August 10.[119] In October he was informed by the authorities that he was not affected by the Civil Service Law, but that he would remain on leave as he had requested July 1.[120] His resignation was ignored. Like Courant, he was kept on the staff in absentia.

When Robert Pohl assumed the administration of all three physics institutes, he arranged first for the astronomer Otto Heckmann and then for Born's pupil Martin Stobbe to hold Born's classes. After Stobbe resigned in anti-Nazi protest, Erwin Fues commuted regularly from the TH Hannover to give the theoretical physics lectures. Fues was appointed to a post in Breslau in 1934. For the next two and one–half years, the theoretical institute was administered by Fritz Sauter, a young Privatdozent from Berlin. Born was officially retired under the Nuremberg Laws on December 31, 1935, and the search for a successor was conducted during 1936. Finally, in 1937, Richard Becker was appointed director; Becker's chair at the TH Berlin was eliminated.[121]

Although not as dramatic as the exodus of 1933, the protracted delay in securing new directors for the Göttingen institutes greatly intensified the impact of the dismissal policy. The intellectual boom of the Weimar years may have been over, but capable, highly regarded men like Hasse, Joos, and Becker were able to restore a degree of normalcy once they were finally in office. The makeshift arrangements, stagnation, and uncertainty in the period between the dismissals and the arrival of the new directors marked an unproductive state of affairs which affected research not only in Göttingen, but also in other centers of physics with which the Göttingen community had been in contact.

3.   The Toll of the Dismissal Policy

The events at Göttingen in 1933 were representative of the implementation of the National Socialist civil service purge at universities and institutes of technology throughout Germany. Other types of academic institutions were also affected, however. In Berlin, perhaps the two most famous scientists who joined the exodus of scientific talent were Albert Einstein, who was ejected from the Prussian Academy of Sciences, and Fritz Haber, who resigned from his Kaiser Wilhelm research institute.

By 1935, approximately one out of five scientists had been driven from their positions. The total among physicists was even higher—about one out of four. Government pressure continued to force researchers from their posts until the outbreak of war, although the drain in the middle and late 1930s was merely a trickle in comparison with the 1933 flood. The annexation of Austria produced another wave of refugees in 1938, both from Austria itself and from Germany, where Austrian Jews had been allowed to continue working. At least as significant as the number of scientists who were compelled to abandon German academia was their remarkably high caliber.

Albert Einstein and Fritz Haber

Following the press release on April 1, 1933, which announced that the Prussian Academy of Sciences had no reason to regret Einstein's withdrawal, a sharp exchange of letters ensued between the physicist and representatives of the Academy. Some members firmly supported Einstein. Walther Nernst, emeritus professor of physics at the university in Berlin, commented sarcastically that there was no reason to require a member of the Academy to be both a great mathematician and a nationally oriented German. Maupertuis, d'Alembert, and Voltaire had been members, and they had even been Frenchmen![1] Max von Laue objected on April 6 that not a single member of the mathematical-physical section of the Academy had been consulted concerning the April 1 announcement. The plenary session before which he spoke, however, voted to approve the secretary's action.[2]

Finally, in early May, Planck returned from vacation in Italy. At

the Academy session of May 11, the day after Einstein's books had
been among those publicly burned as manifestations of the "un-
German spirit," Planck was not afraid to compare Einstein's greatness with that of Kepler and Newton. It was important, he stressed,
that posterity not think that Einstein's Academy colleagues were unable to grasp the great thinker's significance for science.[3] But
throughout the spring of 1933, Planck characteristically tried to
hold passions in check and reconcile opposing sides. He therefore
balanced his remarks on Einstein's greatness with the observation
that, by his political actions, Einstein himself had made it impossible
for the Academy to retain him.[4]

The dean of Germany's physicists harbored no illusions, however,
as to where the Academy's responsibility lay. Even before he returned from Italy Planck wrote that "in the history of the Academy,
the Einstein affair . . . will not be counted among the Academy's
pages of glory." [5]

As a state institution, the Prussian Academy was required to carry
out the provisions of the anti-Semitic ordinances by accepting "voluntary" resignations and avoiding the election of new Jewish members.[6] Had Einstein not resigned, there seems little doubt that he
would have been dismissed under the "politically unreliable" clause
of the Civil Service Law. In a note of April 7, in fact, Einstein was
informed by the Academy that he had let himself be used by opponents not only of the new German government, but of the German people as a whole. This was, the note concluded, "a bitter, pain-
ful disappointment for us, which would probably have necessitated a
parting of the ways even if we had not received your resignation." [7]

Haber's situation was quite different. No one could accuse him of
pacifism or lack of national allegiance, for his energetic efforts
during World War I had led to the introduction and development
of gas warfare—which nearly placed him on the Allied list of war
criminals.[8] In addition, his process for synthesizing ammonia from
nitrogen in the air was used at his instigation to produce the nitrates
essential for war munitions. His Kaiser Wilhelm Institute for Physical Chemistry and Electrochemistry in Berlin-Dahlem was, in fact,
the only Kaiser Wilhelm institute to gear completely to the war
effort.[9] Haber was Jewish, but he was exempt from the law of
April 7 because of his war service and the fact that he had obtained
academic status prior to 1914.

Most of the Kaiser Wilhelm institutes derived their funds from industrial and private sources, although staff members often held academic positions that included the right (but usually not the duty) to teach university classes and train doctoral candidates. Thus, few Kaiser Wilhelm institutes were directly affected by the Civil Service Law. Haber's institute, however, operated with government funds and its personnel had civil service status. Additionally, a very large portion of the staff was Jewish—a fact which the general director of the KWG at the time, Friedrich Glum, had already drawn to Haber's attention. Since the KWG administrators did not intrude upon the prerogatives of the institute directors, Glum could only suggest that Haber try to reduce the percentage of Jewish personnel in his institute. The general director has noted, however, that very little could be done along these lines, for prejudice had often caused the universities to refuse to employ even outstanding Jewish chemists. Capable Jewish researchers, who had nowhere else to go, were therefore attracted to the KWG.[10] Haber's institute thus suffered heavily from the dismissal policy in 1933.

On April 30 (effective October 1), Haber resigned in a letter of protest to the Prussian minister of education. He objected to the dismissal measures which had cost him talented co-workers and he rejected a privileged position in regard to the Civil Service Law. The conclusion of his letter raised a furor in the ministry:

> In a scientific capacity, my tradition requires me to take into account only the professional and personal qualifications of applicants when I choose my collaborators—without concerning myself with their racial condition. You will not expect a man in his sixty-fifth year to change a manner of thinking which has guided him for the past thirty-nine years of his life in higher education, and you will understand that the pride with which he has served his German homeland his whole life long now dictates this request for retirement.[11]

In a speech in Berlin a week later, Rust reacted angrily by serving notice that the prerogatives of institute directors would no longer be inviolate—a major blow to the German academic structure.[12] A few days later, Haber received notice that his resignation had been accepted.[13]

The entire situation appeared even more grave after Planck, in his capacity as president of the KWG, paid a call upon Hitler. After World War II had ended, Planck remembered that he had tried to speak a word on behalf of Haber during the audience. In a response reminiscent of his interview with Breiting in 1931, Hitler proclaimed: "I have nothing at all against the Jews as such. But the Jews are all communists and these are my enemies." When Planck commented that one must make distinctions among Jews, Hitler retorted: "That's not right. A Jew is a Jew; all Jews cling together like burrs. Wherever one Jew is, other Jews of all types immediately gather." The Jews themselves should have produced distinctions, he declared. Since they had not, he had to proceed against all of them on an equal basis. When Planck tried to pursue the subject further, Hitler abruptly changed topics, speaking with ever increasing animation until he was in a rage. "There was nothing left for me to do," the dignified scholar reflected, "but to fall silent and take my leave." [14]

The fact that Hitler was unable to distinguish individual Jews made it impossible to reach him on the subject of the dismissals. As Karl Schleunes has pointed out, the Nazi hierarchy displayed a penchant for dealing with "the Jew" as Nazi propaganda had created him.[15] Jews as antithetical in their outlooks as Einstein and Haber were lumped together as members of an indistinguishable host of enemies.

It was no wonder that during the mid-1930s, the story circulated that Hitler had been even more blunt in his conversation with Planck. It was widely believed that he had said:

> Our national policies will not be revoked or modified, even for scientists. If the dismissal of Jewish scientists means the annihilation of contemporary German science, then we shall do without science for a few years! [16]

The seemingly endless flow of scientific refugees from Germany made such a drastic statement appear all too credible.

The Quantitative Cost

Edward Hartshorne, an American sociologist who went to Germany in the mid-1930s to study the impact of the dismissal policy, compiled what is still the most detailed and trustworthy set of statistics on persons driven from their academic positions. He generated the figures primarily through a comparison of the biennial German catalog of academic personnel with the records of the British refugee relief agency.

In contrasting the staff of the winter semester of 1932–33 with those of 1933–34 and 1934–35, Hartshorne disregarded distinctions between "voluntary" resignations, "retirements," protest resignations, and outright dismissals. He did, however, take into account normal attrition, using death and retirement figures for the 1920s. His conclusion was that a total of 1,145 "university teachers" (exclusive of assistants) from all fields had been driven from their posts. Including assistants and others (such as recent graduates, employees of the Kaiser Wilhelm institutes, museum directors, etc.), the total swelled to 1,684 "dismissed" scholars.[17] Jewish sources claimed 800 dismissed Jewish "university professors and lecturers," a figure which Hartshorne found consistent with his overall tally. Hartshorne's figure of 1,145 represented about 14 percent of the staff of German institutions of higher learning in 1932–33.[18]

A breakdown of the percentage of losses gave some indication of which institutions had been more willing to appoint Jews, liberals, and Marxists prior to the Nazi seizure of power. In general, the universities sustained greater losses than the institutes of technology— 17 percent versus 11 percent (excluding assistants). Among the universities, the highest toll was 32 percent, incurred by both Berlin and Frankfurt. Göttingen had forty-five dismissals for a more moderate 19 percent, while dismissals at strongly conservative Munich amounted to only 8 percent of its 1932–33 staff.[19]

Such general statistics provide no information on the numbers of scientists lost from each institution. It is obvious from the discussion of Göttingen in chapter 2 that a large number of dismissals were in physics and mathematics there and that the 19 percent figure was totally misleading in regard to the losses sustained in these fields. Unfortunately, more detailed figures do not yet exist. Hartshorne did reveal, however, that 406 scientists (including assistants) were dismissed from Germany in the physical and biological sciences, of which 106 were in physics and 60 in mathematics. From other sources, it can be estimated that these sums represented approximately 18 percent of the natural science, 26 percent of the physics, and 20 percent of the mathematics personnel. By comparison, the field of chemistry incurred 86 dismissals for a loss of less than 13 percent. Medicine (usually regarded as a field with particularly heavy Jewish representation at this time) suffered 423 dismissals for an 18 percent toll—about that of the natural sciences overall.[20]

After the first wave of dismissals, a serious talent drain continued to characterize German academia. The reasons were varied and often personal, but the quiet application of the dismissal policy to those who had escaped the initial purge accounted for a number of scientists who were displaced from their positions in the middle and late 1930s.

One prominent example was the TH Berlin's Gustav Hertz, who had shared the 1925 Nobel prize in physics with Franck. Hertz was Jewish, but had served in World War I and was exempted from dismissal. One day (apparently in late 1934 or early 1935) he was informed that he could no longer give examinations—only Aryan professors could do so. He thereupon resigned with the intention of going to work for Phillips Company in Holland, with which he had been employed in the early 1920s. Siemens Company of Berlin offered him the directorship of its research facilities, however, so he stayed in Germany. Through the efforts of some of his students he was accorded the rank of honorary professor in 1935, and he still sat in on some examinations. He was not disturbed and remained in Germany until 1945, when he was taken eastward by the Russians.[21]

The example of the experimental physicist Heinrich Konen illustrated the treatment of those few scientists who had been politically active on behalf of the Weimar Republic. Konen was a well-known spectroscopist and had been energetically involved in the Roman Catholic Center party. He was a very active and influential figure in the politics of organized science.[22] In the spring of 1933, the prime political targets of the Nazis were the communists and socialists; the Catholic party was courted to divide the opposition. But in July 1933, all parties except the National Socialist party were banned, and it soon became a liability to have a record as a former Catholic party politician.

In early 1934, Konen was driven into retirement through the efforts of one of his former assistants.[23] His Weimar political activities were the direct cause of his dismissal, but his enemies also charged him with shady financial dealings and suggested that he was perhaps not quite Aryan. Both ploys were commonly used to remove an opponent in Nazi Germany.[24] Konen retired in isolation to his home in Bad Godesberg where he too was allowed to remain unmolested until the end of the Nazi era.[25] He died in 1948.

As the dismissal policy quietly continued to take its toll, some scientists unaffected by the laws chose to leave Nazi Germany's increasingly restrictive intellectual environment. A case in point was

P. P. Ewald, one of Sommerfeld's early pupils, who held the directorship of the institute for theoretical physics at the institute of technology in Stuttgart. Although he was part Jewish, first his war record and then the Nuremberg redefinition of "part-Jewish" prevented the dismissal of the prominent crystallographer.[26] A succession of conservative, nominally Nazi rectors made it possible for him to work relatively undisturbed for a few years at the institute of technology. In 1936, however, an ardent National Socialist was appointed.[27]

Ewald visited America in the summer of 1936. He was considering emigration, for the situation of Jews in Germany had progressively deteriorated. Ewald has recalled that fear of a European war played an even more important role in his decision making, because it would have forced him to work for Hitler against his friends in England. Returning to Stuttgart, he found the atmosphere of the institution under the new rector dismally oppressive.[28] A compulsory lecture where the young Nazi teaching corps leader read a government pamphlet denying the value of "objective" science proved to be more than the outspoken Ewald could stand—he rose from his seat and walked from the hushed assembly.[29] The consequence was his early retirement from the institute of technology. A year later, with a stipend from the British refugee relief agency, he went to England. In 1939, he went to Belfast and after the war to America.

Max Delbrück left Germany for different reasons. A Göttingen-trained physicist turned biologist, during 1932–37 Delbrück served as an assistant to Lise Meitner, Otto Hahn's co-worker at the Kaiser Wilhelm Institute for Chemistry in Berlin-Dahlem. Partially as a result of the unsettled working conditions in Germany, Delbrück left the country at the same time as Ewald, in September 1937. Unlike Ewald, however, he was not yet planning to emigrate. His reason for accepting a Rockefeller stipend to the California Institute of Technology was simply to buy time in order to watch developments from a distance.[30] The war broke out before his fellowship expired, and he chose to remain in America, where his pioneering work in molecular biology was rewarded with the 1969 Nobel prize in medicine.

In March 1938, Nazi Germany annexed Austria. Political and racial criteria were quickly applied to Austrian academia, and the resultant wave of refugees included three Nobel laureates—Otto Loewi (medicine, 1936), Victor Hess (physics, 1936), and Erwin Schrödinger (physics, 1933). Schrödinger had in 1933 registered an open anti-Nazi protest by resigning from Berlin, gone to England,

and then in 1936 unwisely accepted a post at Graz. Loewi was dismissed on racial grounds and Hess and Schrödinger, who were not Jewish, had to flee because of their political activities.[31] Within Germany, former Austrian citizens also became subject to German law. Delbrück's section chief Lise Meitner had not been allowed to lecture at the university since 1933 because of her Jewish descent, but she had been allowed to stay on at Hahn's Kaiser Wilhelm institute.[32] With the help of Dutch colleagues, Meitner, whom Einstein called "our Madame Curie," was able to escape to Holland in the summer of 1938.[33] Six months later, she and her nephew Otto Frisch (who had been dismissed from Otto Stern's institute in Hamburg) were the first physicists to grapple with Hahn's discovery concerning uranium, which they named "nuclear fission."

Considering the steady attrition of scientists from Germany, Hartshorne's figure of 106 displaced physicists should be revised upward. One researcher has recently reported that over one hundred physicists emigrated to America alone between 1933 and 1941.[34] Hartshorne very briefly reviewed his own statistics in 1938, and one of his revisions was an increase in the estimate of the total percentage of displaced scholars from 14 to 20 percent.[35] Without more precise data, the most one can do is to conclude conservatively that at least 25 percent of the physicists with German positions in 1932–33 were displaced during the Nazi period.

THE QUALITATIVE COST

Naturally, a quantitative measure of the damage done by the dismissal policy is only part of the story. The figure of 25 percent does not indicate whether one is discussing predominately the top or bottom quarter of Germany's physicists. Hartshorne records just three dismissals from Tübingen for a loss of less than 2 percent, the lowest rate of all the universities. Yet among the three who had to leave was the prominent young theoretician Hans Bethe, later a Nobel laureate in physics.

If the Nobel prize is used as a measure of quality, those who abandoned their positions in Germany were of very high caliber indeed. Twenty Nobel winners were driven from their posts, and many of these had been awarded the prize before they left.[36] With the exception of Gustav Hertz, all of them emigrated. The loss of first-rate scientists was particularly evident in physics. Eleven of the twenty displaced laureates were physicists (see table 2).

TABLE 2

Nobel Laureates Who Departed Positions in Germany, 1933–45

Name	Nobel Award		Year of Departure	Country of Birth	Institution Departed
Albert Einstein		1921	1933	Germany	Prussian Academy
James Franck		1925	1933	Germany	Göttingen
Gustav Hertz *		1925	1935	Germany	TH Berlin
Erwin Schrödinger		1933	1933	Austria	Berlin
			1938		Graz
Viktor Hess **	Physics	1936	1938	Austria	Graz
Otto Stern		1943	1933	Germany	Hamburg
Felix Bloch		1952	1933	Switzerland	Leipzig
Max Born		1954	1933	Germany	Göttingen
Eugene Wigner		1963	1933	Hungary	TH Berlin
Hans Bethe		1967	1933	Germany	Tübingen
Dennis Gábor		1971	1933	Hungary	Siemens Co., Berlin
Fritz Haber		1918	1933	Germany	KW Institute for Physical Chemistry, Berlin
Peter Debye **	Chemistry	1936	1940	Netherlands	KW Institute for Physics, Berlin
George de Hevesy		1943	1934	Hungary	Freiburg
Gerhard Herzberg **		1971	1935	Germany	TH Darmstadt
Otto Meyerhof		1922	1938	Germany	KW Institute for Medicine, Heidelberg
Otto Loewi		1936	1938	Germany	Graz
Boris Chain	Medicine	1945	1933	Germany	Charité Hospital, Berlin
Hans A. Krebs		1953	1933	Germany	Thannhauser Clinic, Freiburg
Max Delbrück **		1969	1937	Germany	KW Institute for Chemistry, Berlin

SOURCE: Compiled by the author primarily from *American Men of Science* entries, obituary articles, letters from a number of the principals to the author and correspondence with the Research Foundation for Jewish Immigration in New York.

* Hertz did not emigrate, but went to work for Siemens in Berlin.

What accounts for the remarkably large proportion of leading researchers among the physicists displaced during the Third Reich? A large portion of the explanation lies with the fact that talented Jewish researchers had greater opportunity for success in physics than in many other areas, for example, in chemistry.

Jews began to be widely accepted in German academia only toward the latter part of the nineteenth century.[37] Some fields opened to them more readily than others, depending partially on the number of new positions available in a given field and partially on prejudice. Chemistry was an established discipline, and it was often difficult for a Jew to obtain an academic post in that field. Capable Jewish researchers were not encouraged to embark upon an academic career in chemistry, and those who persevered found only a few avenues for advancement, such as Fritz Haber's institute in the relatively new, hybrid field of physical chemistry.[38]

Jewish researchers more readily found openings in physics, especially in modern physics, which was characterized by concern with quantum phenomena. During the late nineteenth and early twentieth centuries, new academic positions were created in larger proportion in physics (particularly theoretical physics) than in chemistry.[39] Two men whose advice was highly influential in filling these posts were Planck and Arnold Sommerfeld—neither of whom hesitated to promote a Jew when the candidate was highly talented. During the Weimar period, Niels Bohr and the Göttingen circle also contributed to opening the field to Jewish researchers.[40] By the 1920s, Jews met notably less resistance to success in academic physics than in academic chemistry. Since the influence of Planck, Sommerfeld, Bohr, and the Göttingen school was greatest in the very fruitful field of modern physics, many talented Jewish physicists had the opportunity to conduct research of fundamental significance. Hence the number of leading researchers among the refugee physicists was disproportionately high.[41]

While most of the displaced scientists were able to continue their work abroad, magnifying the qualitative cost of the dismissal policy to Germany vis-à-vis other countries, some were not.[42] Otto Stern, the co-discoverer of spatial quantization and the developer of the molecular beam method of atomic research, left Hamburg when the government measures affected members of his institute.[43] The later Nobel laureate was Jewish, but he had been in office long enough to be exempt from dismissal. After his resignation in 1933, he went to the Carnegie Institute, but, as his pupil Isidor Rabi has written, "Stern's stay in Pittsburgh was not a happy one, and he went into premature retirement at a time when his powers were still great." [44] A similar case was that of Martin Stobbe, whose protest resignation in Göttingen effectively ended his academic career.[45] Fortunately, Stern and Stobbe were exceptions, thanks largely to the efforts of the refugee relief agencies which sprang up to aid displaced scholars.[46]

The dismissal policy at all levels of public and professional life was a basic feature of the National Socialist seizure and consolidation of power. Its broad goal was to rid the state bureaucracy of active Nazi opponents and Jews. But since the policy and its aftermath had more effect on academic science than any other Nazi measure, it is disconcerting to realize that the damage to science was only a side effect. When the National Socialists were confronted with persons who were both Jewish and talented scientists, anti-Semitism came first, whatever the effect on science. At no time was the content or caliber of a researcher's scientific work an issue in the dismissal process—a fact with a great many consequences, the most obvious of which was the dramatic exodus of scientific talent. Several other results are revealed in an examination of the relations between the Nazi government and those scientists who remained.

4. The Government and the Physics Professoriate

Scientists who remained in Germany were forced to live amid a great deal of confusion and conflict in university politics, which reflected the internecine bureaucratic power struggles prevalent in the Third Reich. After they seized power, the National Socialists split along administrative lines in their views on personnel policy. Those holding state offices basically adhered to academic, professional principles, and those heading party agencies usually followed ideological precepts. In addition to the rivalry generated in this fashion, the party itself was split on many issues into two factions—the ideologically rigid and the ideologically flexible. The Nazi state officials were generally antagonistic toward the strict ideologues and were more inclined to be cooperative when dealing with pragmatists.[1]

Influential leaders meanwhile guided the physics professoriate in a cautious acceptance of the Nazi government. There were exceptions to the general acquiescence, however, and a growing alienation from the regime led to moments of public and private protest on behalf of traditional, professional values. At the same time, the scientists became increasingly estranged from their colleagues abroad. This isolation was felt particularly strongly by those physicists who had participated in the period of intensive discovery during the 1920s.

THE MINISTRY OF EDUCATION

Throughout 1933 and early 1934, the regional ministries of education were allowed to function as they had in the past, while party members assumed the key posts. Hans Schemm and Bernhard Rust were the two most important figures in these positions. An examination of their views on the dismissal policy and the question of objective scholarship is particularly useful, because Schemm espoused a strongly ideological line, while Rust usually took professional considerations into account.

Hans Schemm was an energetic former elementary school teacher who in 1929 had founded the National Socialist Teachers' League (Nationalsozialistischer Lehrerbund). In late 1932 he had become district party boss of his native region in northeastern Bavaria. He continued to head the Teachers' League, and meanwhile exercised his flair for extremist rhetoric as editor of the National Socialist teachers' newspaper (*Nationalsozialistische Lehrerzeitung*). In March 1933, he was one of the Nazis who assumed a post in the Bavarian government as it fell into National Socialist hands, becoming Bavarian state minister for instruction and culture.

Schemm's position on practically every issue was radically ideological. His stand on the role of Jews in German education and the categorical tone of his speeches are both revealed in this excerpt:

> It is ridiculous to believe that racial foreigners could be allowed to teach German children. Racial foreigners lack instinctive racial sureness in the selection of sustenance . . . only German persons can be teachers among the German people.[2]

His views on objective scholarship were no less extreme. He wanted to eliminate all attempts judiciously to weigh various sides of a question in the classroom, for he believed that the Nazi precepts of race, *Volk,* community, and the dictates of the party were the sole criteria for scholarly work. He stated the essence of his position on this issue in a speech before a meeting of Munich professors, during which he reportedly declared:

> From now on, the question for you is not to determine whether something is true, but to determine whether it is in the spirit of the National Socialist revolution.[3]

Such views were typical among the ideological purists within the Nazi party.

The more moderate Bernhard Rust had also been a teacher. He had joined in right-wing, völkisch activities in the early 1920s, and his steadfast loyalty to Hitler as the chosen leader of the völkisch movement had provided valuable support from northern Germany when Hitler had needed it.[4] Since March 1925, Rust had been party boss of South Hannover-Brunswick, an area which had produced strong pro-Nazi returns in pre-1933 elections. His reward came just days after Hitler's ascent to power. On February 4, he was appointed Prussian minister of education.

Rust gave his views on objective scholarship and the dismissal policy during a speech at the university in Berlin on May 6, 1933.[5] Although he declared that all intellectual endeavor was to take place within a nationalist framework, he also made the ambiguous remark that "without intellectual freedom and intellectual competition, we will not open the pathway to Germany's rise, but seal it off." [6] Those who feared strict Nazi control of scholarly endeavor could perceive a ray of hope in this assertion. On the other hand, Nazis like Schemm, who felt that free competition had been stifled by Nazi opponents during the Weimar period, were able to interpret Rust's declaration as an indictment of Jewish influence in academia. This type of equivocal comment was very characteristic of Rust.

Other statements in this speech made it clear that Rust desired to stress the role of teaching rather than research. Like Schemm and other Nazis, by "teaching" Rust meant leadership in the lecture hall and laboratory on behalf of the new German Reich. Rust, however, held that both teaching and research were vital university tasks. He explained that the number of scholarly publications was not to be the only standard by which an institution would be measured,[7] but he left the clear implication that it would remain *one* of the criteria.

In his emphasis on teaching, Rust's greatest concern was the gap between the outlook of the professors and that of the National Socialist students:

> My dear professors, in these years when this un-German state and its un-German leadership obstructed the path of the German students, you, in your professorial isolation and devotion to your great research work, did not take note of the fact that the young sought in you the leaders of the German nation. The young were marching, but gentlemen, you were not at their head.[8]

The need to close this gap was one justification the Nazis made for the elimination of Jewish and anti-Nazi professors.

In expressing his affirmation of the dismissal policy, Rust took specific issue with Haber's letter of resignation:

> I wish in no way to blame the gentlemen of non-Aryan descent for trying instinctively to attract Privatdozenten and assistants who are more closely related to them by blood. But I cannot allow it. And if a well-known professor of the Kaiser Wilhelm Institute wrote me yesterday that he could not agree in any way to allow conditions to be set on the composition of the research unit which he founded, then I must say: I am not qualified to refuse to carry out the law of the German people as expressed by the Reich government. We must have a new Aryan generation at the universities, or else we will lose the future.[9]

The völkisch views expressed in this passage permeated all of Rust's thought. It was clear that he agreed with the dismissal policy as one tactic in the reconstitution of the universities and institutes. Yet his response to Haber showed that he was disinclined to assume responsibility for that policy. It was very typical for Rust to say that he was "not qualified to refuse" to carry out the prescribed measures, rather than aggressively to defend or claim credit for them. This characteristic lack of forcefulness was largely responsible for the fact that he remained one of the least powerful highly placed Nazis throughout the Third Reich. Another result was that the Ministry of Education became a bewildering battleground of rival Nazi factions. Rust's equivocation was further illustrated in his next comment:

> Personally, I deeply feel the tragedy of persons who inwardly want to consider themselves part of the German Volk community and work within it. Nothing is more bitter to me than when I have to set my name to the dismissal of men who as individuals have often given me absolutely no occasion to do so. But the principle must be carried out for the sake of the future.[10]

Such an apology was rare indeed among high-ranking Nazi officials in the spring of 1933.

Until the establishment of a Reich Ministry of Education in 1934, all the ministers of education generally took their cues from the Reich minister of the interior, Wilhelm Frick, within whose office the dismissal policy had originated and who oversaw all policy concerned with civil servants. Whereas Schemm was mainly concerned with primary and secondary schools and Rust with the universities, Frick set goals for all formal education. In mid-May 1933, Frick made a number of pronouncements on Nazi educational policy. Speaking before the Kaiser Wilhelm Society, he propounded a dictum upon which all National Socialists could agree:

> In learned thinking and research there lies something sovereign which lays claim to the whole being of a person and does not desire to comprehend anything else; therein lies the danger of isolation from the great whole, even the failure to recognize or the denial of the duty to *serve the whole*. Let us therefore, with every respect for the freedom of learning, oppose this danger with the binding consciousness that
> > *service to learning must be
> > service to the Volk*.[11]

Objectivity, the hallmark of scientific investigation, had to be replaced by political and racial consciousness.

One means to attain this end was the policy of "alignment" or "coordination" (*Gleichschaltung*) of the universities with National Socialism. Throughout organized German life, alignment systematically barred Jews from all group or public activity (introduction of the "Aryan paragraph") and gave absolute power over each organization or institution to an ardent Nazi who was held responsible only to higher Nazi authority (the "leadership principle"). Within academia, the dismissal measures represented the first part of this process.

The second part commenced in the fall of 1933. The format was exemplified by the steps taken in Prussia. There, on October 28, Rust decreed that henceforth he, not the faculties, would appoint each rector. The faculties were to become mere advisory bodies and their powers (including distribution of funds) were to be transferred to the rector, who also named the deans. The professors retained only one right. They were allowed to draw up a three-man selection list for each vacant professorship, although even then they had no assurance that their preference would be respected.[12]

A year later, in December 1934, a new ordinance added character (i.e., political) criteria to the requirements for obtaining qualification (*Habilitation*) to teach at a university. Good character was to be displayed by, among other things, a stint in a teachers' camp.[13] On April 3, 1935, a reorganization of higher learning gave each rector the title of Führer of the university. The professors and Privatdozenten were placed together in a teaching corps (*Dozentenschaft*), while the students became the student corps (*Studentenschaft*). Both groups were responsible directly to the rector. The minister not only named the rector, but also the vice-rector, deans, and leaders of the teaching and student corps.[14] The ministry's efforts to keep a tight rein on the daily administration of the universities, however, as well as conflicts between the ministry and the professors, made the "rector as Führer" more propaganda ploy than reality.[15]

As part of the alignment process a national Ministry of Education was created in the spring of 1934. The initiative for this step toward the hierarchical concentration of higher education authority came from party rather than state officials. The impetus derived from a January 1934 meeting in the party headquarters in Munich. The objectives put forward there reflected particularly the views of Rudolf Hess (Hitler's official party deputy) and Alfred Rosenberg (the party ideology chief and editor of the party newspaper). Their goals were very much in line with the strain of thought exemplified by Schemm, who was under consideration for the leadership of the new Reich ministry: liberalism in the form of "objective" scholarship was to be combatted; the ideals of National Socialism were to be taught instead. Professional considerations were to be subordinated to political requirements.[16]

Yet on May 1, 1934, Rust, not Schemm, was named Reich education minister (maintaining his Prussian post with the title of Reichs- und Preussischer Minister für Wissenschaft, Erziehung und Volks- bildung). This appointment at first seems inexplicable, for why would party figures place a weak-willed man of moderate views in a position of such authority? The reasons shed much light on the con- fusion which reigned in Nazi higher education policy.

As Prussian minister, of course, Rust was the logical choice be- cause he already oversaw the majority of the German schools. He was also an old comrade and loyal follower who enjoyed Hitler's protec- tion.[17] More importantly, however, as an administrator rather than ideologue, he would not be competition for Rosenberg.[18] Schemm was as forceful, dynamic, and colorful as Rust was equivocal, passive, and plain—the Bavarian was thus far less easy to manipulate than Rust. In fact, at this time Schemm was perhaps somewhat stronger politically than Hess and Rosenberg in educational affairs and was their most powerful rival in this area. Within a year, however, on March 5, 1935, Schemm died in a plane crash.

Helmut Heiber, a historian of the Nazi period, has described Rust as a lonely figure, "scarcely accessible to his subordinates, isolated from his colleagues." Rust had a decent enough relationship with Hess, but he did not get on well with other Nazi leaders. His rela- tions with Himmler were variable; with Göring and Frick, some- what strained; and with Rosenberg and Goebbels, distinctly poor.[19] Often his subordinates had loyalties outside the Reich Education Ministry (REM), for many of them had been forced upon Rust by other Nazi leaders. Representatives of Göring, Rosenberg, the SS, the SD (Sicherheitsdienst, the powerful security arm of the SS), the army, and so on often worked at cross-purposes, though they were ostensibly all under Rust's authority. Heiber has pointed out that Himmler was quite right in a certain document to mention coopera- tion "with SS comrades who are working" in the REM. It was not that REM officials belonged to the SS, but that SS-men worked in the ministry.[20]

The REM's organizational structure followed the pattern indicated in the full ministry title: the large Offices for Learning (Wissenschaft), Education (Erziehung) and Training of the People (Volksbildung) corresponded roughly to higher, secondary, and elementary education. The ministry also included Rust's personal staff, the central office, and the office for physical education.[21]

Before the creation of the Reich ministry, the Office for Learning had been the Prussian Department of Higher Education (Hochschulabteilung). According to the terms of an agreement between Rust and the army, between 1934 and 1937 there were actually two separate Offices for Learning: W I (the continuation of the Prussian department) headed on paper by the office chief himself, the mathematician K. Theodor Vahlen, but in reality run by the deputy chief, the chemist Franz Bachér; and W II (the army office for research) nominally headed by the chief of the research department in the army weapons office, Erich Schumann, but actually run by the chemist Rudolf Mentzel. Mentzel managed to enjoy at various times the support of both the army and the SS.[22]

By 1937, with rearmament no longer clandestine in Germany, the army abandoned its special outpost in the REM. The two Offices for Learning were merged under Otto Wacker, an ardent SS-man who had been the education minister of Baden since May 1933. Mentzel became his deputy. Apparently Himmler had earmarked Wacker as Rust's successor, but in the face of the "unholy confusion" in the REM, Wacker resigned in 1939 and returned to Baden, where he died in 1940.[23] Mentzel took over the Office for Learning, which he headed for the duration of the war. Although frequent personnel and organizational changes plagued the REM, Mentzel's presence provided a certain amount of continuity in matters affecting physics.[24]

The variety of interests represented within the Reich Education Ministry, combined with Rust's weak personality, hardly provided solid ground upon which to build a new Nazi conception of higher learning. Party ideologues like Rosenberg never intended to work with the state offices, hoping instead to replace them with their own party agencies. Unlike the army and the SS, their goal was not to control higher education, but to remold it entirely. Physics was one of the disciplines which would have to be transformed.

THE PHYSICS PROFESSORIATE

The vast majority of the German physicists were not involved in the conflicts within the REM and between the ministry and the ideologues. Yet the repercussions of the confusion and tension in academic life very much affected the scientists. Their initial cautious acquiescence soon evolved into quiet alienation from the government. Furthermore, their isolation from the international scientific community increased. This double effect—domestic alienation and international isolation—intensified the problems which beset those scientists who remained in Germany.

Response to the Dismissal Policy: Max Planck and Werner Heisenberg

In his speech before the KWG in May 1933, Frick referred to "something sovereign" in learned thinking which claimed a researcher's whole being. Indeed it is not uncommon for a scientist, especially a capable and dedicated one, to feel that his work is truly significant and lasting, while regarding occurrences in the nonscientific world as of lesser concern. Many scientists during the Weimar period, like other professionals, were nearly oblivious to the impending political upheaval. In his memoirs Werner Heisenberg has sought to recapture his reluctance (as well as that of many of his colleagues) to perceive the political atmosphere of the early 1930s:

> The "golden age of atomic physics" now quickly approached its end. The political unrest in Germany grew. Radical groups of the right and left demonstrated in the streets, battled each other in the backyards of the poorer quarter of the city and agitated against one another in public gatherings. Almost imperceptibly the unrest, and with it anxiety, spread also within university life and faculty meetings. For a time, I tried to push the danger away from myself and ignore the incidents on the streets. But in the end, reality is stronger than our wishes . . .[25]

A key figure who also lived in this world of wishful thinking was the initiator of the quantum revolution, Max Planck. Planck apparently believed, along with many others, that the Nazis would be sobered by the responsibilities of power and held in check by their conservative coalition partners. The unfortunate excesses of the early months would shortly pass. It has been reported that when an eminent colleague of Planck came to him and expressed fear for the future, Planck replied,

> Ah, dear colleague, you are letting your thoughts run away with you. If the present university situation displeases you, then take

a vacation for a year. Go on a pleasant research trip abroad. And when you return, all the unpleasant incidental phenomena of the moment will have disappeared.[26]

This view was common among those who sympathized with many of the Nazis' broad goals—an end to the burden of the Versailles treaty, a demand for selfless sacrifice of individual desires in favor of the common good, jobs for the millions of unemployed, and so on. It was also typical of those members of German academia who held the mandarin belief that scholarship was above—and thus beyond the reach of—politics.

Furthermore, Planck was concerned with the long view. During the Einstein affair, the judgment of posterity upon the Prussian Academy of Sciences was what mattered to him. For Planck, the fate of the Academy as an institution was of more lasting importance than the fate of a single individual.

His beliefs in the matter had been consistent throughout his long association with the Academy. In 1915, for example, severance of ties with academies of the Allied powers was advocated. In spite of the prevailing nationalist mood and his own feelings, which were expressed in his support of the extremely nationalistic 1914 declaration "To the Cultured World," Planck opposed the proposal. Part of his argument was:

> Above all, the measures taken against a foreign academy possess a much more protracted effect than those against single persons. For the members of the academies change, but the academies themselves remain.[27]

In 1918, his devotion to the life of the Academy again proved stronger than his personal views when he opposed the cessation of the Academy's activities as a protest against the socialist revolution of November 9. He contended that, as the "most noble learned body of the state," the Academy had to continue its scholarly work.[28]

The perception of the vital issues in life in terms of duty toward state institutions such as the Academy rather than in terms of the fulfillment of personal desires was characteristic of an attitude often pejoratively termed Prussian. Planck's heritage was indeed Prussian (he was born in Kiel in 1858), but he exemplified a good number of his non-Prussian physics colleagues who also interpreted the events of 1933 much as their social peers in the army or bureaucracy did.

Their allegiance was to the state (as distinct from the government), and to the professional institutions of which they were a part.[29]

Concern for the welfare of institutions was not the only factor that made Planck think in historical perspective. By 1933 he had already lived through seventy-five of the most eventful years of German history. It was therefore hardly surprising that he looked beyond the tumult of the moment to the years ahead. The natural circumspection and perspective of age must be considered in weighing Planck's desire to avoid precipitous action.[30]

As the dean of German organized science, Planck's prestige among German physicists was such that he and those who consulted with him set the pace for the response of the German scientists to the dismissal and alignment processes. Their tactics were to delay every final dismissal decision and to avoid confrontation between scientific institutions and the government. In this effort they sensed encouragement from the Prussian Ministry of Education, for Rust's speeches appeared quite moderate and measured in contrast to the rabid Nazi demands of Schemm and the students. Attempts to bridle the activists and the fact that the dismissals were initially couched in terms of "leaves of absence" were taken as signs of hope.[31]

In this atmosphere a policy of voluntary cooperation (usually referred to as Selbstgleichschaltung, self-alignment) was carried out by many institutions, including the KWG in Berlin, of which Planck was president. In its yearly report, published in May, the leaders of the society expressed concern that,

> the government of the national revival, which fully recognizes the significance of pure research for the prosperity of the Fatherland and its position among the peoples of the world, might find the way and means to enable the society not only to maintain its institutes, but to equip them in every manner necessitated by their ceaseless scholarly work.[32]

In order to ensure the support of the state, the KWG general director, Friedrich Glum, undertook reorganizational measures designed ostensibly to depoliticize the society. Glum was able to convince officials in the Interior Ministry that introduction of the leadership principle and the exclusion of all Jews from the senate would provoke sharp criticism abroad. He then managed to drop a number of politically burdensome figures from the senate and to have the society select some new members who tied it more closely to industry.

The Ministry of the Interior and the Prussian Ministry of Education each named six more members of the society's governing body, some of whom were figurehead Nazis suggested by Glum, who has claimed he was seeking to avoid being saddled with party activists.[33]

To a large extent the tactic of self-alignment succeeded. Unlike the universities and many other organizations, the KWG was never fully aligned by the government. Planck and Glum remained in their positions until after the twenty-fifth anniversary of the society in 1936. Planck then decided to retire. In order to ensure the selection of a reasonable successor, some concessions had to be made: the leadership principle had to be accepted, and Glum also had to give up his position. But the new president (who assumed the post in May 1937) was the Nobel prize-winning chemist and industrialist Carl Bosch, whose views on the Nazi government were known to be somewhat critical. Unfortunately, Bosch, who was in ill health, was not able to provide the society with active leadership and died in 1940. He was succeeded by Albert Vögler, an industrialist who had been associated with the society since its founding and who was also rather critical of the regime. Since Vögler's time was largely consumed by his business interests, however, Glum's successor Ernst Telschow actually ran the affairs of the society from 1937 on. Telschow had earned his doctorate with Otto Hahn prior to World War I, but apparently had the confidence of the party and faced a minimum of political interference.[34]

At no time did the KWG suffer financially at the hands of the government. In fact, the organization received increased support in order to expand its operations. One example was the construction of the Kaiser Wilhelm Institute for Physics, which in the Weimar period had existed only on paper. In 1937 the building in Berlin-Dahlem was finally completed with a combination of government and Rockefeller funds. This new institute immediately became the premier physics laboratory in Germany. In view of later events, it is interesting to note that the laboratory's new director was the experimentalist Peter Debye, Dutch-born and an early Sommerfeld pupil. When Debye was forced to leave Germany in 1940, Vögler and Telschow were able to prevent a physicist supported by the German War Office from taking over completely. Dr. Diebner became director "in" the institute, the directorship "of" the institute remained vacant until the end of the war.[35]

As a result of the efforts of the KWG leadership, most of the society's institutes were not greatly disturbed in their work during the early Nazi period. Often Jewish researchers, like Lise Meitner, had to give up formal connections with the universities, but they continued to work in the institute laboratories. Later their positions became untenable and they had to leave Germany if they could. As an exception, however, in 1933 Haber's KW Institute for Physical Chemistry and Electrochemistry in Berlin-Dahlem was occupied and remolded into a model of Nazi research.

Although a good deal of money continued to flow into the institute from the ministry (there was significant new construction in preparation for "forthcoming" work),[36] no account of the institute's activities appeared in the KWG annual reports for 1933 and 1934. The physical chemist Peter Thiessen, who reorganized the institute in the fall of 1935, lamely explained in the annual report for that year that the institute had been silent because much of its work was classified "government research."[37]

The spirit which guided this model of the new Nazi scientific institute was marked not only by the lack of publication of significant work, but also by the "work-community" (Arbeitsgemeinschaft) orientation of the laboratories:

> During the past one and a half years, the work of the institute has been guided by the goal of forming a community. Besides comradeship evenings, during which the entire staff has often been brought together, the institution of a group visit to a camp has helped fulfill this purpose—for which the minister of education placed the teachers' camp at the Tännich Castle at our disposal. Here the male staff [männliche Gefolgschaft] spent a week together during Pentecost 1936. The deepening of our comradeship, which has been achieved through these and other measures fostering work-community, has shown its effectiveness splendidly in the success of our work.[38]

As if aware of how unbelievable this sounded, the writer concluded defensively, "Numerous domestic and foreign visitors have convinced themselves of the efficiency of the work-community." It was quite apparent to those who chose to look, however, that under direct Nazi political control the activities of one of the world's renowned research institutes had degenerated into busy work and beer parties.

Unable to foresee the future course of events, Planck and those following his lead soon were somewhat disillusioned as the summer of 1933 wore on. Capable people were already starting to leave even though the dismissals were not yet final. Planck's distressing conversation with Hitler about Haber took place during this period. Yet his goal was still to avoid confrontation. When colleagues came to him to suggest forms of protest like petitions, Planck tried to dissuade them.[39] Max Born, who visited with Planck when the latter came to the Tyrol for a vacation in the late summer, has remarked that,

> The Prussian tradition of service to the state and allegiance to the government was deeply rooted in him. I think he trusted that violence and oppression would subside in time and everything return to normal. He did not see that an irreversible process was going on.[40]

In his memoirs, Heisenberg has tried to describe the quandary of the scientist who remained in Germany while others were compelled to emigrate.[41] To him, the choice of whether to follow the refugees abroad or to stay on and attempt to make the best of things was not unambiguous. "I almost envied the friends," he has written, "whose basis for living in Germany had been removed from them by force, so that they knew that they had to leave our land." [42]

Heisenberg's discussion of the problem is presented in the form of a dialogue with Planck in the summer of 1933, but the main arguments apply to the entire Nazi period and they reflect Heisenberg's conversations with many others besides Planck.[43] The argument in favor of protest, resignation, and emigration, based on moral outrage and the hope that some good would come through a demonstration of opposition to government policies, was unconvincing to Heisenberg.

The arguments in favor of remaining were more persuasive. One receives the impression from Heisenberg's account that to a man of Heisenberg's (or Planck's) convictions, to emigrate of one's own accord was more akin to desertion of duty than to courageous protest. Their concern was the state of German science, which could not afford losses in addition to those the Nazis had already inflicted.[44] Heisenberg has Planck present the pragmatic considerations of 1933: resignation would not cause the government to reverse itself on the issues; it might not even be reported to the public; and it would unnecessarily add one more scientist to the long list of those seeking a new position abroad—perhaps even keeping some other emigré from securing one of the few available posts. Looking back, these arguments may appear somewhat self-serving, but their practicality was unassailable. The example of Haber's resignation, Rust's displeased response, and the subsequent despoliation of Haber's institute quickly made it clear that protest was not particularly effective on the dismissal issue. The consequence was, however, a dissipation of energy needed to oppose Nazi policies on other issues.

The single most convincing argument for Heisenberg, according to his reconstruction, was that events were leading inexorably toward catastrophe and that leading scientists were desperately needed to stay in Germany—even when it meant making moral compromises— to preserve the traditional scientific values by training the younger generation.[45] In other words, the emphasis was to be placed on "teaching" in the same sense that Rust and Schemm understood it— as leadership in the classroom or laboratory on behalf of a certain set of values. For men like Planck and Heisenberg as well as the Nazis, a key issue in the contest for the universities was professorial appointments, which thus took on significance far beyond considerations of personal prestige.

The Spirit of Independence: Max von Laue

Heisenberg was typical in his decision to remain in Germany. The few scientists who freely chose to resign and emigrate in protest were almost exclusively Jewish (e.g., James Franck and Otto Stern) or foreign-born (e.g., Erwin Schrödinger). As did members of other professional groups, such as the army, scientists perceived loyalty to Germany as loyalty to something above the German government—an attitude which had prevailed since 1918. Loyalty to Germany for scientists meant devotion to the traditions and institutions of German science and efforts to preserve them, even if these efforts entailed moral compromises through apparent—or real—cooperation with the Nazi state.[46]

But there were a few scientists who rejected even a show of cooperation. Foremost among these were Planck's Berlin colleagues, Otto Hahn and Max von Laue, who were as deeply imbued with a Prussian sense of duty as Planck. During the spring and early summer of 1933, von Laue in particular had been among the optimists who saw the forced leaves of absence as temporary and who encouraged others to wait out the storm.[47] Sometime during the summer, he perceived the direction of events and changed his position. His speech as presiding officer at the annual Physicists Conference on September 18, 1933, unmistakably implied a comparison of the Nazi government's attitude toward Einstein and relativity theory with the attitude of the Inquisition toward Galileo. In closing, he pronounced the legendary words of the Italian, "And it still moves!" and was greeted by the applause of his audience.[48] When Fritz Haber died in January 1934, von Laue published a tribute to his former colleague in two widely read and prestigious scientific journals, praising Haber and lamenting Germany's loss.[49] The speech and obituaries earned him reprimands from the Prussian Ministry of Education.[50]

Privately, von Laue's actions were practical consequences of his public stand. In 1937, he sent his son to school in America specifically to remove him from Nazi influence.[51] Von Laue often sent word abroad of the desires of a colleague to leave Germany and find a new position, or acted as a channel of information in other ways.[52]

Apparently he also spent considerable time with Jewish colleagues who did not emigrate from Germany. Most notably, he often visited Arnold Berliner, founder and editor of *Die Naturwissenschaften*, who was dismissed from his position in August 1935. As the situation of the Jews progressively worsened, Berliner became ever more withdrawn. Finally, in 1942, wrote von Laue after the war, "when they wanted to drive him from his apartment, the last refuge, he carried out a decision made long in advance for this case, and parted from this life." [53] Von Laue was one of the few people who attended Berliner's funeral in the Jewish cemetery in Berlin.[54]

Von Laue's uncompromising stance was as well-known abroad as it was in Germany. In fact, he became a symbol for refusal to cooperate with the Nazis. For example, P. P. Ewald, at the close of a visit with Einstein in the mid-1930s, asked if he could deliver any messages for Einstein in Germany. Einstein replied, "Greet Laue for me." Ewald named others, asking if they might also be included in the greetings. Einstein's answer was simply to repeat, "Greet Laue for me." [55]

In a later autobiographical sketch, von Laue indicated that he remained in Germany for a number of reasons, one of which was that he did not wish to occupy one of the positions abroad that were needed so badly by others. But "above all, I wanted also to be there once the collapse of the 'Third Reich'—which I always foresaw and hoped for—allowed the possibility of a cultural reconstruction upon the ruins this Reich created." [56] There is also a ring of truth to the

story that he once remarked to Einstein in America shortly before
the outbreak of the war: "I hate them so much I must be close to
them. I have to go back." [57]

At times one wonders how such an outspoken critic of the government was allowed to remain at large in Nazi Germany. Part of the
answer undoubtedly related to von Laue's eminence as a Nobel
laureate. His age was also a factor, for it was generally Nazi policy
to ignore the older conservative critics, concentrating pressure instead on the younger professors. It is also highly probable that the
physicist had protectors in conservative circles who had connections
in the army.[58]

Von Laue's determination to stay in Germany, yet not compromise,
made him a truly laudable exception among German professors. As
Ewald has written,

> While many respectable scientists yielded to political pressure,
> first outwardly "aligning" themselves and in the end losing their
> spiritual independence, Laue was neither to be threatened nor
> bribed into subservience. . . . Laue was a great patriot and he
> clearly recognized Germany's loss in the eviction of so many of
> her best-trained scientists. But his human loyalty was even
> stronger than the patriotic appeal.[59]

What this meant to others has also been recalled by Ewald:

> To all of us minor figures the very existence of a MAN of
> Laue's stature and bearing was an enormous comfort. Compare
> it to the comfort the presence of just one man gave during the
> war, Churchill. You felt that as long as he stood up, not all was
> lost.[60]

Von Laue remained unbending throughout the war. After the collapse of the Third Reich, true to his goal, he participated in the
reconstruction of German cultural life. He served as a witness in the
de-Nazification trials, helped revitalize the German scientific organizations, and was responsible for reestablishing the laboratories of the
Imperial Institute of Physics and Technology. He also became involved in the opposition of German scientists to work on nuclear
weaponry in Germany.

Public Protest: The Fritz Haber Memorial

In spite of the fact that, unlike von Laue, most German scientists
decided upon at least minimal cooperation with the regime as the

price for the preservation of German science, one symbolic protest did take place, the memorial meeting for Fritz Haber on January 29, 1935.

After leaving Germany in the summer of 1933, Haber had gone to Cambridge, England. His health had long been poor, and he died en route to a resort in Switzerland on January 29, 1934. Von Laue's moving lament for Haber's passing appeared in February. In late June, Max Bodenstein, a former co-worker, gave a memorable lecture in tribute to Haber before the Prussian Academy of Sciences.[61] Aside from these courageous public expressions of esteem, however, no official notice was taken of Haber's demise.

As the first anniversary of his death approached, a desire was expressed in various quarters to honor Haber's memory. A one-year anniversary memorial was in itself quite unusual, even ignoring Haber's Jewish heritage. Planck thus personally took care of the arrangements to hold a meeting under the auspices of the KWG. The invitations went out in mid-January.

On January 15, the Ministry of Education forbade all state employees to attend the memorial. The ministerial decree read in part:

> Professor Dr. Haber was released from his office on the basis of a request in which his inner attitude against the present state was unequivocally expressed, and in which the entire public had to see a critique of the measures of the National Socialist state. The intention of the specified society to arrange a memorial celebration on the occasion of the one-year anniversary of Haber's death must particularly be taken as a challenge to the National Socialist state, since this day is especially remembered only in special exceptional cases of the *greatest* Germans.[62]

An unspoken objection was the fact that January 30, the anniversary of the Nazi seizure of power, had already become a national holiday. To honor a Jewish opponent of the government on the day before would be added provocation.

Planck responded with a letter to Rust on January 18, and the minister replied directly on the twenty-fourth.[63] Apparently Planck had argued that the Prussian Academy of Sciences had been allowed to hold a lecture in Haber's honor, that he (Planck) was loyal to the present state and Führer and that attendance should be allowed. Rust retorted that, whereas the Academy was an international body, the KWG was the most prestigious German research organization. The KWG was therefore expected to act in harmony with the National Socialist state. Planck's expression of personal loyalty was brushed aside, and the ruling against attendance still held. Exceptions could be made in the case of selected individuals, however, because the domestic and foreign press had already reported plans for the affair. Rust's tendency to equivocate thus made it possible for the celebration to take place in spite of his obvious displeasure.[64]

One of the speakers, Karl Friedrich Bonhoeffer, who was to talk on Haber's scientific achievements, was forbidden to appear. As a professor at the university in Leipzig, he was under Rust's authority. Planck made the introductory comments, and a military officer who was familiar with Haber's wartime activities spoke on his services to Germany during that period. Hahn read Bonhoeffer's speech and delivered his own talk on Haber's personality and contributions to the KWG. Since many of those forbidden to come were represented by their wives, the meeting was well attended. Carl Bosch and a number of his I. G. Farben staff were present, as well as some of Hahn's co-workers—Lise Meitner, Fritz Strassmann, Max Delbrück.[65] The ministry made a list of those who appeared and censored press notices pertaining to the memorial.

The significance of the tribute to Haber, according to Hahn, was its demonstration that, "in the first years of the Hitler regime, one could still resist—even though only a little—which was no longer possible later." [66] What the chemist implies is, of course, that no *effective* resistance was possible. Although his disavowal of allegiance to the regime was widely known, Hahn withdrew into what has become known as "inner emigration" and did not openly participate in any other political affairs.

In his book *Politics and the Community of Science,* the political scientist Joseph Haberer has argued that the obituaries of Haber and the memorial meeting did not so much show resistance to National Socialism among German scientists as indicate the lack of it. Much stronger action was morally both required and possible, but the scientists lacked the strength of conscience to perceive it. "More than any [other] institutional or professional community in Germany," he contends, "the scientists disengaged themselves from the problem of their responsibility in the crisis which involved them." [67]

The accuracy of such a categorical judgment is highly problematical for at least two major reasons. First, it assumes that science had a political significance in the 1930s that it did not attain until after the discovery of atomic energy. In spite of their views on the value of their science in Weimar international politics, scientists did not yet perceive themselves as powerful figures of domestic politics. They regarded themselves—and were regarded by political leaders—as more spectators than participants in political affairs.

Second, Haberer's critique presumes a perception of National Socialism which was simply not prevalent in Germany—or even abroad —in the early 1930s. National Socialists were not yet the exterminators of the Jews, the initiators of World War II, the iron-heeled conquerors, nor the Nuremberg criminals. To the politically naïve professionals in the army, civil service, universities, and elsewhere, the Nazis were surely uncouth, uncultured ruffians who had temporarily seized the machinery of a highly organized and powerful state. Still, there were no clear guidelines on how to deal with them, even if one had serious disagreements with their policies. Only in retrospect is it so apparent that the only truly honorable response to National Socialism was uncompromising defiance.

Private Protest

Although the Haber memorial was the only public demonstration of protest by German scientists in the Third Reich, a number of individuals quietly objected to specific government measures affecting science. Physicists were particularly concerned about the reduction in class hours for students and the large number of vacant faculty positions.

Walther Gerlach, noted professor of experimental physics at the university in Munich, like many of his colleagues, was displeased at the drain political activities and labor service placed on the students' study time. When it was proposed that class hours be reduced to allow more time for these activities, he argued firmly against such a course.[68] In June 1934, he filed a formal complaint that irregular interruptions in the form of required political or labor service were lowering the quality of the work performed by the students and assistants in the institute. Beginning students could not make up missed classes because far too many hours were involved. The advanced students could not perform their evening laboratory work because they were required to attend innumerable meetings. Even the assistants often had to refuse to perform experiments because of other duties.[69] Gerlach's protestations were, however, to no avail.

Although the decline in the caliber of the work of the students and assistants portended serious consequences, a more pressing problem for German physicists was the number of vacant professorships. Without effective instruction, the students could not learn physics even if they were left uninterrupted. Thus, in November 1934, the professor of experimental physics in Jena, Max Wien, circulated among his colleagues an informal report on the status of academic physics. His figures revealed that seventeen of one hundred academic posts in physics were vacant, while normally only two or three would be empty at any time. The difficulty was intensified by the fact that seven of the thirty-seven institute directorships were unoccupied, leaving the work at nearly 20 percent of Germany's physical institutes practically at a standstill.[70]

The situation in physics appeared so serious that by late 1934 industrial circles were discussing the possibility of training doctoral candidates within industry itself. Recognizing that such a course of action could only lead to further deterioration in academic physics, professors such as Gerlach and Robert Pohl argued strongly against it.[71] As Pohl pointed out, however, the fact that industrial people would propose such a radical solution to the problems at the universities and institutes of technology represented a powerful critique of the Nazi measures in science that could be used by the academic physicists to buttress their arguments.[72]

The academicians received decisive support for their position from the industrialist-scientist Carl Bosch. In January 1935, Bosch circulated a closely reasoned assessment of the status of German physics and chemistry.[73] The number of vacant academic positions and the apparent tendency of the National Socialist government to fill them with too little regard for professional, scholarly standards was quite alarming. The decrease in the authority of institute directors and professors over the choice of assistants and the criteria for qualification (*Habilitation*) also seemed extremely detrimental to German science. Yet the development of industrial institutes as surrogate universities struck Bosch as a danger to pure research. He called instead for maintenance of the principles and practices which had brought German science world renown in the nineteenth and twentieth centuries. He concluded with a demand that politics be banned from the conduct of physics:

> Science stands outside of state-political controversies to a greater degree than other disciplines. Nature is something unique and there is only one way to penetrate its mysteries, a way which has

always remained essentially the same since the beginning of modern research.[74]

He urged all those agreeing with him to make their views known to the state offices responsible for the economy and for learning. Thereafter the pressures for an industrial degree program quietly dissipated.

International Isolation

Added to the concern for the quality of German physics generated by governmental measures was the growing isolation of German scholars from the mainstream of international science. The trend was manifested in a variety of ways, particularly in the decline (and then the change in composition) of the number of foreigners visiting Germany, holding memberships in learned societies, and subscribing and contributing to scientific journals. In addition, restrictions were placed upon Germans who traveled abroad, and those who did were treated with suspicion.

The figures for the KWG's lodge in Berlin, the Harnack House, gave some indication of the overall tendency (see table 3). The house was founded in 1929 and provided accommodations for visiting scholars from foreign countries and from within Germany. From 1930 to

TABLE 3

Visitors to the Harnack House

Year	Total	German	Foreigners	Americans	
1929–30	40	13 (32%)	27 (68%)	11 (28%)	(41%)
1930–31	202	104 (59%)	98 (41%)	34 (17%)	(35%)
1931–32	240	125 (52%)	115 (48%)	33 (14%)	(28%)
1932–33	230	126 (55%)	104 (45%)	34 (15%)	(33%)
1933–34	287	221 (77%)	66 (23%)	16 (6%)	(24%)
1934–35	359	253 (71%)	106 (29%)	11 (3%)	(10%)
1935	172	119 (70%)	53 (30%)	14 (8%)	(26%)
1935–37	287	180 (63%)	107 (37%)	12 (4%)	(11%)
1937–38	203	103 (51%)	100 (49%)	15 (7%)	(15%)
1938–39	218	117 (54%)	101 (46%)	not reported	

SOURCE: Figures are from April 1 to the following March 31, except April–September 1935 and October 1935–March 1937. Based on the annual report printed each year in *Die Naturwissenschaften*.

NOTE: Figures in parentheses are percentages of the total; second figure under "Americans" is Americans as percentage of all foreigners.

1933, the number of guests remained fairly constant in spite of the economic depression. The total was somewhat over 200, slightly less than half of whom were abroad. In 1933, however, foreign representation dropped by nearly half, while the number of German guests increased considerably. From a ratio of 45 percent foreign to 55 percent German in 1932–33, the proportion became 23 percent foreign to 77 percent German in 1933–34. The 1932–33 ratio was not reestablished until 1937–38, by which time the nationalities of the foreign visitors were quite different from those in the earlier period.

From 1930 to 1933, Americans had provided over thirty guests each year, or approximately one-third of all guests from abroad (by far the largest single foreign contingent). After the Nazis came to power, there were usually less than fifteen Americans per year, accounting for less than one-fourth of the foreigners. This was indicative of an important change. Although countries from all over the world had visited Harnack House before 1933, the heaviest representation had been distinctly Western European and American. By 1937, other areas provided a very large proportion of the visitors. The Union of South Africa, the free city of Danzig, Rumania, and Chile, for example, were as frequently represented as Holland, France, and England.

The Harnack House figures provide documentation of a change which occurred throughout German scholarly life. Up to 1932–33, visitors to Germany had come largely from the countries at the heart of the European learned community. The numerical losses immediately following 1933 were recouped by drawing more heavily upon native Germans and, eventually, visitors from countries outside Western Europe and America.

This trend was particularly significant in physics, for Western Europe and America were the scenes of leading research in many fields during the 1930s. The theoretical physicist Friedrich Hund has recalled:

> the year 1933 took co-workers from the institute, and new ones from abroad no longer came so numerously. At the beginning of the war the circle shrank completely. Heisenberg once related that two students had been in his first seminar at Leipzig; in the last seminar which he and I held together, there were also two.[75]

Heisenberg was typical of many German physicists who missed the extensive international contact they had enjoyed in the 1920s. In 1936 he wrote to Niels Bohr:

Occupation with physics is something which has become very lonely for us in recent years, and it is therefore always a great feast when we can partake of the full life of science for a few days in your circle.[76]

While not all German scientists had been as active in international science as Heisenberg, nearly all were concerned with the problem which beset the various scientific societies. The basic trouble was financial, resulting from the decline in membership which had begun with the onset of the depression in 1930. The Society of German Natural Researchers and Physicians (Gesellschaft Deutscher Natur-forscher und Aerzte), for example, the oldest and largest nationwide scientific body in Germany, had 6,884 members at the end of 1929. By the end of 1931, the figure was 5,691. On December 31, 1933, it was 4,798; by the end of 1935, 4,002; and on the last day of 1937, 3,759. The society ceased to meet during the war.[77]

Other societies had a less serious membership loss, but none escaped the problem. The German Society for Technical Physics (Deutsche Gesellschaft für technische Physik), the Kaiser Wilhelm Society, and the German Physical Society (Deutsche Physikalische Gesellschaft) lost considerable numbers of members in the 1930–33 period. This trend continued until 1935. By recruiting heavily, especially among the Germans themselves, the losses were recouped in 1936–38. (See tables 4, 5, and 6.)

Since the membership decline neither accelerated nor decelerated in 1933 and 1934, it is difficult to assess the precise role played by National Socialism. It appears certain, however, that the losses would have been made up earlier than 1937 if the Nazis had not instituted the dismissal policy. In spite of the dwindling total membership in the German Physical Society from 1930 onward, for example, the number of members abroad had increased steadily (table 6). With the exodus in 1933, the list of members abroad swelled with emigrés who retained their ties to the society, while the total membership shrank still further. A number of refugees and others abroad dropped their membership in 1934 and 1935, however. Among the net loss of thirty-four members in 1935, twenty-nine were in the category which included those abroad. Beginning in 1936, the German Physical Society had a membership that consisted of progressively more resident Germans.

TABLE 4
Membership of the Kaiser Wilhelm Gesellschaft

Date	Number of Members
1 April 1930	892
1 April 1931	902
1 April 1932	829
1 April 1933	786
1 April 1934	693
1 April 1935	656
1 October 1935	675
1 April 1937	800

SOURCE: Based on the annual report printed each year in *Die Naturwissenschaften;* membership not reported after 1937.

TABLE 5
Membership of the Deutsche Gesellschaft für Technische Physik

Year	Number of Members	Year	Number of Members
1930	1,358	1935	1,074
1931	1,268	1936	1,086
1932	1,190	1937	1,174
1933	1,044	1938	1,230
1934	1,040	1939	1,275
		1940	1,234

SOURCE: Based on the annual report printed each year in the *Zeitschrift für technische Physik.*

Most of the twenty-nine members abroad who left the society in 1935 resigned or let their membership lapse by declining to pay their dues. A variety of reasons were involved, from purely financial considerations to explicit protest against National Socialism. Alfred Landé, who had emigrated to America in 1931, suggested in early 1933 that members of the German Physical Society abroad should resign from the organization en masse with a protest declaration against the treatment of the Jews.[78] Such an organized exit from the society never transpired, but individual physicists took action. Dutch-born Samuel Goudsmit was one of those who protested Nazi policies by withholding his dues and donating them instead to a refugee relief fund. He eventually resigned, and his bitter letter of resignation

TABLE 6

Membership of the Deutsche Physikalische Gesellschaft

Year	Total	Percentage of 1930 Total	Members at Large * (% of total)
1930	1,493	100.0	380 (25%)
1931	1,467 **	98.3	383 (26)
1932	1,437	96.2	401 (28)
1933	1,379	92.4	421 (30)
1934	1,355	90.8	410 (30)
1935	1,321	88.4	381 (29)
1936	1,362	91.2	387 (28)
1937	1,352	90.6	386 (28)
1938	1,318	88.3	345 (28)

SOURCE: Based on the membership list printed each year through 1935 in the *Verhandlungen der Deutschen Physikalischen Gesellschaft*, and separately thereafter.

* Includes both members at large and members abroad (section entitled "Mit keinem Gauverein verbunden") as well as members of the Prague district organization, who were listed as foreign members beginning 1934. Does not include Austrians, who were included under the district "Oesterreich." Approximately 80 to 85 percent of the persons in the tabulated category "members at large" did not reside in Germany.

** Due to a printing error in 1931, the membership list for the district "Bayern" was omitted. In 1930, there were 90 members on the list, in 1932 there were 86. Therefore 88 is estimated for 1931, yielding a total of 1,467 for the society that year.

expressed the feelings of many of his colleagues, particularly those who were also of Jewish descent:

I wish to inform you that I am discontinuing my membership in the Deutsche Physikalische Gesellschaft. I am disappointed in that the Gesellschaft has never protested as a whole against the bitter attacks upon some of its outstanding members. Moreover, very few contributions to Physics are coming from Germany nowadays. The main German export being propaganda of hatred.[79]

Leaders of German physics attempted to encourage those abroad to maintain their membership in the Physical Society. The dues and the international connections were necessary to maintain financial and political independence. After convincing the aerodyamics expert Theodor von Kármán to keep his name on the rolls, von Laue wrote that he had also sent letters to others on the subject:

> Up to now only one person besides yourself has answered, and he intimated that he wants to let his official connection with the German Physical Society gradually die away. And from the silence of the others I almost have to conclude that they have the same intention. But tell the German physicists who are still in Brownian motion or have already become sedimentary, that the man who beat the pack because he wanted the donkey to move has never seemed to me to be a model of particular cleverness.[80]

Protest by withdrawing membership was indeed somewhat misplaced, for the German Physical Society was one of the few organizations to escape alignment in the Third Reich. It was never absorbed by a broad Nazi-dominated cover organization (such as the union of technical workers under the autobahn designer Fritz Todt), and never submitted to a Nazi-appointed president.[81] Largely through the efforts of independence-minded presidents Max von Laue, Jonathan Zenneck, and Carl Ramsauer, the Physical Society continued to select its own officers even though it officially accepted the leadership principle in 1940. It also allowed Jews to be members until the same year, provoking consternation among Nazi party agencies.[82] The resignations of those abroad, however, further isolated the German physicists.

The scholarly journals also showed the effects of isolation. *Die Naturwissenschaften,* one of the most important German scientific publications, suffered because many of its regular and best contributors had been among the victims of the dismissal policy. For a time, some of them supported the journal with articles from abroad, but in the fall of 1933, the editor, Arnold Berliner, had already been warned that the publication had too many non-Aryan contributors.[83] By 1935, Berliner had to contend with a scarcity of contributors and a shortage of quality articles.[84] Other journals faced the same problems.[85]

A decline in subscriptions also plagued the scholarly publications. In early 1935, the board of the Society of German Natural Researchers and Physicians decried the trend of foreign libraries, particularly those in Northern Europe, to cancel their orders for German medical and scientific journals. The board requested the German government to support the publications by eliminating export duties on them in order to lower their prices abroad and to increase circulation.[86]

The situation was further exacerbated by the fact that through the Propaganda Ministry's Reich Scholarly Congress Center (Reichswissenschaftskongresszentrale) the Nazi government controlled permission for German citizens to speak at learned meetings abroad.[87] The ministry tried to utilize conferences as propaganda sounding boards, which led other participants to deride Germans who did their government's bidding.[88] German nationals had to secure permission from various ministries—including Rust's unpredictable REM— in order to travel abroad, a process that often involved complications and delays.[89] Once abroad, Germans found themselves in a dilemma: if they spoke out among friends and acquaintances against their government, word might get back and have repercussions at home; if they held their peace, friends and colleagues might suspect that they approved of the Nazi state.

The barrier between German scientists and their colleagues elsewhere became more palpable as the war approached. In late 1937, the leading British journal of scientific affairs, *Nature,* was proscribed in German libraries for reporting events in Germany unfavorably.[90] In the summer of 1938, Heisenberg explained to Bohr that he could not publish his paper for a Warsaw convention in the congress report, because the government frowned on cooperation with meetings having any sort of connection with the League of Nations.[91] And a year later, when Gerlach visited Poland, he reported back to Germany that the library in Posnan was well stocked and that

> almost all the physical journals of all lands are present; furthermore there are the numerous new American physical monographs, which are mostly unknown at home. I looked through some of them at night and regretted that we do not have these books, and that so many scientific books are now appearing abroad in the manner in which they were earlier written in Germany.[92]

Recalling such conditions, Heisenberg has written simply that, "the years before the Second World War have always appeared to me, in so far as I spent them in Germany, as a time of endless loneliness." [93]

The situation was thus depressing for most physicists who stayed in Germany. Alienated from the government by the obvious priorities of the National Socialist dismissal policy; faced with the bewildering morass of personality and interest conflicts in the ministry that had seized control of the university administrations; harassed by measures which portended serious damage to the structure of academic physics; isolated from international contact—the German physicists had no clear focus for political action. Their basic attitude was represented by Planck's passive assumption that service to the state through dedication to the institutions of German science was distinct from service to National Socialism. Their concerns were not those of the politician, but the scientist—teaching conditions, laboratories, assistants, the quality of journals, and so on. Their interests were those of specialists, which, judging by Hitler's conversations with the newspaper editor in 1931, was exactly what the Führer wanted.

Yet the goals of the students, Schemm, and the party ideologues went far beyond this. A small minority of scientists also wanted to turn Frick's dictum around and put service to Volk first. These men were politicians more than scientists. Their concern was not the academic quality of science but its völkisch quality. They wanted to inject Nazi ideology, particularly anti-Semitism, into the conduct and content of physics itself. Their goal was an "Aryan physics."

Foremost among them were two Nobel laureates in physics, Philipp Lenard and Johannes Stark.

5. The Aryan Physicists: Philipp Lenard

Both Lenard and Stark were researchers renowned for their experimental investigations of nature. They were obviously intelligent men capable of objective observation and logical reasoning. Therefore their adherence to the Hitler movement with its emotional appeal and anti-intellectualism has been a mystery to their professional colleagues and later commentators. How, it is often asked, could able and well-established *scientists* declare allegiance to National Socialism? It is necessary to answer this question in order fully to explore the political environment of scientists under Hitler.

From Birth to the Nobel Prize, 1862–1905

Like Adolf Hitler, Lenard was raised not in Germany, but in the Austro-Hungarian Empire. His father was a wine merchant in Pressburg (today Bratislava, Czechoslovakia), where the future Nobel prize laureate was born on June 7, 1862. From his unpublished autobiography, it is apparent that here, as a young boy, he acquired from his favorite grandmother the romantic admiration for the "great figures" (*grosse Geister*) of the past which was profoundly to mark his outlook on life.[1]

His father expected Philipp to take over the family business, but the young man had no interest in the enterprise. After making an unsatisfactory attempt to abide by his father's wishes, Lenard set out in 1883 for Germany, where he decided to study physics.[2] He completed his doctorate under Georg Quincke in Heidelberg in 1886, but after three years (1887–90) as an assistant in the Heidelberg institute he determined to emigrate once again. The twenty-eight-year-old scientist left for England, a country whose language he already understood (he had learned English by reading Darwin's *Origin of Species*[3]) and which he had previously visited in order to see British friends who had studied in Heidelberg.[4]

Lenard was disappointed with England, however, and stayed only about six months. He found the English uncongenial and unreceptive, and he decided that Britain lacked "great personalities" of the stature of those of the past.[5] Lenard's later animosity toward the English may have had its roots in his rebuff during this thwarted emigration, and, in conjunction with his upbringing in a German borderland, it may have been responsible for much of his fierce Pan-German nationalism.

He returned to Germany as an assistant for a short time at Breslau, and then became assistant at Bonn to Heinrich Hertz, the discoverer of radio waves. During his stay on the Rhine (1891–94), Lenard began the careful experiments with cathode rays for which he received the Nobel prize in 1905. After his professor's death in 1894, however, he had to interrupt his research and see Hertz's final book through the publishing process.[6]

Hertz was half-Jewish, a fact which did not disturb Lenard when he was working with him. Neither was Lenard perturbed by the fact that his most faithful backer for academic promotion, the Heidelberg professor of mathematics Leo Königsberger, was also Jewish.[7] Anti-Semitism was not yet an element in Lenard's thinking.

He was, however, upset by the disruption of his experimental work, which persisted in 1895 as he fulfilled the duties of extraordinary professor for theoretical physics in Breslau. He had not really wanted the post, for he knew from his brief stay in Breslau in 1890 that working conditions for experimental physics were very poor there. On the advice of friends, however, he decided that rejection of the offer would jeopardize his chances for future advancement, and reluctantly accepted. Within a year, he had become so restless and desperate for experimental research that he resigned his professorship and acquired a post at the Aachen Institute of Technology as a simple assistant.[8]

This kind of resignation and voluntary demotion was naturally very unusual, and it revealed quite a bit about Lenard's personality, including his deep commitment to experimental work, his willingness to adopt a radical solution to a problem, and his acceptance of the role of maverick. He later complained bitterly that his work was better known and appreciated abroad at this time—especially in England—than it was in Germany. He also contended that academic promotion did not depend upon talent, but upon personally knowing others who would speak well of one when positions became available.[9] He felt special resentment toward the senior professors (the older "authorities"); he felt they were too jealous to reward good work done by younger men.[10]

At Aachen he received the shattering news that Wilhelm Conrad Röntgen had discovered x-rays. Lenard felt that if he had not suffered so many interruptions, he would have made the discovery first. In Aachen, where he had experimental apparatus again, he had been on the verge of the discovery. The disappointment was particularly keen because Lenard had personally advised Röntgen on the way to obtain the unusually high-quality tube needed to generate x-rays. Röntgen did not share the credit for the discovery, however, and Lenard never forgave the older man for slighting him.[11]

Lenard stayed at Aachen for only a year, then went to Heidelberg as extraordinary professor of theoretical physics for two years. Just prior to his arrival in Heidelberg, in September 1896, he visited Liverpool as an honored guest at the meeting of the British Association for the Advancement of Science. Lenard demonstrated his experiments for the English, who were very interested in his pioneering work. Especially interested was J. J. Thomson, director of the Cavendish Laboratory at Cambridge.[12] At Heidelberg, Lenard continued his experimental work with cathode rays, for he had little concern for theoretical physics (especially mathematical physics). Meanwhile, Thomson gravitated to the same subject and laid the basis for his famous argument that cathode rays were negatively charged particles much smaller and less massive than atoms.[13]

In 1898 Lenard was called as professor of physics to Kiel, and set about building a new physics institute in the city. Among the experiments he conducted during this time were a number in 1899 concerning the photoelectric effect, which he published in October 1899, in the proceedings of the Imperial Academy of Sciences in Vienna. He later held that he sent Thomson a copy of his work and that the Englishman printed the same results in December 1899, without giving him credit.[14] Lenard argued that when Thomson finally cited his work in 1903, the Cavendish director noted only a later reprint of Lenard's article rather than the original, thus making Thomson the first to publish on the subject.

Lenard was angry enough to announce his claim to priority in his Nobel lecture, and always afterward resented the Englishman for what he believed to be unethical conduct.[15] He also regarded Thomson as a particularly sloppy experimenter who rushed into print with insufficient and incorrect data, and Thomson came to epitomize for Lenard the "English" manner of research.[16] Thomson became a Nobel laureate in physics in 1906, the year after Lenard.

NOBEL PRIZE THROUGH WORLD WAR I, 1905–18

Lenard was unable to travel to Stockholm to receive his Nobel award until May 1906, for he was recovering from a grave illness. He was afflicted from childhood onward with a periodic swelling of the lymph nodes. The improper treatment he received in Kiel in 1905, however, caused one of his neck muscles to contract so tightly that his head was pulled to one side with his ear firmly pressed against his shoulder. After a time of acute suffering, he was finally operated on by a Heidelberg surgeon who removed the muscle, leaving a scar from the physicist's ear to his breastbone.[17] The illness jeopardized a call to Heidelberg then in progress, for it appeared doubtful that Lenard would be able to teach and work again. The wiry little professor was intensely proud that, despite all expectations but his own, he was able to regain his old powers and was called to Heidelberg in 1907.[18] After this period, however, not only was his own work no longer at the forefront of physical research, but he seemed unable to follow the significant discoveries of others. It was, unfortunately, quite possible that his ordeal dulled his creative powers much more than he was able to perceive.[19]

As a lecturer, Lenard was celebrated throughout Germany. His presentations were carefully prepared and enthusiastically delivered theatrical productions. The Heidelberg chemist Karl Freudenberg has recalled that prior to the beginning of class Lenard would painstakingly arrange a demonstration to run perfectly. As the results occurred before his audience, however, Lenard would step back, throw up his arms in feigned wonder and amazement, and exclaim "Ah!" [20] One of his assistants, Carl Ramsauer, has claimed that in the large lecture hall, Lenard's personality and methods projected the image of a "priest of physics." [21]

Lenard was a master storyteller and his lectures were filled with the great tales of scientific discovery. During the war, when Robert Pohl was called to Göttingen to give the basic lecture course, he stopped in Heidelberg to solicit Lenard's advice. The elder physicist suggested that the way to convey enthusiasm to the students was to re-create for oneself the thrilled mood of those great scientists who had made the tremendous discoveries.[22] Thus Lenard's romantic hero worship obviously played a key role in his lectures.

As Freudenberg has pointed out, however, scientific work is not merely a matter of preplanned demonstrations, and one deceives the students by setting up experiments which run artificially well.[23] Lenard also failed to perceive that, by venerating the past and romanticizing physics, he had himself become one of the older "authorities" against whom he had railed as a young researcher.

He had fallen especially far behind in regard to theoretical physics, which he found ever more disagreeable as the discipline increasingly availed itself of mathematical expertise. His own experiences at Breslau had left him with a distaste for the subject, and the fact that J. J. Thomson originally came to physics from mathematics only reinforced Lenard's antipathy toward the field.

Thomson was an original, perceptive physicist whose talents lay in both theory and experiment, but his son (also a Nobel laureate in physics) has noted some of his shortcomings. He put forth a large number of original ideas, "quite a proportion of which were wrong"; he was not interested in detailed accuracy in experimental work, for sometimes only a qualitative answer would do; and "J. J. always wanted the 'first word' in any line of work, and was somewhat scornful of people who claimed . . . that they had said the last word on a subject." [24] For Lenard, these flaws gradually came to represent those of all theoretical physicists. The tendency of many theoreticians to regard experiment as the servant of theory particularly irritated him.

Lenard espoused a professional code of conduct for physics involving slow, patient, carefully repeated work. Others, who were soon to make up the majority of prominent physicists, preferred to stress the race to open new territories of understanding. Lenard, who turned fifty in 1912, could never understand that the pace of physical investigation had vastly accelerated, and that he and many others had been left behind not only with outdated conceptions of physical reality, but with outmoded ideas on the methodology of physical research.

True to his conception of proper physics, Lenard's pupils had to demonstrate their proficiency in reproducing classical experiments, and in other work they had to proceed step by step according to the professor's instructions.[25] Ramsauer has maintained that Lenard's rigidity in directing his institute revealed an outer protective shell which was one aspect of his character. Another, contrasting aspect was an inner emotional softness, which Lenard showed in thoughtful gifts to students and assistants.[26] Ramsauer's observation hints at another fact. Although Lenard married in 1897, he was always adamantly a loner and had few friends.[27] He reflected sadly in his autobiography that he had always felt a deep need to love other persons, but in most instances had been unable to do so. He was left only with a sense that it was his duty to love others.[28] Possibly his thwarted desire to establish genuine human contact accounted for much of Lenard's extraordinarily subjective understanding of human events. Quite likely the frustration also helped lead him to political activism on behalf of National Socialism, which offered a sense of togetherness, community, and belonging to those who followed Hitler.

The outbreak of war in 1914 had the effect of drastically intensifying Lenard's views. A recent study of German academia during the war has suggested that German professors considered neither France or Russia to be the major foe, but England.[29] A set of exaggerated contrasts between the Germans and British—particularly German freedom (involving selfless subordination of individual desires to the common good) versus English materialistic selfishness, *Helden* (heroes) versus *Händler* (merchants)—reflected the academic values of the nineteenth century. The German academicians held the merchant spirit responsible for what they regarded as the vulgar utilitarian concept of the greatest happiness for the greatest number; the materialistic view of life based solely on external comforts; the balance-of-power political theory; and the predilection for economic methods of oppression rather than an honorable soldierly fight.[30] They saw the war largely as a battle between German Kultur and Western Zivilisation.

Lenard was a vocal exponent of every one of these mandarin shibboleths. In the euphoric feeling of national solidarity of August 1914, Lenard dashed off a pamphlet denouncing England's unwarranted intervention in the conflict. The kernel of the presentation was contained in the following passage, which evidently referred to J. J. Thomson:

> One notices approximately the following from the literature of my discipline in the last ten years: England makes itself look as if it leads all alone; advancements achieved abroad are copiously used, but openly used only where they play no essential role or else they are annexed with the aid of a certain evasion—the source is then found cited somewhere in a tucked-away place deep inside the publication or only in some difficult to locate minor publication. Sometimes direct historical falsification is used. In short, an individual Englishman—even when he is a natural scientist—provides in principle approximately the same picture as that which one gets from English politics.[31]

Lenard claimed that the egoistic English wanted the people of every other country to sit obediently in "menagerie cages" while England ruled the world. France and Russia had been unleashed upon Germany by the scheming islanders in order to weaken all competitors on the Continent.[32]

German scholarship, he maintained, was already subservient to English letters. The great figures of England's past, however—Shakespeare, Newton, Faraday—no longer ruled England, and Germans had to stop imitating the British and begin to seek their own identity. He demanded that the Continent impose an intellectual blockade of England.[33] Shortly after he raised this cry, Lenard signed the notorious appeal "To the Cultured World," which defended German militarism and the violation of Belgian neutrality.[34]

There was no trace at this time of the anti-Semitism which soon dominated Lenard's views. In fact, James Franck has recalled being somewhat startled by a letter from Lenard while at the front: "He said that we should especially beat the Englishmen, because the Englishmen had never quoted him decently." [35] Lenard made a number of personal sacrifices for the war effort, including eschewing cigar smoking (which he loved) because there was a shortage of tobacco for the troops. He also made valuable equipment from his laboratory available for military use.[36] In addition, he was forced to watch his children suffer from poor nutrition, a result of the English blockade.

The physicist later claimed that during this period uncovering the true causes of the war was more important to him than any other task to which he had previously devoted his talents. It seemed clear to him that English materialistic egoism contrasted greatly with German idealistic self-sacrifice, but he had not yet satisfactorily pinpointed the cause of England's decline from a state with great, heroic figures to a country of such lowly, vulgar characteristics. In his search for answers, he read Houston Stewart Chamberlain's *Foundations of the Nineteenth Century* and began to take an interest in racial theories.[37]

RELATIVITY AND BAD NAUHEIM, 1919–20

Germany's surrender in November 1918 came as a shock to Lenard. The only explanation he found comprehensible was the failure of German leadership under Kaiser Wilhelm, whose flight to Holland was the symbolic acknowledgement of his desertion of the German people in their hour of need.[38] The professor was outraged by the execution of hostages in the April 1919 Bavarian Soviet uprising (which he felt certain was instigated by the Jews, a common belief

since a number of the insurgent leaders were Jewish). He was also
dismayed by the Weimar constitution and the new government's acceptance of the "dictated" Versailles treaty. He began to read the
speeches of Anton Drexler and Adolf Hitler printed in the
Münchener Beobachter.[39]

Perhaps Lenard was most indignant, however, over the international acclaim accorded Einstein's general theory of relativity. A
total eclipse of the sun in the tropics, which was observed by a
British team of scientists in May 1919, had provided a measure of
empirical support for the theory. In November, the announcement
that Einstein's work had altered the basis for modern science was
made public, and immediately the retiring physicist was a world
celebrity.[40]

Einstein stood for all the things Lenard had come to abhor. During
the war Einstein had not only refused to sign the appeal "To the
Cultured World," but he had also helped prepare a counter "Manifesto to Europeans" in 1914, calling for European unity in place of
nationalism.[41] As a pacifist and internationalist, he had been a member of the antiwar League of the New Fatherland (Bund Neues
Vaterland), and in private conversation had even expressed hope for
Germany's defeat. He was an active supporter of the fledgling Weimar
government.[42] Furthermore, Einstein was a theoretician whose ideas
had suddenly received overwhelming recognition even though they
were apparently incredibly difficult to comprehend, and in spite of the
fact that their basis in empirical fact was still disputed. To the
Heidelberg professor, however, probably the most objectionable fact
was that Einstein was being lionized and popularized by the hated
English. That Einstein was a Jew was originally a fact of little importance, but it proved essential in eventually turning Lenard to
anti-Semitism.

The unsought publicity made Einstein uncomfortable, but he
found it nearly impossible to escape the press. His every deed and
word were news. As he wrote to Max Born later in 1920, he suffered
from a sort of Midas touch—only everything turned to newsprint
instead of gold.[43]

His extraordinary public exposure and open internationalist
stance on postwar reconciliation made Einstein a highly visible target
for persons opposing his views. The most vocal group was the Work
Group of German Scientists for the Preservation of Pure Scholarship (Arbeitsgemeinschaft deutscher Naturforscher zur Erhaltung

reiner Wissenschaft), led by Paul Weyland, an unsavory and shadowy adventurer.[44] The organization was well funded, and it held public rallies in the latter half of 1920 denigrating Einstein's work and personal character. Max von Laue and other Berlin colleagues of Einstein were so incensed by the half-truths, demagogy, and anti-Semitism displayed at one of these sessions that they wrote a short notice condemning the proceedings and sent it to the larger Berlin newspapers.[45] Weyland's activities also prompted Einstein to respond in the daily press, and he addressed his rather caustic comments on August 27 to "Anti-relativity Theory, Ltd." One of the targets of his criticism was Lenard.[46]

Lenard possessed by far the greatest stature of the German scientists who actively opposed Einstein's work. Although he had once held a high opinion of Einstein's work on the photoelectric effect,[47] the theoretician's subsequent rejection of the aether theory caused Lenard to view relativity with reservations even before the war.[48] In his main criticism of relativity, published in 1918, before the furor swept the popular press, he continued staunchly to uphold the aether theory against what he considered insufficient experimental data in favor of relativity. No intimation of anti-Semitism appeared as yet in his works.[49]

The Heidelberg professor was greatly perturbed by the publicity Einstein and relativity received. He was further angered by what he interpreted as the egosim and arrogance—which he felt were typically British characteristics—displayed by the adherents of the theory. Not just the superlatives applied to Einstein, but also the air of superior inner certainty among the relativity proponents disturbed him. He felt that Einstein's followers refused to listen to any criticism, including his own. In the summer of 1920 he issued a revised edition of his Nobel lecture, in which he stressed his antagonism toward the British. He contrasted the quiet selflessness and willingness to hear other viewpoints exhibited by earlier British scientists with the "one-sided drive toward making their own preferred viewpoint supreme" of the contemporary scientists.[50] The remark could be taken to apply only to J. J. Thomson, but the inference was also clear that many German scientists were acting in an "English" manner.

Lenard allied himself with the Weyland group and allowed his name to be used in connection with it. His own speeches and writings, however, remained quite moderately phrased. He was thus very upset when Einstein deprecated his views publicly in the "Anti-relativity Theory, Ltd." article of August 27, 1920. The Berlin physicist had proposed in the article that protest against his work should be raised at the forthcoming (September 19–24) conference of the Society of German Natural Researchers and Physicians in Bad Nauheim. Lenard perceived the article as a personal affront and was determined to accept the challenge.[51]

The discussion of relativity was actually scheduled under the auspices of the German Physical Society, which was to hold its first post-war general meeting in conjunction with the Society of Natural Researchers and Physicians. The Einstein debate was only one item on the agenda, but with the approach of the Nauheim conference, the growing relativity controversy overshadowed all other issues. The German Physical Society's presiding officer, Arnold Sommerfeld, wrote to Einstein that the Nauheim meeting should issue a condemnation of scientific demagogy and a vote of confidence in him. Einstein preferred to keep the matter on a scientific level, however, and told Sommerfeld he regretted having written the unfortunate article.[52]

The Munich physicist thereupon tried to effect a reconciliation between Lenard and Einstein by writing to both on September 11. To the Berlin theoretician he suggested:

> If you say to him that your reaction was not against learned critics, but against W[eyland]'s alleged comrades-in-arms, and that you would declare this publicly upon his wish, then his wrath will probably be appeased.[53]

Whether Einstein communicated directly with Lenard is not clear, but Lenard's reply to Sommerfeld's note was quite blunt: there would be no apology forthcoming from Heidelberg. Einstein's vituperation would make any sudden change of heart suspicious, Lenard wrote. If an apology were made, it would have to be public since the insult was in the press. The words of Einstein furthermore displayed arrogance of the Berlin members of the Physical Society and represented a low-water mark hitherto unsuspected by Lenard himself, even though he had already thought the organization in need of reform.[54] Since Lenard and Einstein would meet face to face in Bad Nauheim only days later, the convention promised to be an explosive event.

Given the volatile atmosphere of Germany in 1920, the strong emotions displayed by Einstein's detractors threatened to lead to an unseemly anti-Semitic demonstration during the Physical Society sessions. The Weyland group appeared to be organized for the occasion—at least one major physicist, Felix Ehrenhaft of Vienna, was offered money to side with the Einstein opposition.[55] The leaders of the society therefore took the precaution of calling the authorities, who reportedly stationed police outside the meeting hall.[56] Max Planck, who chaired the relativity sessions, had arranged the agenda with an eye toward avoiding an incident. The papers delivered were exclusively scientific and discussion took place on a scholarly level. The presentations were contained within the framework of relativity and assumed that the basic question of the theory's validity had already been favorably resolved. Following a talk on possible new experimental support for Einstein, a short time was allowed for discussion. Unfortunately, no verbatim record of what transpired appears to exist.[57]

Lenard took the floor and raised objections to the "abolition of the aether" announced in connection with the theory. There were two ways of forming a picture of nature, he declared, one based on explaining equations through observations and one based on explaining observations through equations. For the latter (experimental) method the aether was essential. How was it, he asked as an example, that in the relativity theory one could not tell if a train braked to a halt or the surrounding world ceased to move? Einstein asserted that it was a matter of perspective, but the relativity theory was not totally arbitrary because it did explain physical processes. Relativity still violated intuitively obvious (*anschaulich*) pictures of nature, Lenard argued. Einstein answered that what was regarded as intuitively obvious changed with time. Physics was conceptual rather than intuitive, Einstein emphasized, drawing attention to the changes connected with the intuitive perception of Galilean mechanics over the years.

Lenard then offered to compromise by allowing that the aether had failed in certain respects because it had not been handled correctly, as he had pointed out in his works on the subject. And he would grant the relativity principle limited validity. Einstein declared that an essential aspect of relativity was its universal validity. Lenard thereupon objected to the notion of equal value for all coordinate systems, to which Einstein only replied that no system was automatically preferable to any other by reason of its simplicity.

Lenard questioned the use of imaginary experiments (*Gedanken-experimente*) and asked why some which challenged relativity were inadmissible.[58] Einstein gave the argument of a theoretician (which to Lenard was totally unacceptable) that only those imaginary experiments were permissible which in principle could be carried out, even if practically they were not feasible. Lenard thereupon unilaterally concluded that the aether could not yet be abolished, that the relativity principle applied only to gravitation, and that certain problems still caused difficulties for the theory.

Two speakers presented other short objections to Einstein's work, one holding that the relativity theory was correct about everything except abolishing the aether, and the other noting that Einstein and Lenard provided a classic contrast between the theoretical and experimental methods in physics. Einstein rejoined, however, that no antithesis existed between theory and experiment.

Two supporters of Einstein spoke. Max Born asserted that the theory valued observation more than equations, while Gustav Mie pointed out that others before Einstein had presented some of the basic ideas of relativity. Mie's argument in particular foreshadowed a line of reasoning used to disassociate relativity from Einstein's name in the Third Reich. In spite of the efforts of Lenard and Stark later to brand the theory itself un-German, for most National Socialists only Einstein's name was objectionable.[59] Even at Nauheim in 1920, it was not Einstein's work, but his politics, that aroused the greatest animosity. After Born and Mie spoke, the time allotted for the session had expired, and Planck quickly closed the meeting.

Although the official record of this debate suggested that the proceedings were marked by dignity and decorum, apparently the Weyland group staged interruptions when Einstein had the floor. Ehrenhaft has recalled that Einstein was

> interrupted repeatedly by exclamations and uproar. It was obviously an organized interruption. Planck understood this and was pale as death as he raised his voice and told those making the row to be quiet.[60]

Born has written that Einstein was provoked into answering his opponents sharply, and Einstein later declared that he would never again let himself become as agitated by his critics as he was at Nauheim.[61] Sommerfeld was also upset, and wrote to Einstein's wife that in recovering from the convention Einstein had of course regained his "kindness and objectivity, qualities which one can not concede his opponent L[enard]." [62]

As perturbed as they were over the events at Bad Nauheim, Einstein's supporters were probably relieved that nothing worse had transpired. In this connection, the physicist Philipp Frank has suggested in his biography of Einstein that the desire to avoid an unpleasant incident led the Physical Society leadership to miss a valuable opportunity. They could have defused the relativity issue by really attempting to enlighten Einstein's scholarly opponents.[63]

The problem went even deeper than Frank suggests. By curtailing debate and presenting only prorelativity papers, the leadership gave the critics the impression that the society would not tolerate scientific dissent. Lenard, for one, drew the conclusion from the convention that there was no way to challenge relativity theory within the normal scientific channels connected with the Physical Society and its leadership. Other means would have to be found.

ANTI-SEMITISM AND NATIONAL SOCIALISM, 1921–36

Lenard threw himself into the effort to fight the acceptance of Einstein's work with the same intensity he had applied to experimental research and to his later search for the causes of the war. In the 1921 edition of his book on relativity, Lenard appended a section on the Nauheim session concerning Einstein's work. He repeated the conclusions he had announced during that meeting and declared that a theory which could not answer simple questions in simple terms was unsatisfactory.[64] He correctly pointed out that, although a number of competent observers had failed to find the red shift in a gravitational field predicted by Einstein, the only talk on the subject at Nauheim had been given by a Bonn physicist who provided evidence in Einstein's favor.[65] It was typical of the Bonn physics institute, Lenard acidly commented, to turn out shoddy experimental work. And it was characteristic of the Einstein supporters, he implied, to consider only experimental evidence which confirmed their speculations.[66]

In subsequent publications, Lenard showed less and less regard for academic restraint. In July 1922, with a view to the upcoming Hundred Year Celebration at the Natural Researchers and Physicians convention in Leipzig, he published a "word of warning" to German scientists as a forward to another book on aether theory. He noted that the approaching convention had again scheduled a

session on relativity theory. However, he asserted, the relativity theory was no theory at all: it was merely a hypothesis which his book
made superfluous. To broadcast it in the newspaper was one thing;
to honor it in a respected scientific society was another.[67] It was
nothing more than the shrill cry of the marketplace, supported pre-
dominantly by mathematicians who were retreating into a new form
of scholasticism: they sought knowledge in their heads instead of ex-
perimenting with their own hands and observing nature with their
own eyes.[68] Mathematicians who had recently attacked him betrayed
their racial allegiance by doing so, he stressed ironically, for ease in
transforming an objective question into a personal fight was a
"known Jewish characteristic." [69] (Using that criterion, of course,
Lenard's own behavior could easily have been classified as "Jewish.")
In conclusion, Lenard decried Einstein's arrogance at Nauheim in
comparing his own unproven hypothesis (as Lenard insisted upon
terming relativity) with Galileo's honored and time-tested foundation for dynamics. "Respect for the great teacher and judge Nature,"
he emphasized, taking the tone of a moralistic pantheist, "will always remain the first mark of true natural research." [70]

The "word of warning" preface marked an unpleasant milestone
in Lenard's life. Up to this point his emerging anti-Semitism had
been increasingly evident, but it had not infected his scholarly publications. From this point onward, völkisch concepts and terminology
came ever more to the fore and eventually formed the rationale for
his two most lengthy works—Grosse Naturforscher (Great natural
researchers, 1929) and Deutsche Physik (German physics, 4 volumes,
1936–37).

In waging his campaign against Einstein, the Heidelberg professor
went completely beyond the bounds of academic propriety at the
Leipzig convention of September 1922. At the opening of the sessions on relativity, he had his supporters hand out broadsheets which
contained the same extreme sentiments as his recent preface. The
anti-Einstein proclamation also appeared in the newspaper. All of
this shocked and outraged Lenard's professional colleagues.[71]

The extremity of his actions backfired on Lenard. On June 22,
1922, the German Foreign Minister Walther Rathenau had been
assassinated by right-wing radicals. Rathenau was also a Jew and an
internationalist, and Einstein was threatened with a similar fate.
The theoretician therefore avoided public appearances for a time,
and canceled his scheduled speech at Leipzig. Max von Laue gave

a talk in his stead.[72] Lenard's blatantly anti-Semitic attacks on Einstein under these circumstances alienated him from his fellow physicists, and he received noticeably less support at Leipzig than he had at Nauheim.[73] His extremism, it has been noted, put other, less radical aether apologists "in danger of being accused of guilt by association." [74]

In the late fall of 1922, Einstein was awarded the 1921 Nobel prize in physics. The announcement, to be sure, was "for his services to Theoretical Physics, and especially for his discovery of the law of the photoelectric effect" rather than for relativity.[75] Lenard, however, was so displeased that he registered a protest with the Nobel committee and let it reach the press in February 1923.[76] It was apparent that his efforts to discredit Einstein had been in vain. In his autobiography, Lenard later reflected that relativity,

> was a Jewish fraud, which one could have suspected from the first with more racial knowledge than was then disseminated, since its originator Einstein was a Jew. My disappointment was all the greater since a quite predominant number of the representatives of physics more or less conformed to the calculation-doings [Rechengetue] of the Jews.[77]

No other prominent German physicist who opposed Einstein or modern physics, not even Johannes Stark, became as vocally anti-Semitic as Lenard during the early Weimar period. His objection to relativity was not the sole reason. Two other factors must be briefly mentioned, for their effects on Lenard were important even if incalculable. The first was the loss of his son Werner, who died in February 1922, partially as a result of the malnutrition he suffered during the wartime blockade. He was the last of the family name.[78] The second factor was that the professor was one of the many Germans who had traded their gold for government bonds during the war. These bonds (along with his Nobel prize savings) were rendered worthless by inflation. Lenard felt that the money had been stolen from him by the swindling Jewish Weimar government.[79]

The most important single factor in Lenard's progression to völkisch anti-Semitism and ultimately to Hitler, however, was an unprecedented incident at his institute in 1922.[80] The affair came about largely because Lenard maintained that the word "professor" meant one who "professes" his beliefs, and he had not concealed his nationalist views in Heidelberg. He had called openly for the elimination of Rathenau because he felt the minister was doing immeasurable damage to the country. He thus totally refused to observe the period of national mourning ordered for June 27, 1922, the day of Rathenau's funeral.[81]

The leader of the student body (a Social Democrat) tried in the morning of June 27 to have the university or civil authorities force the physics institute to fly its flag at half-mast and to stop work for the day. Failing in this endeavor, he called upon the union leaders, who summoned their members and marched on the institute to talk with Lenard. After shouting for a time for the physicist to come out, the crowd was drenched with cold water from the second story hose. The workers, who by this time numbered in the hundreds, thereupon broke into the institute, caused some minor damage, and forced Lenard to go with them to the union hall, accompanied by a few policemen who had arrived on the scene. Some voices called out for the professor to be tossed into the river Neckar on the way, thus originating the tale that he was nearly martyred during the affair.[82] After he was in the union hall, the crowd began to grow and to appear more threatening.

The municipal attorney arrived on the scene at this point, and he has described the atmosphere which prevailed:

> On the second story we found the Don Quixote-like figure of Lenard so well known to us. He was staring into space, apparently quite uncomprehending how this could happen to him, the world famous Nobel prize winner. Around him stood the union people, who did not know what they should do. Our arrival was a visible relief to them.[83]

Lenard was taken into protective custody to appease the crowd and released later that night. Although he had not been harmed, the episode had a profound impact on his later life. He considered it both a degrading insult and—in Nazi terms—a badge of honor.

Because of his refusal to obey the ordinance calling for a day of mourning, Lenard was enjoined by the academic senate not to enter his institute until further notice. His students gathered 600 signatures on a petition, however, and got him reinstated on July 10 through the Baden Ministry of Education. Lenard thus was drawn into closer contact with the right-wing students and became involved in a number of discussions on Hitler.[84]

Lenard's anti-Semitic views were greatly strengthened in April

1923, at the trial of those accused of leading the assault on the physics institute. The physicist was called as a witness, but the defense attorney, who was Jewish, managed to shift the blame for the event on Lenard's provocation.[85] The Baden ministry therefore opened disciplinary hearings against the professor at the end of May. These hearings resulted in only a written reprimand for his actions, but Lenard submitted his resignation when they began. His students and co-workers once again gathered signatures on his behalf. Among others, they induced the governing board of the German Physical Society to raise objection to his leaving the institute.[86] They found particularly strong support among the staff of the large Imperial Institute of Physics and Technology, which had a reputation for conservatism in both scientific and political matters.[87] In the meantime, the Social Democratic leader of the student corps, who had initiated the events on June 27, was cleared of all blame in a disciplinary hearing chaired by a Jewish professor. The case became a *cause célèbre* for the National Socialists, drawing Lenard further into their fold.[88] The physicist decided not to retire yet.

Not long afterward came the logical culmination of the physicist's increasingly close affiliation with National Socialism—a public profession of allegiance to Hitler and his movement. On April 1, 1924, Hitler was sentenced to prison for his part in the Munich Beer Hall Putsch of November 1923. On May 8, an article composed by Lenard and co-signed by Stark appeared in the *Grossdeutsche Zeitung,* a small, short-lived Pan-German newspaper in Bavaria. The following excerpts illustrate how Lenard's hero-worship combined with racism to lead him to Hitler: we recognize in Hitler and his associates, Lenard wrote,

> the same spirit we have ourselves always striven after and drawn forth in our work, so that it would be profound and successful— the spirit of restless clarity, honest in respect to the exterior world as well as the inner unity; the spirit which hates every work of compromise, because it is untruthful. It is indeed also the same spirit which we—as our ideal—have already recognized and revered early in the great researchers of the past, in Galileo, Kepler, Newton, Faraday. We admire and revere it in the same manner in Hitler, Ludendorff, Pöhner, and their comrades; we recognize in them our closest spiritual relatives.
>
> One ponders how much it means that we are allowed to have

this type of spirit living among us in the flesh. They were rare at all times, these culture-spirits. Indeed, upon their activity rests all inner lofty striving of mankind and all the success of which makes life on this earth worthwhile and beautiful for us. According to experience, these spirits are only embodied with Aryan-Germanic blood, as even the above-named greats of natural research were of this blood . . .

[However, there is a dangerous alien racial spirit at work.] It is exactly the same activity, always with the same Asiatic people in the background, which brought Christ to the cross, Giordano Bruno to the stake, which fires on Hitler and Ludendorff with machine guns and puts them behind prison walls: the struggle of the spirits of darkness against the bringers of light, with the aim of shutting the latter out of effectiveness on this earth . . . [Hitler] and his comrades in struggle, they appear to us as gifts of God from a long darkened earlier time when races were still purer, persons still greater, spirits still less fraudulent. We feel it, and the gifts must not be taken from us. This thought alone must provide sufficient firmness to band the völkisch persons together in their great goal: with Hitler as "drummer" to found a new Germany in which the German spirit would not only be somewhat tolerated again and let out of the dungeons; no, one in which it would be protected, cared for, attended to, and then can finally once again bloom and develop further for the vindication of life on our planet now ruled by an inferior spirit.[89]

Parts of these passages read very much like *Mein Kampf,* the first volume of which did not appear for another year. This similarity is not especially surprising, since both physicist and Führer drew upon contemporary völkisch clichés and were addressing essentially the same readers. The affinity was even closer, however, between the beliefs of Lenard and those of the Nazi party's self-proclaimed ideologue Alfred Rosenberg. The latter's *Mythus des 20. Jahrhunderts* (Myth of the twentieth century) was also written during this time (although not published until 1930). This work was characterized by its romantic mystification of blood and the image of the Aryan-Germanic light-bringers locked in mortal combat with the Jewish powers of darkness.[90] A central theme of the *Mythus* was that Christianity had been "judified" by Paul and the apostles, and was therefore inimical to the true Germanic spirit. Lenard turned from the Christian religion precisely because he accepted this claim and believed the Church (Protestant and Catholic) had degenerated, becoming an instrument of Jewish designs.[91] In fact, one of the reasons for Planck's support of Einstein, Lenard felt, was that Planck's family included many theologians and pastors.[92]

In view of later events, the importance of Lenard and Stark's ideological confession of faith should not be underrated. The contest for the leadership of the völkisch factions was still very much in doubt in 1924.[93] The public declaration of two world-famous scientists on Hitler's behalf would not be forgotten in later years.

Lenard did not become a Nazi party member until 1937, for he simply could not bring himself to overcome his scientist's distaste for joining *any* political party.[94] On May 15, 1926, however, he traveled to a neighboring province to attend a rally for Hitler. Even at sixty-four years of age, he found the experience invigorating.[95] Two years later, after a speech in Heidelberg, Hitler and his party secretary Rudolf Hess called upon Lenard in his home. Their conversation mainly focused on the Germanic religious movement, but the physicist considered it one of the most memorable events of his life.[96]

Lenard's laboratory became a center of right-wing politics. Some of his students and assistants formed a völkisch group in the institute and a number became National Socialists. As Wilhelm Wien's son wrote home in 1925:

> I haven't yet quite figured out whether one first becomes völkisch and then a doctoral candidate, or the reverse. In any case the institute appears to be rather homogeneous in this respect, and in quarrels with the university, the rector, or other officials it is energetically supported by Lenard.[97]

The institute director participated in several Nazi cultural organizations at least as early as 1927, and he was present in 1929 at the founding of Rosenberg's National Socialist Society for German Culture (NS-Gesellschaft für deutsche Kultur, later the Kampfbund für deutsche Kultur).[98] He was also on good terms with the staff of Rudolf Hess, among whom he found understanding support for his goal of "Aryan physics" in the Third Reich.[99] Lenard thus allied himself with the völkisch-ideological wing of the party in fact as well as in outlook.

Lenard had come to place primary importance upon combating the Jewish internal enemy, and, probably influenced by the admiration of Hitler and Rosenberg for their British blood cousins, had restrained his attacks upon the English. Yet he could not completely forget his earlier animosity. In 1925, for example, the *Zeitschrift für Physik* (an organ of the German Physical Society) printed a British article without even translating it into German. This so angered Lenard that he resigned from the society.[100] Afterward, a sign was posted in the Heidelberg physics institute: "Entrance is forbidden to members of the so-called German Physical Society." [101]

After his antirelativity campaign at the 1922 convention in Leipzig and his protest against the award of the Nobel prize to Einstein, Lenard no longer pursued the matter.[102] He turned increasingly to the preparation of historical and review articles and lectures. Almost all of his few research efforts in this period appeared in Wilhelm Wien's *Annalen der Physik,* because the two men shared an antipathy toward the directions modern physics was taking.[103] In 1924 Wien asked Lenard to contribute entries covering phosphorescence, cathode rays, and the photoelectric effect for his *Handbuch der Experimentalphysik.* August Becker, Ferdinand Schmidt, and Rudolf Tomaschek of Lenard's institute co-authored the articles, a project that was not completed until 1928.[104] When Wien died in 1928, Lenard bemoaned the loss of the last distinguished university professor of physics who had not succumbed to the fashionable Jewish-spirited trend in physics. "His calm blue eyes," Lenard claimed, along with his dark hair, indicated a racial mixture which placed him among those devoted to the "highest spiritual development." [105]

Lenard's concern for racial heritage brought him into contact with Hans F. K. Günther, a proponent of Nazi racial theories who held a professorship for "racial science" (*Rassenkunde*) created in 1930 at Jena by the Nazi-controlled government of Thuringia.[106] In early 1927, a letter from Günther induced the physicist to drop a number of other interests and to begin an examination of the great natural scientists of the past.[107] In this project Lenard was able to express his romantic veneration of great personalities; his love for patient, quiet experiment as the starting point for all theoretical considerations; and his thesis that the great contributors to science were exclusively of Aryan-Germanic racial origin. *Grosse Naturforscher* was first published in 1929, and Lenard's expressions of his preconceptions became ever more pronounced in successive editions of the book.[108]

As he embarked on this historical endeavor, the Heidelberg professor submitted his request for retirement. He apparently expressed a clear preference for an experimentalist as his successor, and the faculty appointed a committee to determine a three-man list of candidates for the post. The head of the search committee, the chemistry professor Karl Freudenberg, traveled to Berlin to ask who should be considered. From Planck and Friedrich Paschen, president of the Imperial Institute of Physics and Technology, he received the same advice: James Franck was the man most suitable for the post. Gustav Hertz and Hans Geiger were then ranked second and third.[109] Geiger had studied and worked with Ernest Rutherford in Manchester for nearly six years in the decade before World War I, and had become a prominent experimentalist.

When this list came up for consideration in the appointed faculty session, however, Lenard found it totally unacceptable that two Jews and an Anglophile should be considered to succeed him. He stood up, proclaimed that the list was an affront, and left the meeting; he threatened to withdraw his retirement request unless the list were scrapped.[110] Lenard's isolation in Heidelberg was quite obvious, however, for the list was sent on to the Baden Ministry of Education in Karlsruhe over his protest.

Lenard wrote personally to the ministry describing at some length two schools of physical thought which differed in their conception and evaluation of experimental physics: the one saw experiment as the servant of theory; the other, which had strong support in Heidelberg, saw exact measurement as the foundation for theory. In place of the faculty's candidates, who supported the first school, Lenard recommended Stark or one of his own students as his appropriate successor.[111]

Since the faculty list was eventually accepted by the ministry, Lenard carried out his threat and withdrew his request for retirement on April 16, 1927. In 1929, however, he reached the mandatory emeritus age, and a new list was prepared. Although Geiger was apparently considered again (and perhaps Franck also), the man finally called to replace Lenard was Walther Bothe.[112] The process dragged on so long, however, that it was 1931 before Lenard actually retired.[113] August Becker conducted the lectures until Bothe took over the institute a year later.[114] Apparently partially as a result of the difficulties he encountered with Lenard's assistants, Bothe soon left the institute and went to the Kaiser Wilhelm Institute for Medical Research across town.[115] Becker assumed the directorship of the physics institute as of April 1, 1934, and Lenard's original wish for a successor divorced from modern physics was finally fulfilled.[116]

Although he was already retired when Hitler came to power in 1933, Lenard desired very much to contribute to the "national reconstruction" by redressing what he considered the academic imbalance in physics. On March 21, he wrote a memorandum directly to the Führer offering his services as an advisor in personnel decisions affecting physics.[117] The entire university structure needed renovation, he explained, but the faculty hiring system—which had been left almost entirely up to the professors themselves for the past fifteen years—was "in badly rotted condition." There were not enough really talented persons to fill the required number of posts, but there were enough thoroughly German (*grunddeutsche*) persons who were well enough trained to do the job. Lenard himself would be ready to help in "checking, evaluating, influencing and if necessary rejecting and replacing" candidates for science positions as they came before the ministries.[118]

The Reich Chancellery, to which Lenard addressed his letter, responded that Lenard's letter had been forwarded to the Reich Ministry of the Interior.[119] Quite probably Lenard was contacted by Frick's office during April concerning the position of president of the Imperial Institute of Physics and Technology. Paschen retired and the ministry named Stark as his successor in early May 1933.

Stark's appointment was the occasion for Lenard to rejoice in a virulently anti-Semitic article in the principal Nazi party newspaper. He recalled the Weimar years as a time of struggle for persons like himself:

> It had become dark in physics, and that from the top down. With the powerful penetration of the Jews into positions of authority even at the universities and academies, the observation of nature itself was invalidated and lost in oblivion. Knowledge of the things of the exterior world was supposed to have its foundation in the notions of human heads. These notions, immediately dubbed "theories," were then to be "confirmed" by experimenters. This was carried out quickly and most dutifully with work performed as superficially as possible. "Freedom of research" received a special gloss with the repression of frank statements against such a procedure.[120]

As a result, Lenard claimed, large numbers of people had lost their faith in science. Only faith in technology remained.

He then outlined the view of Einstein which was to be presented to Nazi governmental authorities by Lenard and those who joined his efforts to cleanse German physics of its "Jewish spirit":

> The foremost example of the damaging influence upon natural science from the Jewish side was presented by Mr. Einstein, with his "theories" mathematically blundered together out of good, preexisting knowledge and his own arbitrary garnishes, theories which now are gradually decaying, which is the fate of pro-creations alien to nature. In the process, one cannot spare researchers, even those with genuine achievements, from the charge that they indeed first let the "relativity-Jews" become established in Germany. They did not see—or did not want to see—how very erroneous it was, even in a nonscholarly connection, to consider especially this Jew as a "good German." [121]

The departure of the alien spirit from the universities, and even from the country, he proclaimed, was due not to the professors but to the Führer. The fact that some of those who left had Nobel prizes was inconsequential, for "these prizes have become of increasingly contestable spiritual value in recent times." One should rejoice that a man such as Stark—whom the ruling clique had thought eliminated—was now in such an influential position.[122]

Lenard himself was too old to be very active in the Third Reich. He received a number of honors, was appointed to the senate of the Kaiser Wilhelm Society and the executive committee of the German Research Association, and played a minor role in the conflicts in which his friend Stark became embroiled after 1934. He remained, however, effectively in retirement.

He was not totally inactive, though. In the foreword to a self-educated layman's attack on Einstein in September 1933, he lamented the lack of a sound textbook from which proper physics could be learned. All that was available, he wrote, were collections of "theories" which led the impartial, knowledge-thirsty student astray.[123] A new type of textbook would be necessary if the modern spirit was to be eradicated from physics in the Third Reich. Lenard undertook the preparation of such a primer for students of "Aryan physics." It first appeared in 1936 under the title *Deutsche Physik*.

This examination of Lenard's career indicates that the basis for his allegiance to National Socialism was ideology; he believed fully in the Nazi racial teachings. Although his involvement in anti-Semitic politics was unusual for a scientist, the attitudes he pro-

fessed and the experiences he underwent were fairly typical for early
Nazi activists. His upbringing in a German borderland, his romantic
yearning for great figures to lead the way, and his frustrated need to
feel genuine human contact and belonging were three of the most
common characteristics of converts to the Hitler movement.[124]

Lenard's animosity toward the British was hardly unusual among
German scholars prior to the war, but the manner in which he
projected his hatred onto a new target in the postwar period was
nearly unique. This "displacement" of his resentment onto the Jews
was caused primarily by Lenard's frustration over the relativity affair.
He was embittered by the praise accorded Einstein, because he did
not accept the validity of the theory and could not seem to impress
his objections upon his colleagues.

Alienation from his professional community was a major factor in
Lenard's resort to extremism, but the crucial event in the development of his political activism was the storming of his institute by
workers in 1922. The bitter memory of humiliation and the administrative sanctions imposed upon him led Lenard into direct
contact with the fledgling Nazi movement. His declaration of support
for Hitler and his association with the völkisch elements of the party
soon followed. These actions brought the physicist recognition as a
faithful comrade at the highest levels of Hitler's entourage. It was
therefore hardly surprising that during the Third Reich Lenard's
career was held up as a model of "true" German behavior by those
who wanted to wrest control of science from the professional
community.

Solvay Conference in Brussels, 1927. *Left to right, first row:* I. Langmuir, M. Planck, Mme Curie, H. A. Lorentz, A. Einstein, P. Langevin, C. E. Guye, C. T. R. Wilson, O. W. Richardson; *second row:* P. Debye, M. Knudsen, W. L. Bragg, H. A. Kramers, P. A. M. Dirac, A. H. Compton, L. de Broglie, M. Born, N. Bohr; *third row:* A. Piccard, E. Henriot, P. Ehrenfest, E. Herzen, T. De Donder, E. Schrödinger, E. Verschaffelt, W. Pauli, W. Heisenberg, R. H. Fowler, L. Brillouin.

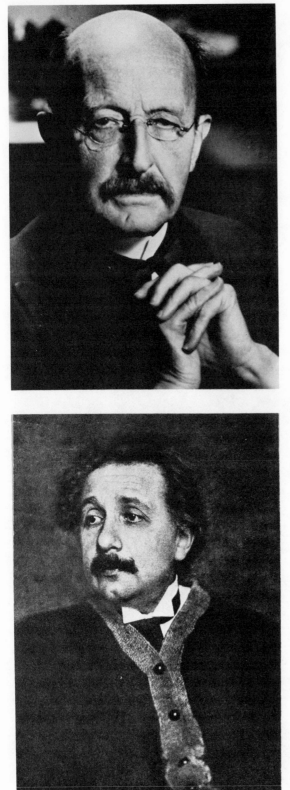

Max Planck (1858–1947).

Albert Einstein (1879–1955).

Fritz Haber (1868–1934).

Lise Meitner and Otto Hahn in the Kaiser Wilhelm Institute for Chemistry, Berlin-Dahlem, 1913.

Max von Laue (1879–1960).

Max Born, James Franck, and Robert Pohl in front of the Göttingen physics institutes.

Arrival at the Stockholm central railroad station prior to receiving the Nobel prize awards, fall 1933. *Left to right:* Werner Heisenberg's mother, Erwin Schrödinger's wife, P. A. M. Dirac's mother, P. A. M. Dirac, Werner Heisenberg, and Erwin Schrödinger.

Award of the 1932 Nobel prize in physics to Werner Heisenberg by King Gustavus V, 1933.

Johannes Stark (1874–1957).

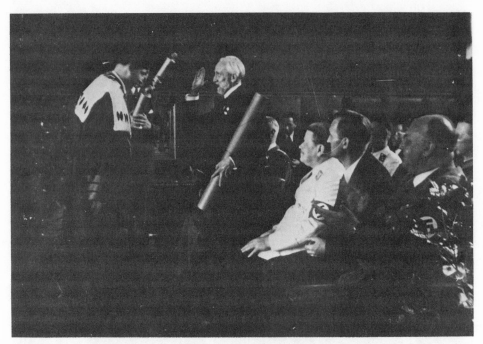

In celebration of his eightieth birthday in Heidelberg on June 7, 1942, Philipp Lenard receives an honorary doctorate from a representative of the new university in German-occupied Pressburg (Bratislava, Czechoslovakia), the city of his birth.

On the same occasion, Lenard receives the congratulations of the rector of Heidelberg University, Dr. Paul Schmitthenner. To the right of Lenard (in white) is Dr. Wilhelm Ohnesorge, the Reich Post Minister, who studied under Lenard in Kiel at the turn of the century.

Arnold Sommerfeld (1868–1951).

Walter Gerlach (b. 1889).

Carl Ramsauer (1879–1955).

6. The Aryan Physicists: Johannes Stark

While Lenard was quietly writing his textbook on physics in Heidelberg, his friend Johannes Stark was actively engaged in efforts to gain control of the organization and direction of German research. His desires were directly opposed to those of the leadership of the physics community, from which he, like Lenard, had been estranged for more than a decade. In order to understand Stark's alienation from his professional colleagues and his recourse to National Socialism, an examination of his earlier career and its political consequences is also essential.

EARLY CAREER AND SUBSEQUENT REJECTION OF MODERN THEORIES, 1874–1929

The son of a landed proprietor, Johannes Stark was born April 15, 1874, on his family's estate at Schickenhof, near Weiden in the Upper Pfalz. After schooling in nearby Bayreuth and then Regensburg, in 1894 he went to Munich, where he studied physics at the university. In 1897, at age twenty-three, he completed his doctorate and remained in Munich as an assistant for three more years.[1]

In 1900, Stark went to Göttingen and stayed there as Privatdozent and assistant to Eduard Riecke for nearly six years. His excellence in experimental investigation was already evident during this period, demonstrated by his discovery of the optical Doppler effect in canal rays in 1905.[2] He was also one of the earliest proponents of modern physical concepts, and in 1907 he suggested that Einstein write a review article on the special theory of relativity for the *Jahrbuch der Radioaktivität und Elektronik,* which Stark had founded in 1904 and edited since then. For more than two years the physicists carried on an active correspondence, and reading it makes it clear that Stark greatly respected his younger colleague.[3] Stark was also one of the first physicists to make use of light quanta in his own work. Later, in 1909, he published a paper which sketched the basis of an experiment to verify Einstein's light quanta hypothesis.[4] The Dutch physicist H. A. Lorentz shortly thereafter named Einstein and Stark together as the advocates of the hypothesis.[5]

Since 1906, Stark had held an untenured extraordinary professorship at the institute of technology in Hannover, but he was unhappy there because of friction with his superior.[6] On April 1, 1909, he became a full professor in Aachen, an appointment he owed in no small part to the active efforts of Arnold Sommerfeld.[7] He thereupon asked if Einstein might want to come to Aachen as his assistant, which Einstein graciously refused because he was engaged in negotiations for a position at Zurich.[8]

Stark was an extremely prolific physicist who published more than three hundred papers in his lifetime.[9] Like most creative scientists, he was quite concerned about his intellectual property rights and priorities. In his many disputes, however, he took an exceptionally unpleasant tone of combative peevishness. James Franck, in summing up Stark's characteristics, has pointed out that he was well known for his sensitivity about being cited properly and the disagreeable manner with which he spoke about others. "He was in every respect a pain in the neck," Franck concluded. "But on the other hand, I must say he had good ideas. And early. He had the idea that photochemistry would be a quantum process. Not as clear as Einstein, but he had it.[10]

Identification of the first person clearly to apply the quantum hypothesis in photochemistry sparked a priority dispute between Stark and Einstein in 1912. Stark claimed in response to an article by Einstein that, although Einstein had arrived at an explanation of photochemistry by a different route, his was the first quantum explanation.[11] Einstein replied somewhat disdainfully that the question of priority was uninteresting, since the matter could be deduced directly from the quantum hypothesis. He pointed out in footnote, however, that he was indeed the first to apply quanta to photochemistry. Stark was not satisfied and insisted that he had still given a simpler—and thus better—presentation.[12]

Without further evidence it is not possible to assess the weight this dispute had in regard to Stark's later animosity toward Einstein. It was, in fact, only one of several public and private squabbles in which he was engaged during this period (including a serious conflict with Sommerfeld), all of which contributed to Stark's increasing alienation from his colleagues.[13]

It is certain, however, that the experience of World War I intensified Stark's nationalism and caused him to view Einstein's open pacifism and internationalism with intense disfavor. In an early wartime letter rejecting an article for his *Jahrbuch* in which the author stressed the international aspects of science, Stark proudly assumed for himself the epithet "chauvinist" in physics.[14] He was disappointed that Sommerfeld's pupil Peter Debye received Riecke's Göttingen chair in 1915, blaming the appointment on Sommerfeld's influence.[15] But in 1917 he was called as professor of physics to Greifswald. Northern Germany was foreign to him, but the faculty was adamantly conservative in both their political and scientific orientation, and Stark's nationalism was undoubtedly appreciated.

Prior to the outbreak of the war, in 1913, Stark had made his second great discovery, the splitting of spectral lines in an electric field. This phenomenon, known as the Stark effect, could not be accounted for by nineteenth-century theory. By the midpoint of the war, however, theoreticians were able to account for it on the basis of the model of the atom propounded by Niels Bohr and by the generalization of Bohr's electron dynamics developed by Sommerfeld.[16]

Stark, however, could not accept the fundamental propositions of the Bohr–Sommerfeld atom. He did not regard the agreement between the new theory and experimental observation as sufficient to outweigh the rejection of classical concepts involved. His acceptance speech for the Nobel prize for 1919 was the forum he chose from which to first voice his objections. Speaking on June 3, 1920, he noted that the Bohr theory, even ignoring its questionable foundations, could not account for the polarity of hydrogen ions he had found in his work. A theory was needed, he suggested, in which the atom would be treated as a whole rather than as a structure with discrete parts.[17]

Later in the year, shortly after the Nauheim convention, Stark presented a more detailed critique of the Bohr model, using as his target Sommerfeld's new book *Atombau und Spektrallinien* (Atomic structure and spectral lines, 1919). His goal was to present an analysis from the point of view of an experimentalist, to determine whether the theory clashed with observation, and to ascertain whether its presuppositions were less numerous than the phenomena they explained. His conclusion was that, although Sommerfeld's use of the special theory of relativity (which had been "largely confirmed by experience") was unobjectionable, the Bohr quantum theory was of dubious validity.[18]

Physicists committed to the Bohr atomic model were also aware of the inadequacies of the theory. They were thus willing to abandon it upon the advent of quantum mechanics in the mid-1920s. Stark, however, also refused to accept the basis of quantum mechanics, though Erwin Schrödinger's theories yielded a good treatment of the Stark effect.[19] In 1929 Stark directed a detailed critique at Schrödinger's work (and Sommerfeld's support of it), even though it was by this time already widely accepted among physicists in the field.[20] Stark was now so isolated that it is highly doubtful that his criticism was taken seriously by anyone involved in the newest developments in atomic physics.[21] Given the parallelism of political and scientific alignments, however, Stark did not totally lack an audience. Those physicists who rejected Weimar generally also rejected relativity and quantum mechanics, and they were willing to listen.[22]

ACADEMIC POLITICS, 1919–21

It is important to note that, like Lenard, Stark began to engage in political activity only after his professional direction diverged from that taken by modern physics. His disagreement with the leaders of the physics community was reinforced by his dissatisfaction with the outcome of the war and the government of Weimar. The 1919–21 period marked for him, as it did for Lenard, the beginnings of the transition from respected member of the scientific community to academic outcast.

Unlike Lenard, Stark was very interested in organizational matters. In 1919 he had two concerns: he was alarmed that the Weimar government might assume binding control of the academic system, and he wanted to reduce the influence of the Berlin physicists in the German Physical Society. As it turned out, Stark found a single means to confront both issues—the formation of an independent association under his own control.

Stark found cause for alarm in a reform proposed in the early summer of 1919 by Undersecretary Carl H. Becker of the Prussian Ministry of Education. The thrust of Becker's plan was a democratization of the universities through a strengthening of the rights and privileges of the younger instructors, who would then be more willing to work with (and have a greater stake in) the republic.[23] In September 1919, Stark had privately printed at least two pamphlets, in which he argued in true mandarin fashion that the educational process was an instrument of unification and was thus above the factionalism of parliamentary parties. The crux of his argument was that, prior to 1918, the institutions of higher learning had leaned heavily on governments that had been founded on real authority.

These governments supported intellectual and cultural endeavor as a matter of course. Now, Stark wrote,

> it is questionable whether after the political upheaval the governments based on changing parliamentary majorities will treat the institutions of higher learning as carefully and considerately as the old governments did. . . . The institutions of higher learning must above all become a power in themselves and for themselves; they must create a self-enclosed organization and maintain, and when possible even broaden, their autonomy in regard to the party governments.[24]

Becker's reform plan included the creation of a panel of experts who would advise the government on the wisdom of accepting the three-man list of a given institution. Stark feared this innovation would lead the ministry to place a heavy reliance on the scholars of the capital city, because their names would be familiar and they could be easily reached for consultation. He therefore proposed instead a professional association (*Fachgemeinschaft*) of all scholars in higher education in each field. A small committee of experts would be chosen by secret ballot every two years by the members of the association, and this committee would assume the role the government and faculty advisory bodies currently played in academic appointments.[25]

It is clear that in his distrust of Weimar Stark grasped the essence of pluralistic party politics, where interest-group pressure is highly important and effective. But his radical response to the problem was quite unrealistic; very few of his fellow academicians were willing to descend into the political mire.

Stark's idea of a professional association nevertheless found some support among physicists who were dissatisfied with Berlin leadership in the organizational affairs of physics. The rift between the members in outlying districts and the Berlin scientists had been growing for some time, paralleling the division between the country as a whole and the burgeoning metropolis. This division culminated in conservative hatred of Berlin in the twenties as a symbol of Weimar liberalism, socialism, and cosmopolitanism. Within the German Physical Society, the move to bridge this gap had begun with the election of Arnold Sommerfeld of Munich as presiding officer in the summer of 1918. He was the first person who was not a resident of Berlin ever to direct the organization's activities.

Sommerfeld's task of conciliation was complicated. The applied and industrial physicists, for example, were displeased with the narrowness of the society. When the organization began in 1845, it had representatives from every subdivision of the field, from mechanics and industrialists to academic scientists. By the beginning of the twentieth century, however, it was oriented toward pure science and most of its leaders were theoretical physicists. Yet at this very time the number of industrial positions for applied physicists was increasing—a trend accelerated by the war. The technical physicists formed their own German Society for Technical Physics (Deutsche Gesellschaft für technische Physik) in June 1919.[26]

Stark had in the meantime decided to use his professional association concept as a counterweight to the Berlin physicists. In the process, he hoped to make himself a key figure in organized German science. He naturally turned to Wilhelm Wien, whose anti-Berlin bias was widely known. In January 1920, Wien counseled him to delay the formation of a new organization until the fall meeting of the German Physical Society. As Paul Forman has pointed out, Wien was not only Stark's ally, but also his chief rival in the campaign against the Berlin physicists. Thus it was unclear to what extent Wien's advice to wait was motivated by his desire to block Stark's attempt to become the leader of that effort.[27] Stark decided not to delay, however, and in April 1920 he began to solicit members for his Fachgemeinschaft deutscher Hochschullehrer der Physik (Professional Association of the German Higher Education Teachers of Physics).

The German Physical Society generally attempted to co-opt dissidents by giving them positions of responsibility. Sommerfeld therefore asked Lenard and Stark (and probably Wien) to participate formally in the deliberations concerning such issues as the recent reorganization of the society.[28] When Stark returned from the Nobel awards ceremony in early June, he informed Sommerfeld that sixty-eight physicists had joined his organization and that he was glad to see that the presiding officer of the Physical Society was one of them. An executive committee would be elected shortly, he promised, and its members would meet in Nauheim to draft a constitution for the association and to take part in the reorganization of the Physical Society.[29]

Six weeks later, Stark announced the unsurprising results of the election (ballots were cast by mail): Stark had forty-five votes; Lenard, thirty-five; Max Wien, thirty-five; Sommerfeld, twenty-two;

Gustav Mie, seventeen; and so on.[30] No votes were received for Berlin physicists; the conservative hue of the executive committee reflected that of the membership. Yet Stark insisted to Sommerfeld that he wanted no "confrontation between Berlin and the Reich." The activities of the Physical Society and Fachgemeinschaft should be complementary, he asserted, yet Sommerfeld must have recognized the potential of the Fachgemeinschaft as a divisive force.[31]

In August and early September, the Einstein controversy eclipsed all other issues facing the physicists. During this period Wien and Stark transferred to new positions at Munich and Würzburg respectively. As a conservative experimentalist, Wien was skeptical of Einstein's work, but he did not take part in aggressive protest against it.[32] Although Stark did not participate directly in the Einstein affair either, it seems certain that members of his Fachgemeinschaft worked with Paul Weyland's anti-Einstein organization. Stark's intentions thus became increasingly suspect among Einstein's friends and supporters, a group in which Sommerfeld was prominent.

Although the anti-Berlin faction was frustrated by the outcome of the relativity debate at Nauheim, it achieved a measure of satisfaction in organizational matters. Stark, however, was not personally victorious. Wien presented a motion at the business meeting of September 21 (two days before the Einstein debate) which "had as its goal the most extensive possible decentralization of the society and an elimination of the special position of the Berlin members." The motion carried, and Wien was elected presiding officer for the next two years.[33]

Even though many of the pro-Berlin Physical Society members were undoubtedly less than enthusiastic about the choice of Wien as presiding officer, the selection of a physicist who lived outside Berlin helped to minimize the rift between the membership in the capital city and the outlying districts. Wien's election scuttled any plans Stark may have entertained to exert pressure on the society. In fact, several members abandoned his Fachgemeinschaft shortly after the Nauheim convention. According to Born:

> After the Nauheim discussions one can not gloss over the fact that there exists a south-German particularism in physics, whose spokesmen are Wien and Stark. You probably also know of Stark's founding of a "professional association of academic physicists," which functions as an adversary of the Physical

Society in such a manner that a large group of colleagues who
at first had joined (including myself) are now collectively declaring their withdrawal.[34]

Despite these setbacks, Stark was not initially inclined to forsake
the Fachgemeinschaft. On the contrary, he veered away from a direct
confrontation with the Physical Society, and attempted to use the
professional association to gain control of the physics advisory bodies
for the two major organizations that financed German scholarship—
the Helmholtz Society for the Advancement of Physical-Technical
Research (Helmholtz-Gesellschaft zur Förderung der physikalisch-
technischen Forschung) and the Emergency Association of German
Science.

The Helmholtz Society was founded on the initiative of the chemical industry magnate Carl Duisberg in October 1920. Its leader at
that time was a prominent figure in Rhineland heavy industry,
Albert Vögler. From the beginning, the society evidenced an emphatically anti-Berlin character.[35] Fritz Haber had provided the
impetus for founding the Emergency Association, which was organized in the spring of 1920 under the leadership of the former
Prussian Ministry of Education career civil servant Friedrich
Schmidt-Ott.[36] Its pro-Berlin orientation was equally unmistakable.

At the end of October 1920, Stark was able to get himself appointed to the board of trustees of the Helmholtz Society on the
strength of his claim to represent a significant group of physicists.
Unknown to Stark at the time, however, Wien had already captured
the vice-chairman's position of top scientist in the organization, as
a result of his prior acquaintance with Duisberg and Vögler.[37]
Stark then sought to have a Fachgemeinschaft committee accepted
as the Emergency Association and Helmholtz Society project-grant
review committee for physics. Schmidt-Ott, however, managed to
forge a compromise with Wien and stymied Stark's efforts in the
spring of 1921. Shortly thereafter, Stark resigned from the leadership of the association and it faded into obscurity.[38]

During his unsuccessful bid to influence physics affairs, Stark displayed his combative nature and his earnestness in organizational
matters. His response to the Becker reform proposals also indicated
his willingness to break with tradition. Opposition to the Berlin
scientists was a major factor in his life from 1920 onward. All these
themes were repeated when, after more than a decade as an aca-

demic outsider, he attempted to dominate the German physics community as a National Socialist.

ACADEMIC OUTCAST, 1921–33

Stark began to withdraw from academic politics in 1921 when his new interest in commercial concerns led him to resign from the university in Würzburg in 1922. He soon changed his mind and wished to return to academia, but during the next eleven years he was unable to secure an academic appointment, although he was considered for several. The bitterness and frustration he experienced encouraged him to take the step into völkisch politics.

At the institute of technology in Aachen and the university in Greifswald, Stark had stressed the importance of technical physics. He had even attempted to have a position for applied physics established at Greifswald.[39] One of the explicit goals of the Fachgemeinschaft was to further technical physics at the universities.[40] Thus Stark's acquisition of part ownership of a porcelain factory was not entirely surprising, nor was the fact that his research interests shifted to technological subjects.[41]

At Greifswald, where, according to Stark, "a fresh spirit blows like the Baltic Sea breeze and I found understanding," [42] the faculty would presumably have understood the lure of new activities. At Würzburg, however, his colleagues were very upset. For one thing, it turned out that Nobel prize funds had been involved in the transaction, and many German physicists regarded this action as a violation of the spirit of the Nobel awards.[43] Although the Nobel Foundation has never placed any restrictions on the use of the prize money, Stark apparently never disputed the view that investment of Nobel funds for profit was unethical. He later claimed in response to his critics that he had only purchased shares in the factory in order to avoid the losses inflicted by inflation and that he had returned them before the end of 1921.[44] In addition, in the summer of 1921 he accepted a paper on optical properties of porcelain as the qualifying work (Habilitationsschrift) for one of his students. His Würzburg colleagues wondered if such investigation really constituted a scientific advance or instead was mere technology.[45] The joke in scientific circles was that those who worked with Stark did not earn a D. Phil. degree, but a "D. Porz." (for porcelain).[46] More serious objections, however, were raised because the student was the engineer Ludwig Glaser, an active member of the Weyland anti-Einstein group. Glaser had delivered one of the Berlin speeches that aroused such deep bitterness the previous year.[47]

Feelings became so intense that by the spring of 1922 Stark was driven to resign his post at Würzburg and to withdraw to his family estate near Weiden.[48] It is highly probable that, at the time he left, Stark had no real intention of retiring. In the spring of 1922, a new president was being sought for the Imperial Institute of Physics and Technology (PTR) in Berlin. Stark's interest in technical matters made him a logical candidate, and he may have had some support on the PTR board. The Reich Ministry of the Interior, however, named the Berlin professor of physical chemistry Walther Nernst to the position. Stark waged a vigorous campaign to reverse the ministry's decision. On June 6, 1922, for example, he wrote to the ministry that Nernst's appointment as president of the PTR "arouses consternation in the circles of the German physicists," noting further that the board of the Imperial Institute had not been consulted in the matter. He also threatened to make the issue public.[49]

His threat was carried out at the close of a scathing indictment of the German physics community which he was already preparing for publication in early June 1922. His book *Die gegenwärtige Krisis in der deutschen Physik* (The present crisis in German physics) attacked both the relativity and Bohr-Sommerfeld quantum theories as injurious to German experimental work. Stark inveighed against the preponderance of theory, indicating that it should be the servant rather than the master of experiment. He also denounced the quantum theory as presented by Sommerfeld as "dogmatic." Proponents of this theory, Stark asserted, were not interested in testing their concepts, but only in confirming and propagating them. Because of the inordinate influence of theory, technical application of physics had suffered.[50]

Although there were some signs of hope for the future, Stark stated, he feared that they would remain nothing but hopes if "the theoretical spirit, which exercises a certain rule in German physics," further strengthened the aversion to application.[51] After noting that his work with ceramics had brought him into close contact with men of practical affairs, he criticized the choice of Nernst as president of the PTR. He could not believe the rumors, he slyly wrote, that Nernst had received the post because of his personal connections with influential government figures. It was just that the position called for a younger man.[52] The implication was obvious that Stark, ten years Nernst's junior, wanted to be that man.

Stark's shrill little book did not help him to obtain the PTR presidency in 1922; it may well have kept him from getting any position at all until 1933. For example, in 1929, Stark wrote to Sommerfeld to ask if it were true that Sommerfeld had rejected consideration of Stark as Wien's successor in Munich. Sommerfeld's reply did not mention their prewar dispute, Stark's opposition to Einstein, or Stark's political activities. Sommerfeld did, however, refer explicitly to Stark's opposition to the Bohr-Sommerfeld and Schrödinger theories and to the unfavorable impression created by his polemical 1922 book.[53]

In the decade following his departure from Würzburg, Stark was considered and rejected for an academic appointment at least six times: at Berlin (1924), Tübingen (1924), Breslau (1926), Marburg (1926), Heidelberg (1927), and Munich (1928).[54] At Berlin, Max von Laue, Fritz Haber, Max Planck, and others signed a faculty report stating that neither Lenard nor Stark could be considered as a successor to Heinrich Rubens in 1924, because their "passionate" opposition to the new directions taken by theoretical physics would endanger the close cooperation among Berlin physicists.[55] Walther Nernst left the presidency of the PTR for the university post instead, and Friedrich Paschen was named to replace him.

By 1927, when Lenard wished to retire and let Stark succeed him, Lenard discovered that his colleagues doubted they could work compatibly with Stark.

> I responded to this, that the Stark to be called now, who yearns for university life, is quite obviously not the same as the Stark who left Würzburg in a perhaps unpleasant manner; and I can add the assurance that this departure absolutely did not occur under circumstances or for reasons which could cause a blemish on his character.[56]

Stark apparently was so desperate for an academic post that he even tried to repair his relationship with Sommerfeld. During the negotiations concerning the selection of Wien's successor at Munich, Stark indicated that he was planning to nominate Sommerfeld and Otto Stern for the 1927 Nobel prize.[57] This ill-conceived effort to gain favor may well have antagonized Sommerfeld even further. By March 1928, Stark realized that he had no hope of obtaining an academic post in Weimar Germany. He therefore withdrew from Weiden to an estate near Munich, where he set up a private laboratory.[58]

Within a year after his unsuccessful bid for the PTR presidency, Stark was involved in völkisch politics. He later claimed to have met and supported Adolf Hitler as early as November 1923, when he turned over leadership of the Upper Pfalz proto-Nazi "national formations" to the Führer in Rosenberg's office in Munich.[59] As Lenard later wrote:

> At that time Stark often refreshed me like an oasis in the spiritual desert of scholars. I could converse about Hitler with him and his kindred-spirited wife—almost with them alone. Our jointly signed public declaration for Hitler stems also from that time, when Hitler was still in prison.[60]

Despite the May 1924 announcement of allegiance to Hitler, Stark resisted joining the party. Once convinced that he had no future in academia, however, he committed himself ever more deeply to political action. Finally, in his words, as "the National Socialist party entered the decisive struggle for power, I closed the doors of my physical laboratory and stepped into the ranks of the fighters behind Adolf Hitler." [61] He joined the Nazi party on April 1, 1930.[62]

From that point until the seizure of power, the physicist turned political activist churned out pamphlets and speeches on behalf of the party.[63] He described and applauded Hitler's goals and personality, attacked the Catholic Church, discussed the deficiencies of Weimar elementary and secondary education, and even tried his hand at a critique of English economic policy.[64] His attacks on the Church and his connections with the Nazi publishing house Franz Eher brought Stark into association with Rosenberg's group of cultural ideologues. His writings on primary education and dealings with the small publisher Deutsche Volksverlag under Ernst Boepple must have placed him in touch with Boepple's boss, Hans Schemm, who was interested in the same educational topics. Because of his close relationship with Lenard, Stark quite likely also came in contact with Lenard's supporters among the staff of Rudolf Hess. Thus, from the beginning of his intimate involvement with the party, Stark, like Lenard, became allied with the more ideologically oriented adherents of National Socialism. It was inevitable that he would become entangled in their rivalries and share their antagonism toward the state bureaucracy after the seizure of power.

Stark's political connections enabled him to obtain the presidency of the PTR after Paschen retired in 1933. Stark certainly did not owe his post to the scientists consulted: von Laue has indicated that they unanimously rejected his candidacy.[65] Wilhelm Frick, the minister of the interior, named Stark president of the PTR on May 1, 1933. The physicist was now in a position to realize the ambitions that had been thwarted during his long exile from academia.

ATTEMPTS TO DOMINATE ORGANIZED PHYSICS, 1933–36

Unaffected by the confusion, consternation, and despair caused by the exodus of many of Germany's finest scientists in the spring and summer of 1933, Stark assumed his position at the PTR. The fall physicists' conference was to be held in Würzburg in September, and he waited until that occasion to make his major pronouncement on the future administration of German physical research.

It was up to the PTR to organize physical investigation, he claimed in his speech, for as the largest single German laboratory its work involved both the scientific and industrial realms. Therefore it should become the central organ mediating between academic physics and the claims of industry and government. Once PTR facilities could be expanded, research beyond the means of individual university institutes could be conducted there. A Reich research service could also be established to direct industrial firms to physicists and institutes suited to a given project. Furthermore, Stark said, the PTR would undertake the centralized direction of the German scientific periodicals.[66]

Although the published account of his speech did not indicate it, Stark apparently turned to a group of publishers at its conclusion and thundered: "And if you're not willing, then I'll use force!" [67] Perhaps the fact that the conference was in Würzburg, the scene of his departure from academia in 1922, made him feel particularly bitter and venomous. This attempt to intimidate his listeners, however, estranged them further, especially in view of von Laue's talk at the same conference, which compared the Inquisition's attitude toward Galileo with that of National Socialism toward relativity.[68] Although Stark clearly intended to attain the preeminence in organized German science that he had failed to achieve in 1919–21, not one of his grandiose plans for the PTR was ever realized.

His failure was due in large measure to von Laue, who emerged as Stark's most active opponent in scientific circles. When Planck and two others proposed Stark's election in the Prussian Academy of Sciences, von Laue spoke against it on December 14, 1933. He did not do so gladly, he said, partially because, in the past years I have often watched with deep regret how obvious—even if sometimes understandable—injustice was done to him in appointments and other academic occasions. That our Academy has not long ago elected him as a member is counted among these.[69]

But that was in the past, he continued, and Stark had revealed at Würzburg that he wanted to become the dictator of physics in Germany. Especially threatening was his plan to control the scientific periodicals by placing them under a general editorship that would determine whether and in which journal every article would appear. The editorship, von Laue had learned, was to be controlled by the PTR, that is, by Stark. If Stark's scheme were successful, theoretical works might no longer appear in Germany. To elect him to the Academy under these conditions, von Laue concluded, would amount to an approval of his plans and their threat to the freedom of research. Stark's candidacy was withdrawn.[70]

His rejection by the Prussian Academy of Sciences weakened any claim Stark could have made to be the spokesman for all German scientists, but it certainly reinforced his assertion that he spoke on behalf of National Socialism rather than the old order. He did not hesitate to present himself as the voice of the New Germany in the British scientific weekly *Nature,* rebuting articles that criticized the Nazi government's attitude toward science. In a February 1934 article, he insisted that the dismissal measures of 1933 served not to restrict German science, but to free it from the unjustifiably great influence of the Jews. It would be a good thing, he noted, to keep scientific research and political agitation separate. *Nature* should stay out of domestic German politics, he warned.[71] In a second article two months later, he further noted that to withhold criticism of the new government "will be to the advantage not only of international cooperation but also of the Jewish scientists themselves." [72] Although some physicists, again notably von Laue, privately informed their colleagues abroad that they did not share Stark's views, no scientist who remained in Germany dared challenge Stark in print.[73] Foreigners who monitored developments in Germany could not escape the impression that those scientists who did not emigrate agreed with Stark's views to some extent.

Stark's rebuff by the Prussian Academy of Sciences did not deter him from his plans to align German research with National Socialism. On April 30, 1934, he sent an outline of his proposals to Hitler. In the name of German scientists, he asked the Führer to assume the presidency of a new Reich academy of science. The vice-president was to be "a leading German scholar." In addition, a Reich research council was suggested, with Reich Chancellor Adolf Hitler as highest director and a Reich research minister (presumably Stark himself) as business director. The council would lay down guidelines for all German research and the expenditure of research funds. The members of the council (representing seven areas: physical, technological, geological, hygienic, psychological, historical, and philological) would serve simultaneously as advisors in technical and personnel matters for the Reich research ministry. The new ministry, the third agency outlined, would oversee nearly all German research centers. Seven undersecretaries, one for each field in the research Council and responsible to the Reich research minister, would administer the centers.[74]

Stark's scheme for this sweeping reorganization of German science had a major flaw, however. It placed Stark on a collision course with the Reich Education Ministry (REM), which had been established under Bernhard Rust on May 1, 1934, just one day after Stark had sent his proposal to the Führer.

At first, it was not obvious that antagonism between Stark and the REM was inescapable. The physicist apparently believed that the creation of the Reich ministry was a step in the right direction, seeing in the birth of an entire department for research the beginning of the central organization of scientific investigation which he had espoused.[75] Also, the members of Rust's staff were apparently able to convince Stark that he could best achieve his objectives by assuming the leadership of one of the organizations transferred on May 1 to the REM from the Reich Ministry of the Interior. Thus Stark was offered the presidency of the Emergency Association of German Scholarship (which was increasingly often referred to as the Deutsche Forschungsgemeinschaft or German Research Association) in Berlin, an agency in which he had wanted to gain influence during the 1920–21 period. In mid-June, 500,000 marks of association funds were frozen and transferred to the PTR—the first indication Schmidt-Ott received that his long tenure as president was about to end. On June 23, Schmidt-Ott appeared before Rust. Rust told him that he would be replaced by Stark because the Führer specifically desired it and gave him a few hours to vacate his office.[76] Stark had finally attained one of his goals of the early twenties—a commanding voice in the allocation of research funds for German science.

Helmut Heiber, in his detailed study of the intricacies of Nazi party infighting, has indicated that the REM helped Stark obtain a position in the Emergency Association in order to shunt him onto a side track where his activities could be watched.[77] The official directive from Rust (dated June 23) ordering Stark to take charge explicitly stated that the physicist was to report to the Education Ministry on any plans related to the association.[78] And his vice-president Eduard Wildhagen, who actually ran the organization since Stark was absorbed in the work of the PTR, was assigned to him by the REM.

Two incidents in the summer of 1934 showed that Stark's appointment had not brought him any support among his scientific colleagues. The first was Stark's formal election to the presidency of the German Research Association. The mathematician Theodor Vahlen, as head of the REM department for higher education, sent a form to fifty-five of the association's members, asking them to approve Stark's accession and to return the form by July 25. Forty-eight yes votes came from the universities and institutes of technology, whose rectors were appointed by the ministry. The Kaiser Wilhelm Society under Planck abstained, and the university in Munich as well as four of the five academies of sciences (the Prussian, Saxon, Bavarian, and Göttingen) voted no. Of the academies, only Heidelberg voted assent. The Munich University vote may have been related to the fact that the Bavarian Academy rejection was the most explicit of all and possibly had been written by Sommerfeld.[79]

The second event came just three weeks later. After Hindenburg's death on August 2, the Nazi party prepared for a plebiscite to sanction Hitler's fusion of the highest state and party offices in his person. On August 11, 1934, Stark sent telegrams to each of Germany's Nobel laureates asking them to sign a public declaration on behalf of the Führer:

> In Adolf Hitler we German natural researchers perceive and admire the savior and leader of the German people. Under his protection and his encouragement, our scientific work will serve the German people and increase German esteem in the world.[80]

Several scientists responded that one should not mix science and domestic politics, an ironic echo of Stark's arguments in *Nature*.

Stark found so little support that he had to abandon the project, and he castigated those who refused to sign for their lack of national outlook and instinct.[81]

By the end of the summer of 1934, Stark was caught up in the intraparty intrigues of the Rust and Rosenberg organizations. The physicist was undoubtedly aware of the implications of his subordinate relationship to the Education Ministry. Thus his naming of Alfred Rosenberg as patron and protector of the association was a calculated move to assert his independence. Since Rosenberg was charged with the supervision of the ideological training of the party, his interests often involved the same administrative areas as those of the Reich Ministry of Education. As suggested earlier, this consideration may have led Rosenberg to support the ineffectual Rust for the post of Reich education minister rather than allow the dynamic Schemm to take over.[82]

The driving force behind the REM's antagonism toward Stark was Rudolf Mentzel, the deputy head of the department of research Rust had established in his ministry to court favor with the army. In early 1934, Mentzel's ostensible chief, the War Office physicist Erich Schumann, had approached Stark with a plan to reorganize German science along military lines. In early July, Schumann again approached Stark with this plan and requested as well to participate in the direction of the German Research Association. Stark's reply was apparently a chilly negative. In September, the physicist practically threw Mentzel and Schumann out of his office.[83] This action, coupled with his choice of Rosenberg as a patron, engendered Mentzel's unwavering animosity.

Mentzel's opposition was much more formidable than Stark had realized. His ties to the army and the SS were strong, and, according to Heiber, "everywhere where it counted in preparing difficulties for Rosenberg and his adherents, Mentzel had his finger in the pie." [84] Stark's choice of Rosenberg as a counterweight to the REM proved to be a major error.

In November 1934, Stark spoke before representatives of the members of the German Research Association in Hannover. He explained his plans for the organization to fulfill the Führer's desire that German science and technology labor to make Germany economically independent of other countries. He praised the Reich minister of education for placing a scientist (i.e., himself) in charge of the association and emphasized that to accomplish its objectives,

the Forschungsgemeinschaft would need two things—financial support and administrative independence.[85] His choice of words implied
that both were in jeopardy.

A measure of Stark's difficulties with the REM was provided on
the following day, November 11. Rosenberg was scheduled to address a party district meeting in Hannover in celebration of the first
annual Tag der deutschen Wissenschaft (Day of German Learning).
The idea was to show the close relationship between the party and
scholarship. Rust, however, as party boss of the district, ordered a
boycott of the meeting. Stark had to step in and give the speech for
Rosenberg in a nearly empty auditorium.[86] The debacle symbolized
Stark's career as a politician.

In early January, Stark employed the leadership principle and
named the new members of the association's executive committee,
but all those associated with the REM or the army found excuses
and declined. When Stark called a meeting on January 12 to discuss
the growing animosity between the association and the REM, the
REM staff managed to cancel the session at the last moment.[87]

A month later, in February 1935, the REM proposed to the Reich
Chancellery that a Reich academy of research, with Hitler as head,
be created under the control of the Reich education minister, to
centralize the administration of German research. Although similar
in this respect to the body Stark had proposed a year earlier, the new
academy would have usurped many of the functions of the German
Research Association.[88] Stark quickly counterattacked. He gained
an audience with the head of the Reich Chancellery, Dr. Hans Lammers, and in a letter on February 21, he warned

> that by Mr. Minister Rust's measures the Jewish-democratic
> influence which ruled German science under the black-red
> [Weimar] system comes back into play.[89]

Lenard sent a telegram in support of Stark, and Hess's staff also expressed dismay that the REM bureaucracy would be placed in charge
of administering German research.[90] The Rust proposal was tabled
by Hitler, and Stark was given a chance to reply to it in detail: he
suggested on March 12 that the Research Association administer itself under supervision of the Reich Chancellery, which would remove it from its increasingly precarious position under the REM.[91]
The REM plan was eventually dropped.

Meanwhile, however, Rust's staff managed to have the German
Research Association's funds frozen effective March 1. Stark com-

plained immediately to Lammers and was supported by Rosenberg, whose office had received considerable financial assistance for its "research" from Stark and his deputy Wildhagen. The REM relented, even though Mentzel did not want to give in, and allowed the funds to be released by the end of the month.[92] Stark had, however, received much less than his financial request in 1935, and only half as much again in 1936.[93] By controlling the purse, the REM had the upper hand in the long run.

Although Mentzel continued to harass the German Research Association, the critical blow to Stark's position actually came from a member of Rosenberg's operation. In early 1936 Rosenberg recommended Walter Frank, whose Reich Institute for the History of the New Germany had been started in October 1935, for vice-president of the association. In an effort to avoid dilution of his own authority, Wildhagen harshly rejected the candidate.[94]

In June Frank was able to wreak revenge upon Wildhagen. In an article in the daily press, he denounced Stark's deputy as the "grey eminence" of German scholarship, one who had been an opponent of National Socialism and a friend of the Jews during the Weimar period.[95] Stark backed his subordinate, but he found that Wildhagen also had enemies on the staffs of Hess and Göring, and that the SS took Frank's side in any internal struggle with Rosenberg. There was very little he could do; his assistant was dismissed on August 15, 1936.[96]

In late September, the physicist received Karl Weigel of the SS ancestral heritage (Ahnenerbe) research section, but he denied the association's aid to the SS; he did not consider their projects scholarly enough. The SS report of this rebuff went through channels to Himmler's staff, and thus added still others to Stark's list of opponents.[97] He had also managed to antagonize the party district leader of Bavaria, Adolf Wagner, in what had been originally a minor matter concerning an associate of Wagner in 1934. By 1936, charges and countercharges had escalated and Wagner was agitating in the REM for Stark's dismissal. A party court battle dragged on until 1938, when Stark was found guilty of using improper channels to oppose Wagner.[98] The judge levied no penalty, for he stated that Stark had "already been punished by dismissal from office as President of the Emergency Association." [99]

Stark was finally toppled by the failure of one of his pet projects— he had spent considerable funds in an attempt to obtain gold from the south German moors. Threatened with a public scandal, Stark made a deal with his ministry antagonists. He would keep the PTR presidency (from which he retired in 1939) and nothing would be said about the gold issue. In return he would abandon the Research Association.[100] On November 19, he received notice from Rust that his resignation was accepted. His successor was none other than Mentzel.[101]

By the end of 1936, Stark's attempt to gather the reins of German science into his hands had been foiled, largely because of party in-fighting. His goals and methods had resulted directly from his experiences prior to 1933. If the grounds for Lenard's allegiance to the Hitler movement could be summed up as "ideology," the basis of Stark's resort to extremism could be epitomized by "disaffection."

Stark was alienated from the direction taken by modern physics beginning with the Bohr-Sommerfeld theories, and his distance from the mainstream of physical investigation grew in the 1920s. Like Lenard, his sense of nationalist solidarity had been intensified by the war, which also caused him to view the postwar parliamentary system with distaste. Ironically, his disaffection from Weimar led him to participate in interest-group politics in order to shield his profession from government interference. By 1921 he had alienated himself still further from the physics community by his unsuccessful attempt to generate a counterweight to the influence of its leaders.

The specific motive for Stark's recourse to political extremism was his resignation from Würzburg in 1922 and his inability—despite his Nobel prize—to secure another position. He felt victimized and found comfort, like Lenard, in association with the völkisch elements which were most energetic in opposing the system. Allegiance to Hitler and party membership followed. Thus, although their racist political activities were unusual for scientists, the experiences, grievances, and attitudes of Lenard and Stark (their political "profiles") were not unusual for early Nazi activists.[102] Their individual reasons for turning to National Socialism gave Lenard and Stark a common need to formulate the distinction between acceptable "German" and nonacceptable "Jewish-oriented" science. For Lenard this distinction was a matter of ideology; for Stark it was a weapon to use against those who had for so long kept him a pariah. For neither was it a matter of science. The "Aryan physics" they espoused, however, colored much of the political environment in which other physicists functioned in Germany from 1936 through the first years of World War II.

7. Aryan Physics

The politicized physics advocated by Philipp Lenard, Johannes Stark, and their small group of associates was never a closely defined set of beliefs. Each proponent of "Aryan," "Nordic," or "German" physics expressed himself in terms of his own personal views and grievances. Therefore, no single programmatic statement on the tenets or goals of this radical movement was ever produced. Certain writings, however, were referred to repeatedly and may be viewed as the Aryan physics "canon."

The Aryan physicists were in basic agreement on some essential premises. They believed in a mechanical, yet organic, nonmaterialistic universe in which discovery could only come through observation and experiment. They asserted that the racial heritage of an observer directly affected the perspective of his work. And they were united in a völkisch outlook pervaded by anti-Semitism.

There was confusion and disagreement on a crucial point, however, namely the proper role of the technological application of physics. Lenard and some of the other Aryan physicists belonged in the antimodern tradition of cultural pessimism. On the other hand, Stark and some others were adamantly in favor of technology. Despite this conflict of views, all were in accord on a course of action designed to infuse völkisch ideology into German academic physics.

THE ARYAN PHYSICS CANON

The basic works of "Aryan physics" were never in any sense codified. Two works each by Lenard and Stark and a collection of speeches given in late 1935 stand out, however, because they were frequently cited by advocates of the movement.

Reflecting the fact that Aryan physics was more politics than physics, the fundamental book of the movement was Lenard's *Grosse Naturforscher* (Great natural researchers, 1929). This survey of the leading scientists of the past opened with antiquity and closed with the end of the nineteenth century. Lenard omitted discussion of figures who had lived after the Great War, in order to avoid including his contemporaries.[1] The sixty-five biographical sketches he included were characterized by his romantic hero worship and his belief that the great contributors to science had been without exception of Aryan-Germanic racial stock. This anthropological-historical approach was in keeping with the general tenor of Nazi ideology: it appealed especially to those who were influenced by the racial theorists—such as Houston Stewart Chamberlain—upon whom the National Socialists relied for intellectual legitimacy. Indeed, Lenard had undertaken the project at the suggestion of one of the party racial experts, Hans F. K. Günther.[2] Alfred Rosenberg in particular liked the book, and even referred to it in one of his speeches.[3]

Rosenberg found noteworthy one of the basic assertions of *Grosse Naturforscher:* from the time of Hipparchus of Nicea (circa 150 B.C.) to Leonardo da Vinci (circa 1500 A.D.) science experienced a "dead time," resulting from the racial degeneration of the Greeks and the politically enforced authority of Aristotle and the Bible.[4] This point is one of the many on which Lenard followed Chamberlain.[5]

Pictures of the great natural researchers were included in the book whenever possible, so that the reader could discern their Nordic physical characteristics.[6] In successive editions the racist terminology became more and more pronounced. The shift was especially noteworthy in regard to Heinrich Hertz, who had been Lenard's professor in Bonn. Hertz was half-Jewish, a fact Lenard mentioned only in passing in the early editions, for he wished to stress his mentor's experimental discovery of radio waves. In later editions, however, he ascribed Hertz's early experimental prowess to his Aryan mother and his later tendency to engage in theoretical work to his Jewish father.[7] Lenard had neatly resolved the problem of explaining why many Jewish scientists performed significant research—the presence of Aryan blood was responsible for their achievements.

If a capable researcher was fully Jewish, however, Lenard used another tactic. Einstein's famous $E = mc^2$ formula relating energy to mass was experimentally irrefutable. Lenard, however, managed to find a precursor of the formula in the work of Friedrich Hasenöhrl, a highly competent, non-Jewish, Austrian physicist who died fighting in World War I. Lenard elevated Hasenöhrl to the stature of Galileo, Newton, Faraday, Darwin, and other scientific greats. Although his discovery went by an "alien name" (Einstein's), Lenard asserted, it was an Aryan creation.[8]

Lenard's second contribution to the Aryan physics canon was the textbook he had begun preparing in 1933. Based on his famed lectures, *Deutsche Physik* (German physics), published in 1936–37, was absorbing reading. Because its introduction was a forthright declaration of racism in physics, it has often been quoted in anthologies dealing with intellectual life in the Third Reich.[9] The infamous opening lines gave the Aryan physics movement its battle cry:

> "German physics?" people will ask. I could have also said Aryan physics or physics of Nordic natured persons, physics of the reality-founders, of the truth-seekers, physics of those who have founded natural research.[10]

But *Deutsche Physik* was not just a polemical brochure, and Lenard himself pointed out that it was necessary to examine more than the introduction to learn what he had to say.[11] The four-volume set was the only major work of Aryan physics that actually dealt primarily with physics instead of politics. It was divided into two portions: the physics of matter (mechanics, acoustics, and heat) and the physics of the aether (optics, electricity, and magnetism). The factor unifying the entire scheme, Lenard wrote, was the concept of energy.[12]

Stark's contributions to völkisch physics were his description of the Jewish inroads into German academic circles and his attack on the notion of internationality in science. His *Nationalsozialismus und Wissenschaft* (National Socialism and scholarship, 1934) took up the story of the Aryan-Jewish conflict in science at the point—about 1900—Lenard's *Grosse Naturforscher* ended. This polemical tract attempted to tie Jews and theoreticians together and to link them with the politics and mentality of the Weimar socialist government. When it was published, Stark was in the process of trying to establish himself as the leader of German science, both by defending National Socialism abroad and by espousing a plan for the central organization of German research. He therefore also stressed the importance of physical research for technology and industry in regard to economic self-sufficiency and war production, because such beliefs strengthened his claim to be heard by the highest Nazi officials.[13]

Stark's second addition to the Aryan physics canon was a speech delivered in Munich in 1941 and published as *Jüdische und Deutsche Physik* (Jewish and German physics, 1941). This talk represented in many respects a closing summary of the Aryan physics position, in which Stark assessed the damage the Jews had supposedly inflicted upon German science in the first three decades of the twentieth century. Stark also criticized quantum mechanics as unproductive formalism, a notably hollow charge in view of the scientific fertility of the new theories. The speech reflected one obvious goal of the Aryan physics effort: what Stark and Lenard had failed to accomplish within scientific circles during the Weimar period, they tried to achieve in the political arena during the Third Reich.[14]

The final component of the standard Aryan physics bibliography was a series of speeches delivered in Heidelberg on December 13 and 14, 1935, on the occasion of the rededication of the physical institute as the Philipp Lenard Institute. The conflict between the Education Ministry and Stark over the German Research Association was nearing its peak, and Education Minister Bernhard Rust did not put in a scheduled appearance. Claiming illness, he sent the head of the Baden Ministry of Education, Otto Wacker, to take his place.[15] Some of the talks placed scholarly topics—such as philosophy, biology, and education—in a völkisch context. The speeches of Stark and Lenard did the same for physics. A student leader, an industrial figure, and two of Lenard's former pupils also spoke.[16]

In a litany characteristic of Aryan physics pronouncements, the episodes of Lenard's life were recounted and honored—particularly his opposition to Einstein and the storming of the Heidelberg institute in 1922. The tenor of the speeches was reflected in the title of the published version: *Naturforschung im Aufbruch* (Natural research bursts forth, 1936). A new era in German research was about to begin, and it would be dominated by the values Lenard held dear, the values at the heart of the Aryan physics philosophy of science.

THE ARYAN PHYSICS WORLD VIEW: NATURE AND EXPERIMENT

Aryan physics focused more sharply upon what it opposed than upon what it favored. It violently denounced mechanistic materialism, which was universally regarded as the underpinning of Marxism. At the same time, because it was molded by the personal antipathies developed by Lenard and Stark in the course of their careers, Aryan physics was opposed to relativity and quantum mechanics. Rejection of modern physics meant that these physicists were forced to rely upon classical Newtonian physics, which since the seventeenth century had been the foundation of the very materialism they abhorred. The attempted solution to this paradox was predicated on the view of reality that permeated National Socialist thought. It was an axiom that all National Socialists rejected any form of materialism and embraced the concept of an all-pervasive spirit animating nature. Communion with this spirit enabled one to divine the natural hierarchical order of things, including the necessity for a Führer to lead a people in its struggle for existence.[17] Lenard exemplified the view of Aryan physics when he dismissed materialism as "material craze" (*Stoffwahn*) and claimed that the great scientific "spirits" (i.e., the great scientists) had never succumbed to it. Materialism was the mark of the lesser figures who followed truly great men like Newton or Darwin.[18]

Lenard prized Newton's work, for he felt that Newton had developed a mechanistic world view without losing sight of nonmaterial factors in reality. The Heidelberg professor believed that the propagandists of the French Enlightenment had, by fraudulently claiming omniscience for science, corrupted Newton's work and divorced spirit from mechanics. This perversion led to a mechanistic materialism that was responsible, among other things, for the desire to rule nature for selfish gain.[19] Lenard called for a new perspective on old truths, a tool to reestablish the connection between matter and spirit. The solution he championed was a version of the aether theory he had first proposed in 1922 as an alternative to relativity.[20]

Nineteenth-century theories had presented the aether as a medium independent of (other) matter through which light rays were propagated as waves.[21] Lenard redefined the aether in the vaguest of terms only as the "something" which regulated the speed of "aether waves," that is, all electromagnetic radiation traveling with the speed of light. He suggested a twist, however, contending that each heavenly body and indeed every piece of matter was endowed with its own special aether.[22] Furthermore, aether and matter were the two realms of existence united by the common bond of energy. In the reaches of interstellar space far from energy phenomena, the aether was uniform and practically synonymous with space itself. In this form, it was called the "meta-aether" (*Uräther.*) [23]

Thus Aryan physics sidestepped such evidence against the existence of the aether as the famous Michelson-Morley experiments of the 1880s, which had attempted in vain to detect the earth's movement through a stationary aether.[24] According to Lenard, the earth, and every atom on the earth, simply took its aether along with it as it moved.

Rudolf Tomaschek of the TH Dresden, one of Lenard's most capable pupils, asserted at Heidelberg in 1935 that the aether was a conception the Jews would like to abolish. The mechanical view of nature it represented was one of the most fundamental tools of

Germanic natural research—the source he quoted for this assertion was no less a racial authority than Houston Stewart Chamberlain.[25] Tomaschek was quick to disassociate mechanics from materialism, however. He defined mechanics not as experience with material objects, but as intuitive (*anschauliche*) ideas subject to quantitative verification.[26]

Besides providing for a mechanical yet nonmaterialistic universe, the aether theory performed another important function in Aryan physics. It placed limits upon human knowledge and left essential facets of nature shrouded in perpetual mystery. In praising the ambiguity of the aether, Lenard proclaimed:

> The concepts which provide solid support for mental images of the aether have indeed been found. But mechanisms in the aether have been sought in vain; everything tentatively thought out in this direction agrees poorly with reality. The aether is apparently more difficult to grasp than matter. It seems already to indicate the limits of the comprehensible. That these limits have been completely exceeded in the attempt to comprehend the world of spirits [*Geister*] is obvious: no human spirit can even understand its own spirit.[27]

The Aryan physics proponents thus placed qualitative boundaries on the quantitative investigation of nature. An indeterminacy was inherent in scientific knowledge because man was innately unable to grasp the spiritual by rational means.

The new atomic theory developed in the 1920s seemed to fit rather well into the Aryan physicists' scheme of things. Quantum mechanics, both Heisenberg's matrix mechanics and Schrödinger's wave mechanics, conformed well enough to Tomaschek's definition of mechanics as ideas subject to quantitative verification. The new theory also held that a fundamental indeterminacy was intrinsic in physical research, thus challenging the notion of strict causality which underlay materialism. In fact, as noted in chapter 1, a number of German quantum scientists in the 1920s were apparently eager to seize the opportunity to abandon causality in order to conform to contemporary antirationalist, antimaterialist cultural thought. The quantum mechanical emphasis on limiting physical investigation to truly observable phenomena, and its recognition of the fundamentally subjective role of the investigator, could easily have been utilized to support such Aryan physics tenets as the importance of observation and the significance of the personality of the observer. If the Aryan physicists needed further recommendation, quantum mechanics was opposed by Einstein, who refused to accept indeterminism as inherent in nature. A political faction in the Soviet Union also rejected it, viewing Heisenberg as aiding the rise of National Socialism by spreading irrationalism in Germany.[28] The total rejection of quantum mechanics by Aryan physics underscored a major deficiency of politicized science: personal animosities overrode all other considerations.

Instead of the Bohr-Sommerfeld atom and the quantum theories which developed from it, the Aryan physicists had only Stark's axial atom in which a doughnut-shaped electron ringed the nucleus. The theory was completely unconvincing, and even though Stark published a good deal on it, no one else appears to have taken it seriously.[29] Even other Aryan physics advocates avoided mention of Stark's atomic model. The movement's image was thus one of a destructive force that offered no constructive alternative to existing atomic theories.

Rejection of relativity and quantum mechanics drastically reduced the appeal of the Aryan physicists among their professional colleagues. Einstein's political stance made his name anathema, of course, but prudent politics would have demanded a broadening of the base of support by claiming quantum mechanics as a Nordic achievement. In fact, thoughts along these lines were published by one of Goebbels's underlings, but the Propaganda Ministry never became actively engaged in the debate concerning ideologically proper physics.[30] Also, one of the foremost proponents of quantum mechanics, Pascual Jordan, stressed pointedly that the new theories provided the foundation for an alternative to materialism. Although his book *Die Physik des 20. Jahrhunderts* (The physics of the twentieth century) was thoroughly professional in tone and gave full credit to Einstein, Bohr, Franck, Hertz, and other Jewish researchers, the Aryan physicists could have used it to their advantage.[31] Lenard and Stark were too committed to opposing physical modernism, however, and could not bring themselves to advocate the politically expedient, even though their ultimate success or failure depended on it.

Aryan physicists found relativity and quantum mechanics unpalatable not only because of the heritage of animosity from the Weimar period but also on epistemological grounds. As theories based on extensive mathematical calculation, relativity and quantum mechanics were regarded as inimical to the proper spirit of natural research. The Aryan physicists declared experiment and observation instead to be the only true bases for physical knowledge.

This view was not as eccentric as it may seem. The conception of a mechanical yet nonmaterialistic universe was the basic ingredient of a respectable philosophy of science known as critical naturalism. The usual naturalist position held that the analysis of one small portion of the universe was sufficient to grasp the workings of all of nature. After initial observations, one needed only to extrapolate from the data in a systematically philosophical and mathematical manner. Critical naturalists rejected this approach because it was too rationalistic. This view was particularly strong among those critical naturalists who embraced the view of "emergent evolution" in the early twentieth century as a means to refute materialism in the life sciences. Emergent evolutionists held that the universe was continually confronting man with new phenomena, which must be progressively discovered. Experiment and observation, not theory and conceptualization, were the foundations of scientific knowledge.[32] Although it would be too simplistic to label Lenard and Stark critical naturalists, this was precisely the Aryan physics understanding of science. It was indicative of the fundamentally organic view of nature held by the Aryan physicists that their position was most coherently stated in a debate among biologists.

In a recent article on Einstein, Gerald Holton has labeled the excessive emphasis on experiment among relativity opponents "experimenticism."[33] The Aryan physicists, however, felt they were struggling against an equally excessive emphasis on theory, which one could in complementary fashion term "theoreticism." They felt theoreticians displayed an arrogant irreverence toward nature, and resented the viewpoint that any disagreement between theory and observation would inevitably be resolved in favor of theory. The notion that theoretical physics was the most advanced portion of the discipline was emphatically denied.[34]

For the Aryan physicists, the theoreticians' attitude of inner certainty and superior knowledge may have been their most irritating characteristic. An early example of this attitude has been related by one of Einstein's students. In 1919, Einstein showed her a newly arrived telegram announcing the results of the famous English eclipse expedition. She exclaimed with joy at the news, but the professor was unmoved. He said he had known the theory was correct. When she asked him what his attitude would have been had confirmation not been forthcoming, Einstein replied, "Then I would have been sorry for the dear Lord—the theory *is* correct." [35]

This weakness for logical certainty was precisely what the Aryan physics adherents rejected as unscientific and un-German. For them the foundation of science was measurable experience, upon which mechanical models of natural processes were based. These models were "proper" theories. Mathematical constructs deriving largely from imagination were abstractions foreign to nature, which deserved only to be called speculations or hypotheses.[36] For this reason, the Aryan physicists emphatically stressed Newton's dictum *hypotheses non fingo,* and "makers of hypotheses" became a common epithet in Aryan physics propaganda.[37]

THE ARYAN PHYSICS WORLD VIEW: THE NATURAL RESEARCHER

Although the Aryan physicists' organic conception of the universe and their consequent stress on observation made them appear to be arguing for an inductive approach to nature, their outlook was fundamentally deductive. Their first principle in the conduct of science was stated succinctly by Lenard: "In reality scholarship—like everything else brought forth by men—is conditioned by race and blood." [38] More than anything else, this völkisch aspect of their outlook stamped Lenard, Stark, and their disciples as renegades within the physics community.

Qualities favored by Aryan physics were ascribed to the Germanic researcher and other characteristics were assigned to his Jewish antithesis. The attributes of the first were responsible for constructive, creative achievements; those of the second were blamed for destructive, dogmatic imitation. The Aryan physics adherents thus ruled out objectivity and internationality in science. Their racist, subjective, nationalistic convictions gave the Aryan physicists the sheen of party orthodoxy.

Völkisch Physics

One of the best-known images of that orthodoxy involved the Aryan culture-bearer and his antithesis, the Jewish culture-destroyer.[39] This racist notion suffused the views of the Aryan physicists. Lenard, Stark, and their followers declared that not only mechanics but also the very concept of science had been created by

the Nordic race, and that the Aryan basis for research rested specifically on experiment and observation. At the 1935 Heidelberg ceremonies rededicating Lenard's institute, H. S. Chamberlain was often
cited to sanction these assertions.[40] At one point, this famous passage
from Chamberlain was quoted:

> Experience—i.e., exact, minute, tireless observation—provides
> the broad unshakable foundation of Germanic scholarship, re-
> gardless of whether it concerns philology or chemistry or any-
> thing else. The capacity to observe, as well as the passion, self-
> sacrifice and honesty with which it is pursued, are essential char-
> acteristics of our race. Observation is the conscience of Germanic
> scholarship.[41]

One of the speakers carefully listed ten characteristics of truly
Nordic researchers, including joy in observation, joy in repetition,
modesty, and "joy in struggling with the object—joy in the hunt." [42]
The Aryan researcher maintained a dialogue with nature. He asked
questions in the form of experiments and observed the answers in
the results.[43]

The Jewish method was censured as alien to nature and science.
Instead of observation, the Jew (the singular was nearly always used)
had a predilection for theory and abstraction. Einstein supposedly
epitomized this aspect of Jewish science.[44] The Jew presented his
theories in the form of complex mathematical calculations without
regard for experimental data. Mathematics had originally been a
Germanic instrument for expressing relationships in nature (as asserted by Chamberlain), but the Jewish academicians had made this
tool their own by the opening of the twentieth century.[45] In the
words of Lenard's pupil Alfons Bühl of the TH Karslruhe:

> This exceedingly mathematical treatment of physical problems
> had undoubtedly arisen from the Jewish spirit. The Jew has
> accepted this numerical, this calculational, as a special achieve-
> ment of physics everywhere he has concerned himself with
> physics. And just as he otherwise—as in business—always has
> only the numerical, the credit and debit calculation before his
> eyes, so it must be designated as a typically racial characteristic
> even in physics that he places mathematical formulation in the
> foreground.[46]

Another speaker at the Heidelberg rededication linked the calculational urge in physics with the Enlightenment impetus toward

materialism and egalitarianism.[47] It was but a short step from this point to the individualism and crass commercialism which were regarded as the primary selfish characteristics of the Jewish spirit in physics.[48] While the Aryan was modest and humble before nature, the Jew was insolent and arrogant.[49] Stark termed the Jew the born advocate (*der geborene Advokat*) of his own cause, a play on a word for lawyer which reflected the popular notion that Germany's Jews had flooded the legal profession.[50] Lenard held the Jewish spirit responsible for the desire to rush into publication with unproven ideas and the need to busy oneself with the newest sensations.[51] His aversion to this approach dated from his unsuccessful priority dispute with J. J. Thomson. Lenard had first regarded it as the "English" commercial method of physics, but he attributed it to the Jews in the postwar period.[52]

Stark's own aversion to theory dated from the same period, and he first applied the term dogmatic in reference to the Bohr-Sommerfeld quantum theory in 1922.[53] In 1934 he stressed that such "dogmatism" was Jewish, thus linking his old antagonist Sommerfeld with the main target of Nazi hatred.[54] Eventually, he delineated a sharp contrast between Jewish dogmatism and Aryan pragmatism in physics. The Jew, he declared, was racially drawn to a deductive approach based on generating ideas from his own preconceptions, cloaking them in mathematical constructions, and then propagandizing them. He only accepted experimental data which supported his theories. The Aryan, on the other hand, was racially conditioned to observe nature itself, formulate his conceptions inductively without regard to self-aggrandizement, and give them up readily if new evidence came to light.[55] This simplistic dogmatic-pragmatic dichotomy was a useful tool with which to discredit theoretical physics as a discipline in the political contest for the power of academic appointment after 1936. A theoretician who was not of Jewish descent could be attacked for "thinking Jewish." The transparently deductive nature of the Aryan physics emphasis on race was not discussed, of course.

Rejection of Objectivity and Internationality

Their racial views obviously placed the Aryan physicists in opposition to the notion of value-free scholarship and research, which formed the core of the concept of objectivity in science. Hitler himself was particularly critical of the objective perspective, because it entailed the political weakness of accepting differing points of view.[56] According to the former Nazi president of the Danzig senate,

Hermann Rauschning, Hitler stated that he believed science was a social endeavor which could only be measured in terms of its impact upon the community. Objectivity in science was merely a slogan invented by professors to protect their interests; the idea of a value-free science was absurd. Instead, Hitler maintained,

> That which is called the crisis of science is nothing more than that the gentlemen are beginning to see on their own how they have gotten onto the wrong track with their objectivity and autonomy. The simple question that precedes every scientific enterprise is: who is it who wants to know something, who is it who wants to orient himself in the world around him? It follows necessarily that there can only be the science of a particular type of humanity and of a particular age. There is very likely a Nordic science, and a National Socialist science, which are bound to be opposed to the Liberal-Jewish science, which, indeed, is no longer fulfilling its function anywhere, but is in the process of nullifying itself.[57]

In full agreement with Hitler, the Aryan physicists argued that since the race and culture of a researcher determined his perspective, objectivity represented a lack of commitment to the truth. It tossed the good and the bad, the proven and the unproven, all into one pot.[58] Pluralism of views was a liberal characteristic foreign to the organic unity of nature. It led to the sterile exercise of splintering science into ever more specialized branches (such as physical chemistry and mathematical physics).[59] The Aryan physicists' opposition to the fragmentation of science paralleled National Socialist opposition to the fragmentation of the body politic into numerous political parties. In both cases espousal of objectivity was regarded as support for factionalism, divisiveness, and narrow self-interest. As Stark claimed in his Heidelberg speech,

> A German natural researcher should not just be a narrow specialist, but should also feel and act as a German racial comrade. He should not lock himself into his laboratory and say: "What is going on out there in politics does not matter to me. I will obey a red or black Minister just as readily as a National Socialist; it is sufficient that I am working in my specialty and producing something." [60]

The true German researcher was to participate in the political life of his people. The models for behavior were, of course, Lenard and Stark.

The Aryan physics emphasis on racial conditioning and rejection of objectivity went hand in hand with a denial of the internationality of science. The results of scientific work had universal validity only if the work was properly scientific, that is, if it was based on the Aryan approach to nature. Any similarity between German and other Western research was due to a common Nordic racial stock.[61] Since Jews, however, had a different racial heritage, they looked at nature in their own particular manner. Because they were a people without a country, their science was truly "international." In Lenard's words:

> The Jews are everywhere, and whoever today still defends the assertion of the internationality of natural science means probably unconsciously the Jewish science, which is of course everywhere with the Jews and everywhere the same.[62]

Thus international science was equated with Jewish science, which was seen as a threat to the unity of creative Aryan research.

Since, according to Aryan physics, research was properly understood only in racial terms, the Aryan physicists often drew parallels between science and art. They argued that insofar as art was a matter of creation and not mere imitation (which was regarded as a special talent of the Jews), it acquired a racial stamp. Science was subject to the same conditions.[63] Both had a social function, that of uniting a people and giving expression to its talents. Science also had another social purpose, however, which was service to the people in its struggle for existence. This purpose was fulfilled in technology.

ARYAN PHYSICS AND TECHNOLOGY

According to the survival-of-the-fittest mentality of National Socialism, the role of technology was to secure the existence of the Volk against the ravages of nature and other peoples. It was of vital importance to the Nazi leaders. The extent to which Aryan physicists could gain influence and power was therefore dependent on their views in regard to technology: their disunity on this subject was an important factor in their failure to achieve the political support necessary to gain hegemony over the German physics community.[64]

The Aryan physicists agreed that all researchers served their

national-racial interest by instinct. They also unanimously supported
the propositions that the Aryan and Jewish races were in conflict
and that the Jews had been gaining ground in physics since the
nineteenth century. But Lenard and some of his pupils held fundamentally antimodern, antitechnology beliefs. To them, every technological advance was a Jewish-oriented, materialistic step away from
organic reality. In contrast, Stark and other Aryan physicists saw
modern technology as the great boon the Germanic race had be-
stowed on mankind. The Aryan physics movement was divided from
the first on the issue of reverence for nature versus mastery of nature.

Reverence for Nature

Most of the tenets of Aryan physics thus far analyzed have been
examples of romantic thought that had a century-old history in
Germany. The romantic rejection of mechanistic materialism, rationalism, theory and abstraction, objectivity, and specialization had
long been linked with belief in an organic universe with stress on
mystery, subjectivity, and unity in nature.[65] In academia, this split
was exemplified in the mandarin deprecation of Zivilisation and
praise for Kultur, noted in chapter 1. Usually, however, physical
scientists in Germany favored the rationalist perspective, while German thinkers in the humanities were much more inclined to be
"cultural pessimists." [66] The Aryan physicists who supported the
romantic tradition were thus exceptions among the physical scientists. On the other hand, the romantic thinkers were emphatically
opposed to empiricism, which they regarded as an analytic process
that dissected and destroyed life. The Aryan physics allegiance to
experiment and observation was thus an anomaly among romantics.
The Aryan physicists made clear their priorities by attempting to
make empiricism conform to the romantic viewpoint. The limitation
the spiritual element in the aether placed on the power of observation and the claim that only researchers of the proper race could
perform experiment in harmony with living nature were two aspects
of this attempt.

Since the technological foundations of industrialization represented the ultimate scientific evil for the cultural pessimists, the
Aryan physicists' aversion to technology was not surprising. Lenard
and Tomaschek were the most prominent Aryan physics opponents
of technology. Lenard, in particular, believed that the Jews were
guilty of overindustrializing Germany for their own profit. They had

caused a variety of evils—from labor unrest and materialism to the foreign hatred of Germany which culminated in World War I.[67] In *Deutsche Physik* Lenard wrote:

> In recent times the successes of technology have produced a particular form of arrogant material craze. The exploitation of practical possibilities provided by the understanding of nature gave rise to the notion of the "mastery" of nature: "Man has slowly become the master of nature." Such expressions in the manner of spiritually impoverished grand technicians have gained much influence through the ostentation made possible by new techniques. And the effect of the all-undermining alien spirit which has penetrated physics and mathematics has been to strengthen that influence.[68]

Man was not nature's sovereign in Lenard's scheme of things; he was a part of nature and subject to it. He had to revere it and respect its mysteries. As Lenard had written in 1922, "Respect for the great teacher and judge Nature will always remain the first mark of true natural research." [69]

But Lenard could not deny the great significance of technology in the modern world even if he loathed its impact. Thus he included James Watt, "the great improver of the steam engine," in his history of great natural researchers. In May 1933, to cite another example, as he cheered Stark's appointment to the presidency of the Imperial Institute of Physics and Technology, Lenard sadly noted that the "masses" believed in technology rather than science. He explained their delusion as a result of excessive Jewish influence in science, which had presumably caused the masses instinctively to lose their faith in it.[70]

Lenard did not, however, perceive the ramifications of his observation. His cultural pessimistic admiration of nature and mandarin belief in the conduct of research for its own sake were convictions the general populace did not share. The German people admired technological achievement rather than the disinterested quest for knowledge. Lenard's views thus estranged him from both the masses and the Nazi leaders.

Mastery of Nature

On the other hand, Stark, Bühl, and a few others rejected the antimodern heritage upon which much of Aryan physics drew. They perceived technology as a source of power and felt that the Germanic peoples deserved credit for its advancement.[71] Such views echoed those of both Hitler and Rosenberg, although these men might have been expected to share Lenard's position. Like Lenard, both men came from central Europe, where Germans were generally regarded as culturally superior because they had introduced technology into the area. Thus mastery over nature was for them a measure of the creative power of the Nordic race.[72] Rosenberg tempered this endorsement of technology, however, with the claim that conscientious experiment kept Germanic research, the basis for technology, from losing contact with organic reality.[73] Hitler also believed that, despite all man's technological achievements, nature still had the upper hand.[74]

While recognizing the possibility that application had been overemphasized, the protechnology Aryan physicists unreservedly stressed its necessity in the economic struggle for existence. Technology played a crucial role not only in peacetime agricultural and industrial production but also in warfare.[75] The Stark faction was thus generally in harmony with the Nazi leaders on the technology issue.

The views of Lenard faction were an obvious embarrassment to the protechnology Aryan physicists. At the Heidelberg ceremonies, Stark tried to handle the situation by asserting that an excess of either pure research or technology could be damaging for German science.[76] The awkwardness of the split was further revealed in the Heidelberg speech of Hans Rukop, director of the Telefunken Corporation in Berlin. The presence of an industrialist was apparently deemed necessary to impress high Nazi officials, yet it hardly seemed appropriate in view of Lenard's convictions. Rukop gave a strictly scientific talk on the progress in television technology and noted that technical physicists must take care to avoid narrowness in their work. In conclusion he quoted from an announcement of Lenard's forthcoming *Deutsche Physik* and remarked lamely that,

> . . . Lenard, whom one perhaps cannot count among the friends of industry, still has the same view as we that in the final analysis what matters is that each one mans his post. If the scholarly physicist finds his satisfaction in researching our world edifice, the technical physicist finds his in cooperation in the great task of feeding, defending, and securing the future of our

German Volk, from which we are all descended. We see our holy duty in the pursuit of these National Socialist goals. Here lies the common root which must bind scholarly and technical physics together.[77]

Prior to the outbreak of World War II, this kind of agreement to disagree characterized the two factions of Aryan physics.

In 1934, Stark had advocated the position that basic research was essential to the important applied work which led to new technological achievement.[78] His conflict with the Reich Education Ministry was just beginning, and his primary purpose was to demonstrate that the ministry should leave the direction of science to experienced scientists like himself.[79] After the initial successes of the German armies in 1939 and 1940, however, this position became the formula for agreement among the Aryan physicists. The words of August Becker, a member of the Lenard faction, indicated the basis for the compromise:

> Doubtless one of the essential reasons for the all-conquering strength of our defense is that German technology and its planning stand in first place in the world. Insofar as its general condition is the practical utilization of nature, does it not rest directly on the foundation of natural research, and does it not entirely reflect the typically German striving toward nature, the tenacity and profundity of digging for ever newer truth, for ever deeper knowledge of natural phenomena, which is exactly what has provided the broad, most important basis for German research? [80]

The split over the role of technology was the most obvious example of how such conflicts destroyed any strength either faction might have given the Aryan physics movement. But it was certainly not the only example. For instance, Lenard was adamantly opposed to relativity theory and Einstein, but he never specifically supported Stark's electron theory. Given other circumstances, he might have been drawn to quantum mechanics by its subjective role for the observer and its insistence on fundamentally observable quantities. Stark meanwhile was totally opposed to the new quantum theory and Sommerfeld, but never specifically supported Lenard's aether and meta-aether concepts. Placed in another situation, he might have been willing to abandon the aether and accept much of relativity. Such mutual cancellation of alternatives among its supporters was the major reason Aryan physics could not produce a coherent doctrine.

Another example of this process was the question of national characteristics. It is interesting to note that most scientists abroad—and many Germans at home—felt that the propensity for abstraction and theory was distinctively German. Ironically, experiment was regarded as the forte of the British, who were much more committed to the aether than their Continental colleagues.[81] Lenard was thus caught in a self-imposed dilemma: the predilection for theory he posited as British (in the style of J. J. Thomson) and Jewish was seen by his colleagues as German, while the inclination toward experiment and the acceptance of aether he saw as truly German was perceived by his colleagues as British. Stark, who greatly admired the English experimental tradition which had produced Ernest Rutherford, sought a way out of the confusion by changing labels—"theoretical" versus "experimental" became "dogmatic" versus "pragmatic." Yet the entire issue was highly typical of the inherent contradictions which undermined any attempt to lend substance to the tenets of Aryan physics.

It is obvious that Aryan physics was, as its name implied, a set of fundamentally incompatible concepts. Aryan physics as a political movement, however, was not thereby barred from a chance to attain control of the physics community in the Third Reich. National Socialism itself was a maze of mutually cancelling contradictions.[82] Aryan physics was a microcosm of National Socialism, a coalition of views just as irrational in form and nihilistic in content. It is a dangerous form of intellectual arrogance to believe that a movement must be rationally consistent in order to achieve political power.

Although the tenets of Aryan physics were often muddled and contradictory, the goal of its advocates was not. They were united in an effort to reduce the influence of and eventually eliminate modern theoretical physics from the German institutions of higher learning. Beginning with the 1935 Heidelberg rededication ceremonies, they attempted to use the terminology of Aryan physics to discredit scientific opponents as "Jewish thinking," and to place their own followers in positions of academic influence.

8. The Aryan Physics Political Campaign

Following the opening of their campaign at Heidelberg in December 1935, the Aryan physicists proceeded to attack theoretical physics from a number of public vantage points. They sought and received particular support from the supervisor of party ideology, Alfred Rosenberg, and from the party publications he controlled. Meanwhile, the conflict between Stark and the Reich Education Ministry continued unabated. When representatives of the majority of German physicists sought to combat the influence of Aryan physics, REM officials were only too happy to assist them. By the end of 1936, the attacks and counterattacks had led to a near standoff, with the Aryan physicists on the defensive.

During 1937–39 one issue—the choice of a successor to occupy Arnold Sommerfeld's chair for theoretical physics at the university in Munich—developed into the focal point of the struggle for control of academic appointment of physicists in the Third Reich. The contest was fought mostly on paper shuffled between bureaucratic desks in the REM and the University Teachers League, an organization subordinate to Rudolf Hess. Stark, however, took to the press, using the principal SS journal in an effort to discredit Sommerfeld's chosen successor, Werner Heisenberg. The attempt to clear his name entangled Heisenberg in a process which dragged on for many months. The appointment of an Aryan physics advocate to the disputed position in 1939 marked the high-water point of the influence of Lenard and Stark.

The Opening Year of the Aryan Physics Campaign

The year 1936 began with a dynamic offensive by the Aryan physicists against theoretical physics as a discipline. This attack started with the aggressively phrased speeches delivered at Heidelberg on December 13 and 14, 1935, in honor of the rededication of the physical institute as the Philipp Lenard Institute. These talks constituted a call for the infusion of völkisch considerations into the physical sciences.[1] Reich Education Minister Bernhard Rust declined to appear, and not one of the heads of the party offices was present. Lenard criticized both state and party agencies for not supporting proper Aryan research. He remarked that even the principal party newspaper (edited by Rosenberg) had praised Jewish-oriented science in its columns.[2]

Rosenberg quickly responded, requesting that Lenard name a science advisor for the *Völkischer Beobachter*. In a letter of January 9, 1936, the retired Heidelberg professor stated his nominee, August Becker. Lenard further recommended that Becker be assisted by Rudolf Tomaschek, Alfons Bühl, and Heinrich Vogt. All four, Lenard claimed, had long been convinced National Socialists and were worthy of trust.[3] All had also been Lenard's pupils, although Vogt was an astronomer. Since Becker was not known as politically radical, however, it was somewhat surprising that he was Lenard's first choice. The explanation undoubtedly lay in the fact that he was completely under Lenard's influence in Heidelberg; his appointment would allow the elder physicist to keep close watch over developments.[4]

Rosenberg apparently acceded to Lenard's wishes, for within weeks an article appeared in the party newspaper contrasting Aryan and Jewish physics. The foreword to Lenard's *Deutsche Physik* and Stark's Heidelberg speech were quoted, although neither was yet in print. The author, purportedly a chemistry student named Willi Menzel (not to be confused with Stark's antagonist Rudolf Mentzel in the REM), must thus have had contact with Aryan physics adherents.[5]

The article specifically labeled Werner Heisenberg a representative of unacceptable physics, and Heisenberg quickly defended himself with an article in the *Völkischer Beobachter* itself. As he later explained, he felt it was necessary to challenge his attackers on their ground.[6] The basis of Heisenberg's argument was that the ultimate goal of natural science was not only to observe nature, but to understand it. Mathematics was particularly useful in the process, but the most important instruments were conceptual systems (*Begriffssysteme*).[7] These systems gave meaning and direction to experiment. Theory, through mathematics, also provided a precision which observation was unable to match. It could occasionally predict the existence of previously undetected physical phenomena. Relativity and quantum theory were experimentally verifiable conceptual schemes, which had in fact predicted the existence of the positron. Furthermore, these theories led away from the naïve materialistic world view of earlier science. Deeper understanding of the epistemological foundations of science was one of the most valuable tasks the younger scientific generation could undertake.[8]

A reply by Stark on the same page was introduced by the editorial comment that it was necessary immediately to refute Heisenberg's article. Stark wrote that experiment, not theory, had led the way in recent physical research, by which he meant the discoveries of the electron, x-rays, and radioactivity at the turn of the century. Neither the quantum theory nor Einstein's relativity were experimentally unexceptionable, and Heisenberg represented the fundamental perspective of Jewish physics with his "conceptual systems" approach. Theory was purely a calculational and representational tool in physics, and its overweening influence in academic appointments must be ended. In an implicitly autobiographical note, Stark added:

> The theoretical physics led by Einstein, Planck and Sommerfeld not only possessed almost all theoretical teaching positions, but no representative of experimental physics could obtain a professorial chair against their objection, not even when he had exhibited recognized experimental achievements.[9]

Stark thus tied Planck and Sommerfeld as well as Heisenberg to Einstein, whose name was practically a byword for "enemy" in the Third Reich. The *Völkischer Beobachter* soon thereafter printed other articles supporting Aryan physics.[10]

Stark had stated the same position in his Heidelberg speech, which another Rosenberg publication, the *Nationalsozialistische Monatshefte* (National socialist monthly), printed in February 1936. This journal had a smaller audience than the party newspaper, but its readers could be expected to have a somewhat greater interest in the ideological claims advanced by Aryan physics proponents. One particular passage in Stark's speech, however, stood out as a purely political ploy. Following a remark on Lenard's role as Einstein's major foe at Nauheim in 1920, Stark wrote:

> Now, Einstein has disappeared today from Germany and no serious physicist still sees his relativity theory as an untouchable revelation. But unfortunately his German friends and supporters still have the opportunity to be further active in his spirit. His main supporter Planck still stands at the head of the Kaiser Wilhelm Society, his interpreter and friend Mr. von Laue still

is allowed to play the role of a physical expert in the Prussian
Academy of Sciences. And the theoretical formalist Heisenberg,
spirit of Einstein's spirit, is supposed to be distinguished with
an academic call. In contrast to these deplorable circumstances, which contradict National Socialist spirit, may Lenard's
struggle against Einsteinism be an exhortation. And it is desirable that the competent experts in the Ministry of Education
allow themselves to be advised by Lenard in the occupation of
physical—even theoretical—professorial chairs.[11]

Stark was at this time angling for the presidency of the Kaiser Wilhelm Society, from which Planck was slated to step down on April 1,
1936. Heisenberg was under consideration to succeed Sommerfeld at
Munich, a position the Aryan physicists wanted to secure for one of
their own followers. Stark obviously hoped to influence both appointments.

Not long after the publication of Stark's article, Lenard's *Deutsche
Physik* appeared. In an initial effort to garner support from high-
ranking officials, Lenard dedicated his work to Wilhelm Frick, Reich
and Prussian minister of the interior, who had elevated Stark and
racial theorist Hans F. K. Günther to positions of influence.[12] The
Aryan physicists were unaware, however, that Frick had for some
time been engaged in a losing struggle with Heinrich Himmler for
control of the German police forces. On June 17, 1936, Hitler gave
Himmler command of the police as well as the SS.[13] Frick thereby
lost most of his political power. The Aryan physicists had chosen the
wrong patron.

Although Frick was unable to give much backing to Aryan physics,
another political ally had been found in Heidelberg. Although
technically under the control of the Reich Education Ministry
through the rector of the university, the Heidelberg student corps
leadership backed Lenard and Stark in their conflict with the REM.
Beginning in 1922–24, Lenard's pro-Nazi stance had won him the
favor of the National Socialist students. They had even considered
staging a torchlight procession (a great honor in Germany) for him
in 1930, but he had told them to wait until they could all come in
Nazi brownshirts.[14] The parade finally took place when Lenard celebrated his seventy-fifth birthday in 1937.

In January 1936, the nominal head of the REM's Department of
Learning, Theodor Vahlen, began publishing *Deutsche Mathematik*,

a journal devoted to Aryan mathematics. The Berlin mathematician Ludwig Bieberbach was the editor, and in each issue political articles preceded the scholarly papers. Student contributors were solicited for the political material, and from the outset the student supporters of Aryan physics used the journal as a forum.[15]

One of these supporters was Heinrich Vogt's assistant at the Heidelberg observatory, Bruno Thüring, who late in 1936 transferred to Munich. In an article in the first issue of *Deutsche Mathematik* he and a group of fellow students typified the National Socialist denial of the notion of value-free science. The students contrasted the "natural harmony of spirit and matter" displayed by the Nordic researchers Kepler and Newton with the "mathematical formalism" of Einstein. Their article concluded, "There is a German physics, a German natural science, concepts which have been absolutely foreign to the liberalistic conception of scholarship of the previous century." [16]

On August 8, 1936, Thüring, Becker, Bühl, and others delivered talks on Aryan research at a Heidelberg meeting of the Reich Expert Group for Science of the radical, activist National Socialist German Students League.[17] The league was a militant party agency, and the Expert Group for Science was led by Fritz Kubach, a young historian of science who became very influential in university politics as a result of his ties with members of Hess's staff.

Under Kubach's direction, a prize contest culminating in publication was held to honor the best piece of work produced by Nazi students in 1936. One winner was a pamphlet on Lenard's career composed by ten Heidelberg students. Although hardly more than a compilation of selections from Lenard's writings, the pamphlet was prepared explicitly to further the "fighting spirit" ignited at Heidelberg in December 1935. Kubach himself provided the foreword, emphasizing that Lenard's long struggle for proper Germanic scholarship was the true model for National Socialist behavior.[18]

In the spring of 1937, Kubach, along with Thüring and their Munich Student League colleague Ernst Bergdolt, took over the editorial leadership of the *Zeitschrift für die gesamte Naturwissenschaft* (Journal for the entirety of natural science). This journal thereby became the official organ of the Reich Expert Group for Science and the unofficial primary journal for proponents of Aryan physics. The editorial announcement of Kubach's assumption of leadership was faced on the opposite page by a picture of Lenard. The first article, written by one of Lenard's last and most politically active pupils, exhibited the tone of aggrieved righteousness that pervaded the writings of Lenard's and Stark's followers.

In reality, the Germany of "democratic freedom" denied all scholarship that honestly and openly built upon the great examples of the past and was based on secure facts of research. Instead, whatever racially alien spirits proclaimed and the racially inimical press prescribed was accepted as true.

Makers of hypotheses were declared Nobel prize winners, Einstein and Marx were the idols of the time. . . .

. . . As a consequence of his intuitive insight, he [Lenard] saw the disintegration in the areas of his own descipline; here he could not calmly await the destruction. Instead, he had to be a perpetual admonisher. On the one hand, this was the reason for his struggle against that "famous" circle around Einstein, against which he courageously spoke and wrote, and on the other hand, this was why he recognized that a cleansing of scholarship would only be possible when a strong hand arising from the Volk once again guided our destiny in Germany. Thus the [old party] fighter became lonely and abandoned in Germany—for much depended on professorships, and these were handed out by the Jew. Indeed, they did not shrink from storming his institute with agitated workers and conducting this honorable man of conviction in triumph through the streets of Heidelberg.[19]

Although Lenard's students, assistants, and pupils who had become professors were the activists and produced a flurry of such publications, Rosenberg was still the highest ranking Nazi supporter of Aryan physics. His support was manifested at the Nuremberg party rally in September 1936. Lenard was the first recipient of the party's new Prize for Scholarship, and Rosenberg delivered a warm presentation speech praising Lenard's long involvement on behalf of truly Germanic scholarship. He concluded with thanks from the party to the "courageous follower of the Führer in a difficult time" and the hope that German academia would produce many more men like him.[20]

By the time of this party rally, however, the initiative was already shifting to the antagonists of Aryan physics. The contest between Stark and the Reich Education Ministry over centralized control of German science was primarily a matter of personal power and prestige. The academic physics community, the target of Aryan physics ideology and politics, had thus far played no part in these intrigues.

However, a brief episode in early 1936, which was linked to the conflict between the REM and Stark, probably awakened the majority of German physicists to the fact that the ministry might be an ally against the Aryan physics campaign. This involved the choice of a successor to Planck as president of the Kaiser Wilhelm Society (KWG). As noted earlier, Stark's Heidelberg speech contained statements apparently designed to influence the KWG succession. On February 3, Minister Rust wrote directly to Hitler that both Krupp von Bohlen-Halbach and Carl Bosch had been suggested as candidates. Now, however, Stark ("who as president of the Imperial Institute of Physics and Technology and the Emergency Association of German Science is overburdened") had offered himself for yet a third presidency. Rust advised against Stark's appointment:

> I must point out against this that Professor Starck [sic] has to my regret been rejected by so many notable leading men and highest State offices that cooperation [with him] would have to encounter grave difficulties.[21]

Hitler decided to let Rust determine the KWG succession, and Bosch was named president as of April 1, 1936.[22]

In addition to this rebuff, the Education Ministry took a step in the spring of 1936 which affected Aryan physics as a whole. On the occasion of the 550th anniversary celebration of the founding of the university in Heidelberg, Rust came into Lenard's bailiwick to deliver the keynote address. He defended the dismissal policy and other government measures as necessary for the good of the nation, thus reminding his Nazi listeners of his claim to lead National Socialist scholarship. He further stole the thunder of his ideological opponents by stressing his antipathy toward objectivity in science and emphasizing that each researcher functions as a portion of nature rather than as an independent abstraction from the world around him. Academic freedom could only be truly free when it realized the need for direction and purpose. He concluded that although the state had introduced many changes since 1933, it was not under the illusion that organizational measures would suffice, for "we are convinced that a real transformation of scholarly life can only come forth from the *idea of scholarship*." [23] Rust thus asserted the claim of the

Reich Education Ministry to determine not only the organization of German scholarship but its ideology as well.

The REM was not the only threat to the Aryan physicists. It was obvious that they still had virtually no support among their scientific colleagues. After the exchange of articles in the party newspaper in February, a number of pieces appeared in the daily press in support of Heisenberg—some of which very sharply denounced any intrusion of political considerations into scientific questions.[24] Other journals picked up the story, and the debate was even reported abroad.[25] A number of physicists also spoke out in scholarly publications on the relationship of theory to experiment in physics, and it was clear from these writings that the professional physics community did not recognize Aryan physics as science.[26]

The activist tone of Rust's speech in Heidelberg was deceptive. Isolated statements there and elsewhere made it apparent to close observers that, although Rust wanted to control the overall direction of science, he did not wish to interfere in the actual conduct of scientific work in the laboratories and classrooms.[27] His appointment of Bosch as head of the Kaiser Wilhelm Society when he might have chosen a Nazi seemed to bolster this view. Thus the majority of German physicists, who wanted only to be left alone to work, sought to ally with the REM against Aryan physics. They apparently did so shortly after the initial Aryan physics attack in the winter of 1936.

Heisenberg had a personal interview with Mentzel, from whom he received an official request to prepare a statement on theoretical physics reflecting the sentiment of the majority of German physicists.[28] Heisenberg had already been working with Max Wien and Hans Geiger for some time on a position paper which would be acceptable to physicists performing technical, experimental, or theoretical physics. Wien (at Jena) was a technical physicist and Geiger (at Tübingen) was an experimentalist. The conservative personal convictions of these men were well known. Both were acquaintances of Heisenberg, and Wien had already evinced concern for the state of German physics in his informally distributed memorandum of November 1934.[29]

The Heisenberg-Wien-Geiger memorandum was apparently circulated in the summer and fall of 1936 (signatures were presumably gathered at the annual physicists convention in September) and was probably submitted to the ministry in late 1936. The exact time frame is somewhat vague, for the only known copy of the document is undated. The most reliable reference to preparation of the memorandum was given by Heisenberg in a letter in November 1937:

> Approximately two years ago when Stark had begun to cast suspicion on modern theoretical physics and its representatives through speeches and articles (compare, for example, *National-sozialistische Monatshefte* 7th year, issue 71, page 5/109), the expert advisor in the Reich Education Ministry, Professor Menzel [*sic*] expressed the wish to me, that a memorandum reflecting the opinion of most German physicists on the position of modern theoretical physics should be worked out for the information of the Reich Education Minister. Upon the express wish of Professor Menzel [*sic*], two representatives of experimental physics, the Director of the Physical Institute of the University of Jena at the time, Privy Councilor Wien, and the present Director of the Physical Institute of the Institute of Technology in [Berlin-]Charlottenburg, Professor Geiger, and I as a representative of theoretical physics, worked out this memorandum in contact with many other colleagues. It was then handed in to the Reich Education Minister with the signatures of the majority of representatives of physics at the German institutes of higher learning.[30]

By October 1936, the recently appointed head of the REM central office had apparently seen a draft of the statement. He noted in an interoffice memo that Mentzel had allowed both Mentzel's own name and that of the education minister to be used in the physicists' memorandum. The ministry should not have given the impression, he pointed out, that it stood on one side or the other. "It would have definitely been more correct," he concluded, "if the expert advisor had not placed his name and that of the Education Minister at the disposal of this type of intervention." [31]

The Heisenberg-Wien-Geiger memorandum was therefore apparently changed slightly before its final submission.[32] The opening paragraph did not mention Mentzel and merely thanked the Reich minister for the opportunity for the signatories to express their views. The text first dealt with the state of physics in Germany: there were too few physicists of the coming generation (*Nachwuchs*); academic appointments faced great difficulties; there was a scarcity of students. The recent damaging attacks on theoretical physics added to the gravity of the situation, because they caused students to shy away from physics, particularly from theoretical physics. They also damaged Germany's image abroad.

The memorandum refuted these attacks in terms very similar to those Heisenberg used in his *Völkischer Beobachter* article. The first and unconditional prerequisite for natural science was experimental investigation; the goal of science, however, was not merely the tabulation of experiments, but the understanding of natural laws. The formulation of natural laws was the task of theory. Both relativity and quantum theory were based on experimental research and led to new understanding of experimental results, just as they provided the impetus toward new experimental discoveries. Theory and experiment thus worked together as equals. The statement closed with the request that discussion in the daily press in which either type of research was denigrated in favor of the other should cease.

The declaration was signed by seventy-five men, including almost all of Germany's most notable physicists. The signers spanned the entire field of physics, running the gamut from quantum theoreticians to purely technical physicists. Politically, they ranged from democrats (such as Erich Regener of the TH Stuttgart, who was finally dismissed in 1938) to conservatives and even National Socialists, who opposed Nazi ideology only when it intruded into physics. Since scientists in the Third Reich were even more reluctant to sign such documents than they might have been in other times, the large roll mustered by Heisenberg, Wien, and Geiger was a strong indication of how seriously German physicists took the threat which political interference posed to their discipline. The specter of a politicized physics apparently acted as an extraordinary unifying force. It must also have been gratifying for some of the more conservative experimentalists to see the theoreticians coming to them for support, even if they joined them in disdaining the unprofessional conduct of the Aryan physics proponents.

THE SOMMERFELD SUCCESSION

The physicists' memorandum was at least partially effective, for the daily press published no more attacks like those of early 1936. Yet the issue was not decided, for the Aryan physicists still had other avenues of publication open to them. Stark's forced resignation from the German Research Association and his replacement by Mentzel in November 1936 considerably weakened the political influence of Aryan physics. Nevertheless, Stark still headed the important Imperial Institute of Physics and Technology in Berlin, and he was far from incapacitated. In fact, the struggle merely switched to another front of more immediate concern, the power of academic appointment. In the process other Nazi agencies interested in university affairs were drawn into the contest between professional and politicized physics.

The National Socialist German University Teachers League

With the establishment of the Reich Education Ministry on May 1, 1934, the administration of scholarship had become centralized under Rust and his staff. Scholarly life, of course, did not come immediately under the domination of National Socialist ideologues. Even though Rust, Vahlen, Mentzel, and other REM figures were "old fighters" who had been with the party since the 1920s, once they assumed a state office they tended to defend the power and prerogatives of that office against any outside encroachment, like most Nazis who took over such positions. The desire for personal prestige played a role in this attitude, as did a certain amount of bureaucratic empire building. One of the major factors involved, however, was that the staffs the Nazis inherited were generally composed of career civil servants who resisted change from any quarter. These professionals held firm beliefs on such matters as proper qualifications and orderly, fixed procedures—views which were perhaps only strengthened by the appointment of Nazi administrators on political grounds and the arbitrariness inherent in the "leadership principle." [33]

Faced with governing academia, the REM figures found it expedient to espouse the maintenance of traditional standards of scholarship. Being convinced National Socialists, however, they also wished to align academia with the Hitler movement. Beyond organizational measures, they sought to accomplish this goal by filling academic positions with qualified scholars who were also Nazis.

On the other hand, figures in the party agencies which became important after the seizure of power usually perceived the goal of National Socialism in terms of replacing rather than maintaining the state apparatus. They were neither constrained by the need to defend preexisting structures nor saddled with staffs of career civil servants. In fact, they were normally aggressive in expanding their authority, so that they were in nearly constant conflict with each other and with the state agencies. Their main concern was the maintenance of political and ideological, rather than professional, standards. Unlike the REM officials, the party figures wished to fill academic positions with committed Nazis who happened to also be scholars.[34]

Thus the criteria of scholarship and political reliability were agreed upon as the basis for academic appointment, although the priorities differed in the state and party offices. The REM was the unchallenged judge of professional qualifications. The question throughout much of the Third Reich concerned which party agency would assess political reliability. As Reece Kelly has shown, the primary contender was the National Socialist German University Teachers League (Nationalsozialistischer Deutscher Dozentenbund), which was created toward the end of 1934 by the Bavarian Minister of Education Hans Schemm. Although the League was to provide the "shock troops of the movement" in the universities, it lacked authority and financial support and, under Schemm, was ineffective.[35]

Some months after Schemm died in the spring of 1935, Hess released the Dozentenbund from its parent organization, Schemm's NS-Lehrerbund.[36] Walter Schultze, a physician and early party member who had most recently been director of public health in the Bavarian Ministry of the Interior, was named its leader. Schultze had only been appointed an honorary professor (of public hygiene) at the university in Munich in 1934. As Kelly has pointed out, Schultze had a rather weak personality, and was probably chosen for this reason by members of Hess's staff who did not want their own positions challenged.[37]

Schultze saw the league as the ideological wing of the Hess organization. Its goal was to remold the German universities by creating a National Socialist scholarship and by providing truly Nazi teachers. According to the draft of an article written by Schultze somewhat later:

> As the official organization of the party for the teachers in higher education, the National Socialist Dozentenbund has the task to jolt these teachers into an awareness of the new intellectual awakening; to lead them into a compact ideological and learned community of militants; to bring into line their ideological stance and their scholarly and scientific work with the ideas of National Socialism; and, through this, to secure the rebuilding of science, scholarship, and the institutions of higher learning.[38]

Schultze went on to catalog the evils of pre-1933 German education in typically ideological terms: "erroneous, misguided Enlightenment," "racially foreign" concepts of individualism and internationalism, "colorless objectivity," "crass utilitarianism," "disintegration of science and scholarship exploited by the Jews." All of these would have to be corrected through indoctrination and the selection of proper university personnel.[39]

Schultze's views were entirely compatible with those of the Aryan physics proponents. Thus it was not surprising that some of these, including at least Thüring and Bühl, became very active in the league's affairs. Also, several active members of the league looked upon Aryan physics favorably even if they were not actual members of the movement. Thus the league came to play a vigorous role in what became the test case for the influence of the Aryan physics movement—the choice of a successor to Arnold Sommerfeld in Munich.

The Munich Faculty and the Reich Education Ministry

In 1935, Sommerfeld reached retirement age after his eminent thirty-year career as professor of theoretical physics at Munich. Upon the recommendation of the mathematics and chemistry department heads, the dean of the faculty requested that Sommerfeld stay on as his own temporary replacement after he became emeritus on April 1. He would be difficult enough to replace under any circumstances, but at the moment his assistant Otto Scherzer was about to leave for the institute of technology in Darmstadt. With both men gone, there would be no theoretical physics at the university.[40]

The request was granted, and the search began for a successor. Since 1927, Sommerfeld had wanted to call his former pupil Heisenberg to Munich.[41] The younger man was one of Germany's finest scientists and would be the perfect candidate to continue the Sommerfeld tradition in both research and teaching. On July 13, 1935, the faculty search committee submitted an impressive three-man list: Werner Heisenberg, Peter Debye, and Richard Becker—all Sommerfeld pupils.[42]

The response of the Reich Education Ministry must have come as a shock to Munich professors. The entire list was rejected without explanation. On November 4, the faculty committee reiterated that it wanted Heisenberg and that he wanted to come to Munich. Eight new names were listed in descending order of preference, but it was clear that the faculty did not intend to abandon Heisenberg without a struggle.[43]

Although contemporary documentation is sketchy, later events indicated that the opposition to Heisenberg was not centered in Berlin. It almost certainly derived instead from Munich, where the Nazi students had long objected to Sommerfeld. The central figure in this affair was the leader of the teaching corps, Wilhelm Führer. A party member since 1930 and an SS-man since 1933, Führer held an untenured lectureship for astrophysics at the university. In July 1935, in addition to his post as teaching corps leader (and thus a state representative through the REM), he was appointed district University Teachers League leader (and thus a party representative through the Hess organization).[44] A year earlier, Führer's allegiance to political rather than professional principles had been amply demonstrated in a dispute with the university's professor of experimental physics, Walther Gerlach. Gerlach was head of a faculty committee to fill the empty chair for astronomy at Munich, and Führer rejected his candidates Hans Kienle and Otto Heckmann on political-ideological grounds. Heckmann was particularly unacceptable, Führer held, because he had been a member of the Catholic youth movement in the Weimar period.[45] Führer's man had then been appointed. The faculty was to give him a stiffer fight over Heisenberg.

While the November faculty list was under consideration in Berlin, Stark made his reference to Heisenberg as "spirit of Einstein's spirit" at the Heidelberg rededication ceremonies. His objection to Heisenberg's appointment at Munich was reprinted in his article in the *Nationalsozialistische Monatshefte* in February 1936. These attacks and the articles in the party newspaper would not alone have convinced the Reich Education Ministry to back away from Heisenberg. At that time the REM was already in conflict with the Rosenberg organization on many fronts, and it was preparing to move against Stark in the German Research Association. Stark's antipathy to Heisenberg could only have made the ministry favor the theoretician more than ever.

At least partially as a result of its conflict with Rosenberg, however, during 1935–38 the REM was seeking better relations with Hess's party headquarters in Munich. The University Teachers League's objection to Heisenberg meant the REM would have to go slowly with his candidacy or perhaps drop it altogether. When Thüring and Bühl also became active in the league and Kubach's segment of the Students League came into life in 1936, the stand of the Hess organization became unambiguously negative on Heisenberg. In fact, if Stark had not been so closely allied with Rosenberg at the time, the REM might have given Heisenberg up entirely for the sake of peace with Hess.

The Heisenberg-Wien-Geiger memorandum and Stark's loss of the presidency of the German Research Association in the autumn of 1936 strengthened the REM's position regarding Heisenberg. In addition, an administrative reorganization within the REM worked in Heisenberg's favor. Since 1934 the ministry had had two departments for learning, one for scholarship, which was headed by Theodor Vahlen, and the other for research, which was led by army physicist Erich Schumann. Mentzel was Schumann's deputy, but since Schumann seldom came to his office, Mentzel was effectively head of the department. In January 1937, the two departments were amalgamated under Otto Wacker (who replaced Vahlen) with Mentzel as his deputy. Vahlen had been much less aggressive than Mentzel in opposing Stark, due in part to his own views, which led him to establish *Deutsche Mathematik* as a journal for Aryan mathematics, and in part to his long association with Stark dating back to their Greifswald years. In compensation for losing his REM position, Vahlen assumed the leadership of the Prussian Academy of Sciences in 1938.[46] Wacker had been Baden minister of education (a position he retained) since 1933, and he was an SS-man. Himmler apparently hoped to have him succeed Rust as education minister. Although Wacker had spoken at the Heidelberg-Lenard celebration, he apparently had no strong feelings on the matter of Aryan physics and generally left decisions regarding the movement to Mentzel.

Mentzel had replaced Stark as head of the German Research Association in November 1936. He now set about the task of founding a Reich Research Council (Reichsforschungsrat) along much the same lines once suggested by Stark.[47] The council was constituted in formal ceremonies attended by Hitler and many high state and military leaders on May 25, 1937. Mentzel's creation drew upon funds supplied under the Four Year Plan administered by Hermann Göring, and was officially headed by General Karl Becker of army research. Wacker was appointed vice-president, but as head of the German Research Association Mentzel actually ran the affairs of the council.[48] The pragmatic Nazi objectives of this organization were succinctly stated in Becker's opening speech:

> The adjustment [of science] has nothing to do with the onset of research upon command. The minister clearly expressed in his founding decree that he would in no way influence the

"how" of research. Only that which is supposed to be researched needs a certain alignment.[49]

With additional funds and power now in Mentzel's hands, the party ideologues—including the advocates of Aryan physics—were threatened with a serious setback.

The position of the REM was so strong in the spring of 1937 that it could defy the University Teachers League and the Students League and appoint Heisenberg as Sommerfeld's successor. In March, Heisenberg informed Niels Bohr that he would finally be married in April. He continued:

> It also now seems certain that I will transfer to Munich in the course of this year. That is good, for I can now have the feeling of building something permanent that will last as long as I am able to work at all.[50]

Two months later Heisenberg received official notice that he had been appointed to the position.[51] It appeared that Aryan physics had suffered a defeat which would end its influence in academic affairs.

The SS and the Heisenberg Affair

This conclusion was premature, however. The proponents of Aryan physics derived new impetus for action from the celebration of Lenard's seventy-fifth birthday on June 7, 1937. In order to receive its Golden Badge of Honor, the aging physicist had finally joined the Nazi party. Again there were speeches and a recital of the main events in Lenard's life, and this time the students gave Lenard a torchlight parade. The basic tenets of Aryan physics were reviewed, and a call was issued for renewed vigor in politicizing academic physics.[52]

With new intensity, the Aryan physicists turned for the first time to the SS. Although this move seems logical enough in retrospect, at the time it caught the opponents of Aryan physics completely off guard. One reason was that the SS had so far stayed clear of involvement in the conflict, and it gave no advance notice that it was about to enter the fray. A second was that Himmler and Rosenberg were rivals on almost all ideological matters, and up to this point Rosenberg had been the prime supporter of Aryan physics. Himmler would be expected to *oppose* Lenard and Stark if he took any notice of them at all. A third reason for surprise was that the SS associations of Wacker and Mentzel seemed to work in favor of the REM. And a fourth was Stark's rebuff of SS Ahnenerbe research in 1936. Yet on July 15, 1937, a full-page article on "white Jews" in science appeared in the SS journal *Das Schwarze Korps* (The black corps). Stark's name appeared at the bottom of the page. How had he managed it?

If the initiative came from the Aryan physicists, as seems likely in view of later events, the contact between Stark and the editors of *Das Schwarze Korps* was very probably established through Ludwig Wesch. Wesch was one of Lenard's last pupils. He had received his doctorate in Heidelberg under Lenard's assistant Ferdinand Schmidt during the Nobel laureate's final semester before retirement (summer 1931). He left Heidelberg for a time, but returned to become an assistant in the physical institute in 1934 and achieve qualification in 1935. In 1937, he became extraordinary professor for theoretical physics in Heidelberg and in 1938 was promoted to full professor. In 1943 he received a full professorship for technical physics and had his own institute for high frequency research. In 1927 (at eighteen) he had been among the leaders of the National Socialist students in Munich, a position he continued to hold while at Heidelberg from 1927 to 1931. In 1931, Wesch joined the SS and later became a member of the SS security service, the Sicherheitsdienst (SD).[53]

The SD was under the direction of Reinhard Heydrich, Himmler's top lieutenant, and it was designed in 1931 to become the elite of the entire SS organization. One of its highest priorities was the intensive völkisch indoctrination of SS members.[54] The SD had originally been assigned intelligence and police functions, but when Himmler wrested control of the state police from Frick in 1936, the SD became increasingly superfluous as the State Secret Police (Gestapo) assumed these missions. The organization thereafter concentrated on internal party intelligence and ideological matters, specifically including scholarly issues.[55] The SD remained significant because its members continued to account for a disproportionately high percentage of SS leaders. SD members formed only 2.3 percent of the SS membership in 1937, but comprised 10.7 percent of the SS officer corps. SD influence was also strong, for example, in *Das Schwarze Korps*, edited by SD-man Gunter D'Alquen.[56]

As a party, SS, and SD member, Wesch was Lenard's most politically dangerous pupil. In the realm of science, however, he was a less than brilliant student. According to the rector of the university after World War II, his rise from institute assistant to full professor was due almost exclusively to his party connections; in Heidelberg his SS and SD activities caused people to fear him.[57] Wesch was thus the Aryan physics proponent most likely to have arranged—or initiated the arrangements—for Stark's contact with the SS following the June 1937 Heidelberg celebration.

The July 15 article in *Das Schwarze Korps* appeared in three segments of approximately equal length.[58] The first segment (under the overall heading "White Jews in Scholarship") was apparently written by the editorial staff—possibly by D'Alquen himself.[59] Here the term "white Jew" was introduced as a synonym for "Jewish in character" as opposed to Jewish by ancestry. Not only must Jewish influence be eliminated from the economy, the article argued, but also from learning, where "white Jews" still exercised great influence. The final paragraph focused on physics as the field where the Jewish spirit most clearly held sway.

The second segment was the heart of the article. It had the separate heading "The Dictatorship of the Gray Theory," which referred, of course, to relativity. Although this section did not have a separate by-line its style and contents mark it unmistakably as the work of Stark—if he did not write it himself, he provided the material in it to a staff member of the journal. After reciting the familiar complaints that Jews and their kindred spirits had lately dominated German physics, the author launched into a frontal attack upon Heisenberg. The theoretician was castigated for "smuggling" a pro-Einstein article into an official party organ in 1936, for taking a vote among physicists on the value of theoretical physics to silence his critics, for becoming a professor in 1928 (when he was too young to have possibly earned such recognition), and for hiring and attracting Jews into his institute in the Weimar period. The fact that he and other proponents of quantum mechanics had won the Nobel prize was a demonstration of Jewish influence comparable to the award of the Nobel prize to Ossietzky. (Carl von Ossietzky was a left-wing pacifist who had been imprisoned in various concentration camps since 1933. The award of the Nobel peace prize to him in 1936 so angered Hitler that in January 1937 he ordered that no German could accept another Nobel award.[60]) After noting that Heisenberg had refused to sign a 1934 declaration supporting the Führer, this section closed with the demand that Heisenberg and others like him be made to "disappear" like the Jews.[61]

The third segment of the article, headed " 'Scholarship' Has Failed Politically," was prefaced by the editorial comment that Professor Stark had been asked to respond to the preceding two segments. This bit of deception enabled the physicist to avoid direct responsibility for the second section of the article. In this final section, Stark stressed the role of Jews in German academia in rather general terms, noting in addition that followers and spouses of Jews multiplied the influence of those of direct Jewish descent. As usual, he denigrated objectivity and internationality of scholarship. Stark did not refer to any other physicist by name—the second segment had made that unnecessary.

The tone and approach of the article represented Stark's heavy-handed attempt to imitate the tactics of his REM opponents of a year earlier. The use of the Ossietzky image, however, was far more ominous. To compare a man with an inmate of a concentration camp in the principal SS journal was a serious matter. Stark apparently hoped not only to prevent Heisenberg's appointment to Munich, but to make it impossible for him to do any further work in Germany.

Heisenberg immediately recognized the gravity of the situation. Nothing better represents the role which chance and personal connections played under the Nazi dictatorship than the absurd-sounding first step he and his family took to deal with it. His mother went to Himmler's mother to seek redress of her son's grievance. The Heisenberg and Himmler families had known each other slightly for a number of years, since the time the physicist's maternal grandfather and the SS leader's father had both been secondary school principals in Munich. In an interview, Heisenberg recalled his mother's account of her visit:

> She said that the elderly Mrs. Himmler said immediately "My heavens, if my Heinrich only knew of this, then he would immediately do something about it. There are some slightly unpleasant people around Heinrich, but this is of course quite disgusting. But I will tell my Heinrich about it. He is such a nice boy—always congratulates me on my birthday and sends me flowers and such. So if I say just a single word to him, he will set the matter back in order."
>
> My mother was very much consoled by the elderly Mrs. Himmler; she was given the assurance that the elderly Mrs. Himmler would give her son Heinrich the sign that this should not go on. Which she did. She was very reliable.[62]

As Mrs. Heisenberg was about to leave, however, Mrs. Himmler suddenly laid a hand upon her shoulder. Or did she believe, Mrs. Himmler asked uncertainly, that perhaps her son Heinrich was not on the right path in life? Heisenberg continued,

> And I believe my mother acted very skillfully. I can now only reproduce her answer from her story. But she must have answered somewhat like this: "Oh, you know, Mrs. Himmler, we mothers know nothing about politics—neither your son's nor mine. But we know that we have to care for our boys. That is why I have come to you." And she understood that.[63]

Mrs. Himmler had advised that Heisenberg should write directly to her son saying that he wanted such attacks to cease and that he would be happy to provide information on his own political background. This the physicist did on July 21, only a week after the article appeared. After referring to Mrs. Himmler's advice and how it was obtained, Heisenberg sketched the background of the split between those who accepted and those who rejected modern physics. Lenard and Stark belonged to the latter group, he wrote, and they were using him as a symbol for the former. He would be willing to participate in a scholarly discussion at any time, but refused to let himself be designated a "white Jew" or "Ossietzky of physics." In particular, he argued, how could he continue as a civil servant under such conditions? If the views of Stark really agreed with those of the government, he would resign. If not, then protection was needed against such attacks. As for his political views, Heisenberg stated candidly that he did not belong to any party and had not participated in the National Socialist revolution; he would like, however, to continue in his state position. He ended the letter with a list of commanding officers and others who could vouch for his patriotism.[64]

By going directly to the SS leader through his family, Heisenberg showed great astuteness. But he could not present a detailed defense until Himmler asked for it. Meanwhile, Heisenberg wrote a rebuttal to Stark's article for the Reich Education Ministry, which was now forced to reconsider his appointment to the Munich professorship.[65] Heisenberg took pains to refute each accusation by Stark which made him appear an enemy of the state, but the REM did not dare take further measures in his favor until it was clear what the SS leadership would do.

On November 11, 1937, Himmler finally answered Heisenberg's

letter.[66] His note was disconcertingly brief and formal, however, and only requested that Heisenberg respond to the charges Stark had leveled against him in his letter to the editor of *Das Schwarze Korps*. Heisenberg wrote back immediately.[67] First, he stated, Stark had implied that as professor in Leipzig Heisenberg had fired a German assistant in order to hire some Jews. Heisenberg explained that the assistant was not interested in modern physics and that the men he hired to replace him were of exceptionally high scientific caliber even though admittedly Jewish. Second, Stark had revealed that Heisenberg had refused to sign a declaration of support for Hitler in 1934. The theoretician conceded the truth of this accusation: he and others had declined due to negative impressions of Stark and the belief that scientists should demonstrate their loyalty in scientific rather than political terms. Third, Stark had claimed that Heisenberg used a vote among physicists on the value of theoretical physics for personal purposes. Heisenberg answered that he had cooperated in preparing the Heisenberg-Wien-Geiger statement at the express wish of Professor Mentzel of the REM. In closing his defense, Heisenberg called Himmler's attention to the memorandum he had written for the REM in July, and suggested that the way to settle the dispute between himself and Stark was in a face-to-face confrontation. When he sent this letter, the matter passed out of Heisenberg's hands. Whether his name would be cleared depended now on the influence of friends and the SS investigation of the case.

His friends and colleagues gave Heisenberg their immediate support. His theoretical physics colleague in Leipzig, Friedrich Hund, for example, wrote to the Reich Education Ministry on July 20, deploring the fact that a German physicist could bring himself to participate in an attack like the article in *Das Schwarze Korps*.[68] Sommerfeld also wrote a letter protesting Stark's action, suggesting that Stark's anger toward Sommerfeld stemmed from the Munich faculty's rejection of Stark as successor to Wilhelm Wien in the late 1920s.[69]

Heisenberg also received support from certain German diplomats. One of his pupils was Carl F. von Weizsäcker, whose father was the head of the political department of the German foreign office. The ambassador to Rome, Ulrich von Hassel, and the elder von Weizsäcker apparently told various authorities that Germany could not afford to lose men of international stature like Heisenberg.[70] This argument was of no small consequence in the Third Reich. As early as 1934 Rosenberg had received a suggestion from a secondary school official that Heisenberg be sent to a concentration camp as an Einstein supporter. Rosenberg replied that he shared this sentiment, but that the physicist was nearly immune to punishment because strong punitive measures would create an unfavorable impression abroad.[71]

Heisenberg obtained further backing in 1937 from some quarters of the SS itself. In Heidelberg, for example, Otto Westphal (a chemist and SS-man) interceded in December on his behalf with the leader of the Students League, Gustav Scheel.[72] Scheel was an SD-man with considerable influence who apparently did not share the infatuation with Aryan physics exhibited by those of his subordinates who followed Kubach. Mentzel also certainly used his SS influence to aid Heisenberg. Throughout the spring of 1938, however, the matter rested with the SD bureaucracy.

In January 1938, Heisenberg had informed Sommerfeld that the REM had completed findings favorable to him and that the SS investigation would probably also be positive.[73] By February, however, he had become aware that the REM was holding its report until the SS position became clear. In a second letter to his teacher he explained this situation along with the remark that the Sommerfeld pupil Fritz Sauter had been denounced in Königsberg as politically untrustworthy. "It is really too bad," he wrote, "that during a time in which physics is making wonderful advances and it is truly fun to participate in them, one is forced to occupy himself again and again with political matters." [74]

By April, the situation looked so unfavorable that Heisenberg disconsolately wrote Sommerfeld that he was seriously considering emigration. A minor SS figure who had promised to try to help him had indicated that Himmler, now the only one who could decide the issue, did not seem inclined to take a stand. There was nothing further to be done.[75]

Heisenberg's case remained unresolved until mid-summer. Important support came in July from Göttingen's aerodynamics expert Ludwig Prandtl, who sat next to Himmler at a dinner sponsored by the German Academy of Aeronautical Research earlier in the year. Prandtl had waited until he felt the SS leader would be free of the pressing duties arising from the annexation of Austria in order to gain a hearing for his defense of Heisenberg. In a letter written on July 12, 1938, Prandtl reminded Himmler that at the dinner the SS leader had expressed the view that Heisenberg should not introduce Einstein's personality into a discussion of relativity if it were necessary to mention the theory in physics classes. Heisenberg had since agreed to this condition, and Prandtl stressed that relativity was regarded as physically correct by the overwhelming majority of physicists. Einstein was a first-class physicist, the Göttingen professor stated flatly, and his personal characteristics were of no concern to science. Experimentalists who could not follow theoretical work should not therefore reject it as simply worthless and slander its representatives. Heisenberg should be freed of Stark's insults effectively and demonstratively. In fact, Heisenberg should be requested to publish an article in the main journal of the Students League, the *Zeitschrift für die gesamte Naturwissenschaft*.[76]

There seems little doubt that Prandtl's strongly worded defense of Heisenberg and theoretical physics played a crucial role in the affair. Less than two weeks later, Himmler wrote to Heydrich that he agreed with Prandtl's letter and felt that the Students League should let Heisenberg publish in their journal.[77] Heisenberg seemed to be a decent young man who would produce a new generation of scientists and should not be silenced. Perhaps, Himmler suggested in conclusion, the SS might even make use of him in its world ice theory research—a notion which showed just how far removed Himmler was from a concern for academic physics. The world ice theory was one of those Nordic myths which had more in common with medieval sagas and science fiction than with serious science.[78]

On the same day, July 21, 1938, Himmler wrote a letter to Heisenberg informing him of his exoneration. The key passages read:

> I have—especially because you were recommended to me by my family—had your case investigated particularly correctly and particularly sharply.
>
> I am happy to be able to inform you that I do not approve the attack of the *Schwarze Korps* through its article, and that I have forbidden the appearance of a further attack against you.
>
> P. S. I would consider it proper, however, if in the future you make a clear distinction for your listeners between the recognition of the results of scholarly research and the personal and political attitude of the researcher.[79]

Thus Heisenberg's name had finally been cleared. However, his exoneration did not automatically guarantee that he would be called to Munich as Sommerfeld's successor, because he still faced strong opposition from the supporters of Aryan physics in that city.

The   Aryan Physics Victory

In the late fall of 1937, Wacker had decided to postpone Heisenberg's final appointment until the investigation of his case had been completed; Sommerfeld was to continue "substituting" for himself.[80] In a letter to Einstein at the close of the year, Sommerfeld surveyed the situation:

> The politics of my most intimate enemies Giovanni Fortissimo [Stark] and Leonardo da Heidelberg, who do not want to grant me Heisenberg as a successor, is forcing me to continue to discharge my office and to tend my now small flock. I can still manage it in any case, even if without the same energy as earlier. I have only very superficially concerned myself with nuclear physics—am therefore by American standards a quite uneducated person. The future looks dismal for German physics; I must console myself with the fact that I actively participated in its golden age 1905–30.[81]

The pessimism was justified, for it still appeared in late 1937 that the Aryan physicists had not only thwarted Heisenberg's call to Munich, but were also going to win support from the SS.

The Aryan physics proponents were confident enough to suggest their own candidates in late 1937 and early 1938. As leader of the district University Teachers League, Wilhelm Führer was the driving force in the opposition to Heisenberg. He was determined to have the position filled not by an "old theoretician," but by an experimentalist.[82] In the fall of 1937, the league nominated as Sommerfeld's successor Karl Uller, who in 1935 had written a treatise on theoretical physics which claimed to refute Einstein. The scholarly evaluations of his work by other physicists, however, were so negative that his candidacy was withdrawn.[83] In early 1938 the league proposed the experimentalist Johannes Malsch. Malsch was a student of Max Wien specializing in high frequency research at Cologne. He was a competent technical physicist, but could not be expected to produce original theoretical work. During the summer, Gerlach struggled to prevent the appointment of Malsch or any other experimentalist, and he finally managed to win the concession from the league that the REM should make a final decision.[84]

Führer and his associates (including Thüring and Kubach, who were also in Munich) could confidently agree to such a compromise because a recent understanding reached between Hess and the REM had expanded University Teachers League influence in Berlin. Following a conference of university rectors in December 1937, Wacker had recognized the deputy to the Führer as the ultimate authority on matters of political reliability in evaluating academic appointments, and the league was to carry out this duty for the party headquarters. The new agreement, which was officially decreed in May, did not specify exactly on what grounds political reliability would be judged, and some differences arose on this issue. But since Wacker was interested in cooperating with the party headquarters in order to reduce the confusion in dealing with party agencies, the ministry could be expected to give in on cases where Hess's staff stood firm.[85] An indication of the party's firm stance on the Munich appointment was that Führer even visited the REM in person to lobby directly for a party appointee.[86]

With Heisenberg's rehabilitation by Himmler in July 1938, the Munich faculty redoubled its efforts to win his appointment to Sommerfeld's chair.[87] In a letter to the REM of November 8, 1938, Sommerfeld and Gerlach gave their views on several potential candidates for the post. They positively evaluated the candidates on the REM's list, but emphasized that the rector and the faculty had never wavered in their desire to call Heisenberg. Now that the matter of the article in *Das Schwarze Korps* had been settled, nothing further should stand in the way. They were perturbed that two candidates put forward by the Munich teaching corps leadership were still under consideration. Malsch simply would not do, and a new candidate, Wilhelm Müller of Aachen, was even less acceptable. Müller was an aerodynamics expert, not a creative physicist, and Prandtl had evaluated him quite negatively as a successor to Sommerfeld.[88]

The Aryan physics faction in Munich was strengthened in 1938–39 by the appointment of Thüring to Führer's post of teaching corps and University Teachers League leader at the university. Führer apparently retained the district leadership. In addition, these men received strong backing from the new dean of the faculty, Friedrich von Faber, a botanist. By the summer of 1939, the REM had decided that in view of all that had happened since 1935, the strong party aversion to Heisenberg, and the current power constellation in Munich, Heisenberg could not be called as Sommerfeld's successor. The officials in the ministry talked with Heisenberg and it was decided to drop his candidacy.[89] Apparently Himmler and Rust agreed instead to demonstrate the theoretician's political exoneration by naming him to some other important post at a later date,[90] but no action was taken until the middle of the war.

In both physics and politics, 1939 was a tumultuous year. The developments following the discovery of nuclear fission in Otto Hahn's Berlin laboratory captivated the attention of scientists. The outbreak of World War II overshadowed academic affairs. The story of the Sommerfeld succession thus ended more quietly than it might have in less unsettled times. Effective December 1, 1939, Wilhelm Müller was named to the Munich theoretical physics chair, prompting Sommerfeld to remark in later years that he had received the "worst thinkable successor." [91]

Müller had never published in a physics journal, had never attended a physicists' conference, and did not even belong to the German Physical Society.[92] His background in aerodynamics involved extensive use of mathematics, but only in problems related to classical physics. His primary qualification to succeed Sommerfeld was his polemical 1936 booklet on "Jews and scholarship," in which he sharply criticized relativity theory as a specifically and typically Jewish affair.[93]

A year after Müller's appointment, Gerlach wrote to the dean that no theoretical physics had been taught at Munich since Sommerfeld ceased lecturing, because Müller only taught classical mechanics.[94] Von Faber's answer demonstrated just how clearly the advocates of Aryan physics had formulated their goal of destroying modern physics at the institutions of higher learning:

> Your assertion that no theoretical physics has been taught for three semesters does not reflect the facts. Everyone can look at the catalog of classes to convince himself that theoretical physics is being taught here. If you only understand theoretical physics to mean the so-called modern dogmatic theoretical physics of the Einstein-Sommerfeld stamp, then I must inform you that this will indeed no longer be taught in Munich. The appointment of Prof. Müller has been achieved precisely to bring about a definitive change. The gratifying way and manner in which Prof. Müller is making theoretical physics honorable again is approved and supported in its entirety by the teaching corps.[95]

Thus in Munich—dubbed by the Nazis the "Capital City of the Movement"—the Aryan physicists had achieved an impressive triumph. Yet their victory marked the peak of the influence of Aryan physics. Less than a week after von Faber wrote his confident lines to Gerlach, the Nordic physics movement suffered a crippling setback which eventually led it to total defeat.

9.   The War Years

The triumph of Aryan physics in Munich in 1939 demonstrated the extent to which political considerations and activities could affect German academic physics. It should be noted, however, that in this very period excellent research was conducted and relativity theory was still taught. Both research and teaching, however, would obviously suffer if the criteria used to determine the Sommerfeld succession were to dominate academic appointments. By 1939, the situation for physics, especially theoretical physics, was critical: poor appointments, reduction of the number of professorships, and unfilled positions were beginning to have a serious impact. Additionally, a number of competent scientists decided to escape political pressures by taking industrial positions, further weakening academic physics.

A number of German physicists—both inside and outside the party—took stock of the situation and determined individually to do something about it. Infighting among the staffs of high Nazi leaders was responsible for many of the political difficulties affecting physics, and little could be accomplished there. But the Aryan physics movement provided a target within the field of physics itself. The Heisenberg case crystallized opposition to political intrusion into the discipline.

In late 1940, this offensive against Nordic physics led to a face-to-face confrontation. Although the result was a severe setback for politicized physics, the movement still maintained strongholds in Heidelberg and Munich. The war and continued political squabbles among party agencies further drained its strength. In 1942–43, after a second confrontation, the movement collapsed completely.

The professional physicists continued to decry the detrimental effects of Aryan physics long after the movement had been defeated. By asserting the ostensible relevance of their work for the war effort, they were able to reestablish professional autonomy in pursuit of pure research and to minimize the loss of younger scientists at the front. The actual goals of the academic physicists were perhaps most clearly revealed in the uranium project, which was eventually dominated by the very group of theoreticians so adamantly opposed by Lenard and Stark.

German Academic Physics by the End of 1939

The damage caused by the dismissal policy and other governmental measures, coupled with the attacks by the ideologues, left German physics badly battered. Nevertheless, the Germans managed some impressive achievements in the 1930s. In 1936 the physicists Samuel Goudsmit at the University of Michigan and Walther Gerlach at the university in Munich corresponded about the state of German physics. Goudsmit held that while physics appeared to be making progress in countries like Italy and America, it seemed to have stagnated in Germany.[1] Gerlach did not quite agree, stating that a good deal of basic research was being performed. As examples of significant advances, he pointed out Erich Regener's investigations in the upper atmosphere, and noted the nuclear studies by Walther Bothe in Heidelberg (which later led to Germany's first cyclotron) and Otto Hahn's laboratory in Berlin (which resulted in the discovery of nuclear fission). He was forced to admit that theoretical work appeared to be on the decline, but he found this retrenchment to be natural since the great burst of creativity in theory during the preceding decades could not be sustained indefinitely. It was now time for the experimentalists to move to the forefront of research.[2] Goudsmit had a point, however, and compared with the German achievements in the past and advances abroad in the 1930s, Gerlach's list was extremely meager.

The situation was particularly disturbing in theoretical physics. When Arnold Sommerfeld in late 1937 wrote to Einstein that the future looked dismal for German physics, he almost certainly had theory in mind.[3] Aside from Heisenberg's cosmic ray investigations in Leipzig and the studies of stellar processes by some of his students (notably Carl F. von Weizsäcker and Hans Euler), theoretical research seemed to have exhausted much of its potential in Germany. In order to keep up with the newest work in the field, therefore, it was all the more important that the Germans be in close contact with their colleagues abroad. Yet as described in chapter 4, this was not the case.

In addition, the question arises whether German theoretical physicists bowed to pressure from the Aryan physics proponents and party ideologues to abandon relativity. This was not the case. There is widespread agreement that the universities never ceased to teach relativity theory. Some scientists, however, remember a specific directive forbidding mention of Einstein's name in lectures or scholarly papers.[4] Others, for example, Heisenberg, do not remember a specific ordinance relating to Einstein, but recall that one was supposed to use an asterisk to denote the use of a Jewish name in all publications. The ideological climate exerted a certain pressure to avoid such names.[5] As a consequence, lectures were not presented as treating "the Einstein theory of relativity," but used the less provocative description, "the electrodynamics of moving bodies." [6] The astronomer Otto Heckmann recalls:

> If one spoke about the matter and did not push the person of Einstein into the foreground, then one did not have to fear any hindrance in Göttingen at that time. I also spoke of the general relativity theory before smaller groups of students at the so-called student "camps." The general relativity theory had often been described to the students in their so-called political schooling as a "Jewish perversion." When one brought the theory into normal view again, they listened eagerly and often with relief.[7]

At least twice during the Third Reich, Sommerfeld wrote Einstein that he had mentioned his name and theories in lectures and that the students had responded enthusiastically. In early 1937, as he announced his coming lectures on the relativistic treatment of some problems, the students loudly expressed their approval. "You can see from this," he assured Einstein, "that you have not been expatriated from the German lecture halls." [8]

Yet the pressures from the ideologues forced some unpleasant concessions. In early 1939 Max von Laue wrote Einstein describing a proposal for one of them. Sommerfeld's pupil Wilhelm Lenz, professor of theoretical physics in Hamburg, wanted von Laue to help get a note on relativity theory into a scholarly journal. The thrust of the article was reminiscent of an argument first broached at Bad Nauheim in 1920. Lenz wanted to rid the theory of its Jewish taint by asserting that its author was the Frenchman Henri Poincaré, an exercise that would make the theory "presentable" in the Third Reich. Lenz hoped thereby to win permission from party officials in Hamburg to lecture openly on relativity, and perhaps even to aid Heisenberg in the Munich affair, which was then entering its final stages. Von Laue was opposed to this kind of political maneuvering on principle, and felt it was "as reprehensible as foolish." [9]

Philipp Frank, a professor of physics in Prague at the time and the author of a biography of Einstein, has recorded another type of concession the ideological climate exacted from professional physicists. Since Lenard's family had been merchants in Pressburg and since many Jewish families practiced the same trade in that city, a number of physicists hoped that perhaps Lenard himself was not fully Aryan. Proof of a tainted ancestry would be a powerful weapon against the patron saint of Aryan physics. Frank was repeatedly asked by his German colleagues to inquire into Lenard's background. He did not actively pursue the matter, but he has recalled that such considerations were a sign of the times.[10]

As distasteful as these activities were, they did not in themselves damage the conduct of physical research and teaching. The attacks in the press and the attitude of many party officials toward theoretical research, however, had a deleterious impact on student enrollment in physics courses. Although limitation on enrollment and lower birth rates for postwar years almost halved the German university student population between 1932–33 and 1936–37, the physical sciences and mathematics experienced an above-average decline of nearly 65 percent in the same period.[11]

The effect upon German physics of National Socialist political infighting and ideological considerations was even more apparent in academic appointments. The Sommerfeld succession was the most dramatic and significant case, but it was not the only instance. Stark retired from the Imperial Institute of Physics and Technology in May 1939, and was succeeded by Abraham Esau, one of the section heads in Mentzel's Reich Research Council. But by the end of the year Aryan physics proponents occupied no less than six physics professorships in Germany: at both the Munich University (Wilhelm Müller for theoretical physics) and the TH Munich (Rudolf Tomaschek for experimental physics), at Heidelberg (August Becker for experimental and Ludwig Wesch for theoretical physics), the TH Karlsruhe (Alfons Bühl for experimental physics), and TH Stuttgart (Ferdinand Schmidt, another Lenard pupil, for experimental physics).[12] Although the positions involved represented less than 10 percent of the eighty-one chairs available in Germany and Austria in 1939, the trend appeared to favor the Aryan physicists.

Because the Aryan physics advocates were very vocal opponents of theoretical physics as a discipline, the Reich Education Ministry supported Heisenberg and theoretical physics on political grounds.

When it was not confronted by party opponents, however, the ministry did not hold theory in high regard.

This diffidence was brought out in the summer of 1938 in a survey of the state of theoretical physics at the German institutions of higher learning. No one signed the unpublished report, but internal evidence points to one of the leaders of the Berlin district organization of the German Physical Society as the author—either Carl Ramsauer (the presiding officer of the Berlin section of the society and head of the German General Electric [AEG] laboratories) or a person associated with him.[13]

The objectives of the document were to provide a statement on the role of theoretical physics in physical research, to respond to the attacks leveled against the discipline by the Aryan physics adherents, and to discuss academic appointments in physics. Judging from its wording, the report was clearly intended to provide the majority of physicists with ammunition against the Aryan physicists and other state and party figures who wished to inject nonprofessional criteria into scientific discussions and academic assignments. Quite likely its author or authors specifically hoped to influence the Heisenberg case. They may also have planned the report to serve as a basis for informal discussion at the fall physicists' conference in Baden-Baden.

The first two sections followed the lines of thought presented by Heisenberg in his 1936 article in the *Völkischer Beobachter* and in the Heisenberg-Wien-Geiger memorandum to the Reich Education Ministry.[14] The third section provided a knowledgeable and unique overview of the serious damage inflicted upon theoretical physics since 1933. A major problem, it stated, was that several positions for theory had been filled by experimentalists unsuited to the task even though they had good reputations in their own fields. These misguided appointments included those at the TH Hannover in 1935, Jena in 1936, and Freiburg in 1937. Two other positions were held by experimentalists as temporary replacements for theoreticians who had left Germany—Berlin (Erwin Schrödinger had left in 1933) and the TH Stuttgart (P. P. Ewald had left in 1937). Another poor appointment was the promotion of Wesch to professor of theoretical physics in Heidelberg; Wesch was a technical physicist rather than a theoretician. The report was written before Sommerfeld's successor in Munich was known, or Müller's name would surely have been included.

The report also noted that the elimination since 1933 of two full professorships of theoretical physics had been particularly damaging. (Richard Becker's chair at the TH Berlin was abolished in 1936 when he was forced to accept Max Born's vacant position in Göttingen, and Walter Weizel's post at the TH Karlsruhe was absorbed into Bühl's professorship in 1936 when Weizel assumed a new position at Bonn.) Although not specified in the report, it was generally known that Becker's theoretical position was stricken from the budget because it was deemed "superfluous" at an institute of technology.[15] To comprehend the impression this action created among the professional physicists, one might consider how a suggestion to eliminate theoretical physics from the California or Massachusetts Institute of Technology would have been received in America.

A final indication of the general prejudice against theoretical physics in the Third Reich, according to the report, was the tendency to allow an extraordinarily long period to elapse between permanent occupants of a particular professional chair. One example given was that of Munich, which in 1938 had already been officially vacant for three years, even though Sommerfeld was still holding lectures on a semester-by-semester basis. Another was Born's position in Göttingen, which took three years to fill. Königsberg and Berlin had the same problem.

Altogether, then, of the thirty-five seats of theoretical physics in German academia (excluding Austria) in 1933, eleven were either unfilled, inappropriately filled, or eliminated by 1938. The report concluded by noting that nine young Privatdozenten were available for academic appointments, so that this situation should not have existed.

Since the survey limited itself to senior faculty members in theoretical physics, it did not mention another phenomenon related to the political environment which affected the entire physics community. A number of researchers—usually younger men—were deserting academia for industry, where they hoped to escape political concerns. Although no quantitative analysis of this migration is available, individual cases are easy to find. One example was the experimentalist Walter Rollwagen, a Gerlach pupil who in 1938 decided to abandon university work to head the laboratory of the Steinheil Optical Works. Unlike the situation in higher education, even when the factory manager was an active Nazi there were no political denunciations.[16] Theoreticians also participated in this migration: Heinrich Welker, a Sommerfeld pupil, and Carl Her-

mann, a co-worker of P. P. Ewald, also found industry employment
to escape political pressures.[17]

Older scientists also sometimes sought industrial havens. Georg
Joos, James Franck's successor at Göttingen in 1935, gave up his
professorship in 1941 and went to work for the Zeiss optical firm in
Jena. He wanted to escape the attacks his defense of theoretical
physics had earned him in Göttingen.[18] Sommerfeld wrote after the
war, however, that Joos had told him that he had to fight against
active Nazis in Jena, too, and that he did not find nearly as much
freedom as he had hoped.[19]

Already by 1938 the situation in academic physics was so alarming
that discussion on that topic formed part of the program at the yearly
fall physicists' conference. Carl Ramsauer presented a booklet on
careers in physics at the main meeting. He stressed the increasing
dearth of physicists in the coming generation and the further deterioration in academic physics it foreshadowed.[20] A partial solution to
the problem was found in accelerating the academic preparation of
physicists by introducing the Diplom-Physiker degree (a step between
the conclusion of the basic physics program and the Ph.D., rather
like a masters degree). But the fundamental difficulty was the attitude of the Reich Education Ministry and the party agencies: physics
appointments had become subject to political intrigues and manipulation. This topic would probably have been brought into sharp relief at the 1939 physicists' conference, but that gathering had to be
cancelled due to the outbreak of the war.

It was very difficult for the physicists effectively to voice their opposition to political interference in scholarly questions. Although the
REM supported them against most party attacks, the 1938 report indicated clearly that the ministry had no real understanding of the
requirements of the physics community. The party agencies—the
Rosenberg office, the staff of the party headquarters, the SS—were
consumed with mutual antagonisms and embroiled in contests over
overlapping areas of authority and interest. It was impossible to
know where or how to defend academic physics from their activities.

It was at this juncture that the Sommerfeld succession was decided. The Aryan physics movement was at least ostensibly within
physics itself and provided a focal point for opposition to political
infestation of the field. As demonstrated by the broad-based support
for the Heisenberg-Wien-Geiger memorandum in 1936, the overwhelming majority of physicists found politicized physics undesir-

able. It was clear that Aryan physics had become a serious danger and could no longer be treated as an irritating aberration. If a Nobel laureate could be prevented from succeeding an outstanding man like Sommerfeld, what might happen in successions involving less prominent figures?

In a sense, therefore, Aryan physics had been *too* successful in Munich. The plight of Heisenberg and Sommerfeld attracted attention and aroused antagonism throughout the physics community. The article in *Das Schwarze Korps*, which was primarily responsible for blocking Heisenberg's appointment, set a precedent which was widely recognized as a real threat to the autonomy of professional physics. The Sommerfeld succession was a tactical victory, but a strategic defeat for Aryan physics.

Stark was following a successful example of political machination in preparing the attack in *Das Schwarze Korps*. But he did not grasp one of the essential features of the Wildhagen affair. Stark's opponents had not attacked him directly, but used character assassination against his subordinate and then suggested guilt by association to contribute to his downfall. Stark, however, attacked Heisenberg directly. He would probably have been more successful in the long run if he could have first discredited some of Heisenberg's pupils and co-workers. Perhaps not even the visit to Himmler's mother would have helped if two or three of Heisenberg's assistants had first been driven from their posts. Stark either did not perceive this basic principle of politics under Hitler, or mistakenly regarded Heisenberg as a mere subordinate of Sommerfeld. Heisenberg was prominent enough in his own right to have supporters with influence.

The article in the SS journal was a strategic mistake for Aryan physics for another reason. Until 1937, Rosenberg had been the high Nazi figure who most strongly backed the movement. By turning to the SS, Rosenberg's chief ideological competitor, the Aryan physicists alienated their primary patron. In December 1937, Rosenberg announced that henceforth the party could not be tied to any dogma in problems dealing with a number of fields, among which was "cosmophysics." [21] From that point onward, the Rosenberg office remained strictly neutral in the conflict between the Aryan physicists and the professionals. Because the ultimate SS decision in regard to Heisenberg was a defeat for Aryan physics, the movement experienced a net loss. They had estranged Rosenberg, yet failed to win Himmler's support. The party advocates of Aryan physics after 1938 had been reduced to Hess's staff, the University Teachers League, and the Students League, all in Munich. Of these, only the party headquarters under Hess was a truly powerful Nazi agency.

In 1939 and 1940, physicists informally discussed the possible ways of avoiding political interference. Some, particularly von Laue, consistently argued that nothing could be done—one should stand clear until the whole structure of National Socialism collapsed. Heisenberg has said that this response always angered him, even though he later agreed it turned out to be perhaps the most morally correct course of action. At the time, he felt one had to try at least to salvage what one could for the future.[22] Others agreed with Heisenberg, and by 1940 a number of physicists decided to fight the Aryan physics adherents in their own camp.

THE OFFENSIVE AGAINST ARYAN PHYSICS

The initiative for the offensive came from within the party itself, primarily through the efforts of the experimentalist Wolfgang Finkelnburg, who was at the TH Darmstadt. Born in 1905, Finkelnburg had received his doctorate in physics in Bonn in 1928. He worked as an assistant in Bonn (1928–29), Berlin (1929–31), and the TH Karlsruhe (1931–35) before transferring as chief assistant to the physical institute of the TH Darmstadt. From late 1933 to late 1934, he was a Rockefeller Fellow at the California Institute of Technology.[23] Later, in the 1950s, he served as director of physics research for Siemens in Erlangen and was elected president of the German Physical Society.

Finkelnburg's political career during the Third Reich was illustrative of that of many young German physicists. He was a bright, energetic, and competent researcher, who, up to 1936, had remained aloof from political involvement. The foreign recognition of Nazi Germany in the 1936 Olympiad, the political successes of Hitler in that year, and the vacillation of the Western powers led him to believe, however, that National Socialism was in power to stay. He therefore sought to accommodate himself to the situation by joining the University Teachers League in late 1936.[24] Unlike the nearby TH Karlsruhe, where the Aryan physics proponent Alfons Bühl was an activist leader in the league, the professors at the TH Darmstadt suffered a minimum of political interference. A number of faculty members joined the party specifically to moderate its activities there. Pressured by the rector to join, Finkelnburg was apparently one of these: although he remained dedicated to the primacy of professional considerations in his field, he requested membership in late 1937. The party accepted him in May 1939.[25]

He later held that in the summer of 1940 he could not escape being appointed the leader of the University Teachers League in Darmstadt. The rector wanted to name an advocate of professional rather than political considerations in academic appointments, and the physicist was his choice.[26] Finkelnburg was able to attach a condition to his acceptance, however: he would be allowed to use his new position to combat the threat posed to professional physics by the Aryan physics adherents.[27]

In early August 1940, the physicist went to Munich to try to dissuade the University Teachers League leadership from supporting Nordic physics. His contention that Aryan physicists were a minority who represented only 5 percent of all physicists was at first rejected, for, he was told, not one of the many physics professors with whom the league had dealt had ever raised this point.[28] It was agreed that a debate would be held in Munich, and both Finkelnburg and Bühl would invite representatives.

After numerous delays, the confrontation took place in Munich on November 15, 1940. Finkelnburg invited Heisenberg's pupil Carl F. von Weizsäcker and Sommerfeld's pupil Otto Scherzer as experts for theoretical physics. Georg Joos came down from Göttingen as a representative of both theoretical and experimental physics (with ties to industrial physics). The young Göttingen astronomer Otto Heckmann was invited as an expert on the general theory of relativity. Hans Kopfermann, who had studied and worked in Göttingen, Copenhagen, and Berlin, journeyed southward from Kiel as a representative of experimental physics. Bühl invited his assistant Harald Volkmann, his Munich Aryan physics colleagues Bruno Thüring, Wilhelm Müller, and Rudolf Tomaschek, and, as a representative of Heidelberg, Ludwig Wesch.

The discussion was led in an impartial manner by Gustav Borger, head of the office for scholarship in the University Teachers League. As a physician, he knew little of the technical matters under debate, and he invited the experimentalists Herbert Stuart from the TH Dresden and Johannes Malsch from Cologne as observers. Although the Aryan physicists at first reckoned Stuart and Malsch as allies, the two men refused to support Nordic physics and stayed neutral during the dispute.[29]

After the initial charges by the Aryan physicists that their opponents were supporters of Jewish theories, the discussion turned to matters more strictly pertaining to physics. The Finkelnburg side then easily carried the day. Heckmann, for example, remembers his particular antagonist Thüring argued that any physics or astronomy working with Euclidian-constructed instruments and leading to non-Euclidian space structures was inherently contradictory. Heckmann simply pointed out that "Euclidian-constructed" theodolites (not using the stars) could prove the earth's surface to be spherical, that is, non-Euclidian.[30] According to Scherzer, Tomaschek was the only Aryan physicist capable of discussing physics coherently.[31] Borger was so disgusted with his political colleagues that he lectured them during the lunch break, whereupon Müller and Thüring left the meeting.[32]

The afternoon session closed with the preparation of five points of agreement as drafted by Scherzer, with the cooperation of von Weizsäcker, Bühl, and Tomaschek.[33] The formula for truce read:

1. Theoretical physics with all mathematical aids is an indispensable component of the whole of physics.

2. The facts of experience summarized in the special theory of relativity belong to the firm stock of physics. The certainty of the application of the theory of relativity in cosmic relationships is nevertheless not so great that further verification is unnecessary.

3. The four-dimensional representation of natural processes is a useful mathematical aid; it does not, however, signify the introduction of a new space and time perception.

4. Any link between the relativity theory and a general relativism is denied.

5. The quantum and wave mechanics are the only methods known at this time with which to comprehend atomic processes. It is desirable to push on beyond formalism and its prescriptive significance to a deeper understanding of the atom.[34]

When Sommerfeld was shown the agreement later that evening, he termed it "thin and trivial." [35] As a declaration of principles of physics, this judgment is undoubtedly true, but as a political statement, the compromise was very substantive. The Aryan physicists

had been forced to discuss physics rather than politics, and the result
was the official recognition of relativity theory and quantum mechanics by a party agency.

One immediate consequence of the Religionsgespräch—the "religious debate," as the Munich confrontation was soon dubbed—was a
splintering of the ranks of the Nordic physics adherents. Lenard apparently charged Bühl with betrayal of the cause for participating in
the arrangement of the conference.[36] Bühl did indeed keep the truce
and published no more on Aryan physics. Tomaschek also held to
the agreement, and from this point on disengaged himself from the
movement, particularly as it was represented by Müller and Thüring
in Munich. The leaders of the University Teachers League, especially Borger, lost confidence in Bühl as an advisor and embraced
neutrality on the issue of Aryan physics. The Dozentenbund thus
came in line with the positions of the Rosenberg office and the SS
in matters of physics, while its views conflicted with those of Hess's
staff and the Students League, which continued to support Nordic
physics.

Despite the outcome of the Munich confrontation, the Aryan
physicists did not give up their fight. They still had backers in the
university of Munich, for example, and could continue to appoint
followers to positions there. Wilhelm Führer had also recently
secured a post in the Reich Education Ministry from which he could
greatly influence academic affairs. Otto Wacker had resigned from
the REM in 1939 and been succeeded as head of the office for scholarship by his deputy Mentzel. Führer, probably in part through his
connections in the Bavarian Education Ministry, assumed Mentzel's
former task of handling professorial appointments in the physical
sciences.[37] In addition, the REM was attempting to cooperate with
the University Teachers League as well as Hess's staff during this
period, and the acceptance of a party-oriented man like Führer
served to strengthen the bonds between party and state. The University Teachers League was under heavy fire from Rosenberg's
office, which had finally achieved independent budgeting in 1938 and
from then on became an increasingly active rival of the league in
political-ideological evaluations of academicians.[38] Both the REM
and the Dozentenbund sought cooperation with Himmler against
Rosenberg's encroachment, and Führer's status as an SS-man made
him useful to both organizations. Thus political maneuvering among
Nazi agencies led to the introduction of an Aryan physics supporter

into a high position in the REM, which up to this time had consistently opposed the movement.

Führer's influence on behalf of Nordic physics now made itself felt: he supported the Aryan physics adherents in Munich and harassed the professional physicists who participated in the confrontation of November 1940.

After Müller's appointment, the Nordic physics contingent in Munich was augmented by two new faculty members. Ludwig Glaser had been one of the vocal antirelativity polemicists in the early 1920s and had qualified under Stark at Würzburg in 1921. After Stark left the university, Glaser stayed on and ran into conflict with a number of members of the faculty. He went on leave in 1928 as an extraordinary professor of physics, and in 1932 he was released from the Bavarian civil service for neglecting to hold classes after his leave expired.[39] In early 1932, he joined the Nazi party.[40] One of Müller's first actions upon arrival in Munich was to drive out Sommerfeld's assistant Heinrich Welker (who took a position in industry) and hire Glaser in his place. In securing Glaser's appointment he was apparently aided by other Aryan physics supporters, for Glaser was an active campaigner on behalf of völkisch physics.[41]

A second Nordic physics supporter given a post in Munich at this time was the philosopher of science Hugo Dingler. A student of the Viennese positivist Ernst Mach, Dingler had questioned the theory of relativity since the early 1920s on epistemological grounds, but had not engaged in racial polemic.[42] In fact, he had praised the Jews in one book and had once termed Einstein a "jewel" of German scholarship because he had raised some fundamental issues.[43] Throughout the Weimar period, Dingler had been an extraordinary professor in Munich and in 1932 finally became a full professor at the TH Darmstadt.

Reportedly forced into retirement in 1934 because of his earlier praise of the Jews, Dingler in the middle and late 1930s began in his books to stress his opposition to "mathematicism" and modern theoretical physics.[44] He also contributed regularly to the *Zeitschrift für die gesamte Naturwissenschaft*.[45] In 1938 he was once again allowed to teach philosophy and history of science in Munich and in late 1940 received a regular university appointment. For a time, he and Müller were the most vocal Aryan physics proponents in the Bavarian capital.

In the summer and fall of 1940, with professional physics in

Munich deteriorating rapidly, Sommerfeld, Gerlach, and their colleagues in mathematics and chemistry attempted to have Müller
appointed elsewhere. Sommerfeld went to Berlin and spoke with
officials in the Reich Education Ministry who were more concerned
with professional than with political qualifications of academicians.
He was encouraged to draft a statement on Müller's lack of suitability
for his position and submit it through the university rector, which
Sommerfeld did. He suggested in particular that Müller be reas-
signed to a post for technical physics and that Carl F. von Weizsäcker
be appointed professor of theoretical physics.[46]

The first response was from the Bavarian ministry: not only would
Müller not be removed, but Glaser would be promoted to an extraordinary professorship for theoretical physics. Gerlach in particular
objected to this proposal and fired off a strongly worded note to
Munich from his army post in Berlin.[47] In late October, Müller invited Stark for a guest appearance in a colloquium, in which both
men gave polemical speeches on behalf of Aryan physics.[48]

Even Tomaschek was having second thoughts about the lack of
genuine theoretical physics in Munich by this time. He therefore
allowed Siegfried Flügge, a young theoretician of Heisenberg's
school, to present a lecture at the institute of technology in early
November. Glaser interrupted the presentation, displayed his lack
of knowledge of the subject under discussion, and resorted to a
political denunciation of those who followed the "Jewish-oriented"
modern concepts.[49]

Ten days later the confrontation arranged by Finkelnburg took
place, after which Tomaschek increasingly disassociated himself
from the Nordic physics adherents in Munich. Due to support from
the dean and from Führer in the REM, Müller was not replaced.
Glaser, however, was appointed in 1941 to the Reich university of
Posnan in eastern occupied territory. Also, Müller changed the name
of the theoretical physics institute to reflect its actual orientation
under his direction: it became the Institute for Theoretical Physics
and Applied Mechanics.

In the spring of 1942, a Sommerfeld pupil, Fritz Sauter, was
brought from Königsberg to the TH Munich. This appointment indicated the extent of Tomaschek's break from his political colleagues
in Munich, for as professor of experimental physics he had been involved in the decision to call Sauter. Müller was particularly displeased by Sauter's arrival, for the theoretician across town lectured

at the same hour as Müller. The Aryan physicist wrote the dean of
the institute of technology requesting that Sauter change his class
time, for, Müller revealed, his students had all abandoned him for
the new man.[50] The request was denied, and Gerlach was able to use
the letter to show convincingly that Müller was not capable of carrying out his tasks as professor of theoretical physics.[51] Nevertheless,
presumably due in part to Führer's influence, Müller was able to
stay at his post until 1945.

Besides supporting Munich Aryan physics advocates, Führer attempted to create difficulties for those professional physicists involved
in the November 1940 conference. Heckmann's call to Hamburg
was delayed, Joos was driven to leave academia for industry, and the
appointment of von Weizsäcker and Finkelnburg to the Reich university in Strasbourg was hindered for a time in 1941.[52]

Finkelnburg's problems stemmed directly from the Munich conference, which had generated Führer's antagonism toward him. In
February 1941, the physicist was assigned to oversee the construction
of the physical institute at the university in Strasbourg, which was to
open as a German Reich university in the fall of the year. An extraordinary professor of theoretical physics was to be called, and one
full and one extraordinary professor of experimental physics were
to have an institute each. Finkelnburg was to be the junior experimentalist. When the individual considered for the senior experimental position declined, Finkelnburg was offered the post by the
Strasbourg dean.[53] As an explicit result of his role in the Munich
conference, however, Finkelnburg's appointment to the full professorship was actively opposed by Führer. Although Mentzel was no
friend of Aryan physics, he joined Führer because he thought
Finkelnburg was too young for such an important position.[54]

Von Weizsäcker, who was to be named the theoretician in Strasbourg, visited Rust and Mentzel on Finkelnburg's behalf in July
1941. He reported that Rust said he had fought consistently against
Führer's demand that the ministry take steps against theoretical
physics as a discipline. But he would also not fight on its behalf.
Rust had a survival-of-the-fittest approach: the truth about the value
of the field would have to prevail on its own. Von Weizsäcker also
got the impression, however, that simple bureaucratic prestige was
at stake, for Führer was now a member of the REM and his su-
periors would have to back him or lose face.[55]

Finkelnburg had associates in Göring's Reich Aviation Ministry

(Reichsluftfahrtministerium) who stepped in on his behalf in 1942.[56] This ministry sponsored some of his research, which it claimed was very important to the war effort. This assertion eventually forced Führer to give in, for he stood in danger of being accused of wanting to sabotage a development crucial to the military.[57] Finkelnburg was finally appointed director of the First Physical Institute in the fall of 1942. Normally a directorship would have entailed a full professorship, but the REM would only grant Finkelnburg an extraordinary professorship. When Strasbourg fell to the Allies in 1944, Finkelnburg was left without a position. After the war he accepted an invitation to go to the United States for a few years as part of the effort to bolster American scientific manpower with foreign talent.[58]

Despite all of his difficulties with the Strasbourg appointment, Finkelnburg continued to work against the Aryan physics movement. In the early months of 1941, with the aid of Gerlach, he uncovered the evidence of Dingler's former praise of Einstein.[59] Later in the year he tried to reduce the influence of Müller and Glaser and was aided by Sommerfeld's former institute mechanic Karl Selmayr.[60] It is not certain what immediate use Finkelnburg made of the information he collected, but by the end of 1941 Rosenberg's office was spreading the word that Dingler had pre-1933 pro-Jewish publications to hide.[61]

These activities, despite their effectiveness in Nazi politics, were not very significant in comparison to those Finkelnburg helped conduct within the German Physical Society, whose members were as concerned as ever with maintaining the prerogatives of professional physics. During the September 1940 general meeting in Berlin, they elected Carl Ramsauer presiding officer. As a former assistant to Lenard, Ramsauer could not be accused of having studied with physics teachers of the wrong race. A long-time university lecturer, he was familiar with the procedures and values of academia. He had been director of the German General Electric laboratories in Berlin for more than a decade and thus also knew the needs of industry. The fact that this position also made him independent of state support added to his attractiveness, because it allowed him to take action against government and party policies damaging to physics without as much fear of reprisal. The acting president of the society, Jonathan Zenneck of the TH Munich, had strongly supported Ramsauer's election for this reason.[62] Ramsauer had also already served as Berlin district presiding officer for two years and knew the needs of the society.

The new presiding officer saw his task as two-fold: preserving the traditional autonomy of the society and energetically reversing the decline of German physics. He later wrote:

> It was here primarily a matter of the filling of important physics teaching chairs with political incompetents, which was becoming ever more frequent, and of the defamation of German theoretical physics as a Jewish machination. The poor appointments lamed the scholarly work of old research centers for years ahead and at the same time damaged the coming generation of experimental physicists in the long run. The defamation of theory tended to drive precisely the most successful theoreticians from Germany and also to damage the coming generation of theoreticians in the long run, in that young physicists were systematically frightened away from occupying themselves with theoretical physics.[63]

Ramsauer heard of Finkelnburg's opposition to the Aryan physicists and decided in the spring of 1941 to use his right under the Nazi leadership principle to appoint Finkelnburg his deputy.[64] The younger man hesitated to accept, for the added repsonsibility was great and the possibility was real that acceptance could damage his academic career by leading him into further conflict with the party. In May, he finally agreed to serving in the society leadership. Shortly thereafter, Gerlach expressed his appreciation for Finkelnburg's decision, but pointed out that Müller had been appointed dean in Munich.[65] There was much work to be done.

In the fall of 1941, Ramsauer, Finkelnburg, and others worked out a memorandum which was submitted to the Reich Education Ministry on January 20, 1942. Portions of this document were published after the war to show that German scientists had not been totally passive under Hitler.[66] A cover letter from Ramsauer, which stressed that German physics had been overtaken by Anglo-Saxon (especially American) physics, was accompanied by six enclosures.

The first enclosure was perhaps the most important.[67] It contained a series of arguments which attempted to document the generally recognized decline of German physics vis-à-vis Anglo-Saxon work. The first argument was based on a citation index prepared in 1935 in America for use by librarians. In 1897, 64 percent of the citations in the five leading journals of Germany, England, France, America, and Russia were of German sources. Only 3 percent were of American pieces of work. By 1933, the corresponding figures were 36 percent German and 33 percent American. America appeared to be on the verge of overtaking the German lead in footnoted sources, which indicated it was performing increasingly significant research. A second argument pointed out the growing number of Nobel prizes in physics going to Americans, while a third noted that the American *Physical Review* was recognized as the leading physics journal of the world. A fourth point referred to nuclear physics, the field in the forefront of physics research in the 1930s and 1940s. According to a German abstracting journal, the comparative number of articles on the subject were as follows:

	1927	1931	1935	1939
Germany	47	77	129	166
USA and England	35	77	329	471

A final measure of America's challenge to Germany was the number of particle accelerators: thirty in America, four in England, one each in Japan, Germany, the Soviet Union, France and Denmark. The closing remark of this enclosure was that the American lead in accelerators could have been offset by the German preeminence in theoretical work if theory had not been denigrated as it had been, for example, in the treatment of men like Heisenberg.

The second enclosure contained a chronological list of articles which attacked theoretical physics. Its point was that theory had indeed been under fire. The authors included Bühl, Stark, Thüring, Dingler, Müller, and Glaser. The third enclosure was an argument on behalf of the importance of theoretical physics and pure research to the whole of physics and applied work. Ramsauer and his German Physical Society co-workers stressed that the antagonists of theoretical research had no alternative to offer.

The fourth attachment was a direct response to the claim that modern physical theory was a product of the Jewish spirit. According to this attachment, theory was not a Jewish, but a German characteristic. Modern theories were defended as products of the true German spirit. In their published lectures on "German and Jewish Physics," the report noted, Stark and Müller had insisted that theoreticians did not begin with experimental data, would not submit their theories to experimental proof, and overestimated the value of conceptual-mathematical work. In response to the first two points, Ramsauer (who specifically disclaimed the role of an Einstein follower) argued that if the experimental evidence refuted the relativity theory, no serious scientist would support it. He also pointed out that Heisenberg's quantum mechanics was consciously concerned with constructing knowledge on the basis of fundamentally measurable quantities. Furthermore, Ramsauer held that the theoreticians did not overestimate the value of conceptual-mathematical work, but noted instead that Stark and his associates underestimated its worth.[68]

The fifth enclosure to the memorandum was an excerpt from a statement by Ludwig Prandtl, the Göttingen aerodynamics expert, on the senselessness of Müller's call to Munich. Prandtl termed the appointment an act of sabotage against the further technical development of a crucial field.[69] The sixth attachment was a report on the Munich confrontation arranged by Finkelnburg. Added to the five points of agreement was a short note that a series of appointments by the Reich Education Ministry had gone to authors of antitheoretical articles, that Müller had been appointed specifically to destroy theoretical physics in Munich, and that the position for theoretical physics at the TH Berlin had been eliminated. These steps damaged German physics as a whole and thereby the German economy and war technology. The responsibility for failing to prevent all this was laid at the feet of the REM.[70]

Ramsauer and his co-workers expected some sort of reaction to their sharply worded critique of the situation, but the REM did nothing—an indication of the passivity of Rust's organization.[71] They had also submitted copies of the memorandum to various persons in industry and the military, however, and here they found some response. In the summer of 1942, the head of the Aviation Ministry, Air Marshal Erhard Milch, ordered the German Academy of Aeronautical Research to prepare an evaluation of the Physical Society report.[72] Prandtl handled the matter, and the report was certainly favorable to Ramsauer's position. By this time, the research department of the Aviation Ministry had been backing Finkelnburg in his Strasbourg difficulties for some months. From the summer of 1942 onward, Göring's organization supported the professional physicists against further political interference and gave them a platform from which to reach other influential government offices.

Ramsauer drew upon Aviation Ministry support a number of times, and he gave a particularly consequential talk before the Acad-

emy of Aeronautical Research on April 2, 1943.[73] He reiterated most
of the points made in his memorandum to Rust, emphasizing the
Anglo-Saxon lead in physics and noting what this portended for the
war effort. Germany needed to restore proper academic appointment
criteria and academic prestige, and mobilize its physicists for the
war effort. In particular, physicists should not be drafted for combat
duty and physics students should be allowed to continue their studies. They should also be freed from tasks which could be performed
by less qualified personnel. Proper utilization of human resources
was essential to physics and the prosecution of the war. Ramsauer
argued: 3,000 soldiers less would not harm the army, 3,000 physicists
more could decide the war.[74]

This talk was published as a classified document, which made the
rounds of high Nazi offices. When Goebbels saw it in May, he found
it convincing and disturbing. He blamed Rust for failing to protect
science against insults and interference and for not providing it with
sufficient material support.[75]

In late August 1943, a board meeting of the German Physical Society adopted a program for the German physics community designed
to reassert the discipline's independence and restore professional excellence. The program grew directly out of the memorandum to
Rust and Ramsauer's talk before the Aviation Academy. It laid heavy
stress on revitalizing the academic (particularly university) institutes,
appointing professors on a scholarly basis, and removing those who
were not active in research. The study of physics needed to be promoted by popular publications, and financial support was essential
for young physicists. The secondary school teachers of physics would
also have to be persuaded of the value of physics so that they might
encourage students to seek a university education in the field.[76] All
in all, the Physical Society reform program was a sweeping challenge
to political influence in academic affairs.

At the board meeting of August 22–24, 1943, it was also decided
that one of Ramsauer's suggestions should be put into practice immediately. An information office of the Physical Society was established to publish a new popular journal. Ernst Brüche, a pupil and
co-worker of Ramsauer for many years, was assigned the task of edit-
ing the periodical. The Propaganda Ministry of Goebbels and the
Ministry of Armaments under Albert Speer cooperated in order to
obtain the scarce paper for the venture.[77] The first issue of the
Physikalische Blätter (Physical papers), that of January–February

1944, became available in May 1944. It was indicative of the defeat of politicized physics that the last issue of the Students League journal, which supported Aryan physics, appeared at the same time as the new Physical Society publication made its debut.

THE DECLINE OF IDEOLOGY AND THE CLOSE OF THE WAR

The major impact of World War II on Nazi higher education politics was to affirm the significance of utilitarian and reduce the importance of ideological values. This effect was abundantly clear in the highest Nazi circles as early as 1940. When Rosenberg attempted to expand his mandate for ideological supervision of the party in early 1940, for example, Hitler took specific objection to his subordinate's inclusion of the phrase "scientific research and training" in the commission he was to sign. The Führer ordered it removed.[78]

The Aryan physics adherents were severely handicapped under these circumstances by their image as ideologues. The protechnology faction of the movement suffered a considerable loss of influence when Stark retired as president of the Imperial Institute of Physics and Technology in May 1939. Although Müller and Glaser agreed with Stark on the subject of the technical application of science, they had aroused considerable opposition in Munich. The split among the Aryan physicists following the Munich confrontation weakened the entire movement. Had it not been for Führer's influence in the REM, the Aryan physics effort might well have completely ended in 1941.

In contrast, the advent of war significantly strengthened the professional physicists. The discovery of nuclear fission brought greater influence especially for Heisenberg and his immediate associates, for they could claim that their work was important for the war effort. As a result, although the German atomic research program began as a military undertaking, the academicians came to dominate the effort. Various institutes became involved, and the center for the project was the Kaiser Wilhelm Institute for Physics in Berlin-Dahlem.[79]

As David Irving has shown, the fact that the theoreticians in the Berlin institute prevailed over other scientists associated with the project was fortuitous for the Allies. Up to mid-1942, the Germans had kept pace in nuclear research with their counterparts in England and America. From then on, however, as the theoreticians came to the fore, the German scientists carefully compared each experimental step with theory before proceeding, thus "gaining in those three years knowledge that could have been won in as many months had the will been there." [80] The Heisenberg group lacked the background and inclination to transform uranium research from a laboratory experiment into an industrial enterprise. This was one of the major reasons for the project's failure to achieve a self-sustained chain reaction, much less an atomic bomb.

In addition, some measurements by one of the foremost German experimentalists, Walther Bothe, led the group mistakingly to believe that carbon was unsuitable as a moderator for an atomic pile. The Germans thereupon relied solely on heavy water, the production of which was effectively sabotaged by British and Norwegian raids upon the only large heavy water plant in Europe. The theoreticians were completely unaware that, as Irving concluded, "the German scientists had lost the art of experiment." [81]

Overshadowing the entire uranium project was, of course, Hitler's edicts on long-term research and production items. Given the *Blitzkrieg* ideology of a short war, it is doubtful that an order for the necessary large-scale, sustained effort could have been given before the battle of Stalingrad. It is also unlikely that one given afterward could have mustered enough men and matériel to achieve practical use of atomic energy by 1945.[82] Yet their reputations for effective research and promise of eventual success brought the academicians the backing of Göring through Mentzel's Reich Research Council. In 1942, Abraham Esau, the council's section chief for physics, became Göring's deputy for nuclear physics research. By the end of the same year, the academicians began to receive the support of Speer as well.[83]

The theoreticians were not solely to blame for the dilatory pace of what should have been a crash project. The experimentalist Gerlach, who succeeded Esau in late 1943, was one of the strongest proponents of conducting pure research under the guise of military usefulness. His goals for the uranium program were the same as those of the theoreticians—to reassert the primacy of professional research and to prevent the loss of young scientists at the front.[84] Thus the objectives of the scientists working on the high-priority nuclear energy project were in complete accord with those of other professional physicists.

In the final years of the war it was obvious to the highest Nazi leaders that reports of Allied superiority in science were all too justi-

fied. After reading a copy of Ramsauer's talk before the Aviation
Academy which was handed to him in May 1943, Goebbels related
the decline in German science directly to German losses in air and
submarine warfare. He felt the physicist's suggestions should be carried out. Even though it would take time, it was better than doing
nothing.[85]

As Ramsauer had strongly urged, on July 29, 1943, Göring created
a planning board to determine research priorities and to withdraw
scientists from combat. He appointed Werner Osenberg, an SS-man
and engineering professor working on naval research, as head of the
board. The board overlapped the authority of Mentzel's Reich Research Council, and for a time little was accomplished. But Osenberg
managed to get additional support and began to consolidate scientific
manpower.[86] Unfortunately, by 1944 conditions were quickly becoming chaotic. According to a postwar British intelligence report, only
4,000 of the 6,000 scientists scheduled to be withdrawn from the
fighting could actually be recalled; 2,000 had already been killed or
could not be located in the spreading confusion. The effort was too
little, too late.[87] In a report written for American intelligence in
1945, Ramsauer expressed similar views. Germany had lost the war
of the laboratories largely because it lacked a clear organization for
scientific research.[88]

The British report noted a fact which Ramsauer discreetly ignored; namely, the remarkable extent to which the academicians
succeeded in using military contracts to support purely academic research.[89] The key was simply to designate even the most esoteric
projects as essential, since the Nazi officials who signed the appropria-
tions were unable to discern the difference. Toward the end of 1946,
von Laue wrote to his son concerning the charge that German scientists had collaborated with the Nazis by performing war research.

> The single actually established fact in Goudsmit's letter is that
> uranium research was designated as "decisive for the war effort"
> [*kriegsentscheidend*] in official files. But what would you say,
> if I now write to you that my books on x-ray and electron inter-
> ference also bore the imprint "decisive for the war effort"? That
> I even once wrote an evaluation of Heisenberg's cosmic ray book
> in which I put down that it was "decisive for the war effort"?
> Otherwise it would have been impossible to get these books

printed. And if someone wanted to research persistently through the files of the final years of the war, he would notice that absolutely everything conducted in science was "decisive for the war effort." Otherwise the state and party agencies would have granted neither the means nor the co-workers necessary. Many, many young people owe to this designation the activity which allowed them to avoid going to the front and thus kept them alive. This is the only meaning which the ominous word "kriegsentscheidend" had in the years 1942–45.[90]

The opponents of professional physics, of course, recognized the true state of affairs. In late 1942 one of Göring's deputies received a letter denouncing Mentzel for supporting Heisenberg and his associates. The anonymous critic charged specifically that "this huge swindle with the so-called uranium machine" was Mentzel's worst deed.[91] But by then no one was really listening to the followers of Lenard and Stark.

As early as the spring of 1941, the Reich leader of the University Teachers League had noted the strong position of the professional physicists in the universities and in the war industry. The 1940 confrontation between the two "battling camps" around Lenard and Heisenberg had indicated that there were a number of misunderstandings which could be eliminated. But an ideological clarification of the situation was still necessary.[92]

Official clarification did not come for another eighteen months, when a second confrontation between the professional and Aryan physicists occurred. In the meantime, however, the issue was effectively decided by the fact that the party agencies most concerned with political and ideological evaluations of professors, the Teachers League and Rosenberg's office respectively, had decided on neutrality in regard to physics. This was at a time when the two organizations were locked in bureaucratic combat on a number of fronts, for Rosenberg was intent on absorbing the league into his own agency. Neither, however, could risk the charge that it was impeding the war effort.[93]

The positions of the Dozentenbund and the Rosenberg office were expressed during deliberations concerning Heisenberg's appointment as professor of theoretical physics at the university in Berlin, which would follow his appointment as director "at" the Kaiser Wilhelm

Institute of Physics in late 1942. The party Chancellery requested
political and ideological reports on the physicist. Rosenberg's representative emphasized in his "ideological evaluation" that:

> It can not be the goal of the party to take sides with one of the
> two factions in the conflict of opinions between the Lenard and
> Heisenberg orientations in theoretical physics. At all costs,
> atomic physical research in Germany must be kept from falling
> behind that performed abroad. Prof. Heisenberg's achievements
> in this area doubtlessly justify his call to the Kaiser Wilhelm
> Institute; the attainment of a settlement between the different
> orientations in theoretical physics must be left to free profes-
> sional discussion.[94]

The views of the Teachers League representative were the same.[95]
The officials of both agencies evidenced a specific concern for the
deterioration of German atomic physics vis-à-vis that of other countries. From the wording of their evaluations, in fact, it is highly
probable that they had seen the Physical Society's memorandum
to Rust.

A second confrontation between the professional physicists and
their antagonists took place at the resort of Seefeld in the Tyrolean
Alps in early November 1942. About thirty physicists were present,
and Heisenberg has said the occasion was simply a "victory celebration." [96]

Tomaschek, Bühl, and Thüring found themselves quite outnum-
bered and succumbed quickly to the arguments of their opponents.
Ramsauer also attended and talked on the American superiority in
physics. Von Weizsäcker and Sauter later prepared a set of minutes
which claimed that apparent differences of opinion were due only
to misunderstandings: quantum mechanics and the special theory of
relativity were both secure contributions to physics. Both sides further agreed that relativity had its roots in work that predated Einstein and would have been discovered by someone else had not Einstein developed it.[97]

By the end of 1943, Heisenberg was able to get an article published in the Students League organ *Zeitschrift für die gesamte
Naturwissenschaft*. Although he had drafted the essay, "The Evaluation of 'Modern Theoretical Physics,' " in 1940, he did not submit
it until May 1943. Heisenberg took issue with Aryan physics both
on scientific and political grounds, defending quantum mechanics,

relativity theory, and the political independence of physicists. Dingler's response to Heisenberg, which appeared in the pages immediately following, could not destroy the impression that the professional physicists were totally victorious.[98]

Their triumph was actually clear even before the Seefeld conference. In June 1942, Lenard celebrated his eightieth birthday. Among
the greetings he received was a note from the REM, to which he replied with a note of thanks and a statement which could serve as the
epitaph of the Aryan physics movement:

> What I had striven strongly to achieve six years ago—especially
> improved school instruction in regard to knowledge of nature—
> it appears to me that the time for that has not yet come. I have
> also become more patient with increasing age and I am glad to
> leave much to the future. There remains for us only the
> Führer.[99]

With the high priorities available for research "decisive for the
war effort" and with their Aryan physics opponents silenced, the
professional physicists grew increasingly confident during the last
years of the war. The image of Planck on a rostrum in 1934 hesi-
tantly rendering the obligatory "Heil Hitler!" symbolized the uncertainty and timidity of the German scientists immediately following the Nazi seizure of power. Ten years later Ramsauer, as president
of the German Physical Society, also spoke before a scholarly audience. At the end of his talk, with various minor Nazi dignitaries in
attendance, he came to an embarrassed silence. As his student Ernst
Brüche remembered:

> What did he want to say yet? In the painful silence the first
> rows could hear his soft interjection: "Curses!" But then his
> countenance brightened, for he had found what still had to be
> said and what had refused to occur to him: "Heil Hitler!" [100]

Despite all due allowance for differences in personalities and lapses
in memory, the contrast could not be stronger. By the closing stages
of the war, the German scientists once more felt in control of their
dealings with the government.

Of course, there were many aspects of life in the war years beyond
the scientists' control. One of these was the disturbance of their work
caused by the Allied bombings of major urban areas. Many institutes
were damaged and some were destroyed, for very few academic in-

stitutes were transferred out of the cities. Those institutes associated
with atomic energy research were notable exceptions. Most of their
personnel and equipment were moved to the vicinity of the village
of Hechingen in the Black Forest. But not even all of these could be
relocated in time to avoid destruction of valuable papers and equipment. Von Laue provided a vivid description of the destruction of
Otto Hahn's institute.

The fire in the Kaiser Wilhelm Institute for Chemistry on
February 15, 1944, was also severe. About eight o'clock in the
evening, if I remember correctly, an air raid alarm began which
lasted until ten P.M. We, that is Mama, Hilda, Mr. and Mrs.
Koch, and perhaps Mr. Arenz, were in the bomb shelter. I no
longer remember exactly how it went there that day. It could
have been that then too, as so often happened, the electric lights
failed, so that we had to light a pitiful candle. It could have
been that we heard bombs whistle and then crash. At any event,
things went well for our area. But as we came into the garden
again and looked around, the red glow of a fire stood against
the sky in the direction of Dahlem. Koch and I got on our bi-
cycles and rode first to the Kaiser Wilhelm Institute for Physics.
There was only minor damage there, perhaps just the windows.
But someone said to us: "The chemistry institute is burning."
And indeed, a large piece of the southern outside wall of Hahn's
institute was missing, for a high-explosive bomb had exploded
right in the director's room. Besides this, the rafters and the
uppermost story of the same side were brightly aflame, a terrible-
beautiful sight. Since many persons were already extinguishing
and saving what they could, I left Mr. Koch alone there and
rode to Hahn's house in order to inform Mrs. Hahn. She then
came back with me to see the fire. It was by no means the only
one in Dahlem; on the contrary, dozens of smaller and larger
villas were aflame. Then I participated in the salvaging of the
library and the equipment. The entire Kaiser Wilhelm Institute for Physics helped out; many were also there from the Institute for Physical Chemistry. I saw even Ministerial Director
Mentzel carrying books. While the military fire brigade fought
the fire on top—in my opinion they got things wrong and sought
to save a part of the roof which could not be saved, while in
other places the fire invaded sections which could have been

held—hot water from a broken water pipe dripped into the cellar, which contained a large portion of the library. The water was already several centimeters high by the time I left, and it was a singular sight to behold how a pair of men from the fire police sat in a corner of the room and, calmly, as if everything around them were in order, telephoned someplace else. In the courtyard of the institute, Heisenberg orchestrated [*dirigierte*] the placing of the salvaged books into a shed—on this day Hahn was in Hechingen preparing the transfer of his institute. Toward two or three o'clock in the morning the fire slackened off considerably and I went home. I heard the next day that the fire department very quickly brought the whole thing to an end.[101]

Such scenes were repeated in every major city, causing dislocation of institute personnel, destruction of research papers and apparatus, and sometimes loss of life. In addition, with the advance of Allied troops, transportation and communications systems were breaking down, and in many areas civil authority ceased to function. By the spring of 1945, scientific research had practically collapsed in Germany.

One of the few projects which continued to function through April 1945 was the atomic energy program. A list of those scientists associated with the effort had been prepared by Allied intelligence, so that Hahn, Heisenberg, von Laue, von Weizsäcker, and others were rounded up in May and sent to France.[102] Eventually they were brought to Farm Hall in England, where they stayed until the end of the year.

In captivity the German scientists first heard the news not only that the Allies had constructed a reactor which sustained a chain reaction, a step they had nearly reached themselves, but that the Allies were years ahead and had already produced—and used—the first atomic bombs. On August 7, the day after they discovered how far behind they had been, von Laue wrote a long letter to his son.

This letter is concerned with a history making event of unforeseeable consequences. Even though I was far from Hiroshima as the bomb exploded, I experienced the news of the occurrence in the midst of colleagues who have worked on the uranium problem for years and who are, like myself, living under excep-

tional circumstances—namely "detained for His Majesty's plea-
sure." . . .

Around 7:45 P.M. yesterday, as always, we began our evening
meal, which both of the English officers guarding us, Major
Rittner and Captain Brodie, regularly share. . . Earlier the
major had already indicated something to Hahn about a radio
report that the Americans had used an atomic bomb. At the
table he expanded upon this information and naturally a lively
discussion immediately ensued. We did not really want to believe it. Some of us thought that if there were any truth to the
matter, then the name "atomic bomb" had to signify something
other than what we understood it to mean. At any rate, it could
have nothing to do with uranium fission.

But then we heard the English radio news at nine o'clock.
And quite plainly it was reported that the English and Americans had used uranium fission to construct a bomb in a collective, laborious, and exceedingly expensive process requiring
years to complete. I don't need to go any further into the announcement . . .

The effect of this announcement upon the German physicists
assembled here was naturally very profound. Certainly I was—
if I may start with myself—a relative nonparticipant. Throughout the entire uranium research I always played the role of an
observer who was usually, but not always, kept abreast of events
by the participants. Also Otto Hahn, whose mood is causing
Major Rittner serious concern, remained quite calm and said
only that he was glad to have not participated in the construction of such a murderous weapon. But Walter [sic] Gerlach,
as the erstwhile "Plenipotentiary of the Reich Marshall for
Nuclear Physics," was very agitated and behaved like a defeated
commander. He was also painfully disturbed by a couple of in-
temperate remarks by one of the younger men. Harteck, Hahn,
I, and Heisenberg sought to calm him yesterday evening and
this morning, and we finally succeeded. But his mood and that
of others of our circle remained influenced by the news. The
bomb dominated the conversation today and the newspapers
were nearly "devoured." Heisenberg established repeatedly that
no exact picture of the process leading to the bomb could be
pieced together on the basis of the knowledge presented here
and in the previous reports. The reports have intentionally been
prepared so that this is impossible.

The main question naturally, is why we did not arrive at the bomb in Germany. There is this to say: (1) the German physicists would never have received the means which England and America made available to their scientists for this purpose. Neither the work force nor the money would have been obtainable in anything approaching such quantities. For this reason alone, no physicist seriously considered requesting such means. That the increasingly severe, continuous bombardment of all cities would have been a further obstacle is proven by Churchill's statement that the production of the atomic bomb was not located in England due to the danger of air raids. (2) Our entire uranium research was directed toward the creation of a uranium machine as a source of energy, first, because no one believed in the possibility of a bomb in the foreseeable future, and second, because no one of us wanted to lay such a weapon in the hands of Hitler.[103]

The last remark expresses a sentiment which surely applied to von Laue and Hahn, but did it apply to the others? Since 1945, opinion has been divided. Goudsmit presented the argument in 1947 that the German scientists had very much wanted to build a bomb, but had simply failed due to an arrogance which blinded them to their errors. A contrary thesis was the basis for the journalist Robert Jungk's bestseller in 1954: the German atomic scientists had knowingly conspired to keep the bomb from Hitler. In 1967, David Irving struck a good balance between these two viewpoints. He concluded that the Germans devoted their energies solely to the construction of a nuclear reactor because they thought a bomb was beyond anyone's grasp. They never reached the point of decision for initiating a nuclear weapons project.[104]

As von Laue noted, the German scientists felt the matériel and manpower would not possibly be available, so they never requested them. This tendency to anticipate and be stymied by problems outside their closed world of experience was a consistent characteristic of German scientists from the dismissal policy through the end of the war. The advent of the atomic bomb made them aware, as had nothing during the Nazi period, that they could no longer find refuge from their political environment by retreating into their professional community. The world for them, as for everyone else, had been irrevocably changed.

What of the Nazis? In 1945 Rust committed suicide; Mentzel later

faced de-Nazification proceedings. The Aryan physics proponents—
including Becker, Dingler, Führer, Glaser, Müller, Thüring, Tomaschek, and Wesch—left their academic positions. Several also were
tried in de-Nazification courts. Lenard initially withdrew to a village
near Heidelberg, but finally gave himself up. The authorities were
going to try him in a de-Nazification court, but the chemist Karl
Freudenberg, acting rector of the university, convinced them they
would find no honor in humiliating the aged physicist.[105] He died in
Messelhausen near Bad Mergentheim on May 20, 1947.

Stark, however, was not similarly spared, although he had retired
before the outbreak of war. During his trial in Bavaria von Laue,
Sommerfeld, and Heisenberg testified against him. Found guilty on
July 20, 1947 of being a major Nazi offender (*Hauptschuldiger*), he
was sentenced to four years hard labor. In an appeal he managed to
get the classification reduced and the sentence suspended, but he
regarded the affair as his opponents' final act of revenge.[106] He died
on his private estate on June 21, 1957.

As targets of party attacks in the 1930s, Sommerfeld, von Laue,
and Heisenberg had reputations as proven anti-Nazis. The Allied
authorities sought their opinions not only against Aryan physics proponents, but also in support of physicists who wanted to continue
working in postwar Germany. Their approval thus was particularly
important for the younger men who, like Finkelnburg, had joined
the party, but had held to professional values in physics. Older scientists who had held positions of authority under the Nazis, such as
Ramsauer, also had to seek the recommendation of Sommerfeld and
von Laue.[107] The German physicists were all anxious to document
their purely academic activities during the Nazi era, and, ironically,
they began to espouse one of the central assertions of Aryan physics:
adherence to professional values was actually opposition to National
Socialism. A major question which must be answered, however, is the
extent to which this assertion was true.

10.   Conclusion

The foremost concern of the members of the physics community during the Nazi years was the protection of their autonomy against political encroachment. The vast majority of the scientists under Hitler were neither anti-Nazi nor pro-Nazi. They were committed solely to independence in the conduct of professional affairs.

The challenges to the autonomy of the physicists came primarily from two quarters. The National Socialists in the state administration sought to rid the government of undesired elements and concentrate control of academic affairs in the hands of the ministers of education. The National Socialists in party agencies, and the small band of disaffected followers of Lenard and Stark, wanted to remold the standards and conduct of the entire discipline. The efforts of the government authorities achieved considerable success. The desire of the ideologues to create an Aryan physics met with failure.

It was not at all clear at first that the design of the Nazi government in 1933 was to force the emigration of Germany's Jews. The Civil Service Law of April 7 was couched in confusing terms with qualifiers such as the cutoff date of September 30, when procedures were supposed to return to normal. This, coupled with the staggered manner in which the dismissals and forced leaves were announced, made effective protest nearly impossible. As was demonstrated in the case of the Göttingen physics and mathematics faculty, no clear focus for action could be decided upon. The academicians were also severely hampered by the superficial legality of the Nazi measures. Yet, in contrast to popular belief, the scientists did not passively accept their fate. The resignations of Einstein, Franck, Haber, Schrödinger, and Stern were demonstrative attempts to face the basic issue. The ineffectiveness of resignation lay in the fact that it accomplished the Nazi purpose of removing opponents from the scene.

An alternative was to fight through legal channels to stay on. As Courant discovered, however, this was a losing battle. When he realized his position was untenable, he was forced to accept one of the diminishing number of posts abroad. The international communication available to German scientists (particularly physicists) through journals, meetings, and the fame of the German universities made emigration a more viable option for them than for members of many other segments of German society.

The relative ease of emigration was all too apparent to those leaders of the German physics community unaffected by the Nazi ordinances. Planck, von Laue, Sommerfeld, Heisenberg, and others signed petitions, counseled those who were included in the provisions of the decrees, and sought as best they could to hold their community together. The watchword was that those who could should stay. The goals of these leaders were to minimize individual hardships, reverse the dismissals and resignations when possible, and, above all, to maintain the international standing of German science. The Nazis, or at least the Nazi excesses, were regarded in 1933 and early 1934 as transitory phenomena. The worst of National Socialism would pass, these men felt, but the importance of science for Germany's reputation would endure.

To a certain extent, the appeals of the physics community's leaders were heeded. The scientists who joined the exodus of talent were overwhelmingly the individuals affected by the new laws. A few non-Jews, notably Erwin Schrödinger and Martin Stobbe, followed their colleagues into exile. Most remained at their posts, and even a number of Jewish scholars who were not forced to leave, such as Gustav Hertz and Lise Meitner, chose to stay as long as they could.

Despite the best efforts of the leaders of the physics community, severe losses were inflicted upon their discipline. The figure of 25 percent of those holding academic physics positions in 1932–33 was significantly higher than that for the natural sciences as a whole. The number of potential students lost is impossible to calculate. Even more important, many of the emigrés vacated positions at the top of the profession: by 1934, one out of every five institute directorships was vacant. In 1935, the situation was still so serious that talk began in industrial circles of compensating for the losses by establishing a Ph.D. program in industrial laboratories. This was one of the most telling indications of the real impact of the dismissal policy upon German academia. Although the suggestion was dropped, a continued drain of talented researchers and a large number of critical vacancies plagued academic physics throughout the Nazi years.

The cost of the dismissals was magnified by the high quality of those who emigrated. It was even greater than apparent at the time, because many of the most talented of the emigrés were young men whose abilities were not yet widely known. The refugees settled for the most part in Western Europe and America, thus further raising the cost of dismissal policy for Hitler's Germany. The scientists Germany lost were gained by her rivals.

Although the leaders of the physics community may at first have not perceived the destructive nature of National Socialism, the damage wrought within their own discipline was something they could understand. In the years following 1933 they cooperated with those Nazis in the government who seemed inclined to entertain at least minimal professional considerations in their deliberations. The scientists sought especially to use the government to support their own interests, an attitude which intensified during the war years. But at no time did the leading figures in the physics community seek to embrace National Socialism on its own terms. In addition to the obvious loss of many capable researchers, the disruption of at least an entire academic year, individual hardship, and a long, unproductive period of vacancies in key posts, one of the direct consequences of the dismissal policy was the alienation of the leaders of the physics community from the regime.

One more consequence of the Nazi expulsion policies should be noted here—the successful Allied program to construct an atomic bomb. What became the gigantic Manhattan Project was initiated in a letter from Einstein to President Franklin Roosevelt in August 1939. Einstein had been convinced that he should alert the president about the potential of atomic energy by Leo Szilard and Eugene Wigner, both of whom had given up positions in Berlin, and Edward Teller, who had left Göttingen in 1933.[1] The list of emigrés who participated in the bomb program is extensive, including not only Szilard, Teller, and Wigner, but also Hans Bethe, Felix Bloch, James Franck, Lother Nordheim, and Euguene Rabinowitch, to name some of those mentioned in this book. Enrico Fermi and Niels Bohr, both of whom had fled the introduction of Hitler's racial policies in other lands, also played key roles. Other refugees participated in the British bomb project, which contributed significantly to the American effort.[2]

The refugees not only initiated the push to develop a bomb, they were its driving force. Their great fears were that it was feasible to construct such a weapon, and that Hitler would gain access to it and use it. Their experiences in Germany had convinced them that German science was the best in the world, and that if a bomb could be built, the Germans could—and would—build it.

As it turned out, the Germans did not live up to expectations. By the end of the war, they had not yet reached the milestone achieved by the American project at the end of 1942; they had not yet contrived a nuclear reactor that could develop a self-sustained, con-

trolled chain reaction. They therefore had not yet been forced to
decide whether or not to initiate the construction of a bomb.

In wider perspective, the German atomic energy project was
foiled by the Nazi economic policies that restricted long-term projects. In a more narrow view, it failed because of the predominant
influence of theoreticians who had no understanding of how to conduct projects on an industrial scale, and because Germany lacked
the experimentalists needed to counteract the influence of the theoreticians. In addition, the Germans were not laboring under any sense
of urgency. They did not fear the success of an American and
British project. If they could not succeed in applying nuclear energy,
they were certain that no one else could. They, too, believed German
science was the best in the world.

Obviously, that was no longer true, at least not in physics. A
pertinent question here is whether National Socialism caused the
decline of German physics. The dismissal of many excellent researchers clearly was a handicap to the maintenance of high–
quality work in Germany, and the governmental policies toward the
universities and the campaign of the Aryan physicists did make life
difficult for those who stayed. But the fundamental reasons for the
decline were internal developments within physics which lie outside
the scope of this book. Particularly significant was the rise of American science, especially in the field of nuclear physics. Coupled with
this was a fact hinted at by Born as early as 1931, when he wrote
von Kármán that he no longer had anything "really new" to offer
the Americans.[3] Gerlach also indicated the development when he
wrote Goudsmit that following the outburst of creative activity in
theory prior to 1930, it was only natural for theory to decline in
significance while experiment came to the fore. But Gerlach failed
to add that this development applied primarily to Germany, where
successes in theory had caused experimental work to take a back seat,
leaving German physics poorly equipped to compete internationally
in the 1930s.

The result was evident to Ramsauer and others who worked to
terminate political interference in professional matters during the
war. It also noticeable in the atomic energy project. National
Socialism was *not* responsible for the phenomenon, but Nazi policies
exacerbated and obscured an already deteriorating situation.

The profound sense of international isolation shared by most
scientists under Hitler was felt particularly keenly by the theore-

ticians, perhaps because it reinforced a fear that German physics was slipping out of the mainstream of research. They thus enthusiastically welcomed the advent of nuclear fission, which, although an experimental discovery, raised a host of theoretical problems which brought them back into the thick of things. The theoreticians, notably the group associated with Heisenberg, were able to reassert their central position in the physics community and gain the decisive voice in the unsuccessful nuclear energy project.

Ironically, there was thus some truth to the complaint of Lenard and Stark that the overweening influence of theoreticians in the Weimar period had worked to the detriment of German physics. Given the dismissal statistics, it was also apparent that they were correct in claiming substantial Jewish participation in the field. Their remedy involved destroying the influence of Planck, von Laue, Sommerfeld, and Heisenberg and redefining the criteria for professorial appointment on the basis of ideological consciousness. Since the National Socialists gave clear priority to politics before professional excellence, the Aryan physicists appeared to have a chance to become predominant.

Why, then, did Aryan physics fail?

The answer has two components—the Aryan physics adherents' lack of success in obtaining backing from political sources, and their inability to win the support of the professional physics community. Both failings were due ultimately to the limitations imposed upon Aryan physics by the personalities of Lenard and Stark. In essence, the movement they produced was both poor politics and poor physics.

One reason that the Aryan physics movement might have succeeded also had a great deal to do with its failure. This was the fact that the highest Nazi leaders were unconcerned with academic physics. Their lack of concern for the impact of the dismissal policy on science and their hesitation to determine ideological correctness in physics were two sides of the same coin. This indifference meant that the professional physicists could not turn to the highest party circles for support against Lenard and Stark, but it also meant that the Aryan physicists were forced to pursue their aims alone in the jungle of competing second echelon Nazi agencies and interests. Under these circumstances, Stark's penchant for making personal and political enemies became a severe political handicap.

During the war years, Aryan physicists also labored under the burden of the ideologue image that Lenard and Stark had projected in the 1930s. With respect to German professionals, such as educators, clergymen, engineers, and other technicians, ideological pressures eased as Hitler's war turned from Blitzkrieg into a prolonged struggle. The Nazis had to rely more and more heavily on specialists who could cope with the details which refused to obey political edicts.

Thus Lenard and Stark were at a disadvantage in their struggles against their professional rivals during the war. Had they been better politicians, they might earlier have been able to perceive the realities of the Third Reich and bend in order to gain the support of the highest Nazi leaders. If Stark had not rejected the opportunity to support the SS Ahnenerbe research, for example, it is entirely possible that his offensive against Heisenberg would have met with Himmler's favor. With Himmler's growing power, the result could well have been an Aryan physics movement as politically powerful as Lysenko biology was in the Soviet Union.

But such political acumen was foreign to Lenard and Stark. The narrowness of their political vision had been defined by völkisch activities in the 1920s. Until the progress of the war brought powerful backers to the aid of the professional physicists, Lenard and Stark had had their choice of patrons. Their selection of Interior Minister Wilhelm Frick (who lost to the SS leader Heinrich Himmler), party ideology chief Alfred Rosenberg (who lost to Goebbels and Himmler) and the Führer's Deputy Rudolf Hess (whose departure in 1941 left support for Aryan physics in the hands of minor Brown House officials) displayed a consistent tendency to choose losers in the higher echelon power struggles of the Third Reich. This was not coincidental. The preference for Frick, Rosenberg, and Hess stemmed from the association of Lenard and Stark with these men in the early years of the party. Ideological concerns had been a key element of the movement before Hitler developed a mass following. After the seizure of power in 1933, however, the tenets of National Socialism were molded or destroyed by the demands of expediency. What mattered in the Third Reich was skill in bureaucratic intrigue and the ability to gain the Führer's ear. Most early party leaders, including Frick, Rosenberg, and Hess, tended to cling stubbornly to the ideals of a movement rather than adjust to the realities of wielding power. They thus came to grief, as did Lenard and Stark. Although its program was first announced in 1935–36, nothing more clearly demonstrated that Aryan physics was a relic of the Weimar years than its advocates' selection of patrons.

At one crucial point the Aryan physicists attempted to break the pattern. The move in 1937–38 to win Himmler's support, however, foundered because they had chosen a poor target. Werner Heisenberg had access to a great deal of support. If a lesser figure had first been attacked and the SS had become involved on the side of Aryan physicists, later events might well have transpired in their favor. By blocking Heisenberg's appointment but fostering SS neutrality, the Nordic physics proponents won their battle, but lost their war.

Aryan physics advocates were unable to convince enough supporters that modern theoretical physics was opposed fundamentally to National Socialism, and that the professionals who supported it were somehow un-German and thus disloyal. The Nazi leaders viewed science in much the same terms as the professional physicists themselves did, as divorced from political affairs. Nazi staff members saw the Aryan physics issues as an internal dispute within the physics discipline, and they did not feel competent to judge the technical matters under debate. Inability to convince these officials that their struggle had practical consequences was one of the key failures of the Aryan physicists.

While the Aryan physics movement failed to evoke interest within political circles because it was seen as a matter of physics, the physics community found it unappealing as a matter of politics. The dismissal policy had been implemented by the National Socialists for ideological and pragmatic reasons not directly related to physics. As such, it might have been acceptable to the leaders of the physics community had it been coupled with an active effort to reinforce Germany's position as a (or perhaps even *the*) leader in world physics.

Instead, Aryan physics stood for the rejection of Germany's most admired contributions to twentieth-century physics. This fact was rooted firmly in the careers of Lenard and Stark. Both men were exceptionally outspoken individuals. Both felt slighted—"betrayed" might more accurately convey the depth of their emotion—by their colleagues in prewar priority disputes. After World War I, these two experimentalists were further alienated from the German physics community by unsuccessful conflicts with its leaders—Lenard principally in opposition to Einstein's relativity theory and Stark in disagreement with the new quantum theory and organizational matters. Their sense of frustration and ostracism predated and was an essential factor in their departure from accepted professional behavior.

Because the Aryan physics generated by Lenard and Stark in the mid-1930s was an attempt to redress their early personal grievances, it offered nothing of substance to most members of the physics community. In place of the recognized leaders of German physics, the Aryan physicists merely offered themselves as examples of truly German researchers. As substitutes for the achievements of relativity and quantum mechanics, the Nordic physicists had no widely acceptable scientific alternatives. The coalition nature of their movement led to a set of tenets that canceled each other out, so that their only affirmative principle was the introduction of racism into physics.

The contradictions and personal grievances expressed in Aryan physics were of little concern to most German physicists. But the blatant manner in which the Aryan physicists advocated violating the principle that only professional considerations should enter into academic appointments was unacceptable to the overwhelming majority of the physics community. Even though subtle damage had often been inflicted on this rule in the past, professional physicists did not wish to see it abolished.

Undoubtedly part of their opposition to the intrusion of political criteria into professional matters stemmed from a fear of losing their personal prerogatives. But much more was at stake, for the resort to outside authority in scientific matters has far-reaching implications. If the standards for scientific achievement are not controlled by a uniquely competent group of peers sharing essentially similar values, there is no way to avoid the claim that there is not one truth, but many.[4] This was indeed one of the assertions of Aryan physics (although Germanic truth was supposedly higher than Jewish truth).

Such a claim posed, however weakly, a fundamental challenge to the rationale of modern science and had to be met forcefully. Thus Heisenberg, Wien, and Geiger were able to unite physicists of widely varied persuasions in their petition to the Education Ministry. The support Ramsauer received in the German Physical Society during the war years was further evidence of the strong desire of the professionals to protect their discipline from political intrusion. Due to the incoherent nature of the Third Reich, however, no one was ever quite sure who or what represented true National Socialism. Therefore, contention against such radicals as Lenard, Stark and their followers did not automatically mean opposition to the Nazis, a fact pointed out consistently by the professional physicists whenever they sought government support against their Aryan physics rivals.

We thus come to the question raised at the close of chapter 9: To what extent did adherence to professional values constitute opposition to National Socialism? The answer must be that it was not opposition at all. The maintenance of professional values amounted only to the denial of *active* support, not denial of support per se. To combat Lenard and Stark not because they were Nazis, but because they threatened the effectiveness and standards of German science, was professional opposition. But professional opposition to Nazi theory was not the same as political opposition to the Nazi regime, as Himmler clearly recognized when he exonerated Heisenberg. And in an environment like that created by the Third Reich, political opposition is the only opposition worthy of the name.

The obvious question is, therefore, why did the scientists not put up greater resistance to the Nazis? It is not enough to say that their scientific code of behavior precluded political involvement. Why did they not go beyond the bounds of professional behavior and take the risks inherent in political action?

In a postwar letter to his son, von Laue wrestled with the question of resistance on the part of those who stayed. He was particularly disturbed by the attitude of the British and even more strongly disturbed by Americans who maintained to the Germans that they had obviously not performed their duty in resisting Hitler, because they were still alive. Von Laue felt that such logic was nonsense. Open protest had been tantamount to suicide, he argued, and was therefore useless. If there were to be any hope for the German people, it would come through those who acted pragmatically according to the saying "learn to be silent without exploding." It was not easy to do, he admitted, and sometimes he had been too incautious. But it was the ethically correct course of action for those who chose to remain.[5] Coming from a man who rejected even the appearance of compromise, the argument carries some weight.

But the emphasis on practical considerations dissipated the energy needed to oppose the Nazis, leading to what one observer has termed "prudential acquiescence" on the part of the scientists.[6] Although largely accurate, the problem with this phrase is its connotation that the judgments of men like Planck and Heisenberg were little more than excuses for inaction. It implies that they were men of little or no conviction. This was not the case. The truth was not that the scientists were political cowards, but that they did not know how to be political heroes. Their actions were in complete accord with a set of standards we have come to recognize as too narrow. Resistance would have broken their code as effectively as open devotion to the Nazi cause.

The scientists were—to a large extent intentionally—politically naïve when Hitler came to power in 1933. They regarded the Nazis at first as one more form of government with which to have to deal as they continued to serve the state. The spurious notion that service to the state was distinct from service to the government had prevailed since 1919 among large segments of German society. Academia had been one of these, and it could in fact be argued that to some extent the intensity with which scientists turned inward to their work and professional obligations was already a form of "inner emigration" during the Weimar period. Thus the fundamental problem facing Planck, von Laue, Sommerfeld, and Heisenberg as leaders of the physics community was a matter of perception. Nearly as important was the fact that the academic physicists had no political leverage. The engineers, chemists, and even industrial and technical physicists (men like Ludwig Prandtl) could point to the economic or war-related significance of their work. Atomic physics was generally regarded as a subject more akin to science fiction or academic philosophy than practical affairs. This is an important fact obscured by the advent of the atomic bomb and guided missiles. It makes Hitler's alleged response to Planck, "then we will do without science for a few years" more understandable and perhaps even credible.

Given these conditions, the basic choice was to emigrate or to stay. For those who stayed, some form of accommodation would have to be reached with the regime. For many, especially young men like Finkelnburg, it was self-alignment in collaboration with the government or the party. For some, particularly older and prominent men like Planck and Ramsauer, it was a form of prudential acquiescence. For many others it was inner emigration away from political involvement. For a very few it was a form of resistance, as shown by the demonstrative refusal of Hahn and von Laue to compromise and their insistence on doing what they could to counter the persecution of the Jews.

If the pluralism of Nazi authorities made a degree of resistance possible, it was not evident in the physics community. The political naïveté of the physicists led them repeatedly to overestimate the dangers and difficulties involved (from the danger of participation in the Fritz Haber memorial to the difficulty in obtaining matériel and manpower for an atomic bomb). Although a certain amount of professional interests could be pursued by playing the government off against the party, without a concerted plan even a relatively cohesive community such as that of the physicists was baffled. The best that could be accomplished was to avoid the alignment of the German Physical Society and take advantage of the situation when the discovery of nuclear fission and the course of war drew important support from Göring and Speer.

One of the major reasons that Hahn and von Laue were in such a minority was that most scientists seemed to predicate their actions on predictable consequences. This was not a phenomenon limited to scientists, of course, or even to scholars. But how this affected resistance to Hitler has been aptly described by the physicist Leo Szilard:

> I noticed that the Germans always took a utilitarian point of view. They asked, "Well, suppose I would oppose this, what good would I do? I wouldn't do very much good, I would just lose my influence. Then why should I oppose it?" You see, the moral point of view was completely absent, or very weak, and every consideration was simply, what would be the predictable consequence of my action. And on that basis did I reach the conclusion in 1931 that Hitler would get into power, not because the forces of the Nazi revolution were so strong, but rather because I thought that there would be no resistance whatsoever.[7]

His observation is very much to the point. Trying to ascertain predictable consequences is a fundamental principle of scientific research. Often, however, this effort is paralyzing in politics, because the consequences of an action are unforeseeable. In such cases, the sole basis for action must be moral and social responsibility. Von Laue accepted this fact gradually, as Einstein described to Born in 1944:

> We must not allow ourselves to be surprised if the scientists are no exception (in the great majority) and *if* they are different, it is not attributable to intellectual capability but human stature, as in the case of Laue. It was particularly interesting in his case to observe how he tore himself loose step by step from the traditions of the herd under the effect of a strong feeling of justice.[8]

His uncompromising spirit of moral courage made von Laue an important symbol to men like Ewald in Germany and Einstein and Born abroad.

Despite the example of von Laue, the basic reason so few scientists exhibited any evidence of resistance was that their goal of professional autonomy did not demand it of them. They were able to meet threats to their independence on professional grounds, and, given the predictably negative results, few were willing to risk the transition from professional to political opposition.

Most of the scientists under Hitler shied away from the moral repercussions of this fact once they had decided to remain in Germany. Their concern was to deny that their work had political import, which was the major point on which the physics community was united against Lenard and Stark. The striving of Ramsauer and others during the war to regain autonomy for physicists was an escape into professionalism in order to avoid a political reality they could no longer completely ignore.

A major effect of National Socialism upon the German physics community was thus to drive the scientists under Hitler to make an ever stronger affirmation of the political irrelevance of their work. At the same time, they stressed ever more strongly how important their labors were for the war effort. The inherent contradiction was driven home to them not by the Nazi leaders, but by the news that the atomic bomb had been used against the Japanese. It became clear that no longer could scientists claim that pure science was divorced from technology and political power.

To the end, the scientists under Hitler were unable to perceive that it was not the strength of its defenders which kept professional physics from being politically overwhelmed, but the weakness and lack of political adeptness among its assailants. The thought is a healthy reminder that scientists are subject to the same pressures and failings as other men, even though the product of their labors has transformed our world.

Notes

CHAPTER 1

1. American Institute of Physics, Center for History and Philosophy of Physics, Oral History Collection (hereafter cited as AIP), transcript of interview with P. P. Ewald by Charles Weiner, 17 and 24 May 1968, p. 54.

2. Hans Rosenberg, *Bureaucracy, Aristocracy, and Autocracy: The Prussian Experience, 1660–1815* (Cambridge, Mass.: Harvard University Press, 1958), pp. 182–88.

3. Fritz Ringer, *The Decline of the German Mandarins: The German Academic Community, 1890–1933* (Cambridge, Mass.: Harvard University Press, 1969), pp. 86–90.

4. Rosenberg, *Bureaucracy, Aristocracy, and Autocracy,* pp. 183–84.

5. Ringer, *Decline of the German Mandarins,* p. 5.

6. Ibid., pp. 23–24.

7. Joseph Ben-David, *The Scientist's Role in Society: A Comparative Study* (Englewood Cliffs, N.J.: Prentice-Hall, 1971), pp. 117–25.

8. See Frank Pfetsch, "Scientific Organisation and Science Policy in Imperial Germany, 1871–1914: The Foundation of the Imperial Institute of Physics and Technology," *Minerva* 8 (October 1970) : 557–80.

9. See Max Planck, ed., *25 Jahre Kaiser Wilhelm-Gesellschaft zur Förderung der Wissenschaften* (Berlin: Springer, 1936).

10. Ringer, *Decline of the German Mandarins,* pp. 102–03.

11. Ibid., pp. 128–43.

12. Ibid., pp. 213–19.

13. See Paul Forman, "The Environment and Practice of Atomic Physics in Weimar Germany: A Study in the History of Science" (Ph.D. diss., University of California, Berkeley, 1967), pp. 161–68.

14. Paul Forman, "Scientific Internationalism and the Weimar Physicists: The Ideology and Its Manipulation in Germany after World War I," *Isis* 64 (June 1973) : 169–71. In this connection, see also Brigitte Schröder-Gudehus, "Deutsche Wissenschaft und internationale Zusammenarbeit 1914–1928" (Ph.D. diss. University of Geneva, 1966) (Geneva: Dumaret & Golay, 1966), pp. 33–49.

15. See Siegfried Grundmann, "Der deutsche Imperialismus, Einstein und die Relativitätstheorie (1914–1933)," in *Relativitätstheorie und Weltanschauung* (Berlin [East]: VEB Deutscher Verlag der Wissenschaften, 1967), pp. 208–32. On Einstein's travels and the reaction to them, see also Ronald Clark, *Einstein: The Life and Times* (New York and Cleveland: World Publishing Co., 1971), pp. 267–305.

16. Bernhard Breslauer, ed., *Die Zurücksetzung der Juden an den Universitäten Deutschlands* (Berlin: 1914), as cited by Alexander Busch, *Die Geschichte des Privatdozenten,* Göttinger Abhandlungen zur Soziologie, vol. 5 (Stuttgart: F. Enke, 1959), p. 160. See also David L. Preston, "Science, Society

and the German Jews, 1870–1933" (Ph.D. diss., University of Illinois, 1971), pp. 113–24.

17. See Ringer, *Decline of the German Mandarins*, pp. 220–21.

18. The man quoted was the nineteenth-century art critic Julius Langbehn. Fritz Stern, *The Politics of Cultural Despair: A Study in the Rise of the Germanic Ideology*, (Garden City, N.Y.: Doubleday, Anchor Books, 1965), p. 160. For other aspects of antimodern and antirationalist thought in the Weimar period, see Kurt Sontheimer, *Antidemokratisches Denken in der Weimarer Republik: Die politischen Ideen des deutschen Nationalismus zwischen 1918 und 1933* (Munich: Nymphenburger Verlagshandlung, 1962).

19. Paul Forman, "Weimar Culture, Causality and Quantum Theory, 1918–1927: Adaptation by German Physicists and Mathematicians to a Hostile Intellectual Environment," *Historical Studies in the Physical Sciences* 3 (1971) : 7.

20. Constance Reid, *Hilbert* (New York: Springer, 1970), pp. 182–83.

21. George W. Gray, *Education on an International Scale: A History of the International Education Board, 1923–1938* (New York: Harcourt, Brace, 1941), pp. 26, 29–30.

22. Herman Weyl, "Emmy Noether," in *Gesammelte Abhandlungen*, ed. K. Chandrasekharan (Berlin, New York: Springer, 1968), 3 : 444; see also Augusta Dick, *Emmy Noether, 1882–1935*, Supplement 13 to *Elemente der Mathematik* (Basel: Birkhäuser, 1970).

23. Friedrich Hund, "Höhepunkte der Göttinger Physik II," *Physikalische Blätter* 25 (1969) : 210.

24. For an excellent review of Franck's career, see Heinrich Kuhn, "James Franck," *Biographical Memoirs of Fellows of the Royal Society* (hereafter cited as *Biog. Mem. F.R.S.*) (London: Royal Society, 1965), 11 : 53–74.

25. A phrase popularized by Robert Jungk, *Brighter than a Thousand Suns: A Personal History of the Atomic Scientists*, trans. James Cleugh (New York: Harcourt, Brace, 1958), pp. 10–28.

26. Werner Heisenberg, *Der Teil und das Ganze: Gespräche im Umkreis der Atomphysik* (Munich: R. Piper, 1969), p. 90.

27. Alexander Deubner, "Die Physik an der Berliner Universität von 1910 bis 1960," *Wissenschaftliche Zeitschrift der Humboldt Universität zu Berlin* (1959–1960), Beiheft 14, p. 87.

28. Wilhelm Westphal, "Das Physikalische Institut der TU Berlin," *Physikalische Blätter* 11 (1955) : 556.

29. For an overview of Weimar cultural achievements and attitudes, see Peter Gay, *Weimar Culture: The Outsider as Insider* (New York, Evanston: Harper & Row, 1968); also the collection of essays "Germany 1919–1932: The Weimar Culture," in *Social Research*, vol. 39 (Summer 1972).

30. Peter Debye, Wolfgang Pauli, Werner Heisenberg, and Hans Bethe.

31. Max Born, "Sommerfeld als Begründer einer Schule," *Die Naturwissenschaften* 16 (1928) : 1036.

32. Blatant anti-Semitism in academic appointments at Munich caused one Jewish Nobel laureate in chemistry, Richard Willstätter, to resign his professorship there in 1924. See Willstätter, *From My Life*, trans. Lilli S. Hornig (New York, Amsterdam: W. A. Benjamin, 1965), pp. 364–65.

33. Adolf Hitler, *Mein Kampf* 352–354th printing (Munich: Zentralverlag der NSDAP, Frz. Eher Nachf., 1938), pp. 469–70.

34. Ibid., p. 452.

35. Joachim Fest, *The Face of the Third Reich: Portraits of the Nazi Leadership*, trans. Michael Bullock (New York: Random House, Pantheon Books, 1970), p. 250.

36. Edouard Calic, ed., *Ohne Maske: Hitler-Breiting Geheimgespräche* (Frankfurt/Main: Societäts-Verlag, 1968), p. 42.

37. Ibid., p. 113.

38. Ibid., p. 115. Hitler apparently expressed similar news on the manipulation of experts in conversation with the Nazi leader of the Danzig senate. Hermann Rauschning, *Gespräche mit Hitler* (New York: Europa Verlag, 1940), p. 173.

39. See Karl Dietrich Bracher, Wolfgang Sauer, and Gerhard Schulz, *Die nationalsozialistische Machtergreifung: Studien zur Errichtung des totalitären Herrschaftssystems in Deutschland 1933/34* (Cologne: Westdeutscher Verlag, 1960) (hereafter cited as *NS-Machtergreifung*); Bracher, *The German Dictatorship*, trans. Jean Steinberg (New York, Washington, D.C.: Praeger, 1970).

40. On this point, see, for example, Alan Bullock, *Hitler: A Study in Tyranny*, rev. ed. (New York: Harper & Row, 1962), p. 257.

41. Walther Hofer, ed., *Der Nationalsozialismus: Dokumente 1933–1945* (Frankfurt/Main: Fischer Bücherei, 1957), p. 268.

42. Ibid., pp. 28–31.

43. Lucy S. Dawidowicz, *The War against the Jews, 1933–1945* (New York: Holt, Rinehart and Winston, 1975), p. 56.

44. Bracher, Sauer, Schulz, *NS-Machtergreifung*, p. 496.

45. A particularly vivid contemporary account was given by the correspondent for the London *Times*, "Boycott of Jews," *The Times*, London, 3 April 1933, p. 14.

46. See Clark, *Einstein*, pp. 458–62.

47. Grundmann, "Der deutsche Imperialismus, Einstein und die Relativitätstheorie," p. 249. On the Einstein affair see also an earlier East German account, Friedrich Herneck, *Albert Einstein: Ein Leben für Wahrheit, Menschlichkeit und Frieden* (Berlin [East]: Buchverlag der Morgen, 1963), pp. 199–213.

48. Published in Grundmann, "Der deutsche Imperialismus, Einstein und die Relativitätstheorie," p. 249.

49. Ibid., p. 250.

50. Ibid.

51. Printed in Einstein, *Mein Weltbild* (Amsterdam: Querido, 1934), pp. 120–21.

52. Axel Friedrichs, ed., *Die nationalsozialistische Revolution 1933*, vol. 1, *Dokumente der deutschen Politik*, ed. Paul Meier-Benneckenstein, 4th ed. (Berlin: Junker und Dünnhaupt, 1939), p. 167.

53. Walter Strauss, "Das Reichsministerium des Innern und die Judengesetzgebung, Aufzeichnungen von Dr. Bernhard Lösener," *Vierteljahrshefte für Zeitgeschichte* 9 (1961) : 266.

54. For a discussion of the preparation and overall goals of this crucial law, see Hans Mommsen, *Beamtentum im Dritten Reich*, No. 12 of Schriftenreihe der *Vierteljahrshefte für Zeitgeschichte* (Stuttgart: Deutsche Verlags-Anstalt, 1966), pp. 39–61, 151–55. The law itself appeared in the *Reichsgesetzblatt*, I, 175.

55. See the exchange of letters on this subject between von Hindenburg and Hitler in Joachim Remak, ed., *The Nazi Years: A Documentary History* (Englewood Cliffs, N.J.: Prentice-Hall, 1969), pp. 146–48.

56. *Reichsgesetzblatt*, I, 195.

57. *Reichsgestezblatt*, I, 245.

58. With the "Deutsches Beamtengesetz" of 26 January 1937, *Reichsgesetzblatt*, I, 39. See Mommsen, *Beamtentum im Dritten Reich*, pp. 91–123, 203–21.

59. See Raul Hilberg, *The Destruction of the European Jews* (Chicago: Quadrangle, 1967), pp. 45–53; Strauss, "Judengesetzgebung," pp. 272–77; Dawidowicz, *War against the Jews*, pp. 66–69.

60. Hilberg, *The Destruction of the European Jews*, p. 48.

61. Despite flaws, perhaps the best insight into the implementation and overall impact of the dismissal process is provided by Fritz Köhler, "Zur Vertreibung humanistischer Gelehrter 1933/34," *Blätter für deutsche und internationale Politik* 11 (July 1966): 696–707. Also useful for an overview is Helge Pross, "Die geistige Enthauptung Deutschlands: Verluste durch Emigration," in *Nationalsozialismus und die deutsche Universität*, ed. Freie Universität Berlin (Berlin: Walter de Gruyter, 1966), pp. 143–55. A sense of the enormity of the impact of the dismissals on German academic life is provided by the Notgemeinschaft deutscher Wissenschaftler im Ausland, *List of Displaced Scholars* (London: privately printed, 1936; Stockholm: privately printed, 1972).

CHAPTER 2

1. Kuhn, "James Franck," *Biog. Mem. F.R.S.*, p. 57.

2. "Das neue Beamtengesetz, Schluss mit dem Parteibuch-Beamtentum," *Göttinger Tageblatt*, 7 April 1933, p. 1.

3. See chap. 1.

4. Josef Wulf, ed., *Literatur und Dichtung im Dritten Reich: Eine Dokumentation* (Gütersloh: S. Mohn, 1963), pp. 41–42; see also Hans-Wolfgang Strätz, "Die studentische 'Aktion wider den undeutschen Geist' im Frühjahr 1933," *Vierteljahrshefte für Zeitgeschichte* 16 (1968) : 347–72.

5. See the commentary in the *Vossische Zeitung*, "Das neue Studentenrecht," in the evening edition, 13 April 1933, p. 4; Hans Peter Bleuel and Ernst Klinnert, *Der deutsche Student auf dem Weg ins Dritte Reich: Ideologien—Programme—Aktionen, 1918–1935* (Gütersloh: S. Mohn, 1967), pp. 246–47; Wolfgang Zorn, "Student Politics in the Weimar Republic," *Journal of Contemporary History* 5, 1 (1970) : 128–43. On the relationship between the Göttingen NSDAP branch, in which students early played a crucial role, and the larger party organization, see Jeremy Noakes, *The Nazi Party in Lower Saxony, 1921–1933* (London: Oxford University Press, 1971).

6. See the famous listing in the *Manchester Guardian Weekly*, "Nazi 'Purge' of the Universities," 19 May 1933, p. 399.

7. Kuhn, "James Franck," p. 63.

8. Mrs. Elizabeth Lisco and Mrs. Dagmar von Hippel (Franck's daughters) to the author, 19 February 1972.

9. Ibid. Also present was Kurt Hahn, head of the well-known Salem boarding school. Kuhn was at a number of discussions, but does not remember whether he was in the Franck home on this particular evening, Kuhn to Mrs. Lisco, 9 March 1972, quoted in part by Mrs. Lisco to the author, 14 March 1972.

10. Franck to the Preussischer Minister für Wissenschaft, Kunst und Volksbildung, Bernhard Rust, 17 April 1933, Kuratorium der Georg August Universität, Göttingen (hereafter cited as KUG), Akte Franck, p. 94.

11. Mrs. Lisco to the author, 6 March 1972.

12. "Freiwilliger Amtsverzicht Prof. James Francks," Göttinger Zeitung, 18 April 1933. Neither the Göttingen curator's office nor the Franck family has the original document.

13. Ibid.

14. "Professor Franck legt sein Amt nieder," Vossiche Zeitung, Berlin, evening edition, 18 April 1933, p. 7; "Treatment of Jews in Germany, Nobel Prizewinner's Protest," The Times, London, 19 April 1933, p. 11.

15. "Ein Nobelpreisträger legt sein Lehramt nieder," Berliner Tageblatt, morning edition, 19 April 1933, p. 3.

16. Hilsch, tape-recorded interview with the author in Göttingen, 5 May 1971.

17. Mrs. Lisco and Mrs. von Hippel to the author, 19 February 1972.

18. Haber to Franck, February 1931, cited by Mrs. Lisco in letter to the author, 22 March 1972.

19. The selection list also included Hans Geiger and Otto Stern. From letters to Franck cited by Mrs. Lisco to the author, 22 March 1972.

20. Based on a comparison of the signatories in "Der Rücktritt Professor Francks," Göttinger Tageblatt, 24 April 1933, p. 3, with Wilhelm Ebel, Catalogus Professorum Gottingensum, 1734–1962 (Göttingen: Vandenhoek & Ruprecht, 1962). The exception among the physicists and mathematicians was Werner Weber, an assistant to the mathematician Edmund Landau. Weber came from Oldenburg-Birkenfeld, a province near the French border which had a strong National Socialist vote in elections before 1933. Herbert Busemann, tape-recorded interview with the author in Santa Ynez, California, 10 May 1972.

21. "Der Rücktritt Professor Francks," Göttinger Tageblatt, 24 April 1933.

22. "6 Göttinger Professoren beurlaubt: Weitere werden folgen," Göttinger Tageblatt, 26 April 1933, p. 3.

23. Albert Einstein-Hedwig und Max Born, Briefwechsel 1916–1955 (Munich: Nymphenburger Verlagshandlung, 1969), pp. 158–59 (hereafter cited as Einstein-Born-Briefwechsel).

24. Ibid., p. 19; the Einstein-Born friendship was partially founded on mutual opposition to German political aims during the war. Born, My Life and My Views (New York: Charles Scribner's Sons, 1968), p. 29.

25. Lothar Nordheim, tape-recorded interview with the author in La Jolla, California, 15 April 1972.

26. Einstein-Born Briefwechsel, p. 58.

27. Ibid., p. 60. See below, chap. 5.

28. Born to von Kármán, 7 November 1922, California Institute of Tech-

nology Archives (hereafter cited as CIT-Ar), von Kármán Papers, Box 4—Born.

29. Cf. Born to Einstein, 21 October 1921, *Einstein-Born Briefwechsel*, p. 88.

30. Born, *My Life and My Views*, p. 37.

31. *Einstein-Born Briefwechsel*, p. 157.

32. Born to von Kármán, 27 March 1931, CIT-Ar, von Kármán Papers, Box 4 —Born. See also Born to Einstein, 22 February 1931, *Einstein-Born Briefwechsel*, p. 153.

33. *Einstein-Born Briefwechsel*, pp. 155–56.

34. Hund, tape-recorded interview with the author in Göttingen on 26 July 1971.

35. Born to [Justus] Valentiner, 24 May 1933, KUG, Akte Born, p. 132.

36. Born to Einstein, 2 June 1933, *Einstein-Born Briefwechsel*, pp. 162–63.

37. Ibid., p. 164.

38. Ibid., p. 161.

39. Einstein to Born, 30 May 1933, ibid., p.. 159.

40. F[erdinand] Springer to Courant, 19 April 1933. in the private papers of Richard Courant in the possession of his family (hereafter cited as Courant Papers).

41. Courant to H. Kneser, 28 April 1933, Courant Papers.

42. Neugebauer in a tape-recorded interview with Constance Reid, author of *Hilbert*, in Princeton, N.J., on 14 November 1971, the transcript of which Mrs. Reid kindly showed the author. Confirmed in letter from Neugebauer to the author, 5 February 1972. Mrs. Reid's forthcoming biography of Courant should shed more light on this and related matters.

43. Busemann, interview with the author, 10 May 1972.

44. Berlin Document Center (hereafter cited as BDC), Research, Korrespondenz "Wi," Richard Edler von Mises.

45. Courant to Kneser, 28 April 1933, Courant Papers.

46. Ibid.

47. Courant to Kneser, 29 April 1933, Courant Papers.

48. Courant to Flexner, 2 May 1933, Courant Papers.

49. The curator to Courant, 5 May 1933, Courant Papers.

50. Kneser to Courant, 20 May 1933, Courant Papers.

51. E.g., Carl Ludwig Siegel to the Minister für Wissenschaft, Kunst und Volksbildung, 24 May 1933, Courant Papers.

52. "An den Herrn Minister für Wissenschaft, Kunst und Volksbildung," May 1933, Courant Papers. This is a copy of the version of the petition which was circulated to various persons for their signatures. No copy of the petition in its final form (the text was almost certainly left unchanged) is among the Courant Papers or the files of the curator's office in Göttingen.

53. Neugebauer to Friedrichs, 8 June 1933. Courant Papers. According to this letter, the final list of signatories was: Artin, Betz, Bessel-Hagen, Blaschke, Caratheodory, Friedrichs, Hasse, Heisenberg, Herglotz, Hilbert, Hund, Koppenfels, Laue, Maier-Leibnitz, Mie, Neugebauer, Planck, Prandtl, Rellich, Schaffeld, Schauffler, Schrödinger, Seyfarth, Sommerfeld, Straubel, Trefftz, van der Waerden, and Weyl. Jungk mistakenly refers to twenty-two signatories in *Brighter than a Thousand Suns*, p. 35.

54. Courant, "Reminiscences from Hilbert's Göttingen," colloquium given in the Department of History of Science and Medicine, Yale University, 13 January 1964, transcribed from a tape-recording, mimeographed, pp. 19–20.

55. Prandtl to Valentiner, 1 June 1933; Valentiner to Prandtl, 3 June 1933, KUG, Akte Prandtl, pp. 203–04.

56. "Bericht zu den Anträgen des Professor Prandtl, Göttingen, vom 6. Dezember 1934," Deutsche Forschungsgemeinschaft (hereafter cited as DFG), Bad Godesberg, Akte Prandtl. I am indebted to Steffen Richter of the Lehrstuhl für die Geschichte der Naturwissenschaften und Technik in Stuttgart for drawing my attention to this report.

57. "Was ist Göttingen ohne Prandtl?" *Göttinger Tageblatt,* 7 June 1933, p. 1.

58. [Johannes] Weniger, undated reply to memorandum of 11 January 1935, DFG, Akte Prandtl.

59. H. Kneser, K. O. Friedrichs, and L. Prandtl to the Minister für Wissenschaft, Kunst und Volksbildung, 25 June 1933, KUG, Akte Courant, p. 111.

60. Courant to Valentiner, 18 May 1933, KUG, Akte Courant, p. 108.

61. Friedrichs to the author, 24 January 1972.

62. Radio Bremen, *Auszug des Geistes: Bericht über eine Senderreihe* (Bremen: Verlag B. D. Heye, 1962), p. 200.

63. On the financial restriction involved in emigration, see Hilberg, *European Jews,* pp. 90–97.

64. [Johann] Achelis to the curator, 17 October 1933, KUG, Akte Courant, p. 124; Valentiner to Courant, 20 October 1933, Courant Papers.

65. Granted by the Minister für Wissenschaft, Kunst und Volksbildung to Courant, 1 November 1933, Courant Papers.

66. Preussischer Minister für Wissenschaft, Kunst und Volksbildung to Born (through the Göttingen curator), 9 October 1933, KUG, Akte Born, p. 151.

67. Lothar Nordheim to the author, 27 April 1972.

68. Mrs. Lisco and Mrs. von Hippel to the author, 19 February 1972.

69. Nordheim to the author, 16 February 1972. Edward Teller, who was also forced to leave Göttingen at this time, remembers the seminar in Franck's home quite vividly: "It sticks in my mind that one topic which we discussed was the energy level scheme (at very low energies) of the ammonia molecule which later played such a great role in the invention of the maser." Teller to the author, 18 July 1972.

70. Kroebel, "Zum Tode von James Franck," p. 422.

71. Rabinowitch to the author, 8 May 1972.

72. Kuhn to Mrs. Lisco, 9 March 1972, quoted by Mrs. Lisco to the author, 14 March 1972.

73. Mrs. Lisco to the author, 6 March 1972; Helge Pross, "Die geistige Enthauptung Deutschlands: Verluste durch Emigration," in *National-Sozialismus und die deutsche Universität* ed. Freie Universität Berlin (Berlin: W. de Gruyter, 1966), p. 149. See also Horst Widman, *Exil und Bildungshilfe: Die deutschsprachige akademische Emigration in die Türkei nach 1933* (Frankfurt/Main: Peter Lang, 1973).

74. Walter Heitler to the author, 1 February 1972.

75. On Rumer, see *Einstein-Born Briefwechsel*, p. 144; Nordheim, interview with the author, 15 April 1972.

76. [Max] Reich to Nordheim, 28 April 1933, in the private possession of Nordheim.

77. Nordheim to the author, 29 February 1972.

78. Stuckart to Nordheim, 11 September 1933, and Valentiner to Nordheim, 20 September 1933, both in the private possession of Nordheim; Nordheim to the author, 16 February 1972.

79. Teller to the author, 18 July 1972; *Einstein-Born Briefwechsel*, p. 161.

80. Teller to the author, 18 July 1972.

81. Heitler to the author, 22 February 1972.

82. Heckmann to the author, 7 April 1972.

83. Weyl to Paul Epstein, 21 October 1936, CIT-Ar, Epstein Papers, Box 2—Emergency Committee in Aid of Displaced German Scholars; confirmed by Heckmann to the author, n.d. (received 2 June 1972).

84. Stobbe to H. A. Kramers, 2 June 1937 and 18 October 1937 SHQP (10, 12); on Stobbe's death, letter to the author from Steven Siegel, Research Foundation for Jewish Immigration, New York, 25 July 1975.

85. Busemann, interview with the author, 10 May 1972.

86. Lewy to the author, 4 April 1972.

87. Busemann, interview with the author, 10 May 1972.

88. Reid, *Hilbert*, p. 204.

89. Karl F. Herzfeld to "Sehr geehrter Herr Kollege!" 21 February 1934, and Herzfeld to Samuel A. Goudsmit, 23 May and 5 November 1936, all in the private correspondence of Samuel A. Goudsmit in his private possession (hereafter cited as Goudsmit Papers—Correspondence).

90. Reid, *Hilbert*, p. 204.

91. Busemann, interview with the author, 10 May 1972; Courant to von Kármán, 12 November 1933, CIT-Ar, von Kármán Papers, Box 7—Courant.

92. Weniger to A. Gnade, 16 August 1934, Hoover Institution on War, Revolution and Peace in Stanford, California, Nationalsozialistischer Deutscher Dozentenbund, Box 2.

93. Gnade to Weniger, 8 September 1934, and Vahlen to the Notgemeinschaft der deutschen Wissenschaft, 28 August 1934, ibid.

94. Weyl, "Emmy Noether," 3 : 431–32.

95. Ibid., pp. 434–35.

96. Ibid.

97. Reid, *Hilbert*, p. 205; Weyl to Courant, 11 October 1933, Courant Papers.

98. Abraham Adolf Fraenkel, *Lebenskriese: Aus den Erinnerungen eines jüdischen Mathematikers* (Stuttgart: Deutsche Verlags-Anstalt, 1967), p. 165.

99. Busemann, interview with the author, 10 May 1972.

100. Courant to von Kármán, 12 November 1933, CIT-Ar, von Kármán Papers, Box 7—Courant; cf. Emil J. Gumbel, "Arische Naturwissenschaft?" in *Freie Wissenschaft: Ein Sammelbuch der deutschen Emigration*, ed. Emil J. Gumbel (Strasbourg: Sebastian Brant, 1938), pp. 255–56.

101. Reid, *Hilbert*, p. 205.

102. Courant to Valentiner, 6 February 1934, Courant Papers.

103. Courant to H. Hasse, 28 April 1934, Courant Papers.

104. Franz Neumann, "The Social Sciences," in *The Cultural Migration: The European Scholar in America,* ed. Franz Neumann et al. (Philadelphia: University of Pennsylvania Press, 1953), p. 17.

105. Courant to H. Hasse, 28 April 1934, Courant Papers.

106. Courant to the Preussischer Minister für Wissenschaft, Kunst und Volksbildung, 23 June 1934, KUG, Akte Courant, p. 147.

107. Vahlen to Courant, 10 July 1934, Courant Papers; Reichs- und Preussischer Minister für Wissenschaft, Erziehung und Volksbildung to the curator, 12 December 1935, KUG, Akte Courant, p. 174; curator to the Regierungspräsident in Hildesheim, 14 December 1935, KUG, Akte-Courant, p. 172.

108. [Otto] Wolff to Franck, 28 April 1933, and Valentiner to Franck, 15 May 1933, in the Franck family papers, now deposited in the Dept. of Special Collections of the University of Chicago Library (hereafter cited as Franck Papers).

109. Mrs. Lisco to the author, 14 March 1972.

110. Haber to Franck, 15 May 1933, Franck Papers, quoted in Mrs. Lisco to the author, 22 March 1972. See also below, chap. 3.

111. Franck to Valentiner, 22 July 1933, Franck Papers.

112. Mrs. Lisco and Mrs. von Hippel to the author, 19 February 1972.

113. Mrs. Lisco to the author, 6 March 1972.

114. Werner Kroebel, "Zum 70. Geburtstag von James Franck," *Die Naturwissenschaften* 39 (1952) : 386.

115. Werner Kroebel, "Zum Tode von James Franck," *Die Naturwissenschaften* 51 (1964) : 422.

116. [Wilhelm] Stuckart to Franck, 11 December 1933, and 8 February 1934; and Bernhard Rust to Franck, 8 February 1934, all in Franck Papers.

117. Bothe to the Dekan der mathematisch-naturwissenschaftlichen Fakultät, 29 September 1933; Bothe to the Rektor, 25 September 1934, and 8 November 1934, all in the Archiv der Universität Heidelberg (hereafter cited as AUH), Akte Bothe.

118. Reichs- und Preussischer Minister für Wissenschaft, Erziehung und Volksbildung to Joos, 7 May 1935, KUG, Akte Joos.

119. Born to the Minister für Wissenschaft, Kunst und Volksbildung, 10 August 1933, KUG, Akte Born, p. 139.

120. Achelis to Born, 9 October 1933, KUG, Akte Born, p. 151.

121. Wilhelm Westphal, "Das Physikalische Institut der TU Berlin," *Physikalische Blätter* 11 (1955) : 557. Becker felt that his transfer had been a disciplinary measure (*Strafversetzung*). He left Berlin very much against his will and only later accepted the smaller city. Rudolf Hilsch, interview with the author, 5 May 1971; Friedrich Hund, interview with the author, 26 July 1971.

CHAPTER 3

1. Philipp Frank, *Einstein: Sein Leben und seine Zeit* (Munich, Leipzig, Freiburg i. Br.: Paul List, 1949), p. 379. On Nernst, see Kurt Mendelssohn, *The*

World of Walther Nernst: German Science in Triumph and Crisis (Pittsburgh: University of Pittsburgh, 1973).

2. Siegfried Grundmann, "Der deutsche Imperialismus, Einstein und die Relativitätstheorie," pp. 251–52; and Herneck, *Einstein*, p. 204.

3. Grundmann, "Der deutsche Imperialismus, Einstein und die Relativitätstheorie," pp. 251–52.

4. Herneck, *Einstein*, p. 207.

5. Quoted with elipses by Grundmann, "Der deutsche Imperialismus, Einstein und die Relativitätstheorie," p. 252.

6. H. Frühauf, "Max Planck als beständiger Sekretär," in *Max Planck zum Gedenken*, ed. Die deutsche Akademie der Wissenschaften zu Berlin (Berlin: Akademie Verlag, 1959), p. 10.

7. Einstein, *Mein Weltbild*, p. 125.

8. See Morris Goran, *The Story of Fritz Haber* (Norman: University of Oklahoma Press, 1967), pp. 81–82.

9. See the account of Haber's wartime activities by his co-worker Willstätter, *From My Life*, pp. 264–67, 272–73, 279–81.

10. Friedrich Glum, *Zwischen Wissenschaft, Wirtschaft und Politik* (Bonn: Bouvier, 1964), p. 440.

11. Printed in Otto Hahn, "Zur Erinnerung an die Haber Gedächtnisfeier vor 25 Jahren, am 29. Januar 1935, im Harnack-Haus in Berlin-Dahlem," *Mitteilungen der Max Planck–Gesellschaft zur Förderung der Wissenschaften* (1960), pp. 3–4. Hans Kopfermann, a former doctoral student of James Franck in Göttingen, and an assistant (non-Jewish) in Haber's institute from 1924 to 1932, was at Bohr's institute in Copenhagen during 1932–33. After a ten-day trip through Göttingen, Berlin, and Rostock in early May 1933, he reported his impressions to Bohr, who was in America at the time. Kopfermann specifically blamed the loss of Haber, and Haber's co-workers Michael Polanyi and Herbert Freundlich, on the KWG leadership's panic and on Planck's hesitation to return from Sicily. (It was well known that Planck was extremely reluctant to allow business to intrude upon his yearly vacation.) H. Kopfermann to Bohr, 23 May 1933, Archive for History of Quantum Physics-Bohr Scientific Correspondence (22,2) (hereafter cited as BSC). Glum has maintained that he was not even consulted in the Haber affair, because Haber dealt directly with the ministry. Glum, *Zwischen Wissenschaft, Wirtschaft und Politik*, p. 433. On the other hand, von Laue later remarked that he had tried to get Planck to return from Italy on Haber's behalf, but his attempt failed because Glum reported to Planck that the KWG was in no danger. This was true only as far as the central administration was concerned. Max von Laue to his son Theodore H. von Laue, 12 October 1952, in the private possession of Theodore H. von Laue (hereafter cited as von Laue Papers).

12. See below, Chap. 4.

13. Goran, *Fritz Haber*, p. 162.

14. Max Planck, "Mein Besuch bei Hitler," *Physikalische Blätter* 3 (1947): 148. The audience was apparently held in the middle or late part of May, and the fact that it occurred was common knowledge among the Berlin scientific community in mid-June. By the end of July, an account of the confrontation

was circulated among those concerned with refugee affairs in America. Charlotte Schoenberg to R. G. D. Richardson, 27 July 1933 (copy), Library of Congress, Papers of Oswald Veblen (hereafter cited as Veblen Papers).

15. Karl A. Schleunes, *The Twisted Road to Auschwitz: Nazi Policy toward German Jews, 1933–1939* (Urbana, Chicago, London: University of Illinois Press, 1970), p. 78.

16. Edward Y. Hartshorne, *The German Universities and National Socialism* (London: Allen & Unwin, 1937), p. 112.

17. Ibid., p. 93.

18. Ibid.; "Jewish Self-Help," *The Times,* London, 18 April 1934, p. 18. In comparison, see the figures for the changes within the civil service of the state administration in Bracher, Sauer, and Schulz, *NS-Machtergreifung,* pp. 507–08.

19. Hartshorne, *German Universities and National Socialism,* pp. 94–95.

20. These estimates are rough approximations. Figures for the 1931 staff exclusive of assistants are available in Christian von Ferber, *Die Entwicklung des Lehrkörpers der deutschen Universitäten und Hochschulen 1864–1954,* vol. 3, Untersuchungen zur Lage der deutschen Hochschullehrer (Göttingen: Vandenhoeck & Ruprecht, 1956), pp. 211–16: natural science, 1,765; physics, 322; mathematics, 239; chemistry, 542; medicine, 1,897. However, Hartshorne's figures are based on 1932–33, and they include assistants. The percentages here are arrived at by assuming negligible change in the number of personnel between 1931 and 1932–33 and by accepting Hartshorne's contention (pp. 87–88) that assistants comprised approximately one-fifth of the staff of the Hochschulen. Each of von Ferber's figures is thus assumed to equal approximately 80 percent of the actual total staff (i.e., von Ferber's figure = .80 × total). Each of his figures is therefore divided by a factor of .8 and the resulting quotient is divided into Hartshorne's figure to compute a percentage of the total staff dismissed in each field. By this method the figures to one decimal place are: natural science, 18.4 percent; physics, 26.3 percent; mathematics, 20.0 percent; chemistry, 12.7 percent; medicine, 18.2 percent. There is a great need to reinvestigate Hartshorne's sources, carry them beyond 1935, and present them in greater detail. These tasks are presently being carried out in part by the staff of the Research Foundation for Jewish Immigration in New York. Some preliminary work has also been carried out by Charles Weiner of the Massachusetts Institute of Technology and David Sutherland of Ohio University.

21. Sources for History of Quantum Physics in the Archive for History of Quantum Physics (hereafter cited as SHQP), transcript of interview with Gustav Hertz, 14 May 1963, p. 31, and 15 May 1963, p. 6. Cf. Wilhelm Westphal, "Das Physikalische Institute der TU Berlin," *Physikalische Blätter,* 11 (1955) : 556–57; and Hans Ebert, "The Expulsion of the Jews from the Berlin-Charlottenburg Technische Hochschule," *Yearbook of the Leo Baeck Institute* 19 (1974) : 155–71.

22. For Konen's views on politics and learning, see Konen, "Staat und Wissenschaft," in *Volkstum und Kulturpolitik: Eine Sammlung von Aufsätzen,* ed. Konen and J. P. Steffes (Cologne: Gilde, 1932), pp. 168–84.

23. As related by Konen himself, according to Walter Weizel, who was called to Bonn's theoretical physics chair in 1936. Weizel to the author, 28

March 1972. See also Paul E. Kahle, *Bonn University in Pre-Nazi and Nazi Times, 1923-1939* (London: privately printed, 1945), p. 7.

24. Walther Gerlach (who prepared a deposition on Konen's behalf in this affair) to the author, 7 March 1972. On the Nazi tactic of charging corruption as a means of discrediting and intimidating opponents, see, e.g., Eva Lips, *Savage Symphony* (New York: Random House, 1938), pp. 31-34.

25. K. F. Herzfeld to S. A. Goudsmit, 6 November 1935, Goudsmit Papers— Correspondence; and Konen to Sommerfeld, 17 May 1935, SHQP (31,13). Kahle (*Bonn University*, p. 7) reports that Konen was engaged in industry after his dismissal, and the physicist may well have been a consultant to one or more firms.

26. He was considered one-quarter Jewish through one of his grandfathers— the other, also of Jewish descent, had been baptized as a child (*liegend getauft*). Ewald to the author, 14 March 1972 and 27 April 1973.

27. AIP, transcript of interview with Ewald by Charles Weiner, 17 and 24 May 1968, pp. 28-29.

28. Ibid., pp. 31-34, 46. Ewald had warm personal ties to the British. See ibid., p. 46, on his relationship with Sir William Bragg.

29. Ibid., p. 47; Ewald to the author, 27 April 1973.

30. Letter from Delbrück to the author, 31 March 1972.

31. Both Loewi and Hess had to hand over their Nobel prize money in order to exit from Austria. See Ferdinand G. Smekal, *Oesterreichs Nobelpreisträger*, 2d ed. (Vienna: Frick, 1969), pp. 122-23, 132. The writer in *Current Biography Yearbook* (1963) p. 182, indicates that Hess was dismissed "first, because he had a Jewish wife, and secondly, because he had been a representative of the sciences in the independent government of Chancellor Kurt von Schuschnigg. A sympathetic Gestapo officer warned the Hesses that they would be taken to a concentration camp if they stayed in Austria, and they escaped to Switzerland four weeks before the order came for their arrest." The discoverer of cosmic rays took a post later in 1938 at Fordham University in New York.

Schrödinger, as a declared opponent of National Socialism in 1933, had time to take no more than hand luggage with him as he fled Austria in 1938. Schrödinger to the Herrn Dekan der Mathematisch-Naturwissenschaftlichen Fakultät der Universität Berlin, 24 June 1947, SHQP (37,2). See also Walter Heitler, "Erwin Schrödinger," *Biog. Mem. F.R.S.* (1961), 7 : 224. Schrödinger went to Dublin, where he made his seminal contribution to the field of molecular biology with his famous 1943 lectures which were published as *What Is Life?* See Donald Fleming, "Emigré Physicists and the Biological Revolution," in *The Intellectual Migration: Europe and America, 1930-1960*, ed. Donald Fleming and Bernard Bailyn (Cambridge, Mass.: Harvard University Press, 1969), esp. pp. 172-77. This article also contains considerable information on Delbrück, another central figure in molecular biology.

32. Johannes Asen, *Gesamtverzeichnis des Lehrkörpers der Universiät Berlin, 1810-1945* (Leipzig: O. Harrasowitz, 1955), p. 128, indicates Meitner's *venia legendi* was revoked 6 September 1933.

33. The friends included Peter Debye, Dirk Coster, Adriaan Fokker, and W. J. de Haas. Meitner had only an hour and a half to pack and leave Berlin.

Otto Frisch, "Lise Meitner," *Biog. Mem. F.R.S.* (1970), 16 : 410–11. See also Coster to S. A. Goudsmit, 27 June 1938, Goudsmit Papers—Correspondence. The Einstein statement is noted in Herneck, *Einstein*, p. 212.

34. Charles Weiner, "A New Site for the Seminar: The Refugees and American Physics in the Thirties," in *The Intellectual Migration,* ed. Fleming and Bailyn, pp. 190–91.

35. Hartshorne, *The German Universities and the Government* (Chicago: private edition of University of Chicago Libraries, 1938), pp. 13–14.

36. On the basis of the article "Nazi Persecution of Liberals Rises," *New York Times,* 5 March 1934, p. 10, Hartshorne (*German Universities and National Socialism,* p. 100) lists five Nobel winners "who appear to have been dismissed": Meyerhof, Franck, Einstein, Haber, and Hertz. The article was, however, incorrect, since Hertz did not resign his post until 1935, and Meyerhof was not forced from his Heidelberg institute for physiology until 1938. On Meyerhof, see Dorothy Needham, "Prof. Otto Meyerhof, For. Mem. R. S.," *Nature* 168 (24 November 1951) : 895–96.

Hartshorne is usually quite reliable, and his acceptance of the *New York Times* article has led to much confusion and error. A recent example concerning Hertz and Meyerhof is Karl Dietrich Bracher, *The German Dictatorship* (New York: Praeger, 1970), p. 269, where one finds this statement: ". . . outstanding scholars, including numerous Nobel Prize winners (alone in 1933, Otto Meyerhof, James Franck, Albert Einstein, Fritz Haber, Heinrich [*sic*] Hertz), were driven into emigration . . ." Heinrich Hertz was the gifted Jewish physicist who discovered radio waves; he had died in 1894.

37. On the general subject of the entrance of Jews into German academia, see Alexander Busch, *Die Geschichte des Privatdozenten* (Stuttgart: F. Enke, 1959), pp. 148–62. On their entry into the scientific field, see David Preston, "Science, Society and the German Jews, 1870–1933" (Ph.D. diss., University of Illinois, 1971), pp. 113–16, 185–96.

38. Willstätter, for example, often alludes to the vicissitudes of Jewish chemists in German academia. See his references to Adolf von Baeyer's advice to have himself baptized, the disproportionately large number of Jews in the Berlin-Dahlem Kaiser Wilhelm institutes, and his resignation from the university in Munich to protest against anti-Semitism in university appointments. *From My Life,* pp. 83–84, 222, and 360–69.

39. E.g., from 1900 to 1910, the overall increase in positions (exclusive of assistants) was 41 percent in chemistry (254 to 360) and 49 percent in physics (117 to 185). The increase at the universities was only 26 percent in chemistry (175 to 221); however, it was 59 percent in physics (67 to 107). From von Ferber, *Entwicklung des Lehrkörpers der deutschen Universitäten,* p. 197. Different figures for physics only (based on *Minerva* rather than von Ferber's study) are provided in Paul Forman, John L. Heilbron, and Spencer Weart, *Physics circa 1900: Personnel, Funding, and Productivity of the Academic Establishments,* vol. 5 of *Historical Studies in the Physical Sciences,* ed. Russell McCormach (Princeton, N.J.: Princeton University Press, 1975), pp. 12–13.

40. On relative influence in academic appointments in physics in the 1920s, see Forman, "Physics in Weimar," p. 107.

41. An approach to the problem based on the relative weaknesses of the academic barriers to opportunity in various fields is sounder than one ascribing a special cultural heritage of "abstraction" (and hence talent for mathematics and physics) to Jewish scientists. The assertion that Jewish researchers had a predilection for abstract thought, however, and that abstraction was thus somehow "Jewish" in nature, became one of the major tenets of certain Nazi scientists. A discussion of reasons for the high percentage of Jews in theoretical physics has been undertaken by Preston, "Science, Society and the German Jews," pp. 196–209.

42. A few appeared to be stimulated by the change of environment. See Leo Szilard, "Reminiscences," in *The Intellectual Migration,* ed. Fleming and Bailyn, pp. 95–141; cf. also Weiner, "New Site for the Seminar," pp. 220–27.

43. Clark, *Einstein,* p. 526. Otto Frisch was one of those who had to leave Hamburg.

44. Isidor I. Rabi, "Otto Stern, Co-discoverer of Space Quantization, Dies at 81," *Physics Today* 22 (October 1969) : 105.

45. See above, chap. 2.

46. The story of these efforts can be found in Norman Bentwich, *The Rescue and Achievement of Refugee Scholars: The Story of Displaced Scholars and Scientists, 1933–1952* (The Hague: Martinus Nijhoff, 1953); Stephen Duggan and Betty Drury, *The Rescue of Science and Learning: The Story of the Emergency Committee in Aid of Displaced Scholars* (New York: Macmillan, 1948); and Charles J. Wetzel, "The American Rescue of Refugee Scholars and Scientists from Europe, 1933–45" (Ph.D. diss., University of Wisconsin, 1964).

CHAPTER 4

1. Much attention has been given in recent historical literature to the intra-party and party-state power struggles of the Third Reich. Most directly to the point is Peter Diehl-Thiele, *Partei und Staat im Dritten Reich: Untersuchungen zum Verhältnis von NSDAP und allgemeiner innerer Staatsverwaltung 1933–1945,* Münchener Studien zur Politik, vol. 9, ed. Gottfried-Karl Kindermann, Nikolaus Lobkowicz, and Hans Maier (Munich: C. H. Beck, 1969). The best analysis of the impact of this conflict upon higher education is Reece C. Kelly, "National Socialism and German University Teachers: The NSDAP's Efforts To Create a National Socialist Professoriate and Scholarship" (Ph.D. diss., University of Washington, 1973).

2. Hans Schemm, *Hans Schemm spricht: Seine Reden und sein Werk,* ed. G. Kahl-Furthmann (Bayreuth: Gauleitung der Bayerischen Ostmark, 1936), p. 178.

3. Ernst Niekisch, *Das Reich der niederen Dämonen* (Hamburg: Rowohlt, 1953), p. 197.

4. Jeremy Noakes, *The Nazi Party in Lower Saxony, 1921–1933* (London: Oxford University Press, 1971), pp. 46–47, 97–99.

5. Found in Friedrichs, ed., *Die nationalsozialistische Revolution 1933,* pp. 278–85.

6. Ibid., p. 284.

7. Ibid., p. 281.

8. Ibid.

9. Ibid., p. 283.

10. Ibid.

11. Aufgabe der Wissenschaft ist Dienst am Volke," *Völkischer Beobachter,* Munich, 24/25 May 1933, p. 1. Emphasis and indented spacing in the original.

12. Bracher, Sauer, and Schulz, *NS-Machtergreifung,* pp. 568–69.

13. Reichshabilitationsordnung of 13 December 1934. See Bracher, Sauer, Schulz, *NS-Machtergreifung,* pp. 568–69; and Hartshorne, *German Universities and National Socialism,* pp. 103–04. Character-political criteria were also applied to incoming students, whose number was limited by the Ministry of the Interior on 28 December 1933 to 15,000 (compared to 20,000 the year before). For a succinct presentation of the directives affecting entrance and enrollment of students, see Hartshorne, ibid., pp. 72–86, and Hartshorne, "Numerical Changes in the German Student Body," *Nature* 142 (23 July 1938): 175–76. After 15 April 1937, German Jews could no longer obtain a doctorate in Germany, much less go on to qualification and teaching. For the measures affecting Jews specifically, see Albrecht Götz von Olenhusen, "Die 'nichtarischen' Studenten an den deutschen Hochschulen: Zur nationalsozialistischen Rassenpolitik, 1933–1945," *Vierteljahrshefte für Zeitgeschichte* 14 (1966) : 175–206.

14. Bracher, Sauer, Schulz, *NS-Machtergreifung,* p. 569.

15. As has been convincingly argued by Hellmut Seier, "Der Rektor als Führer: Zur Hochschulpolitik des Reichserziehungsministeriums, 1934–1945," *Vierteljahrshefte für Zeitgeschichte* 12 (1964) : 105–46. The ministry did manage to consolidate university finances under its firm control. See Klemens Pleyer, *Die Vermögens– und Personalverwaltung der deutschen Universitäten: Ein Beitrag zum Problemkreis Universität und Staat* (Marburg: N. G. Elwert Verlag, 1955), pp. 146–68.

16. See Hans Maier, "Nationalsozialistische Hochschulpolitik," in *Die deutsche Universität im Dritten Reich: Eine Vortragsreihe der Universität München* (Munich: R. Piper, 1966), pp. 87–88.

17. Hitler's personal backing kept Rust in office despite later attacks. Rosenberg wrote in his diary on 1 January 1940: "The Führer is unhappy, but in memory of the old days does not want to let him [Rust] fall." *Das politische Tagebuch Alfred Rosenbergs aus den Jahren 1934/35 und 1939/40,* ed. Hans-Günther Seraphim (Göttingen, Berlin, Frankfurt/Main: Musterschmidt, 1956), p. 95. See also Helmut Heiber, *Walter Frank und sein Reichsinstitut für die Geschichte des neuen Deutschlands,* vol. 13, Quellen und Darstellungen zur Zeitgeschichte (Stuttgart: Deutsche Verlags-Anstalt, 1966), pp. 641–42; and Peter Hüttenberger, *Die Gauleiter: Studien zum Wandel des Machtgefüges in der NSDAP,* no. 19, Schriftenreihe der *Vierteljahrshefte für Zeitgeschichte* (Stuttgart: Deutsche Verlags-Anstalt, 1969), pp. 15–20, 80.

18. It is noteworthy that the third figure in contention for the post was also an administrator, Dr. Rudolf Buttmann, head of the cultural department of the Reich Ministry of the Interior, who later took over the Bavarian State Library. See Heiber, *Walter Frank,* pp. 162, 641.

19. Ibid., pp. 641–42.

20. Ibid., p. 124. On the bewildering conflict of loyalties within the REM, see ibid., pp. 123–24, 641–53. On relations between the Reich and provincial (*Länder*) ministries, see Rolf Eilers, *Die nationalsozialistische Schulpolitik: Eine Studie zur Funktion der Erziehung im totalitären Staat*, vol. 4, *Staat und Politik*, ed. Ernst Fraenkel, et al. (Cologne and Opladen: Westdeutscher Verlag, 1963), pp. 54–65.

21. Heiber, *Walter Frank*, p. 643.

22. Ibid., pp. 116, 645–46; Glum, *Zwischen Wissenschaft, Wirtschaft und Politik*, pp. 449–51; and Samuel Goudsmit, *Alsos* (New York: Schuman, 1947), pp. 142–45.

23. Heiber, *Walter Frank*, p. 643.

24. E.g., as discussed below in chaps. 6 and 8.

25. Heisenberg, *Der Teil und das Ganze*, p. 174.

26. Frank, *Einstein*, p. 381. See also Joseph Haberer, *Politics and the Community of Science* (New York etc.: Van Nostrand Reinhold, 1969), pp. 128–33.

27. Frühauf, "Max Planck als beständiger Sekretär," p. 7. Although Planck was certainly a patriot, he was not a political chauvinist. His nationalism was rooted in a concept of self-sacrifice and service rather than a desire for Germany to conquer other peoples.

28. Ibid., pp. 7–8. See also Armin Hermann, *Max Planck: In Selbstzeugnissen und Bilddokumenten* (Reinbek bei Hamburg: Rowohlt, 1973), p. 58.

29. Views like Planck's were also held by some emigré scientists. The mathematician Busemann, who emigrated to Copenhagen with Franck and others, has recalled Franck's position on the January 1935 plebiscite in the Saar. If he were a Saar resident, Franck maintained to Busemann, he would vote for reunification with Germany and then emigrate because of his Jewish descent. The territorial plebiscite was a decision of long-lasting consequence, he contended, while the Nazi government was transitory. Busemann, interview with the author, 10 May 1972. Other examples would not be difficult to find.

30. This basic human point is too lightly considered by Haberer in his critique of Planck's leadership during the early Nazi period. Haberer, *Politics and the Community of Science*, pp. 128–33, 164–65.

31. As emphasized in the Kopfermann report, Kopfermann to Bohr, 23 May 1933, BSC (22,2). Planck's central role in events was stressed by another visitor to Berlin at this time. The mathematician Harold Bohr was given the impression that Planck was the only person whose efforts to alleviate the situation might meet with some success. Bohr to R. G. D. Richardson, 30 May 1933 (copy), Veblen Papers.

32. "Tätigkeitsbericht der Kaiser Wilhelm Gesellschaft zur Förderung der Wissenschaften (April 1932 bis Ende März 1933)" (hereafter cited as "Tätigkeitsbericht der KWG"), *Die Naturwissenschaften* 21 (26 May 1933) : 417.

33. Glum, *Zwischen Wissenschaft, Wirtschaft und Politik*, pp. 441–42. The full list is found in "Tätigkeitsbericht der KWG," *Die Naturwissenschaften* 22 (1 June 1934) : 339.

34. Glum, *Zwischen Wissenschaft, Wirtschaft und Politik*, pp. 486–91. For a public exposition of Bosch's views on science and government, see his speech before the Society of German Natural Researchers and Physicians, "93.

Versammlung Deutscher Naturforscher und Aerzte zu Hannover am 16. bis 20. September 1934," *Mitteilungen der Gesellschaft Deutscher Naturforscher und Aerzte* 10, No. 5/6/7 (October 1934) : 21–24.

35. See Peter Debye, "Das Kaiser Wilhelm-Institut für Physik," *Die Naturwissenschaften* 25 (23 April 1937): 257–60; and David Irving, *The Virus House: Germany's Atomic Research and Allied Countermeasures* (London: W. Kimber, 1967), p. 51.

36. "Tätigkeitsbericht der KWG," *Die Naturwissenschaften* 25 (11 June 1937) : 370.

37. "Tätigkeitsbericht der KWG," *Die Naturwissenschaften* 24 (10 January 1936) : 21.

38. "Tätigkeitsbericht der KWG," *Die Naturwissenschaften* 25 (11 June 1937) : 370–71.

39. In early July, Hahn suggested that thirty distinguished German professors make a common protest against the treatment of Jewish colleagues. Planck's response was: "If you bring together thirty such gentlemen today, then tomorrow one hundred and fifty will come out against them because they want to have their positions." Hahn, "Eine persönliche Erinnerung an Max Planck," *Mitteilungen der Max Planck-Gesellschaft zur Förderung der Wissenschaften* 5 (1957) : 244. See also Hahn, *My Life: The Autobiography of a Scientist*, trans. Ernst Kaiser and Eithne Wilkins (New York: Herder and Herder, 1970), p. 145.

40. Born, "Max Karl Ernst Ludwig Planck," *Obituary Notices of the Royal Society* 6 (1948) : 179–80. As late as October, Planck was still trying fruitlessly to get Schrödinger's resignation from the university in Berlin reversed or changed into a leave of absence. Heisenberg to Sommerfeld, 9 October 1933, SHQP (83).

41. Heisenberg, *Der Teil und das Ganze*, pp. 206–12. These memoirs have been criticized as very misleading from a historical standpoint. The sharpest criticism has come from Paul Forman, "*Physics and Beyond* by W. Heisenberg" [the English translation], *Science* 172 (14 May 1971) : 687–88. Considerably milder is Rudolf Peierls, "Atomic Germans," *The New York Review of Books* 16 (1 July 1971) : 23–24. As is nearly always the case with memoirs (and interviews), the criticism is largely justified, and care must be taken in using them.

42. Heisenberg, *Der Teil und das Ganze*, pp. 209–10.

43. Heisenberg often spoke and corresponded with Planck and von Laue during the upheaval of 1933. See Heisenberg to Bohr, 30 June 1933, BSC (20,2). The tone of Heisenberg's reconstruction agrees well with that of a contemporary account of a discussion with Planck on the subject. H. Bohr to R. G. D. Richardson, 30 May 1933 (copy), Veblen Papers.

44. Philipp Frank has captured the tone well in his biography of Einstein: "Max Planck belonged to those German professors who said again and again, 'The new rulers are following a great and noble goal. We academicians, who understand nothing of political business, ought not to make any difficulties for them. Our task is, as much as it is possible, to see to it that in the process as little harshness as possible is suffered by individual scholars, and above all that the level of scholarship in Germany is preserved' " (Frank, *Einstein*, p. 381).

45. Heisenberg, *Der Teil und das Ganze*, pp. 208–09. The stress on the word "catastrophe" by Heisenberg's Planck makes it clear that as Heisenberg wrote

his memoirs, he had not only the academic disaster of 1933 in mind, but also the ultimate calamity of World War II. Similarly, Heisenberg's repeated emphasis on the issue of moral compromise is an indication of how keenly he has felt the concessions he saw as the cost of remaining in Germany. Ibid., pp. 209–12.

46. Some of the younger conservative physicists believed they could temper the radicalism of National Socialism by cooperating with it. A well-known case was Pascual Jordan at the university in Rostock. Jordan, who has served as a conservative member of the West German parliament, has been attacked in the postwar period for his actions. See Gerhard Becherer, "Die Geschichte der Entwicklung des Physikalischen Instituts der Universität Rostock," *Wissenschaftliche Zeitschrift der Universität Rostock, Math.-Naturwiss. Reihe* 16 (1967): 831. Kopfermann reported to Bohr in May 1933 that some younger physicists wanted to try to deradicalize the Nazi movement by joining it; he had just visited Rostock and probably had Jordan in mind. Kopfermann to Bohr, 23 May 1933, BSC (22,2). Jordan's postwar explanation of his actions to Bohr states that this was indeed his aim. Jordan to Bohr, May 1945, BSC (21,3).

47. Kopfermann to Bohr, 23 May 1933, BSC (22,1); also R. Ladenburg to Bohr (concerning a letter from von Laue), 24 May 1933, BSC (17,3).

48. Max von Laue, "Ansprache bei Eröffnung der Physikertagung in Würzburg am 18. September 1933," *Physikalische Zeitschrift* 34 (15 December 1933) : 889–90. The applause was deplored by Johannes Stark in Stark to von Laue, 28 August 1934, Deutsches Museum (in Munich), Sondersammlung 164/6–164.

49. Von Laue, "Fritz Haber," *Die Naturwissenschaften* 22 (16 February 1934) : 97; "Sitzung der Physikalischen Gesellschaft zu Berlin am 9. Februar 1934," *Verhandlungen der Deutschen Physikalischen Gesellschaft* 15 (31 March 1934) : 7–9.

50. Von Laue, "Mein physikalischer Werdegang: Eine Selbstdarstellung," in *Gesammelte Schriften und Vorträge* (Brunswick: Friedrich Vieweg, 1961), 3 : xxvii–xxviii.

51. Ibid., p. xxvi; Theodore H. von Laue (son of the physicist) to the author, 4 February 1972, and tape-recorded interview with the author in Riverside, California, 23 February 1972.

52. E.g., von Laue to S. A. Goudsmit concerning P. P. Ewald, 16 May 1936, Goudsmit Papers-Correspondence. Von Laue also arranged on one of his trips for Ewald's daughter Rose, later Mrs. Hans Bethe, to come to America. Ewald to the author, 23 March 1972.

53. Von Laue, "Arnold Berliner," *Die Naturwissenschaften* 33 (15 November 1946) : 258.

54. P. P. Ewald, "Max von Laue," *Biog. Mem. F.R.S.*, 6 (1960) : 147.

55. P. P. Ewald, "Vor fünfzig Jahren," *Beiträge zur Physik und Chemie des 20. Jahrhunderts*, ed. O. R. Frisch et al. (Brunswick: Friedrich Vieweg, 1959), p. 146. See also interview with Ewald, AIP, p. 54.

56. Von Laue, "Mein physikalischer Werdegang," p. xxx.

57. Clark, *Einstein*, p. 526.

58. This is the understanding of his son. Theodore H. von Laue, interview with the author, 23 February 1972. On the intricacies of how a well-known, conservative scholar could remain independent yet unmolested in Nazi Ger-

many, see Gerhard Ritter, "Der deutsche Professor im 'Dritten Reich,'" *Die Gegenwart* 1 (24 December 1945) : 23–26.

59. Ewald, "Max von Laue, 1879–1960," *Acta Crystallographica* 13 (July 1960) : 515.

60. Ewald to the author, 23 March 1972.

61. Max Bodenstein, "Gedächtnisrede auf Fritz Haber," *Sitzungsberichte der Preussischen Akademie der Wissenschaften: Oeffentliche Sitzung zur Feier des Leibnizischen Jahrestages am 28. Juni 1934* (Berlin: Verlag Akademie der Wissenschaften, 1934), pp. cxx–cxxix.

62. Bundesarchiv Koblenz (hereafter cited as BA), R 43 II/1227a, p. 87. Also printed in Hahn, "Zur Erinnerung an die Haber-Gedächtnisfeier vor 25 Jahren," p. 8.

63. Only Rust's letter is available, Hahn "Zur Erinnerung an die Haber-Gedächtnisfeier vor 25 Jahren," pp. 8–9.

64. Ibid. Meanwhile various organizations, particularly those controlled by autobahn designer Fritz Todt, forbade their members to attend. See ibid., pp. 10–11.

65. Ibid., pp. 12–13. Hahn had relinquished his associate professorship at the university in 1934; Rust's orders thus did not affect him. The staff positions in his institute were funded independently of the civil service.

66. Hahn, *Von Radiothor zur Uranspaltung, Eine wissenschaftliche Selbstbiographie* (Brunswick: Friedrich Vieweg, 1962), p. 94.

67. Haberer, *Politics and the Community of Science*, p. 141.

68. Gerlach to the Philosophische Fakultät, II. Sektion, 24 April 1934, in the private possession of Walther Gerlach (hereafter cited as Gerlach Papers).

69. Gerlach to the Dekannat der Philosophischen Fakultät der Universität, II. Sektion, 22 June 1934, Gerlach Papers.

70. Max Wien, "Die Physik an den deutschen Hochschulen," undated manuscript with a signed cover letter to "Sehr geehrter Herr Kollege!" 19 November 1934, Gerlach Papers.

71. Gerlach to Dr. [Ernst] Hochheim, 7 January 1935; and Pohl to Gerlach, 11 January 1935, both in Gerlach Papers.

72. Pohl to Gerlach, 11 January 1935, Gerlach Papers.

73. Report by Carl Bosch, Berlin, 30 January 1935, Gerlach Papers.

74. Ibid., p. 9. Political criteria for qualification had been introduced during the previous month.

75. Hund, "Göttingen, Kopenhagen, Leipzig in Rückblick," in *Werner Heisenberg und die Physik unserer Zeit,* ed. Fritz Bopp (Brunswick: Friedrich Vieweg, 1961), p. 7.

76. Heisenberg to Bohr, 5 July 1936, BSC (20,2).

77. Compiled from the society's biennial reports in the *Mitteilungen der Gesellschaft Deutscher Naturforscher und Aerzte* (July 1931), p. 8; (February 1933), p. 8; (August 1935), p. 9; (April 1937), p. 14; (February 1939), p. 13.

78. Landé to Epstein, 23 March 1933, CIT-Ar, Epstein Papers, Box 4—Landé.

79. Gerlach (who was serving as an officer of the society at the time) to Goudsmit, 10 February 1936; Goudsmit to Gerlach, 24 June 1936; and the

quote from Goudsmit to Walter Schottky (the treasurer), 17 December 1937, all in Goudsmit Papers–Correspondence.

80. Von Laue to von Kármán, 15 June 1935, CIT-Ar, von Kármán Papers, Box 22—Laue.

81. On the alignment of engineers and technicians under the Nazis, see Karl-Heinz Ludwig, *Technik und Ingenieure im Dritten Reich* (Düsseldorf: Droste, 1974), pp. 109–41. The society's refusal to bow to pressure and remove von Laue from its board caused the resignation of at least one Nazi physicist —Johannes Stark. Stark to the Vorstand der Deutschen Physikalischen Gesellschaft, 26 May 1934, and Zenneck to Stark, 21 June 1934, Zenneck Nachlass, Deutsches Museum, Munich.

82. On 9 December 1938, following the pogrom of 9–10 November, the society announced to its members that "under the compelling prevailing circumstances" membership might have to be withdrawn from Jewish colleagues. The Nazi University Teachers' League (Dozentenbund) thereupon commented sarcastically: "They seem to be very far behind the times in the Ger. Physical Society, and still very devoted to their dear Jews. It is indeed remarkable that membership of Jews can no longer be maintained intact only 'under the compelling prevailing circumstances'!" Informationsdienst der Reichsdozentenführung, series 2, vol. 2 (February 1939), p. 27, in BA, Zsg 3/3629. I am indebted to Reece Kelly of Fort Lewis College, Durango, Colorado, for this information.

83. Berliner to Sommerfeld, 31 October 1933, SHQP (29,8); and more explicitly, Berliner to Sommerfeld, 8 December 1933, Deutsches Museum, Munich, Sommerfeld Nachlass (hereafter cited as Sommerfeld Nachlass).

84. But Berliner vowed that he would never allow a decline in the quality of the journal, which he had founded, in order to maintain its existence. Berliner to Sommerfeld, 15 April 1935, SHQP (29,8). Six months later he was forced to step down as editor because he was Jewish. He sent the mathematician Paul Epstein a card with a simple handwritten message under his name printed "Dr. Arnold Berliner": "had to leave the Nw, his lifelong work, on 13/8 because he had become unbearable for the publisher." Berliner to Epstein, 23 August 1935, CIT-Ar, Epstein Papers, Box 1—Berliner.

85. Otto Blumenthal, editor of the *Mathematische Annalen,* wrote to von Kármán that although he would respect von Kármán's wishes and inform the publisher that von Kármán no longer wished to receive the *Annalen,* he had to request somewhat illogically that von Kármán try to recruit subscribers and contributors for the journal. Very little material was being submitted, and Blumenthal was concerned that the quality of the *Annalen* would suffer. Blumenthal to von Kármán, 3 April 1934, CIT-Ar, von Kármán Papers, Box 3—Blumenthal.

86. "Entschliessung des Vorstandes in Sachen 'Preise der Deutschen Zeitschriften und Bücher,'" *Mitteilungen der Gesellschaft Deutscher Naturforscher und Aerzte* 11, No. 1/2 (March 1935) : 4. It has been noted also that, "One of the main reasons for the boycott of German periodicals (at least in England) was the fact that no fixed yearly price was stated. They appeared in volumes at a given price, but the number of volumes per year was not fixed. This made it impossible for librarians to budget properly. Besides, they were expensive." Ewald to the author, 23 April 1973.

87. See the short but informative account of science in prewar Nazi Germany by Morris Goran, "Swastika Science," *The Nation* 148 (3 June 1939) : 641–43.

88. Cf. Emil J. Gumbel, "Arische Naturwissenschaft?" in *Freie Wissenschaft: Ein Sammelbuch der deutschen Emigration* (Strasbourg: Sebastian Brant, 1938), p. 253.

89. Ewald has recalled that only members of an official delegation led by a REM-designated Führer who agreed to follow the leader's instructions could attend scientific meetings. He attended the Harvard Tercentenary in 1936 on his way back to Germany from Ann Arbor. He did not have permission to do so, however, and therefore was cautious about revealing his identity in Cambridge. Interview with Ewald, AIP, p. 34.

90. "Proscription of *Nature* in Germany," *Nature* 141 (22 January 1938) : 151.

91. Heisenberg to Bohr, 14 June 1938, BSC (20,2).

92. Gerlach report of 18 May 1939, DFG, Akte Gerlach, as quoted by Steffen Richter, *Forschungsförderung in Deutschland 1920–1936: Dargestellt am Beispiel der Notgemeinschaft der Deutschen Wissenschaft und ihrem Wirken für das Fach Physik*, Technikgeschichte in Einzeldarstellungen, no. 23 (Düsseldorf: Verein Deutscher Ingenieure, 1972), p. 58.

93. Heisenberg, *Der Teil und das Ganze*, p. 226.

CHAPTER 5

1. Philipp Lenard, "Erinnerungen eines Naturforschers," unpublished autobiography concluded September 1943, p. 147, Lehrstuhl für die Geschichte der Naturwissenschaften und Technik, Stuttgart.

2. Ibid., pp. 2–3.

3. Ibid., p. 60.

4. Ibid., p. 32.

5. Ibid., pp. 3–4.

6. Ibid., pp. 53–55.

7. Ibid., p. 64. See also Leo Königsberger, *Mein Leben* (Heidelberg: Winter, 1919), p. 207.

8. See Lenard, "Erinnerungen," pp. 52–57, 62–71.

9. Ibid., pp. 70–71.

10. Ibid., pp. 57–59, 61.

11. Ibid., pp. 47–48, 56. Cf. Johannes Stark, "Zur Geschichte der Entdeckung der Röntgenstrahlen," *Physikalische Zeitschrift* 36 (15 April 1935) : 280–83. Lenard did not refer to x-rays as Röntgen-rays, the usual designation in Europe. He called them simply "high frequency rays," Lenard, "Erinnerungen," p. 74. See also the statements of one of Lenard's most able assistants: Carl Ramsauer, *Physik-Technik-Pädagogik: Erfahrungen und Erinnerungen* (Karlsruhe: Braun, 1949), p. 115.

12. Lenard, "Erinnerungen," pp. 91–93.

13. Lord Rayleigh, *The Life of Sir J. J. Thomson* (1942; reprint ed., London: Dawsons of Pall Mall, 1969), pp. 76–114.

14. Lenard, "Erinnerungen," p. 105. On Lenard's scientific activities in Kiel, see Charlotte Schmidt-Schönbeck, *300 Jahre Physik und Astronomie an der*

Kieler Universität (Kiel: F. Hirt, 1965), pp. 112–16. A number of brief passages from Lenard's autobiography are quoted in these pages.

15. Nobel Foundation, ed., *Nobel Lectures: Physics, 1901–1921* (Amsterdam, London, New York: Elsevier, 1964), p. 122.

16. Lenard, "Erinnerungen," pp. 39, 87, 92. Also see Lenard, *Ueber Kathodenstrahlen: Nobel-Vortrag gehalten in öffentlicher Sitzung der Königl. Schwedischen Akademie der Wissenschaften zu Stockholm,* 2d ed. (Berlin and Leipzig: Walter de Gruyter, 1920); and Ludwig Wesch, "Lenards Werk—Vorbild zukünftiger Forschung," *Zeitshrift für die gesamte Naturwissenschaft* 8 (May/June 1942) : 104–06.

17. Lenard, "Erinnerungen," p. 114.

18. Ibid., p. 6.

19. A historical analysis of Lenard's early work is in preparation by Bruce R. Wheaton and is to appear in *Historical Studies in the Physical Sciences,* vol. 9.

20. Karl Freudenberg, tape-recorded interview with the author in Heidelberg, 16 July 1971.

21. Ramsauer, *Physik-Technik-Pädagogik,* p. 108.

22. Robert Pohl, tape-recorded interview with the author in Göttingen, 7 May 1971.

23. Freudenberg, interview with the author, 16 July 1971.

24. George P. Thomson, *J. J. Thomson and the Cavendish Laboratory in His Day* (Garden City, N.Y.: Doubleday, 1965), pp. 169–70.

25. Ramsauer, *Physik-Technik-Pädagogik,* pp. 110–11.

26. Ibid., p. 114.

27. Lenard, "Erinnerungen," pp. 82–83, 95.

28. Ibid., p. 11.

29. Klaus Schwabe, *Wissenschaft und Kriegsmoral: Die deutschen Hochschullehrer und die politischen Grundfragen des Ersten Weltkrieges* (Göttingen, Zurich, Frankfurt/Main: Musterschmidt, 1969), p. 26.

30. Ibid., p. 28; see also Ringer, *Decline of the German Mandarins.*

31. Lenard, *England und Deutschland zur Zeit des grossen Krieges* (Heidelberg: Winter, 1914), p. 5. This pamphlet was reprinted with minor alterations (mostly involving punctuation and emphases) as *Ideelle Kontinentalsperre* (Munich: Frz. Eher, Nachf., 1940).

32. Lenard, *England und Deutschland,* pp. 9, 12.

33. Ibid., p. 15.

34. See text in G. F. Nicolai, *Die Biologie des Krieges* (Zurichi Füssli, 1919), pp. 7–9. For an English translation, see Samuel Harden Church, *The American Verdict on the War: A Reply to the Appeal to the Civilized World of 93 German Professors* (Baltimore: Norman, Remington, 1915), pp. 26–32.

35. SHQP, transcript of interview with Franck, 10 July 1962, p. 2.

36. Ramsauer, *Physik-Technik-Pädagogik,* p. 117.

37. Lenard, "Erinnerungen," p. 7.

38. Ibid., p. 156. A few excerpts (with minor omissions) from this portion of the autobiography have been published in Schmidt-Schönbeck, *300 Jahre Physik,* pp. 117–18.

39. Ibid., pp. 158–59.

40. Clark, *Einstein,* pp. 228–39.

41. Ibid., pp. 180–82. The text of the manifesto is printed in Otto Nathan and Heinz Norden, eds., *Einstein on Peace* (New York: Simon and Schuster, 1960), pp. 4–6. The character of Einstein's internationalism was perhaps most succinctly stated to his Austrian-born colleague Paul Ehrenfest in Leiden (23 August 1915): "Isn't the small group of scholars and intellectuals the only 'fatherland' which is worthy of serious concern to people like ourselves? Should *their* convictions be determined solely by where they happen to live?" Quoted in Martin J. Klein, *Paul Ehrenfest*, vol. 1, *The Making of a Theoretical Physicist* (Amsterdam, London: North Holland Publishing Co., 1970), p. 301.

42. Nathan and Norden, *Einstein on Peace*, pp. 9, 16, 24–26.

43. Einstein to Born, 9 September 1920, *Einstein-Born Briefwechsel*, p. 59.

44. Clark, *Einstein*, p. 256; Frank, *Einstein*, p. 270; von Laue wrote to Sommerfeld, 25 August 1920, that Weyland had identified himself as a profiteer, *Einstein-Sommerfeld Briefwechsel*, ed. Armin Hermann (Basel, Stuttgart: Schwabe, 1968), p. 65.

45. Von Laue to Sommerfeld, 25 August 1920, *Einstein-Sommerfeld Briefwechsel*, p. 65. The article is quoted in Clark, *Einstein*, p. 259.

46. Albert Einstein, "Meine Antwort über die anti-relativitätstheoretische G.m.b.H.," *Berliner Tageblatt*, 27 August 1920, p. 1.

47. Clark, *Einstein*, p. 256.

48. Philipp Lenard, *Ueber Aether und Materie: Vortrag gehalten in der Gesamtsitzung der Heidelberger Akademie der Wissenschaften am 4. Juni 1910* (Heidelberg: Winter, 1911). A recent and balanced presentation of the aether concept is given by Kenneth F. Schaffner, *Nineteenth-Century Aether Theories*, Selected Readings in Physics, ed. D. Ter Har (Oxford, etc.: Pergamon Press, 1972).

49. See Philipp Lenard, *Ueber Relativitätsprinzip, Aether und Gravitation* (Leipzig: S. Hirzel, 1918). Lenard was hardly alone in his desire to defend the aether theory. See Loyd S. Swenson, *The Ethereal Aether: A History of the Michelson–Morely–Miller Aether–Drift Experiments, 1880–1930* (Austin: University of Texas Press, 1972), pp. 185–87, 190–212; also Stanley Goldberg, "In Defense of Ether: The British Response to Einstein's Special Theory of Relativity, 1905–1911," *Historical Studies in the Physical Sciences*, 2 (1970) : 88–125.

50. Lenard, *Ueber Kathodenstrahlen*, p. 99.

51. Lenard to Sommerfeld, 2 September 1920, Sommerfeld Nachlass.

52. Sommerfeld to Einstein, 3 September 1920, and Einstein's reply, 6 September 1920, *Einstein-Sommerfeld Briefwechsel*, pp. 68–69.

53. Sommerfeld to Einstein, 11 September 1920, ibid., p. 71.

54. Lenard to Sommerfeld, 14 September 1920, Sommerfeld Nachlass.

55. Felix Ehrenhaft, "My Experiences with Einstein," unpublished manuscript, p. 3, cited by Clark, *Einstein*, p. 263.

56. Clark, *Einstein*, p. 263; Frank, *Einstein*, p. 275.

57. The following account is from the published record in "Vorträge und Diskussionen von der 86. Naturforscherversammlung in Nautheim vom 19.–25. September 1920," *Physikalische Zeitschrift* 21 (1/15 December 1920) : 666–68.

58. An evident misprint here makes Einstein appear to be both asking and answering the same question, ibid., p. 667.

59. See chap. 9.

60. Ehrenhaft, "My Experiences with Einstein," quoted by Clark, *Einstein*, p. 264.

61. Born's commentary and Einstein to Born, undated, *Einstein-Born Briefwechsel*, pp. 60, 67.

62. Sommerfeld to Mrs. Einstein, 7 October 1920, *Einstein-Sommerfeld Briefwechsel*, p. 72.

63. Frank, *Einstein*, p. 276.

64. Philipp Lenard, *Ueber Relativitätsprinzip, Aether und Gravitation: Mit einem Zusatz betreffend die Nauheimer Diskussion*, 3d ed. (Leipzig: S. Hirzel, 1921), p. 39.

65. The talk was by Leonhard Grebe, "Ueber die Gravitationsverschiebung der Fraunhoferschen Linien," *Physikalische Zeitschrift* 21 (1/15 December 1920) : 662–66.

66. Lenard, *Ueber Relativitätsprinzip, Aether und Gravitation*, 3d ed., pp. 43–44.

67. Philipp Lenard, *Ueber Aether und Uräther: Mit einem Mahnwort an deutsche Naturforscher*, 2d ed. (Leipzig: S. Hirzel, 1922), p. 5.

68. Ibid., pp. 6–7.

69. Ibid., p. 9.

70. Ibid., p. 10.

71. Cf. Clark, *Einstein*, pp. 294–95; Frank; *Einstein*, pp. 308–09; Rudolf Stern, "Fritz Haber: Personal Recollections," *Yearbook of the Leo Baeck Institute* 8 (1963) : 82.

72. Frank, *Einstein*, p. 309.

73. Ibid.

74. Swenson, *The Ethereal Aether*, p. 203.

75. Nobel Foundation, *Nobel Lectures, Physics*, p. 477. The official document read: "independent of the value that may be credited to the relativity and gravitation theory after eventual confirmation, bestows the prize . . ." Gerald Holton, "Einstein, Michelson and the 'Crucial Experiment,' " *Isis* 60 (Summer 1969) : 148. Jeremy Bernstein has argued cogently that a major reason for the wording of the Nobel award—and indeed for the mixed reception of all of Einstein's work—was that it was difficult to fit him into the normal spectrum of scientific achievement. Bernstein, *Einstein*, Modern Masters Series, ed. Frank Kermode (New York: Viking, 1973), pp. 187–90.

76. Lenard, "Wissenschaft, Volk und Rasse," *Volk und Rasse* 9 (May 1934) : 132.

77. Lenard, "Erinnerungen," p. 136, as quoted also in Schmidt-Schönbeck, *300 Jahre Physik*, p. 119.

78. Lenard, "Erinnerungen," pp. 9, 130.

79. Ibid., pp. 84–85.

80. The following account draws upon Ernst Brüche and Hugo Marx, "Der Fall Philipp Lenard—Mensch und 'Politiker,' " *Physikalische Blätter* 23 (1967) : 262–67. There are a number of documents on this incident in the archives of the university in Heidelberg, and Marx apparently drew upon them in preparing his earlier "Der Fall Lenard," *Rhein-Neckar-Zietung*, 20 November 1964.

Marx was the city attorney on duty during the day of the incident and witnessed much of what transpired.

81. Lenard, "Erinnerungen," p. 159.

82. For example, "When one the day of the funeral of the assassinated Jew Rathenau all civil operations were supposed to cease, he [Lenard] instinctively took no notice of this ordinance and placed himself in danger of assault by a Marxist band under Jewish leadership—and very little kept him from being thrown into the Neckar at that time" (Johannes Stark, "Philipp Lenard als deutscher Naturforscher," in *Naturforschung im Aufbruch,* ed. August Becker [Munich: J. F. Lehmanns, 1936], p. 13).

83. Brüche and Marx, "Der Fall Philipp Lenard," p. 265.

84. Lenard, "Erinnerungen," p. 161.

85. Ibid., p. 162.

86. Open letter by August Becker and Ferdinand Schmidt, 11 June 1923, Deutsches Museum, Sondersammlung, Nachlass Lenard, N 9/1. According to Lenard, the number of signatories reached 1,100, "Erinnerungen," p. 162.

87. Cf. Lenard's thank you note for unanimous support from the institute, Lenard to W. Nernst, 2 July 1923, Deutsches Museum, Nachlass Lenard, N 9/1.

88. Lenard, "Erinnerungen," p. 163. Cf. "Demokratische Universitätsjustiz," *Völkischer Beobachter,* 22 August 1923.

89. Lenard and Stark, "Hitlergeist und Wissenschaft," *Grossdeutsche Zeitung,* 8 May 1924, p. 1. The article was reprinted with a few minor errors in Stark, "Philipp Lenard als deutscher Naturforscher," in *Naturforschung im Aufbruch: Reden und Vorträge zur Einweihungsfeier des Philipp Lenard Instituts der Universität Heidelberg am 13. und 14. Dezember 1935,* ed. August Becker (Munich: J. F. Lehmanns, 1936), pp. 14–15; and Stark, same title, in *National-sozialistische Monatshefte* (February 1936), pp. 106–12.

90. Alfred Rosenberg, *Der Mythus des 20. Jahrunderts: Eine Wertung der seelisch-geistigen Gestaltenkämpfe unserer Zeit,* 95th–98th printing (Munich: Hoheneichen, 1936). See also Robert Cecil, *The Myth of the Master Race: Alfred Rosenberg and Nazi Ideology* (New York: Dodd Mead & Co., 1972), pp. 82–104.

91. Lenard, "Erinnerungen," p. 8. The physicist also supported the "Christian" anti-Semitism of Theodor Fritsch (publisher of *Der Hammer*), and—for a time—the Germanic "Christian" faith of Artur Dintner, which fed into the infamous Deutsche Christen movement. On these racist groups, see George L. Mosse, *The Crisis of German Ideology: Intellectual Origins of the Third Reich,* Universal Library (New York: Grosset & Dunlap, 1964), esp. pp. 112–13, 141–44, 306–07.

92. Lenard, "Erinnerungen," p. 137.

93. See Wolfgang Horn, *Führerideologie und Parteiorganisation in der NSDAP (1919–1933)* (Düsseldorf: Droste, 1972), pp. 153–208.

94. Lenard, "Erinnerungen," pp. 157–58; BDC–NSDAP Zentralkartei, Philipp Lenard.

95. Lenard, "Erinnerungen," p. 165.

96. Ibid., p. 166.

97. Karl Wien to his family, 26 May 1925, Wien Family "Chronik, 1914–1928,"

translated and quoted by Forman, "Financial Support and Political Alignment of Physicists in Weimar Germany," *Minerva* 12 (January 1974) : 60.

98. Lenard, "Erinnerungen," p. 157. On the Kampfbund, see Reinhard Bollmus, *Das Amt Rosenberg und seine Gegner: Zum Machtkampf im nationalsozialistischen Herrschaftssystem*, Studien zur Zeitgeschichte, published by the Institut für Zeitgeschichte, Munich (Stuttgart: Deutsche Verlags-Anstalt, 1970), pp. 27–39.

99. Lenard, "Erinnerungen," p. 138. See below, chaps. 8, 9.

100. Wesch, "Lenards Werk," p. 106.

101. SHQP, interview with James Franck, 10 July 1962, p. 13; Ernst Brüche, tape-recorded interview with the author in Mosbach/Baden, 2 July 1971.

102. Lenard, "Erinnerungen," p. 138.

103. See August Becker, "Philipp Lenard und seine Schule," *Zeitschrift für die gesamte Naturwissenschaft* 8 (May/June 1942) : 144. This article (pp. 143–52) gives a complete list of work done by and under Lenard and his assistants from 1887 to 1942. On Lenard's feelings toward Wien, see his congratulations to Wien on the latter's sixtieth birthday, 13 January 1924, part of which is printed in Forman, "The Environment and Practice of Atomic Physics in Weimar Germany," p. 180. On the outlook toward modern physics shared by the two men, see Forman, "Financial Support in Weimar Germany," pp. 57–61.

104. Becker, "Philipp Lenard und seine Schule," p. 144; Lenard, "Erinnerungen," p. 134.

105. Lenard, "Wilhelm Wien," *Völkischer Beobachter*, 12 September 1928, p. 2.

106. On Günther, see Mosse, *The Crisis of German Ideology*, pp. 302–04; and Mosse, ed., *Nazi Culture: Intellectual, Cultural and Social Life in the Third Reich*, trans. Salvator Attanasio et al. (New York: Grosset & Dunlap, 1966), pp. 58–59, 61–65.

107. Lenard, "Erinnerungen," pp. 140–41.

108. See chap. 7.

109. Freudenberg, interview with the author, 16 July 1971.

110. Ibid.

111. Lenard to the Ministerium des Kultus und Unterrichts in Karlsruhe, 1 April 1927, copy, Archiv der Universität Heidelberg (hereafter cited as AUH) —Akte Lenard. Lenard's candidates were, in order: Johannes Stark, Clemens Schaefer (at Breslau, also a conservative in politics and physics), Ernst Gehrcke (at the PTR in Berlin, also a vocal critic of Einstein), Carl Ramsauer, and August Becker. W. Wien, F. Himstedt, and J. Zenneck had joined Lenard in furthering Stark's candidacy. Lenard to the Ministerium des Kultus und Unterrichts in Karlsruhe, 16 April 1927, copy, Zenneck Nachlass, Deutsches Museum, Munich.

112. Freudenberg, interview with the author, 16 July 1971; Geiger to Rutherford, 28 August 1931, Cambridge University Library, Rutherford Collection.

113. Minister des Kultus und Unterrichts to Lenard, 23 September 1931, AUH —Akte Lenard.

114. Minister des Kultus und Unterrichts to Bothe, 14 July 1932, AUH— Akte Bothe.

115. Freudenberg to the rector, 12 February 1946, AUH—Akte Lenard; Freudenberg, interview with the author, 16 July 1971.

116. Becker to the rector, 20 March 1934, and Minister des Kultus und Unterrichts to the rector, 15 June 1935, both in AUH—Akte Becker.

117. Lenard to Adolf Hitler, 21 March 1933, BA, R 43II/936, vol. 1, pp. 23–26.

118. Ibid., p. 25.

119. Staatssekretär in der Reichskanzlei to Lenard, 8 April 1933, BA, R 43II/936, vol. 1, pp. 27–29.

120. Lenard, "Ein grosser Tag für die Naturforschung," Völkischer Beobachter, 13 May 1933, Zweites Beiblatt.

121. Ibid.; Frank, Einstein, p. 376, gives a rough paraphrase of this paragraph of the article.

122. Lenard, "Ein grosser Tag für die Naturforschung."

123. In Johannes Heinsohn, Einstein Dämmerung: Kritische Betrachtungen zur Relativitätstheorie (Leipzig: Otto Hillman, 1933), p. 6.

124. See Peter H. Merkl's analysis of 581 undistinguished Nazis, Political Violence under the Swastika (Princeton, N.J.: Princeton University Press, 1975).

CHAPTER 6

1. Nobel Foundation, Nobel Lectures, Physics, p. 436.

2. Ibid., p. 430.

3. Armin Hermann, "Albert Einstein und Johannes Stark: Briefwechsel und Verhältnis der beiden Nobelpreisträger," Sudhoffs Archiv 50 (September 1966) : 267–85.

4. See Stark, "Elementarquantum der Energie, Modell der negativen und der positiven Elektrizität," Physikalische Zeitschrift 8 (1 December 1907) : 881–84; and Stark, "Zur experimentellen Entscheidung zwischen Aetherwellen- und Lichtquantenhypothese," Physikalische Zeitschrift 10 (22 November 1909) : 902–13. Cf. Max Jammer, Conceptual Development of Quantum Mechanics (New York: McGraw-Hill, 1966), p. 37.

5. H. A. Lorentz, "Alte und neue Fragen der Physik," Physikalische Zeitschrift 11 (15 December 1910) : 1249–50.

6. Hermann, "Einstein und Stark," p. 277.

7. Hermann, "Die frühe Diskussion zwischen Stark und Sommerfeld über die Quantenhypothese," Centaurus 12 (1967) : 40–42.

8. Hermann, "Einstein und Stark," pp. 277–78.

9. Nobel Foundation, Nobel Lectures, Physics, p. 436.

10. SHQP, interview with Franck, 10 July 1962, p. 12.

11. Original article by Einstein: "Thermodynamische Begründung des photochemischen Aequivalentgesetzes," Annalen der Physik 37 (26 March 1912) : 832–38; and "Nachtrag zu meiner Arbeit: 'Thermodynamische Begründung des photochemischen Aequivalentgesetzes,'" Annalen der Physik 38 (12 July 1912) : 881–84. Stark's claim: "Ueber die Anwendung des Planckschen Elementargesetzes auf photochemische Prozesse: Bemerkung zu einer Mitteilung des Hrn. Einstein," Annalen der Physik 38 (23 May 1912) : 468–69.

12. Einstein: "Antwort auf eine Bemerkung von J. Stark: 'Ueber eine Anwendung des Planckschen Elementargesetzes,'" *Annalen der Physik* 38 (12 July 1912) : 888. Stark: "Antwort an Hrn. A. Einstein," *Annalen der Physik* 39 (24 September 1912) : 496.

13. For example, with Paschen and Lunkenheimer, see Hermann, "Einstein und Stark," p. 279; and with Sommerfeld, see Hermann, "Diskussion zwischen Stark und Sommerfeld," pp. 45–53, and Stark and Wilhelm Müller, *Jüdische und deutsche Physik, Vorträge zur Eröffnung des Kolloquiums für theoretische Physik an der Universität München* (Leipzig: Helingsche Verlagsanstalt, 1941), pp. 53–54.

14. Stark to [Max] Iklé, 22 February 1915, Lehrstuhl für die Geschichte der Naturwissenschaften und Technik, Stuttgart, Akte Stark (hereafter cited as Akte Stark, Stuttgart).

15. Hermann, "Diskussion zwischen Stark und Sommerfeld," p. 53.

16. See Jammer, *Conceptual Development of Quantum Mechanics,* pp. 106–09.

17. Nobel Foundation, *Nobel Lectures, Physics,* pp. 434–35.

18. Stark, "Zur Kritik der Bohrschen Theorie der Lichtemission," *Jahrbuch der Radioaktivität und Elektronik* 17 (23 December 1920) : 172.

19. See Jammer, *Conceptual Development of Quantum Mechanics,* pp. 266, 279–80.

20. Stark, "Zur physikalischen Kritik von Schrödingers Theorie der Lichtemission," *Annalen der Physik* 1 (7 May 1929) : 1009–40.

21. The lack of response to his critique was interpreted differently by Stark in a pamphlet written after World War II: "In a detailed discussion (Ann. d. Phys.), I presented the physical impossibility of this theory in the interpretation represented by Sommerfeld. Sommerfeld could provide no factual answer to my factual critique." Stark, *Zur Auseinandersetzung zwischen der pragmatischen und der dogmatischen Physik* (Eppenstatt bei Traunstein, Upper Bavaria: privately printed, 1949), pp. 4–5.

22. This group included, of course, Lenard, as well as many of the Imperial Institute of Physics and Technology staff (such as Ernst Gehrcke), members of Clemens Schaefer's physics institute in Breslau, and others. Schaefer wrote Stark specifically that his entire institute was enormously pleased by Stark's "slaughter" of Sommerfeld. Schaefer to Stark, 20 October 1930, Staatsbibliothek Preussischer Kulturbesitz (hereafter cited as StBPK), Nachlass Stark, quoted in Paul Forman, "Financial Support and Political Alignment of Physicists in Weimar," p. 60.

23. See Becker, *Gedanken zur Hochschulreform* (Leipzig: Quelle & Meyer, 1919). The mixed fate of this reform plan is discussed in Forman, "Physics in Weimar," pp. 60–63.

24. Stark, *Die Organisation der akademischen Kreise* (Greifswald: privately printed, 1919), pp. 6–7. A copy is included in Akte Stark, Stuttgart.

25. Stark, *Das alte und das neue Berufungsverfahren* (Greifswald: privately printed, 1919), pp. 14–22. Also available in Akte Stark, Stuttgart.

26. See "Zur Gründung der Deutschen Gesellschaft für technischen Physik,"

Zeitschrift für technische Physik 1 (1920) : 4–6; Forman, "Physics in Weimar," pp. 143–44.

27. Forman, "The Helmholtz-Gesellschaft: Support of Academic Physical Research by German Industry after the First World War" (unpublished manuscript generously made available to me by Forman), p. 246. The letter from Wien to Stark, 28 January 1920, is found in StBPK, Nachlass Stark.

28. Sommerfeld to Lenard, 7 May 1920; Lenard to Sommerfeld, 2 September 1920; and Stark to Sommerfeld, 10 June 1920, all in Sommerfeld Nachlass.

29. Stark to Sommerfeld, 10 June 1920, Sommerfeld Nachlass.

30. Stark to Sommerfeld, 23 July 1920, ibid. Others receiving votes were M. Born, A. Bestelmeyer, and W. König (each 13); W. Hallwachs, F. Himstedt, and R. W. Pohl (each 12); and F. Krüger (10). Bestelmeyer to Stark, 9 July 1920 (StBPK, Nachless Stark), cited by Forman, "Helmholtz Gesellschaft," pp. 246, 255. The radical nature of Stark's concept of a professional organization is revealed by the fact that Born would not only join, but also receive some votes in such a conservative-dominated venture.

31. Stark to Sommerfeld, 23 July 1920, Sommerfeld Nachlass.

32. For Wien's views on relativity, see Wien, *Die Relativitätstheorie vom Standpunkt der Physik und Erkenntnislehre* (Leipzig: J. A. Barth, 1921).

33. "Geschäftssitzung der Deutschen Physikalischen Gesellschaft in Bad Nauheim am 21. September 1920," *Verhandlungen der Deutschen Physikalischen Gesellschaft* 1 (31 December 1920) : 84–86.

34. Born to Felix Klein, 21 November 1920 (Universitätsbibliothek Göttingen, Handschriftenabteilung, Nachlass Klein), quoted in Steffen Richter, *Forschungsförderung in Deutschland, 1920–1936: Dargestellt am Beispiel der Notgemeinschaft der Deutschen Wissenschaft und ihrem Wirken für das Fach Physik*, no. 23, Technikgeschichte in Einzeldarstellungen (Düsseldorf: Verein Deutscher Ingenieure, 1972), p. 14.

35. Forman, "Helmholtz-Gesellschaft," pp. 36–39, 46–49.

36. Kurt Zierold, *Forschungsförderung in drei Epochen, Deutsche Forschungsgemeinschaft—Geschichte, Arbeitsweise, Kommentar* (Wiesbaden: Franz Steiner, 1968), pp. 8–13.

37. Forman, "Helmholtz-Gesellschaft," pp. 39–40, 119–21.

38. As it turned out, the role of the Helmholtz Society in support of German physics became decreasingly important. It experienced a brief resurgence in the late 1930s, as the physicists in the organization regained the control of the fund-dispensing mechanisms they had lost to the applied scientists in the early 1920s. Ibid., pp. 118–66, 190–200.

39. Stark, *Die gegenwärtige Krisis in der deutschen Physik* (Leipzig: J. A. Barth, 1922), p. 28. Ironically, this interest in technology was quite likely inspired by a suggestion from Sommerfeld. See Sommerfeld to Stark, n.d. [February 1909], Hermann, "Diskussion zwischen Stark und Sommerfeld," 42–43.

40. Forman, "Helmholtz-Gesellschaft," pp. 248–49.

41. See, for example, Stark, *Die physikalisch-technische Untersuchung keramischer Kaoline* (Leipzig: J. A. Barth, 1922).

42. Stark, *Die gegenwärtige Krisis*, p. 28.

43. Sommerfeld to the Rektorat der Universität München, 26 July 1937, Archiv der Universität München (hereafter cited as AUM), Akte Sommerfeld, E II–N, 121–22.

44. Stark, *Zur Auseinandersetzung zwischen der pragmatischen und dogmatischen Physik*, pp. 7–8.

45. Stark, *Die gegenwärtige Krisis*, p. 28.

46. Walther Gerlach, tape-recorded interview with the author in Munich, 8 July 1971.

47. Ludwig Glaser, "Lebenslauf," private papers of the mechanic Karl Selmayr in A. Sommerfeld's Institute for Theoretical Physics in Munich, presently in the possession of the author (hereafter cited as Selmayr Papers). The date of Glaser's qualification was 27 June 1921.

48. The exact date and circumstances of Stark's departure from Würzburg are not clear. It is possible that he submitted his resignation in the fall of 1921, but that it did not become effective until the spring of 1922. In the *Führerlexikon 1934/35*, for which entries were solicited from those persons listed, one finds under Stark's name: "1920–22 Prof. at the University Würzburg, spring 1922 voluntary withdrawal from teaching position." During the Nazi years, it was claimed that Stark was dismissed because of his stand against Einstein. This seems unlikely, for he did not come out against Einstein until the summer of 1922. Georg Rost of Würzburg explained in a letter to Sommerfeld in 1940 that Stark's and Glaser's records were reviewed by the party Dozentenführer of Bavaria in 1937 to verify Stark's claim, and that it was clearly established that opposition to Einstein played no role in the fact that Stark "was dismissed [*entlassen*] from the Bavarian civil service." Rost to Sommerfeld, 4–6 June 1940, Sommerfeld Nachlass. The documents available today in the Würzburg archive shed no light on the matter, the Würzburg archivist (Prof. P. Baumgart) to the author, 20 September 1973.

49. Stark to the Reichsministerium des Innern, 6 June 1922, Deutsches Museum, Sondersammlung 1942/5. Nernst solicited letters of support from his colleagues, e.g., Planck to Nernst, 23 June 1922, ibid., 1942/6. Wien, however, indicated that he was not pleased with the manner in which the appointment had been effected, even though he had no quarrel with Nernst personally. His letter implied that he would have preferred a less theoretically oriented scientist as PTR president. Wien to Nernst, 28 June 1922, ibid., 1942/5.

50. Stark, *Die gegenwärtige Krisis*, pp. 20–23.

51. Ibid., p. 27.

52. Ibid., p. 31.

53. Sommerfeld to Stark, 18 February 1929, Sommerfeld Nachlass.

54. Dekanat der philosophischen Fakultät der Universität München to the Akademischen Senat der Universität München, 15 November 1928, copy, Sommerfeld Nachlass.

55. The Berlin faculty records are in East Germany, but a brief excerpt from this report appears in Werner Haberditzl, "Der Widerstand deutscher Naturwissenschaftler gegen die 'deutsche Physik' und andere faschistische Zerrbilder der Wissenschaft," in *Naturwissenschaft, Tradition, Fortschrittt*, Beiheft zur

Zeitschrift NTM (Berlin [East]: VEB Deutscher Verlag der Wissenschaften, 1963), p. 321.

56. Lenard to the Ministerium des Kultus und Unterrichts in Karlsruhe, 1 April 1927, copy, AUH—Akte Lenard. See above, chap. 5.

57. Stark to Sommerfeld, 7 December 1927, Sommerfeld Nachlass.

58. Stark to Ludwig Glaser, 6 March 1928, Sommerfeld Nachlass.

59. Stark, *Adolf Hitler und die deutsche Forschung* (Berlin: Pass & Garleb, 1934), p. 8.

60. Lenard, "Johannes Stark zum 70. Geburtstag," *Völkischer Beobachter*, Munich, 15 April 1944, p. 4. On the joint declaration of allegiance to Hitler, see above, chap. 5.

61. Stark, *Adolf Hitler*, p. 8.

62. BDC-NSDAP Zentralkartei, Johannes Stark.

63. Stark was an active speaker and political agitator in the Upper Bavarian area near his estate. Stark to the Zentralamt des Obersten Gerichtes der N.S.D.A.P., 1 July 1936, BDC-Oberstes Partei-Gericht, Johannes Stark, pp. 14–17, esp. pp. 14–15.

64. See Stark, *Adolf Hitlers Ziele und Persönlichkeit* (Munich: Deutscher Volksverlag, 1930); *Nationalsozialismus und katholische Kirche* (Munich: Zentralverlag der NSDAP, Frz. Eher, Nachf., 1931); *Zentrumspolitik und Jesuitenpolitik* (Munich: Zentralverlag der NSDAP, Frz. Eher, Nachf., 1932); *Nationalsozialismus und Lehrerbildung* (Munich: Zentralverlag der NSDAP, Frz. Eher, Nachf., 1931); *Nationale Erziehung* (Munich: Zentralverlag der NSDAP, Frz. Eher, Nachf., 1932); *Der Kapitalexport und seine Rückwirkung auf das Kapitalausführende Land: An Hand der englischen Entwicklung untersucht* (Leipzig: Deutsche wissenschaftliche Buchhandlung, 1932). In spite of the last title here, Stark never subscribed to the Anglophobia which afflicted Lenard. In 1931, for example, he nominated Rutherford for the Nobel prize in physics. Stark to the Nobelkomitee für Physik, 18 January 1931, Cambridge University Library, Rutherford Collection.

65. "Bemerkung zu 'J. Stark: Zu den Kämpfen in der Physik während der Hitler–Zeit,'" *Physikalische Blätter* 3 (1947) : 272. The answer of Niels Bohr to a query about Stark was probably typical of the response of the scientists consulted: it was difficult to judge Stark, because his work lay in a direction so divorced from the future development of physics; yet hopefully theoretical work would continue at the PTR if Stark were to become president. Bohr to Paschen, 18 April 1933, BSC (24,2).

66. Stark, "Organisation der physikalischen Forschung," *Zeitschrift für technische Physik* 14 (1933) : 433–35. The Verein Deutscher Ingenieure (VDI, Union of German Engineers) wanted very much to expand the PTR to exploit the wave of spending anticipated with the advent of the Nazi government. C. Matschoss to Zenneck, 30 January 1933, and Frick to the Reichskommissar für Arbeitsbeschaffung, copy, 7 February 1933, both in Zenneck Nachlass, Deutsches Museum, Munich. On the VDI under Gottfried Feder at this time, see Karl-Heinz Ludwig, *Technik und Ingenieure im Dritten Reich* (Düsseldorf: Droste, 1974), pp. 73–90, 96–118.

67. Otto Scherzer, "Physik im totalitären Staat," in *Deutsches Geistesleben und National Sozialismus: Eine Vortragsreihe der Universität Tübingen,* ed. Andreas Flitner (Tübingen: Rainer Wunderlich, 1965), pp. 52–53; Ernst Brüche, tape-recorded interview with the author in Mosbach/Baden, 2 July 1971; von Laue, "Bemerkungen zu 'J. Stark,' " p. 272.

68. See above, chap. 4.

69. Von Laue, "Bemerkungen zu 'J. Stark,' " p. 272.

70. Ibid., pp. 272–73. Cf. H. Frühauf, "Max Planck als beständiger Sekretär," p. 10. (Two days after this speech, von Laue was dismissed as a consultant to the PTR, von Laue, "Bermerkungen zu 'J. Stark,' " p. 272.)

71. Stark, "International Status and Obligations of Science," *Nature* 133 (24 February 1934) : 290.

72. Stark, "The Attitude of the German Government Toward Science," *Nature* 133 (21 April 1934) : 614. Stark even wrote to Rutherford about the *Nature* article, indicating that he spoke for the majority of German scholars. Germans understood when the English scientists welcomed Jews who had "withdrawn" (*zurückgezogen*) from Germany, he explained, but found it incomprehensible that a scholarly journal would take a stand on the internal affairs of another country. Stark to Rutherford, 28 February 1934, Cambridge University Library, Rutherford Collection. Stark also expounded at length on scientific internationalism and freedom of research in more racist terms in a pamphlet intended for domestic consumption: *Nationalsozialismus und Wissenschaft* (Munich: Zentralverlag der NSDAP, Frz. Eher, Nachf., 1934). See below, chap. 7.

73. Von Laue to A. V. Hill, 6 June 1934, Deutsches Museum, Sondersammlung, 1964/6–163. Even von Laue was cautious not to send this anti-Stark letter through the mail. A Dutch colleague who purposely remained ignorant of its contents carried it out of Germany for him. Adriaan Fokker to Hill, 8 June 1934, Deutsches Museum, Sondersammlung, 164/6–163.

74. Stark to Hitler, Bundesarchiv Koblenz, Rep. 43 II/1227a, pp. 61, 63, 65.

75. On 29 June 1934, Stark was reported to have said in a speech: "Now that a Reich Ministry for Learning, Education, and Volksbildung has been created, the organization of scholarship and research can be planned and quickly carried out under the leadership of Reich Minister Rust. As soon as the transfer of the cultural-political department from the Reich Ministry of the Interior to the Reich Ministry of Education was administratively completed at the end of last week, Mr. Reich Minister Rust immediately laid down the guidelines for the organization of research in his ministry—next to a department for higher education a special department for research and technology will be organized in the new ministry." "Reichsregierung und wissenschaftliche Forschung: Eine neue technisch–physikalische Reichsanstalt in München," *Bayerische Staatszeitung,* 29 June 1934, p. 5. On the organization of the REM, see above, chap. 4.

76. Schmidt-Ott, *Erlebtes und Erstrebtes, 1860–1950* (Wiesbaden: Franz Steiner, 1952), p. 293; Zierold, *Forschungsförderung in drei Epochen,* pp. 154, 157.

77. Helmut Heiber, *Walter Frank und sein Reichsinstitut für die Geschichte*

des neuen Deutschlands, vol. 13, Quellen und Darstellungen zur Zeitgeschichte (Stuttgart: Deutsche Verlags-Anstalt, 1966), p. 796. Stark apparently planned to use his new office to further the establishment of a second PTR in Munich, "Reichsregierung," *Bayerische Staatszeitung,* 29 June 1934, p. 5.

78. Quoted in Zierold, *Forschungsförderung in drei Epochen,* p. 173.

79. Ibid., pp. 176–77. The Bavarian Academy reply: "As outstanding as the achievements of President Prof. Dr. Johannes Stark are in his special field, he is still relatively one-sided even in that field. We can not therefore expect that he will possess the overview which is indispensable for a president of the Emergency Association in its extraordinarily manifold tasks and which his predecessor possessed in such unusually great measure." Ibid. Von Laue had written to Schmidt-Ott a month earlier that he and the majority of German physicists regretted to see him leave the association. Von Laue continued: "Under the present circumstances the change in the presidency will also, I fear, form the prelude to difficult times for German scholarship, and physics will probably have to suffer the first and hardest blow." Von Laue to Schmidt-Ott, 27 June 1934, in Armin Hermann, "50 Jahre Forschungsförderung der DFG," *Physik in unserer Zeit* 2 (January 1971) : 20.

80. Stark to Nernst, n.d., Deutsches Museum, Sondersammlung, 1946/7; Stark to Heisenberg, 14 August 1934, in the private possession of Werner Heisenberg (hereafter cited as Heisenberg Papers).

81. Nernst to Stark, 13 August 1934, and Stark to Nernst, 21 August 1934, Deutsches Museum, Sondersammlung, 1946/7; Stark to von Laue, copy, 21 August 1934, Deutsches Museum, Sondersammlung, 1964/6–164; Stark to Heisenberg, 21 August 1934, Heisenberg Papers. Von Laue wrote to Richard von Mises, a prominent Berlin mathematician who had been forced to emigrate, that he, Planck, and Nernst had all refused Stark's request to sign the public declaration. He added that in some ways the physicists were better off than the mathematicians, ". . . for we do not take the threat of Robusti [i.e., Stark] too seriously. He also has opponents in the party and among the ministers. He would have been disposed of long ago if he did not have the personal support of Hitler. It is at least good that now as president of the Emergency Association he is bringing *all* the scholars down upon his head. As he does, we will let him fend for himself." Von Laue to von Mises, 7 September 1934, Harvard University Archives, von Mises Papers, Box 2. Von Laue's understanding of Stark's political weaknesses was accurate, but his perception of Stark as an irritant rather than a threat was to alter after Lenard and Stark launched their Aryan physics campaign at the end of 1935.

82. See chap. 4. Rosenberg titled himself, on the basis of a directive by Hitler on 24 January 1934, the Beauftragte des Führers für die Ueberwachung der gesamten geistigen und weltanschaulichen Schulung und Erziehung der NSDAP (Representative of the Führer for the Supervision of the Entire Spiritual and Weltanschauliche Schooling and Education of the NSDAP). This title was carried over to his staff, and since it was as cumbersome in German as it is in English the usual designation was simply Amt Rosenberg (Rosenberg office).

83. Stark, "Zu den Kämpfen in der Physik während der Hitler-Zeit," *Physikalische Blätter* 3 (1947) : 271; Heiber, *Walter Frank,* p. 809.

84. Heiber, *Walter Frank*, p. 644. See also above, chap. 4.

85. Stark, *Adolf Hitler und die deutsche Forschung*, pp. 13–23, esp. pp. 20–22.

86. The speech is printed in Stark, ibid., pp. 7–11. See also Zierold, *Forschungsförderung in drei Epochen*, p. 184.

87. Stark, "Zu den Kämpfen in der Physik," p. 271.

88. The proposal is printed in Zierold, *Forschungsförderung in drei Epochen*, pp. 194–97.

89. Stark to Lammers, 21 February 1935, printed in ibid., pp. 198–99.

90. Lenard to Hitler, 23 February 1935: "The old faithful one [*Getreue*] warns very much against Rust's Research Academy and asks urgently for postponement of the decision. Letter follows." BA, Rep 43 II/1227a, p. 165. This and a portion of Hess's objections in Zierold, *Forschungsförderung in drei Epochen*, p. 199.

91. Stark's proposal in Zierold, *Forschungsförderung in drei Epochen*, pp. 200–05; see also Heiber, *Walter Frank*, p. 811.

92. Heiber, *Walter Frank*, p. 813 (see BA, R 43 II/1227a, pp. 97–99, 103). On Rosenberg's support from Research Association funds, see Reinhard Bollmus, *Das Amt Rosenberg und seine Gegner, Zum Machtkampf im nationalsozialistischen Herrschaftssystem*, Studien zur Zeitgeschichte (Stuttgart: Deutsche Verlags-Anstalt, 1970), pp. 70–71; and Zierold, *Forschungsförderung in drei Epochen*, p. 188.

93. The Research Association received 4.4 million marks instead of the 19.2 million requested for 1935. In 1936, it was given only 2 million. Zierold, *Forschungsförderung in drei Epochen*, p. 180. Half of the 1935 and 1936 funds were under the administrative control of the REM, Heiber, *Walter Frank*, p. 813.

94. Heiber, *Walter Frank*, pp. 587, 779–80.

95. On Frank's article, "Die graue Eminenz der Notgemeinschaft, auf dem Wege zum 30. Januar der Wissenschaft," *Westfälische Landeszeitung*, 19 June 1936, see Heiber, *Walter Frank*, pp. 822–27.

96. Ibid., pp. 806–07, 838–42; Bollmus, *Amt Rosenberg*, p. 96.

97. "Unterredung mit Präsident Professor Stark von der Deutschen Forschungsgemeinschaft, 22.9.36–12.30," Aktennotiz by Karl T. Weigel 22 September 1936; Strobel to Reischle, 23 September 1936, both in BDC-Research, Ahnenerbe: Karl T. Weigel; and Reischle to Himmler, 24 September 1936, BDC-Research, Ahnenerbe: Johannes Stark.

98. Some hundred pages of documents relating to this affair are in BDC-Oberstes Partei-Gericht, Johannes Stark. Cf. Heiber, *Walter Frank*, pp. 843–44.

99. Schneider to Hess, 16 November 1937, BDC-Oberstes Partei-Gericht, Stark, p. 95.

100. Heiber, *Walter Frank*, pp. 845–46.

101. Zierold, *Forschungsförderung in drei Epochen*, p. 212.

102. See Merkl, *Political Violence under the Swastika*, pp. 311–82, 446–97.

CHAPTER 7

1. Lenard, *Grosse Naturforscher, Eine Geschichte der Naturforschung in Lebensbeschreibungen,* 2d ed. (Munich: J. F. Lehmanns, 1930), p. 7. References are to this expanded edition unless otherwise indicated. The word *Naturforscher* is normally translated as "scientist." But the Aryan physics adherents deliberately contrasted this older word with the newer term *Naturwissenschaftler* (also translated as "scientist"), in order to indicate that they placed emphasis on experimental research *(Forschung)* rather than intellectual knowledge *(Wissen).* "Naturforscher" is thus translated as "natural researcher" here.

2. See above, chap. 5.

3. In a speech in Munich on 7 November 1934, Rosenberg, *Gestaltung der Idee, Blut und Ehre,* vol. 2, *Reden und Aufsätze von 1933–1935,* ed. Thilo von Trotha (Munich: Zentralverlag der NSDAP, Frz. Eher, Nachf., 1936), pp. 200–01.

4. Lenard, *Grosse Naturforscher,* pp. 17–18.

5. See above, chap. 5. For Chamberlain's explanation of the Jewish-Catholic suppression of Germanic science, see Chamberlain, *Die Grundlagen des neunzehnten Jahrhunderts,* 2d ed. (Munich: F. Bruckmann, 1900), pp. 762–63.

6. See Lenard's introductory remarks on the pictures, *Grosse Naturforscher,* p. 9. This reason for the illustrations was also stressed in Lenard, "Gedanken zu deutscher Naturwissenschaft," *Volk im Werden* 4 (1936) : 383–85.

7. Cf. *Grosse Naturforscher,* 2d ed., pp. 315–16, with the 6th ed. (1943), p. 330.

8. *Grosse Naturforscher,* 2d ed., p. 318. An overview of Hasenöhrl's work in the field of relativity is presented in Lewis Pyenson, "The Göttingen Reception of Einstein's General Theory of Relativity" (Ph.D. diss., Johns Hopkins University, 1973), pp. 112–17. The attempt to divorce Einstein's name and ideas from the results of his theories was not new to Lenard with *Grosse Naturforscher.* This approach had been foreshadowed by apologists for relativity as early as the 1920 Nauheim debate (see above, chap. 5). In 1921, Lenard introduced Hasenöhrl's name in a preface to a hundred-year-old paper by Johann Georg von Soldner dealing with stellar displacement in a gravitational field. He claimed the paper showed that one could account for such displacement without recourse to relativity theory or new conceptions of space or time, as Hasenöhrl had done. J. Soldner, "Ueber die Ablenkung eines Lichtstrahls von seiner geradlinigen Bewegung durch die Attraktion eines Weltkörpers, an welchem er nahe vorbeigeht," *Annalen der Physik* 65 (1921) : 593–604. Lenard's introduction (20 July 1921) is found on pp. 593–600.

9. E.g., Leon Poliakov and Josef Wulf, eds., *Das Dritte Reich und seine Denker: Dokumente* (Berlin-Grunewald: Arani Verlag, 1959), pp. 294, 297 (a misprint here lists item IV incorrectly; it comes from *Deutsche Physik,* vol, 1, p. ix). Also George L. Mosse, *Nazi Culture* (New York: Grosset & Dunlap, 1966), pp. 201–05; Remak, *The Nazi Years,* pp. 59–60.

10. Lenard, *Deutsche Physik,* vol. 1, *Einleitung und Mechanik* (Munich: J. F. Lehmanns, 1936), p. ix. (Vols. 1–3 were published in 1936; vol. 4 in 1937.)

11. Lenard, "Vergangenheit und Zukunft deutscher Forschung," in *Naturfor-*

schung im Aufbruch: Reden und Vorträge zur Einweihungsfeier des Philipp Lenard Instituts der Universität Heidelberg am 13. und 14. Dezember 1935, ed. August Becker, (Munich: J. F. Lehmanns, 1936), p. 25.

12. Lenard, *Deutsche Physik,* 1 : 4.

13. Stark, *Nationalsozialismus und Wissenschaft* (Munich: Zentralverlag der NSDAP, Frz. Eher, Nachf., 1934), pp. 17–18. Cf. above, chap. 6.

14. Stark and Müller, *Jüdische und deutsche Physik,* pp. 21–56.

15. "Rede des Herrn Minister des Kultus und Unterrichts Dr. Wacker," in Becker, *Naturforschung im Aufbruch,* p. 7.

16. The speakers were, in order: August Becker (Lenard's pupil and head of the institute), Wacker, Stark, F. Kreuzer (student leader), Lenard. On the second day: Becker, Lothar Tirala (professor of medicine in Munich), Wolfgang Schulz (professor of philosophy in Heidelberg), Ernst Krieck (professor of philosophy in Heidelberg, who spoke on Nazi educational ideals), J. Stein (director of a Heidelberg university clinic), A. Seybold (director of the botanical institute in Heidelberg), Hans Rukop (head of Telefunken in Berlin, who gave a talk on advances in television technology), Rudolf Tomaschek (a Lenard pupil, professor of physics at the TH Dresden at the time), Alfons Bühl (a Lenard pupil, professor of physics at the TH Karlsruhe).

17. Cf. Daniel Gasman, *The Scientific Origins of National Socialism: Social Darwinism in Ernst Haeckel and the German Monist League,* History of Science Library, ed. Michael A. Hoskin (London: MacDonald, 1971; New York: American Elsevier, 1971), esp. pp. 161–63. This book is particularly pertinent since some of Lenard's views rather closely paralleled those of the Monists.

18. Lenard, *Deutsche Physik,* 1 : 12. Hitler, too, believed that great discoveries were the work of great men (whom he termed "persons" as opposed to individuals). Hitler, *Mein Kampf,* pp. 495–96.

19. Lenard, *Grosse Naturforscher,* pp. 92–93. Concerning Newton's outlook on matter and spirit, see Frank E. Manuel, *A Portrait of Isaac Newton* (Cambridge, Mass.: Harvard University Press, 1968).

20. Lenard, *Ueber Aether und Uräther: Mit einem Mahnwort an deutsche Naturforscher,* 2d ed. (Leipzig: S. Hirzel, 1922).

21. For a detailed study of the aether, see Edmund T. Whittaker, *A History of the Theories of Aether and Electricity,* 2 vols. (New York: Philosophical Library, 1951–54). A more recent overview is Schaffner, *Nineteenth-Century Aether Theories.*

22. Lenard, *Deutsche Physik,* vol. 3, *Optik, Elektrostatik und Anfänge der Elektrodynamik,* p. 7. Since the presentation in *Deutsche Physik* was Lenard's last word on the subject, it will be discussed here. On the point in the text, however, cf. *Ueber Aether und Uräther,* esp. pp. 23–24.

23. Lenard, *Deutsche Physik,* vol. 4, *Magnetismus, Elektrodynamik und Anfänge von Weiterem,* p. 266.

24. See Swenson, *The Ethereal Aether.*

25. Tomaschek, "Die Entwicklung der Aethervorstellung," in Becker, *Naturforschung im Aufbruch,* p. 73. Tomaschek quoted from the following passage: "also among us a reaction is now and then aroused against the too one-sided predominance of a purely mechanical interpretation of nature; but let transitory

currents not lead us astray. We must of necessity come back again and again to mechanism, and as long as the German rules, he will force this view of his upon the non-Germans also. I am not speaking of theories. . . . I can in no way bring myself to regard the mechanical as a theory and thus as belonging to 'scholarship': I believe rather that I must conceive of it much more as a discovery, as a firmly established fact." Chamberlain, *Die Grundlagen des neunzehnten Jahrhunderts,* pp. 775–76.

26. Tomaschek, "Die Entwicklung der Aethervorstellung," p. 73.

27. Lenard, *Deutsche Physik,* 1 : 12.

28. Clark, *Einstein,* pp. 338–47, discusses Einstein's attitude toward quantum mechanics, but he is at his best when presenting nontechnical issues. Better discussions are found in Martin J. Klein, "Einstein and the Wave-Particle Duality," *The American Natural Philosopher* 3 (1964) : 1–49; and Bernstein, *Einstein,* pp. 191–206, 215–21. On the Soviet reaction to Heisenberg's ideas, see David Joravsky, *Soviet Marxism and Natural Science, 1917–1932* (New York: Columbia University Press, 1961), p. 293. For a recent Marxist discussion of materialism and modern physics, see Herbert Hörz, *Physik und Weltanschauung: Standpunkte der marxistischen Philosophie zur Entwicklung der Physik* (Leipzig, etc.: Urania Verlag, 1968). Also useful is Loren R. Graham, *Science and Philosophy in the Soviet Union* (New York: Knopf, 1972), pp. 69–110.

29. See Stark, *Die Axialität der Lichtemission und Atomstruktur* (Berlin: A. Seydel, 1927); *Atomstruktur und Atombindung* (Berlin: A. Seydel, 1928); *Fortschritte und Probleme der Atomforschung* (Leipzig: J. A. Barth, 1931); *Erfahrungen und Theorien über Licht und Elektron* (Traunstein, Upper Bavaria: Stifel, n.d. [ca. 1950]). For a statement on the axial atom mixed with political terms, see Stark, "Experimentelle Fortschritte der Atomforschung," *Zeitschrift für die gesamte Naturwissenschaft* 4 (November 1938) : 289–313.

30. "More important to us in the scientific realm is the presentation of the Heisenberg 'uncertainty theory' than the pseudo-scientific, because superficial, so-called relativity theory of the communist Einstein" (Wilfrid Bade, *Kulturpolitische Aufgabe der deutschen Presse* [Berlin: Junker und Dünnhaupt, 1933], p. 30).

31. Pascual Jordan, *Die Physik des 20. Jahrhunderts: Einführung in den Gedankeninhalt der modernen Physik* (Brunswick: Friedrich Vieweg, 1936).

32. For the emergent evolutionist position, see the argument by the American zoologist Herbert S. Jennings, *The Biological Basis of Human Nature* (New York: Norton, 1930), esp. pp. 371–72. For a critique of this view, see William McDougall, *Modern Materialism and Emergent Evolution,* 2d ed. (London: Meuthen, 1934), pp. 109–39. For a more recent and broader overview of critical naturalism, see Harry Girvetz et al., *Science, Folklore and Philosophy* (New York and London: Harper & Row, 1966), pp. 346–65.

33. Gerald Holton, "Einstein, Michelson and the 'Crucial' Experiment," *Isis* 60 (Summer 1969) : 147.

34. Lenard, *Deutsche Physik,* 1 : xiii.

35. The student was Ilse Rosenthal-Schneider. Gerald Holton, "Mach, Einstein, and the Search for Reality," *Daedalus* 97 (Spring 1968) : 653. Another example involves Max Born. The negative results of the Michelson-Morely

experiments were widely thought to be the basis for Einstein's development of
relativity, even though this idea has since been refuted (see Holton, "Einstein,
Michelson and the 'Crucial' Experiment"). Thus the announcement of a positive result by Dayton Miller, president of the American Physical Society, was
a serious challenge to the theory (see Swenson, *The Ethereal Aether*, pp. 190–
212). Yet when he heard of the American work, Born only scoffed, "The Michelson experiment is one of those things which are 'practically' *a priori;* I do not
believe a word of the rumor." Born to Einstein, 6 August 1922, *Einstein-Born
Briefwechsel*, p. 106. The feeling of superiority among theoreticians in the
1920s and some of its social implications have been discussed by Forman, "Physics in Weimar," pp. 132–37.

36. Lenard, *Deutsche Physik,* 1 : 5–7.

37. Ibid., 1 : xii; Lenard, *Grosse Naturforscher,* p. 91. It is noteworthy that
Goethe's antipathy toward Newton was one of the reasons why Goethe was
seldom mentioned by the Nordic physics adherents, even though he appealed
to them on other points. See, for example, A. Seybold, "Die Gemeinschaftsarbeit
physikalischer und biologischer Forschung—eine Aufgabe der deutschen Wissenschaft!" in Becker, *Naturforschung im Aufbruch*, pp. 55–60. For a recent exposition of the role of abstraction and experience in Goethe's thoughts on science,
see "Das Naturbild Goethes und die technisch-naturwissenschaftliche Welt,"
Werner Heisenberg, *Schritte über Grenzen: Gesammelte Reden und Aufsätze*
(Munich: R. Piper, 1971), pp. 243–62.

38. Lenard, *Deutsche Physik,* 1 : ix.

39. See, for example, Hitler, *Mein Kampf,* pp. 317–33.

40. Lothar Tirala, "Nordische Rasse und Naturwissenschaft," in Becker,
Naturforschung im Aufbruch, p. 31; and Tomaschek, "Die Entwicklung der
Aethervorstellung," p. 73. Cf. Lenard, *Deutsche Physik,* 1 : ix.

41. Chamberlain, *Die Grundlagen des neunzehnten Jahrhunderts*, p. 786.
Quoted by Tomaschek, "Die Entwicklung der Aethervorstellung," p. 73.

42. Tirala, "Nordische Rasse und Naturwissenschaft," p. 32.

43. Ibid., p. 30.

44. Lenard, *Deutsche Physik,* 1 : ix–x.

45. Ibid., p. 7.

46. Bühl, "Die Physik an den deutschen Hochschulen," in Becker, *Naturforschung im Aufbruch*, p. 79.

47. Wolfgang Schulz, "Deutsche Physik und nordisches Ermessen," in Becker,
Naturforschung im Aufbruch, pp. 46–48.

48. Stark, *Nationalsozialismus und Wissenschaft,* p. 11.

49. Ibid., and Lenard, *Deutsche Physik,* 1 : x.

50. Stark, *Nationalsozialismus und Wissenschaft,* p. 11.

51. Lenard, *Deutsche Physik,* 1 : x–xii.

52. See above, chap. 5.

53. See above, chap. 6.

54. Stark, *Nationalsozialismus und Wissenschaft,* pp. 12–13.

55. Stark, "The Pragmatic and the Dogmatic Spirit in Physics," *Nature* 141
(30 April 1938) : 770–72; Stark, "Physikalische Wirklichkeit und dogmatische
Atomtheorien," *Physikalische Zeitschrift* 39 (1 March 1938) : 189–92; the argu-

ment is most succinctly presented in Stark and Müller, *Jüdische und deutsche Physik*, pp. 22–25. Tomaschek also stressed the notion of dogma among Jewish physicists, "Die Entwicklung der Aethervorstellung," pp. 72–74.

56. See Hitler, *Mein Kampf*, pp. 120, 124, 129, 200, 371.

57. Rauschning, *Gespräche mit Hitler*, pp. 210–11.

58. Bühl, "Die Physik an den deutschen Hochschulen," p. 80.

59. Named specifically in this connection by Lenard, *Deutsche Physik*, 1 : 3, 11.

60. Stark, "Philipp Lenard als deutscher Naturforscher," in Becker, *Naturforschung im Aufbruch*, p. 13. "Red" meant the color of the Socialist party; "black," that of the Catholic Center party.

61. Bühl, "Die Physik an den deutschen Hochschulen," p. 80; and Lenard, *Deutsche Physik*, 1 : ix. Lenard also referred to a physics of the Arabs and the Japanese. No mention was made anywhere of the Slavic scientists.

62. Lenard, *Deutsche Physik*, 1 : ix.

63. E.g., Stark, *Nationalsozialismus und Wissenschaft*, p. 10.

64. See below, chap. 9.

65. On romanticism and National Socialism, see Peter Viereck, *Meta-politics: The Roots of the Nazi Mind*, rev. ed. (New York: Capricorn Books, 1965), pp. 16–47. Viereck also gives considerable space to Rosenberg, whose views contained many elements of romanticism. On this subject, see also the introduction in Robert Pois, ed., *Race and Race History and Other Essays by Alfred Rosenberg* (New York, etc.: Harper & Row, 1970), pp. 17–20; and Cecil, *The Myth of the Master Race*.

66. See Joseph Ben-David, *The Scientist's Role in Society*, pp. 111–14. Cf. Stern, *The Politics of Cultural Despair*; Ringer, *Decline of the German Mandarins*, pp. 83–90; See above, chap. 1.

67. Lenard, "Erinnerungen eines Naturforschers," unpublished autobiography concluded September 1943, p. 159.

68. Lenard, *Deutsche Physik*, 1 : 13.

69. Lenard, *Ueber Aether und Uräther*, p. 10.

70. Lenard, "Ein grosser Tag für die Naturforschung," *Völkischer Beobachter*, 13 May 1933, Zweites Beiblatt. Cf. above, chap. 5.

71. Stark, *Nationalsozialismus und Wissenschaft*, pp. 15–16.

72. Rosenberg, *Der Mythus des 20. Jahrhunderts*, pp. 142–43; Rosenberg, *Gestaltung der Idee*, pp. 322–23; Hitler, *Mein Kampf*, pp. 314–16.

73. Rosenberg, *Weltanschauung und Wissenschaft*, Heft 6 of Nationalsozialistische Wissenschaft, Schriftenreihe der NS-Monatshefte (Munich: Frz. Eher, 1937), p. 6.

74. Hitler, *Mein Kampf*, p. 314.

75. Stark, *Nationalsozialismus und Wissenschaft*, pp. 16–17.

76. Stark, "Philipp Lenard als deutscher Naturforscher," pp. 11–12.

77. Hans Rukop, "Physikalische Probleme in der Wissenchaft und in der Industrie," in Becker, *Naturforschung im Aufbruch*, pp. 11–12.

78. Stark, *Adolf Hitler und die deutsche Forschung*, p. 22.

79. See above, chap. 6.

80. August Becker, *Naturerkenntnis und Wehrkraft: Experimentalvortrag*

gehalten im grossen Hörsaal des Philipp-Lenard-Instituts am 2. Juni 1940, Heft
4 of Kriegsvorträge der Universität Heidelberg (Heidelberg: Winter, 1940),
p. 15.

81. See Goldberg, "In Defense of Ether," pp. 88–125.

82. David Schoenbaum, *Hitler's Social Revolution: Class and Status in Germany, 1933–1945* (Garden City, N.Y.: Doubleday, Anchor Books, 1967), p. 288.

CHAPTER 8

1. See above, chap. 7.

2. Lenard, "Vergangenheit und Zukunft deutscher Forschung," pp. 24–25.

3. Lenard to Rosenberg, 9 January 1936, in Poliakov and Wulf, eds., *Das Dritte Reich und seine Denker,* pp. 295–96.

4. Becker, as a matter of fact, did not join the party until 1940. Vogt joined in 1931, Bühl in May 1933, Tomaschek in 1937, BDC-NSDAP Zentralkartei. Becker was the eldest of the group (b. 1879), had qualified under Lenard at Kiel in 1905, transferred with his mentor to Heidelberg in 1907, had become extraordinary professor for theoretical physics there in 1914, had served as acting institute director 1931–32 and 1934–35, and had become full professor of experimental physics and director of the physical (Philipp Lenard) institute in 1935. Dismissed during the de-Nazification process of 1945–46, he petitioned for retirement in 1946, claiming he had never been a convinced Nazi. He believed in the primacy of experiment, but did not share Lenard's racist views in physics. His error, he wrote, was that he had been too weak to free himself from Lenard's influence throughout his life. He had only joined the party under pressure. Petition of August Becker, 10 March 1946, AUH, Akte Becker. Judging by the impressions others had of Becker, this self-appraisal was quite accurate. See SHQP interview with James Franck, 10 July 1962, p. 13; Karl Freudenberg, interview with the author, 16 July 1971.

5. Willi Menzel, "Deutsche Physik und jüdische Physik," *Völkischer Beobachter,* Berlin, 29 January 1936, p. 5.

6. Heisenberg, tape-recorded intervew with the author in Munich, 13 July 1971.

7. Heisenberg's "conceptual system" is an excellent expression for one meaning of the word "paradigm" as initially used by Thomas Kuhn. Kuhn later introduced the term "disciplinary matrix" for this meaning, in order to denote a set of conceptions shared by the members of a given scientific discipline. Thomas Kuhn, *The Structure of Scientific Revolutions,* 2d ed. (Chicago and London: University of Chicago Press, 1970), pp. 182–87.

8. Heisenberg, "Zum Artikel 'Deutsche und jüdische Physik,'" *Völkischer Beobachter,* Berlin, 28 February 1936, p. 6.

9. Stark, "Stellungnahme von Prof. Dr. J. Stark," *Völkischer Beobachter,* Berlin, 28 February 1936, p. 6.

10. E.g., two articles by Christian J. Hansen, "Kant und die deutsche Naturwissenschaft," *Völkischer Beobachter,* Berlin, 11 March 1936, p. 5; and "Intellektualistische Wissenschaft," *Völkischer Beobachter,* Berlin, 14 March 1936, p. 5.

11. Stark, "Philipp Lenard als deutscher Naturforscher," *Nationalsozialistische Monatshefte,* Heft 71 (February 1936) : 109.

12. Lenard, "Vergangenheit und Zukunft deutscher Forschung," p. 25.

13. See Hans Buchheim, "The SS—Instrument of Domination," in Helmut Krausnick, et al., *Anatomy of the SS State,* trans. Richard Barry et al. (New York: Walker & Co., 1968), pp. 153–62.

14. F. Kreuzer (leader of the Heidelberg student corps), "Lehrer und Student," in Becker, *Naturforschung im Aufbruch,* p. 17.

15. See Fritz Kubach, "Studenten in Front!" *Deutsche Mathematik* 1 (1936) : 5–8. Other mathematicians connected with the Aryan mathematics effort included Erhard Tornier (Berlin), Oswald Teichmüller (Göttingen), Max Steck (Munich) and Werner Weber (Berlin). Cf. "Deutsche Mathematik," *Nature* 137 (11 April 1936) : 596–97. A detailed study of the effort to delineate an Aryan mathematics is presently being conducted by Sanford Segal of the University of Rochester.

16. Bruno Thüring, "Deutscher Geist in der exakten Naturwissenschaft," *Deutsche Mathematik* 1 (1936) : 10–11.

17. Reichsfachgruppe Naturwissenschaft des Nationalsozialistischen Deutschen Studentenbund (NSDStB). See Thüring, "Kepler-Newton-Einstein—ein Vergleich," *Deutsche Mathematik* 1 (1936) : 706–11; Becker, "Das Philipp Lenard-Institut," *Deutsche Mathematik* 1 (1936) : 703–04; Bühl, "Naturwissenschaft und Weltanschauung," *Deutsche Mathematik* 2 (1937) : 3–5.

18. Fritz Frey, et al., *Philipp Lenard der deutsche Naturforscher: Sein Kampf um nordische Forschung,* published by the authority of the Reich Student Leader (Munich: J. F. Lehmanns, 1937), pp. 3, 5. For Kubach's praise of Aryan physics, see, e.g., his review of *Deutsche Physik* in *Deutsche Mathematik* 1 1936), p. 52.

19. Ludwig Wesch, "Philipp Lenard—Vorbild und Verpflichtung," *Zeitschrift für die gesamte Naturwissenschaft* 3 (May/June 1937) : 42–44. See also in this issue, Thüring, "Physik und Astronomie in jüdischen Händen," pp. 55–70.

20. *Der Parteitag der Ehre vom 8. bis 14. September 1936, Offizieller Bericht über d. Verlauf d. Reichsparteitages m. sämtl. Kongressreden* (Munich: F. Eher, 1936), p. 32.

21. Rust to Hitler, 3 February 1936, BA, R 43 II/1227, pp. 15–16.

22. Staatsekretär u. Chef der Reichskanzlei Heinrich Lammers to Rust, 8 February 1936, BA R 43 II/1227, p. 17.

23. Bernhard Rust and Ernst Krieck, *Das nationalsozialistische Deutschland und die Wissenschaft* (Hamburg: Hanseatische Verlagsanstalt, 1936), p. 22. Rust's emphasis.

24. One of the most thoughtful was Robert Wieman, "Die Rechte der Physik," *Berliner Tageblatt,* 1 March 1936, 4th section, p. 17. The most strongly phrased was perhaps Max von Laue, "Experimentelle und theoretische Physik," *Ostdeutsche Tagespost* (in Beuthen), 29 March 1936 and 31 March 1936, printed in von Laue, *Gesammelte Schriften und Vorträge,* vol. 3 (Brunswick: Friedr. Vieweg & Sohn, 1961), pp. 78–81. Also noteworthy was "Weltanschauliche Naturwissenschaft?" in the *Frankfurter Zeitung,* 6 May 1936, p. 2.

25. See "Streit zwischen experimenteller und theoretischer Physik," *Hochland* 33 (1936): 282–85; Otto D. Tolischus, "Nazis Would Junk Theoretic Physics,"

New York Times, 9 March 1936, p. 19. One newspaper which gave particularly detailed coverage was the Jewish *Jüdische Rundschau* in Berlin. See, e.g., "Philosophie und Physik," 31 January 1936, p. 6; "Deutsche und jüdische Physik," 3 March 1936, p. 3; "Rasse und Denken," 13 March 1936, p. 4; "Nordisches und jüdisches Denken," 17 March 1936, p. 4.

26. See the article of Walther Gerlach, an experimentalist, "Theorie und Experiment in der exakten Wissenschaft," *Die Naturwissenschaften* 24 (13 November 1936) : 721–41. Cf. also the works of a political conservative, but physical modernist, Jordan, *Die Physik des 20. Jahrunderts;* and "Gibt es eine 'Krise' der modernen physikalischen Forschung?" *Die Tatwelt* 12 (1936): 59–68.

27. See the carefully worded article "Parole: Wissenschaft," in the *Frankfurter Zeitung,* 10 November 1936, p. 3.

28. The interview probably took place in late February 1936, i.e., at the time Heisenberg was preparing his article for the *Völkischer Beobachter.* Heisenberg to Sommerfeld, 14 February 1936, Sommerfeld Nachlass.

29. See above, chap 4.

30. Heisenberg to Himmler, 7 November 1937, in the private possession of Werner Heisenberg (hereafter cited as Heisenberg Papers).

31. [Werner] Z[schintzsch] to the Minister, 2 October 1936, BA R 21 (Rep. 76)/203, p. 29; another copy is in BDC-Research, Korr. "Wi," Werner Heisenberg.

32. The following discussion follows "An den Herrn Reichsminister für Erziehung, Wissenschaft und Volksbildung," undated, in the private possession of Friedrich Hund (hereafter cited as Hund Papers).

33. This has been discussed by Hans Mommsen, *Beamtentum im Dritten Reich* (Stuttgart: Deutsche Verlags-Anstalt, 1966), esp. pp. 62–126. See also Edward N. Peterson, *The Limits of Hitler's Power* (Princeton, N.J.: Princeton University Press, 1969).

34. On the differences in orientation among the Nazi party and state officials concerned with higher education, see Kelly, "National Socialism and German University Teachers," esp. pp. 241–67.

35. Ibid., pp. 222–23. A survey of the organizations in this area is provided in pp. 144–61.

36. On 24 July 1935; see NSDAP Parteikanzlei, *Verfügungen/Anordnungen/Bekanntgaben,* vol. 1 (Munich: Zentralverlag der NSDAP, Frz. Eher, Nachf., 1943), p. 671. Membership in the league was opened to nonparty members on 26 June 1936, ibid. On Schemm's Lehrerbund, see Rolf Eilers, *Die nationalsozialistische Schulpolitik, Staat und Politik,* vol. 4, ed. Ernst Fraenkel et al. (Cologne and Opladen: Westdeutscher Verlag, 1963), pp. 128–34.

37. Kelly, "National Socialism and German University Teachers," pp. 224–26.

38. From the draft of an unpublished article probably written in early 1942, translated and quoted in ibid., pp. 243–44.

39. Ibid., p. 244.

40. O. Schmauss to the Rektorat der Universität München, 24 March 1935, Archiv der Universität München (hereafter cited as AUM), Akte Sommerfeld, E II-N, p. 86.

41. Sommerfeld to Heisenberg, 17 June 1927, and Heisenberg to Sommerfeld, 21 June 1927, Sommerfeld Nachlass.

42. "Zur Wiederbesetzung des Lehrstuhls für theoretische Physik," n.d. [13 July 1935], Gerlach Papers. The story of the Sommerfeld succession must be pieced together from scattered sources, for the specific documents relating to the case in the university archive were gathered together in one file (Akte 288), which is missing from the archive. I am indebted to Craig Zwerling, who photocopied some of them in 1965 when working with copies in the Gerlach Papers (before Gerlach's own copies became lost).

43. "An das Dekannat der Philosophischen Fakultät," 4 November 1935, Gerlach Papers. Debye dropped from consideration as he entered negotiations for the directorship of the Kaiser Wilhelm Institute for Physics in Berlin. He was shortly thereafter awarded the Nobel prize for chemistry (1936). Becker was rejected by the ministry because he was already earmarked for Göttingen, where he was transferred against his will in 1937. Westphal, "Das Physikalische Institut der TU Berlin," pp. 557; Rudolf Hilsch, interview with the author, 5 May 1971.

44. "Personalnachweisung," BDC-Research, REM-Akte Wilhelm Führer. Nazi student hostility toward Sommerfeld dated back at least to 1927, when Sommerfeld had turned down an offer to go to Berlin as Planck's successor. In return for staying in Munich, he was recommended for the honor of rector of the university. The Nazis waged a successful campaign to defeat his appointment, apparently because they were convinced that he was Jewish. "Zur bevorstehenden Wahl der Rektor Magnificus an der Universität in München," *Münchener Beobachter,* 8 July 1927; also "Nicht Sommerfeld, sondern—Schüpfer," *Berliner Tageblatt,* 22 July 1927.

45. Wilhelm Führer to the Rektorat der Universität München, 14 August 1934, copy; copies of the faculty three-man nomination list, 26 July 1934; Gerlach to Heinrich Vogt, 22 June 1934, and Vogt to Gerlach, n.d.; and handwritten notes on a conversation between Gerlach and Führer on 28 July 1934, in which Führer's preference for political-ideological criteria at the expense of professional considerations is quite clear. All in Gerlach Papers.

46. Vahlen's appointment as president was contrary to the statutes of the Academy and sparked the resignations of Planck and the other three standing secretaries. See Hermann, *Max Planck,* p. 97.

47. See above, chap. 6.

48. On the formation and operation of the council, see Zierold, *Forschungsförderung in drei Epochen,* pp. 215–24.

49. *Ein Ehrentag der deutschen Wissenschaft: Die Eröffnung des Reichforschungsrats am 25. Mai 1937* ([Berlin]: Pressestelle des Reichministeriums für Wissenschaft, Erziehung und Volksbildung [1937]), p. 26.

50. Heisenberg to Bohr, 18 March 1937, BSC (20,2).

51. Heisenberg, "Der Kampf um die sogenannte 'Deutsche Physik,'" Heisenberg Papers.

52. See Rudolf Weigel, ed., *Philipp Lenard, der Vorkämpfer der deutschen Physik,* no. 17 of the Karlsruher Akademischen Reden (Karlsruhe: C. F. Müller, 1937). Cf. also, Ludwig Wesch, "Philipp Lenard—Vorbild und Verpflichtung," pp. 42–45.

53. "Lebenslauf vom 5.1.36," AUH, Akte Ludwig Wesch; BDC-NSDAP Zentralkartei, Ludwig Wesch.

54. Alwin Ramme, *Der Sicherheitsdienst der SS: Zu seiner Funktion im*

faschistischen Machtapparat und im Besatzungsregime des sogenannten General-gouvernements Polen, Militärhistorische Studien der Deutschen Akademie der Wissenschaften zu Berlin, vol. 12 ([East] Berlin: Deutscher Militärverlag, 1970), p. 84.

55. See Buchheim, "The SS—Instrument of Domination," pp. 166–72.

56. Ramme, *Der Sicherheitsdienst der SS,* pp. 84 and 79.

57. Freudenberg to Rektor, 25 May 1945, AUH, Akte Ludwig Wesch. The American scientific intelligence team leader, Samuel Goudsmit, described Wesch as "the top Nazi in Heidelberg," *Alsos* (New York: Schumann, 1947), p. 84. On Wesch's espousal of Aryan physics, see e.g., "Lenards Werk—Vorbild zukünftiger Forschung," *Zeitschrift für die gesamte Naturwissenschaft* 8 (May/ June 1942) : 100–14.

58. The following is based on Stark, et al., " 'Weisse Juden' in der Wissenschaft," *Das Schwarze Korps,* Berlin, 15 July 1937, p. 6.

59. Heisenberg was informed that D'Alquen was behind the article, Heisenberg, interview with the author, 13 July 1971.

60. Kurt R. Grossmann, *Ozzietsky: Ein deutscher Patriot* (Munich: Kindler Verlag, 1963), pp. 359–428.

61. On the thwarted 1934 declaration, see above, chap. 6.

62. Heisenberg, interview with the author, 13 July 1971.

63. Ibid.

64. Heisenberg to Himmler, 21 July 1937, Heisenberg Papers.

65. Heisenberg to Wacker, 28 July 1937, ibid.

66. Himmler to Heisenberg, 4 November 1937, ibid.

67. Heisenberg to Himmler, 7 November 1937, ibid.

68. Hund to the Herrn Reichsminister für Wissenschaft, Erziehung, und Volks-bildung, 20 July 1937, Hund Papers.

69. Sommerfeld to the Rektorat der Universität München, 26 July 1937, AUM, Akte Sommerfeld. On the call to Munich, see above, chap. 6.

70. Heisenberg, "Der Kampf um die sogenannte 'Deutsche Physik,' " Heisenberg Papers; Ernst von Weizsäcker to Sommerfeld, 30 September 1937, Sommerfeld Nachlass.

71. Excerpts from this exchange of letters are found in Haberditzl, "Der Widerstand deutscher Naturwissenschaftler gegen die 'Deutsche Physik,' " p. 323.

72. O. Westphal to Scheel, 2 December 1937, Heisenberg Papers.

73. Heisenberg to Sommerfeld, 16 January 1938, Akte Stark, Stuttgart. During the winter of 1938, Heisenberg was twice questioned by a panel from Himmler's staff. The first session was in Leipzig and the second in the Gestapo headquarters in Berlin. Both times he was treated with respect, and during the first meeting had been able to answer the objectons of a young experimental physicist among his interrogators. Heisenberg, interview with the author, 13 July 1971. Perhaps for this reason he felt the SS report would be in his favor.

74. Heisenberg to Sommerfeld, 12 February 1938, Akte Stark, Stuttgart.

75. Heisenberg to Sommerfeld, 14 April 1938, ibid. On Heisenberg's reasons for not emigrating—not wanting to abandon his younger colleagues and pupils, reluctance to leave his homeland, hope that something could be done to avoid the impending catastrophe—see his retrospective account of a "conversation" with Enrico Fermi in the summer of 1939, *Der Teil und das Ganze,* pp. 231–34.

76. Prandtl to Himmler, 12 July 1938, Heisenberg Papers.

77. Himmler to Heydrich, 21 July 1938, BDC-Research, Ahnenerbe, Werner Heisenberg; also in Goudsmit, *Alsos*, p. 116.

78. On the world ice theory and related Nordic myths, see Louis Pauwels and Jacques Bergier, *The Morning of the Magicians*, trans. Rollo Myers (New York: Avon, 1968), pp. 214–98, esp. 224–32. On the relationship between science fiction and National Socialism, see Manfred Nagel, *Science Fiction in Deutschland*, Untersuchungen des Ludwig–Uhland–Instituts, vol. 30 (Tübingen: Tübinger Vereinigung für Volkskunde, 1972), pp. 176–92.

79. Himmler to Heisenberg, 21 July 1938, Goudsmit Papers—Alsos; also printed in Goudsmit, *Alsos*, p. 119.

80. Wacker to the Bayerisches Staatsministerium für Unterricht und Kultus, 16 November 1937, and Wacker to Sommerfeld, 16 November 1937, both in AUM, Akte Sommerfeld, E II-N, p. 127.

81. Sommerfeld to Einstein, 30 December 1937, *Einstein-Sommerfeld Briefwechsel*, p. 118. The play on Stark's name (Stark means "strong" in German) was first introduced by Einstein in the Weimar period, ibid., p. 119. Max von Laue referred to Stark as "Giovanni Robusto."

82. Christian Gerthsen to Gerlach, 17 November 1938, Gerlach Papers.

83. Heinrich Ott to Gerlach, 8 November 1937, Gerlach Papers. See Karl Uller, *Das Grundgesetz der Wellenfortpflanzung aus bewegter Quelle in bewegtem Mittel: Der Michelson-Versuch und die Raumzeitlehre von Einstein* (Berlin: M. Oldenbourg, 1935).

84. Gerlach to Peter Debye, 8 July 1938, Gerlach Papers.

85. See Kelly, "National Socialism and German University Teachers," pp. 361–70.

86. Gerthsen to Gerlach, 17 November 1938, Gerlach Papers.

87. E.g., Sommerfeld to the Rektor der Universität München, 1 September 1939, SHQP (32,8).

88. Draft of Sommerfeld and Gerlach to the Dekanat der Naturwissenschaftlichen Fakultät der Universität München, 8 November 1939, SHQP (32,8).

89. Heisenberg, interview with the author, 13 July 1971.

90. Himmler to Heisenberg, 7 June 1939, Goudsmit Papers—Alsos.

91. Sommerfeld, "Autobiographische Skizze," in *Gesammelte Schriften*, ed. Fritz Sauter, vol. 4 (Brunswick: Friedr. Vieweg & Sohn, 1968), p. 679.

92. Draft of the faculty committee (Sommerfeld, Gerlach, Carathéodory, Wieland) to the Rektorat der Universität München, 1 September 1940, Sommerfeld Nachlass.

93. Müller, *Judentum und Wissenschaft* (Leipzig: Theodor Fritsch, 1936), pp. 48–55.

94. Gerlach to Friedrich von Faber, 15 October 1940, Gerlach Papers.

95. Von Faber to Gerlach, 6 November 1940, Gerlach Papers.

CHAPTER 9

1. Goudsmit to Gerlach, 24 June 1936, Goudsmit Papers-Correspondence.

2. Gerlach to Goudsmit, 7 November 1936, ibid.

3. Sommerfeld to Einstein, 30 December 1937, *Einstein-Sommerfeld Brief-wechsel,* p. 118.

4. Gerlach, interview with the author, 8 July 1971; Otto Scherzer, tape-recorded interview with the author in Darmstadt, 14 July 1971.

5. Heisenberg, interview with the author, 13 July 1971.

6. Friedrich Hund, interview with the author, 26 July 1971; Otto Heckmann, letter to the author, 7 April 1972. For a list of course offerings, see the compilation printed biannually in the *Physikalische Zeitschrift* throughout this period.

7. Heckmann to the author, 7 April 1972.

8. Sommerfeld to Einstein, 27 August 1934 and 16 January 1937, *Einstein-Sommerfeld Briefwechsel,* pp. 113–17.

9. Von Laue to Einstein, 27 February 1939, in the Archives of the Albert Einstein Estate at Princeton. See Walter Sullivan, "The Einstein Papers: A Man of Many Parts," *The New York Times,* 29 March 1972, p. 1; also Craig Zwerling, "The Influence of the Nazis on Physics in the German Universities" (senior thesis, Harvard University, 1966), pp. 43–44. Von Laue indicated that the article was to be printed soon in *Die Naturwissenschaften* and that he could not keep it from appearing. However, examination of *Die Naturwissenschaften, Physics Abstracts, Chemistry Abstracts,* and the comprehensive *Bibliographie der deutschen Zeitschriftenliteratur* has not revealed such an article. Perhaps Lenz reconsidered.

10. Frank, *Einstein,* pp. 384–85. The Aryan physicists checked Sommerfeld's heritage for "non-Aryan" ancestors, Thüring to the Herrn Rektor der Universität München, 28 March 1939, AUM, Akte Sommerfeld, E II-N, pp. 165–66. None were found. Staatsministerium für Unterricht und Kultus to the Herrn Leiter der Dozentenschaft, 18 April 1939, ibid., p. 169.

11. Edward Y. Hartshorne, "Numerical Changes in the German Student Body," *Nature* 142 (23 July 1938): 175; and Hartshorne, *The German Universities and the Government,* p. 15.

12. For an example of the Aryan physics views held by Schmidt, the only one of these not previously mentioned, see Schmidt, review of *Deutsche Physik* by Philipp Lenard, *Deutsche Mathematik* 2 (April 1937): 161–63.

13. "Bericht im Anschluss an die Aussprache vom 15. Juni 1938," n.d., Heisenberg Papers.

14. See above, chap. 8.

15. Westphal, "Das Physikalische Institut der TU Berlin," p. 557.

16. Zwerling, "Influence of the Nazis on Physics," p. 58. This is based on an interview with Rollwagen by Zwerling.

17. On Welker, who went to the Flugfunkforschung Institut at Oberpfaffenhofen, see ibid., pp. 58–59. On Hermann, P. P. Ewald to the author, 27 February 1972.

18. Richard Grünberger, *A Social History of the Third Reich* (London: Weidenfeld & Nicolson, 1971), p. 310.

19. Sommerfeld to Prof. A. Albert, 6 December 1946, Sommerfeld Nachlass.

20. "Bericht über die 14. Deutsche Physiker- und Mathematikertagung in Baden-Baden, vom 11.–16. September 1938," *Zeitschrift für technische Physik* 19

(1938) : 614. The booklet was co-prepared by Herbert Stuart and Wilhelm Orthmann of the German Physical Society Berlin district leadership, and published in cooperation with the German Work Front (Deutsche Arbeitsfront), headed by Hess's rival in internal party administration, Robert Ley. See Ramsauer, *Der Physiker* (Berlin: Akademisches Auskunftsamt in Verbinding mit dem Amt für Berufserziehung u. Betriebsführung in der Deutschen Arbeitsfront, 1938).

21. Institut für Zeitgeschichte (hereafter cited as IfZ), microfilm MA-141/3, Rosenberg's memorandum of 7 December 1937. Cf. "Nazis Lift Anathema on Einstein's Theory," *New York Times,* 12 December 1937, p. 5.

22. Heisenberg, interview with the author, 13 July 1971.

23. Finkelnburg, "Lebenslauf," 19 November 1941, in the private papers of Wolfgang Finkelnburg in the possession of his widow (hereafter cited as Finkelnburg Papers).

24. Finkelnburg, "Darlegung," [spring 1946] Finkelnburg Papers. Also, Hans Rau (professor of experimental physics at the TH Darmstadt), "Ueber die politische Betätigung von Professor Dr. Wolfgang Finkelnburg," 5 April 1946, ibid.

25. Rau, "Ueber die politische Betätigung von Professor Dr. Wolfgang Finkelnburg."

26. Finkelnburg, "Darlegung," Finkelnburg Papers.

27. Finkelnburg, "Der Kampf gegen die Partei-Physik," n.d., p. 2, manuscript in the private possession of Ernst Brüche in Mosbach/Baden.

28. Ibid.

29. Otto Scherzer, "Physik im totalitären Staat," in *Deutsches Geistesleben und National Sozialismus,* ed. Andreas Flitner (Tübingen: Rainer Wunderlich, 1965), pp. 56–57. Cf. Ernst Brüche, " 'Deutsche Physik' und die deutschen Physiker" *Physikalische Blätter* 2 (1946) : 235.

30. Heckmann to the author, 7 April 1972.

31. Scherzer, "Physik im totalitären Staat," p. 57; Scherzer, interview with the author, 14 July 1971.

32. Scherzer, "Physik im totalitären Staat," p. 57.

33. Heckmann to the author, 7 April 1972; Scherzer to the author, 7 November 1973.

34. Circular letter with the five points, n.d., Gerlach Papers. An abbreviated translation is found in Goudsmit, *Alsos,* p. 152.

35. Heckmann to the author, 7 April 1972.

36. Finkelnburg, "Der Kampf gegen die Partei-Physik," p. 3.

37. Führer had held a post in the Bavarian ministry (Hans Schemm's old bailiwick) since 5 September 1936. BDC-Research, Ahnenerbe, Wilhelm Führer.

38. On this conflict from the Rosenberg perspective, see Herbert Rothfeder, "A Study of Alfred Rosenberg's Organization for National Socialist Ideology" (Ph.D. diss., University of Michigan, 1963), pp. 267–77; from the Dozentenbund side, see Kelly, "National Socialism and German University Teachers," pp. 411–43.

39. [Friedrich] Harms to Sommerfeld, 12 and 13 February 1940, and Georg Rost to Sommerfeld, 4–6 June 1940, all in the Sommerfeld Nachlass.

258 NOTES TO PAGES 180–82

40. BDC–NSDAP Zentralkartei, Ludwig Glaser.

41. See, e.g., Ludwig Glaser, "Juden in der Physik: Jüdische Physik," *Zeitschrift für die gesamte Naturwissenschaft* 5 (October/November 1939): 272–75; Glaser, "Die Sommerfeldsche Feinstrukturkonstante als prinzipielle Frage der Physik," *Zeitschrift für die gesamte Naturwissenschaft* 5 (December 1939) : 289–331.

42. See, e.g., Hugo Dingler, *Physik und Hypothese: Versuch einer induktiven Wissenschaftslehre nebst einer kritischen Analyze der Fundamente der Relativitätstheorie* (Berlin and Leipzig: Walter de Gruyter, 1921); *Relativitätstheorie und Oekonomieprinzip* (Leipzig: S. Hirzel, 1922); *Der Zusammenbruch der Wissenschaft und der Primat der Philosophie* (Munich: Ernst Reinhardt, 1926). For a complete listing of Dingler's works and an exposition of his attempt to provide an axiomatic foundation for the exact sciences, see Wilhelm Krampf, ed., *Hugo Dingler: Gedenkbuch zum 75. Geburtstag* (Munich: Eidos-Verlag, 1956).

43. Dingler, *Die Kultur der Juden: Eine Versöhnung zwischen Religion und Wissenschaft* (Leipzig: Der neue Geist Verlag, 1919); "Albert Einstein: Zu seinem 50. Geburtstag am 14. März," *Münchener Neueste Nachrichten,* 14 March 1929, p. 1.

44. Especially in *Die Methode der Physik* (Munich: Ernst Reinhardt, 1938). On his forced retirement, see Krampf, *Hugo Dingler,* pp. 5, 13.

45. See, e.g., Dingler, "Die 'Physik des 20. Jahrhunderts': Eine prinzipielle Auseinandersetzung (Zu einem Buche von P. Jordan)," *Zeitschrift für die gesamte Naturwissenschaft* 3 (December 1937) : 321–25; "Zur Entstehung der sog. modernen theoretischen Physik," *Zeischrift für die gesamte Naturwissenschaft* 4 (December 1938/January 1939) : 329–41.

46. Sommerfeld to Gerlach, 24 August 1940, Gerlach Papers; draft of Sommerfeld, [Heinrich] Wieland, [Constantin] Carathéodory to the Rektorat der Universität München, 1 September 1940, Sommerfeld Nachlass.

47. Gerlach to the Staatsministerium für Unterricht und Kultus, München, 18 September 1940, Gerlach Papers.

48. "Die Erscheinungen der elementaren Strahlungen," *Völkischer Beobachter,* Munich, 23 October 1940. These talks were published as Stark and Müller, *Jüdische und deutsche Physik.*

49. Glaser to K. Clusius, 6 November 1940, and W. Meissner to Gerlach, 3 December 1940, Gerlach Papers.

50. Copy of Müller to the Dekan der Fakultät für allgemeine Wissenschaften Prof. Dr. Boas, 28 April 1942, Gerlach Papers.

51. Gerlach to Menzel [sic] in the REM, 24 June 1942, Gerlach Papers.

52. On Heckmann, see above, chap. 8. Cf. also Finkelnburg, "Der Kampf gegen die Partei-Physik," p. 4. In a letter to the author, 7 April 1972, Heckmann noted that personal intrigues against him in the name of political affairs had made it impossible for him to advance from Göttingen to a new position between 1933 and 1941.

53. Finkelnburg to Joos, 4 July 1941; Finkelnburg memorandum of 6 July 1941; Georg Niemeier (dean of the Strasbourg faculty) to Finkelnburg, 14 July 1941; and the Gauleiter of Hessen-Nassau, [Jakob] Sprenger, to Rust, 18 July 1941; all in Finkelnburg Papers.

54. [Friedrich] Drescher-Kaden to Finkelnburg, 21 July 1941, Finkelnburg Papers.

55. Von Weizsäcker to Finkelnburg, 24 July 1941, ibid.

56. Major Prof. Dr. Doetsch in the Technical Office of the RLM to Finkelnburg, 12 February 1942, ibid.

57. Finkelnburg to Gaudozentenbundsführer Dr. Guthmann, 24 September 1942, ibid.

58. On this subject, see Clarence Lasby, *Project Paperclip: German Scientists and the Cold War* (New York: Atheneum, 1971).

59. Finkelnburg to Gerlach, 21 January 1941, and Gerlach to Finkelnburg, 27 January 1941, Gerlach Papers.

60. Karl Selmayr to Finkelnburg, 6 October 1941; Finkelnburg to Selmayr, 12 October 1941; Selmayr to Finkelnburg, 22 October 1941; etc. all in the private papers of Sommerfeld's institute mechanic Karl Selmayr, presently in the possession of the author.

61. [Heinrich] Härtle to [Hugo] Rössner (in Vienna), IfZ, microfilm MA 129/6, frames 52115–116.

62. Zenneck to Gerlach, 27 February 1942, Gerlach Papers; Ramsauer, "Zur Geschichte der Deutschen Physikalischen Gesellschaft in der Hitlerzeit," *Physikalische Blätter* 3 (1947) : 111.

63. Ramsauer, "Zur Geschichte der Deutschen Physikalischen Gesellschaft in der Hitlerzeit," p. 111.

64. Ibid., p. 112.

65. Gerlach to Finkelnburg, 3 June 1941, Gerlach Papers.

66. See Ramsauer, "Eingabe an Rust," *Physikalische Blätter* 3 (1947) : 43–46, from which the necessary protestations of allegiance to the government have been omitted, as one would expect. A copy of the original version is in AUH, upon which the following is based.

67. This enclosure was only briefly summarized in the published version.

68. A damning review of the inconsistencies of *Jüdische und deutsche Physik* was published by Walter Weizel in *Zeischrift für technische Physik* 23 (1942) : 25. Weizel insisted that the theories of modern physics were true products of German learning.

69. Printed in Ramsauer, "Eingabe an Rust," pp. 45–46.

70. Ibid., p. 46.

71. Ramsauer, "Zur Geschichte der Deutschen Physikalischen Gesellschaft in der Hitlerzeit," p. 113.

72. Prandtl to Gerlach, 22 June 1942, Gerlach Papers.

73. Ramsauer, *Ueber Leistung und Organisation der angelsächsischen Physik: Mit Ausblicken für die deutsche Physik* (Berlin: Schriften der Deutschen Akademie der Luftfahrtforschung, 1943), limited edition, a copy of which is in Goudsmit Papers-Alsos.

74. Ibid., p. 21. Engineers faced the same problem of minimizing political and ideological influences in their profession during the war. See Ludwig, *Technik und Ingenieure im Dritten Reich*, pp. 382–93.

75. Joseph Goebbels, *The Goebbels Diaries*, ed. and trans. Louis P. Lochner (London: Hamilton, 1948), 15 May 1943, pp. 434–35, and 22 May 1943, pp. 444–45.

76. "Programm der Deutschen Physikalischen Gesellschaft für den Ausbau der Physik in Grossdeutschland," *Verhandlungen der DPG* 25 (1 September 1944) : 1–6.

77. Ernst Brüche, *25 Jahre Physik Verlag in Mosbach* (Mosbach in Baden: Physik Verlag, 1972), pp. 3–4; Speer to the author, 23 March 1972.

78. In Rosenberg's diary entries of 27 January and 7 February 1940. See Rothfeder, "A Study of Alfred Rosenberg's Organization," p. 121.

79. The most widely known and dramatic account is Jungk, *Brighter than a Thousand Suns;* a useful discussion is Goudsmit, *Alsos;* the most thorough and balanced presentation is Irving, *The Virus House.*

80. Irving, *The Virus House,* p. 274.

81. Ibid., p. 270.

82. See Alan S. Milward, *The German Economy at War* (London: University of London Athlone Press, 1965).

83. See Irving, *The Virus House,* esp. pp. 137–40, 180–81; also Albert Speer, *Inside the Third Reich,* trans. Richard and Clara Winston (New York: Macmillan, 1970), pp. 225–29. It has caused some astonishment that one faction among the physicists (led by Manfred von Ardenne) received considerable support for nuclear energy research from the Reich Minister of Post, Wilhelm Ohnesorge. Since the post office in Germany handles all telegraph and telephone communication as well as mail, it should not really be surprising that research funds for physics were available, even if nuclear research was rather far afield. What may be more surprising, however, is that Ohnesorge had associated with Lenard since attending the physicist's lectures in Kiel. The Reich minister delivered the keynote address during the celebration of Lenard's eightieth birthday in 1942. Lenard, "Erinnerungen," p. 202.

84. Irving, *The Virus House,* pp. 180–81, 209.

85. Goebbels, *The Goebbels Diaries,* 15 May 1943, pp. 434–35.

86. Ludwig, *Technik im Dritten Reich,* pp. 243–47; Irving, *The Virus House,* pp. 161–62, 231.

87. Major E. W. B. Gill, "German Academic Scientists and the War," Field Information Agency, Technical (F.I.A.T.), 28 August 1945, pp. 5–7, in the IfZ, documentation for *The Virus House* by David Irving, document sheets no. 311232–254, here 311237–239.

88. Ramsauer, "The Failure of the German War Effort in Physics Research and Development," 19 August 1945, in Goudsmit Papers-Alsos.

89. Gill, "German Academic Scientists and the War," p. 10.

90. Max von Laue to Theodore H. von Laue, 27 November 1946, von Laue Papers. Actually, it was fortunate for Heisenberg that atomic energy research in Germany was "decisive for the war effort" in name only. When Heisenberg delivered a speech in Zurich in December 1944, the Allies sent an OSS agent to listen to him. The agent was reportedly prepared to assassinate Heisenberg if the physicist intimated that the Germans were close to developing an atom bomb. Louis Kaufman, et al., *Moe Berg: Athlete, Scholar, Spy* (Boston and Toronto: Little, Brown & Co., 1975), pp. 195–98.

91. Irving, *The Virus House,* pp. 138–39.

92. Memorandum accompanying Schultze to Lammers (State Chancellery), 19 March 1941, Bundesarchiv (hereafter cited as BA) R 43 II/941, pp. 38–39.

93. In von Weizsäcker's call to Strasbourg, the neutrality of the Dozentenbund and the Rosenberg office on matters affecting physics overrode the desire of the party headquarters to block the appointment of such a politically unsuitable Heisenberg pupil. Kelly, "National Socialism and German University Teachers," pp. 386–90.

94. Partei-Kanzlei (Bechtold) to [Wolfgang] Erxleben, 8 July 1942, and quote from Erxleben to Bechtold, 9 September 1942, IfZ, MA 116/5 Heisenberg.

95. Erxleben to [Gustav] Borger, 10 July 1942, and Borger to the Partei-Kanzlei, 9 September 1942, IfZ, MA 116/5, Heisenberg.

96. Interview with the author, 13 July 1971.

97. Minutes of the Seefeld conference 1–3 November 1942, written 6 November 1942 by Rudolf Fleischmann; and von Weizsäcker to Sauter, 21 June 1943, with "Vorläufiger Bericht über das Physiker-Lager in Seefeld (Tirol) im November 1942," all in Goudsmit Papers-Alsos.

98. Heisenberg, "Die Bewertung der 'modernen theoretischen Physik,'" *Zeitschrift für die gesamte Naturwissenschaft* 9 (October/December 1943) : 201–12; Dingler, "Ueber den Kern einer fructbaren Diskussion über die 'moderne theoretische Physik,'" *Zeitschrift für die gesamte Naturwissenschaft* 9 (October/December 1943) : 212–21.

99. Lenard to the Herrn Reichsminister für Wissenschaft, Erziehung und Volksbildung, 8 June 1942, BA R 21 (Rep. 76)/833, vol. 3.

100. Ernst Brüche, ed., *Physiker Anekdoten: Gesammelt und mitgeteilt von Kollegen* (Mosbach/Baden: Physik Verlag, 1952), p. 45; Brüche, tape-recorded interview with the author in Mosbach/Baden, 2 July 1971.

101. Max von Laue to Theodore H. von Laue, 26 May 1945, von Laue Papers.

102. The list was prepared by the Manhattan Project's liaison office in London with the help of Moe Berg, the same agent who had been ready to assassinate Heisenberg in Zurich. Kaufmann, *Moe Berg*, pp. 171–72.

103. Max von Laue to Theodore H. von Laue, 7 August 1945, von Laue Papers. Cf. a similar account by one of the younger participants, Erich Bagge, Kurt Diebner, and Kenneth Jay, *Von der Uranspaltung bis Calder Hall* (Hamburg: Rowohlt, 1957), pp. 56–58.

104. Goudsmit, *Alsos*, p. xi; Jungk, *Brighter Than a Thousand Suns* (the German edition was published in 1954); pp. 91–92; Irving, *The Virus House*, p. 268.

105. Freudenberg, interview with the author, 16 July 1971.

106. The details of the trial from Stark's point of view were given in Stark, *Zur Auseinandersetzung zwischen der pragmatischen und der dogmatischen Physik.*

107. Ramsauer to Sommerfeld, 8 March 1946, Sommerfeld Nachlass.

CHAPTER 10

1. The letter is printed with background information in Nathan and Norden, eds., *Einstein on Peace*, pp. 286–97.

2. On the Manhattan Project, see Richard Hewlett and Oscar Anderson, *A History of the United States Atomic Energy Commission* (University Park, Pa.: University of Pennsylvania Press, 1962), vol. 1, *The New World, 1939/1946.*

3. See chap. 2. In another 1931 letter to von Kármán, Born explained that a modern physicist must have contact with the Americans every couple of years, because the most important experiments were performed there and also because the theoreticians produced extremely respectable achievements. Born to von Kármán, 4 June 1931, CIT-Ar, von Kármán Papers, Box 4—Born.

4. Kuhn, *The Structure of Scientific Revolutions*, p. 268.

5. Max von Laue to Theodore H. von Laue, 12 November 1946, von Laue Papers.

6. Haberer, *Politics and the Community of Science*, pp. 163–81.

7. Leo Szilard, "Reminiscences," in *The Intellectual Migration*, ed. Fleming and Bailyn, pp. 95–96.

8. Einstein to Born, 7 September 1944, *Einstein-Born Briefwechsel*, pp. 202–03.

Selected Bibliography

I. Unpublished Sources

A. Archival Material

(Only the files or collections most pertinent to the text are included here.)

American Institute of Physics, Center for History and Philosophy of Physics, New York (AIP):
Transcript of interview with Felix Bloch, 15 August 1968.
Transcript of interviews with P. P. Ewald, 17 and 24 May 1968.

Archiv der Ruprecht Karl Universität, Heidelberg (AUH):
Personnel files of August Becker, Walther Bothe, Philipp Lenard, Ludwig Wesch.

Archiv der Ludwig Maximillian Universität, Munich (AUM):
Personnel file of Arnold Sommerfeld, E II-N.

Archive for History of Quantum Physics, Berkeley (AHQP):
Niels Bohr Scientific Correspondence (BSC), 1930–45.
Paul Ehrenfest Scientific Correspondence (EHR).
Sources for History of Quantum Physics (SHQP), Correspondence and transcribed interviews.

Berlin Document Center, Berlin-Zehlendorf (BDC):
NSDAP Zentralkartei.
Oberstes Partei-Gericht (OPG).
Partei Kanzlei.
Research.
SS Führer.

Bundesarchiv, Koblenz (BA):
R 3   Ministerbüro Speer.
R 21   Reichsministerium für Wissenschaft, Erziehung und Volks- bildung, 1934–45.
R 43 II Reichskanzlei, 1933–45.

California Institute of Technology Archives, Pasadena (CIT-AR):
Delbrück Papers.
Epstein Papers.
Von Kármán Papers.

Cambridge University Library, Cambridge, England:
Ernest Rutherford Collection, correspondence between Ernest Rutherford and Johannes Stark.

Deutsche Forschungsgemeinschaft, Bad Godesberg:
File Pr 2/07 concerning Ludwig Prandtl.

Deutsches Museum, Handschriften-Sammlung der Bibliothek, Munich:
    Nachlass Philipp Lenard.
    Nachlass Arnold Sommerfeld.
    Nachlass Jonathan Zenneck.
    Special collections 1942/5, 1942/6, and 1946/7 concerning Walther
        Nernst.
    Special collections 1961–17 to 1961–22 concerning Friedrich Pockels.
    Special collection 1964/6 concerning Max von Laue.
Harvard University Library, Cambridge, Mass.:
    Von Mises Papers.
Hoover Institution on War, Revolution and Peace, Stanford:
    Nationalsozialistischer Deutscher Dozentenbund, Forschungsstipend-
        ien, Gutachterschreiben.
Institut für Zeitgeschichte, Munich (IfZ):
    Records of the Rosenberg office contained in the microfilm collec-
        tions MA 116 (also found at the Yivo Institute for Jewish Re-
        search in New York) and MA 141 (National Archives Microcopy
        No. T-81).
    Research materials collected for *The Virus House* by David Irving.
Kuratorium der Georg August Universität, Göttingen (KUG):
    Personnel files of Max Born, Richard Courant, James Franck, Georg
        Joos, Ludwig Prandtl.
Lehrstuhl für die Geschichte der Naturwissenschaften und Technik,
    Stuttgart:
    Philipp Lenard, "Erinnerungen eines Naturforschers," unpublished
        autobiography concluded September 1943.
    Akte Stark, a selection of papers from the Sommerfeld Nachlass
        concerning Johannes Stark.
Library of Congress, Washington, D.C.:
    Oswald Veblen Papers.

B. PAPERS IN PRIVATE POSSESSION

*(Unless otherwise indicated in the notes, the author possesses a copy
of each document cited from the following sources.)*
Richard Courant (obtained with the permission of Mrs. Courant from
    Mrs. Constance Reid, San Francisco).
Wolfgang Finkelnburg (through Mrs. Finkelnburg, Erlangen).
James Franck (through Mrs. Elizabeth Lisco and Mrs. Dagmar von
    Hippel, Brookline, Mass. The Franck family papers are now deposited
    in the Dept. of Special Collections of the University of Chicago
    Library.)
Walther Gerlach, Munich.
Samuel A. Goudsmit, Brookhaven National Laboratory, Long Island.

Alsos papers (Goudsmit Papers-Alsos). Private correspondnce (Goudsmit Papers-Corr).
Werner Heisenberg, Munich.
Friedrich Hund, Göttingen.
Max von Laue (through Theodore H. von Laue, Worcester, Mass.).
Lothar Nordheim, La Jolla, California.
Karl Selmayr (through Mr. Craig Zwerling, New York).

C. TAPE-RECORDED INTERVIEWS CONDUCTED BY THE AUTHOR

Ernst Brüche, Mosbach/Baden, 2 July 1971.
Herbert Busemann, Santa Ynez, California, 10 May 1972.
Karl Freudenberg, Heidelberg, 16 July 1971.
Walther Gerlach, Munich, 8 July 1971.
Werner Heisenberg, Munich, 13 July 1971.
Rudolf Hilsch, Göttingen, 5 May 1971.
Friedrich Hund, Göttingen, 26 July 1971.
Theodore H. von Laue, Riverside, California, 23 February 1972.
Lothar Nordheim, La Jolla, California, 15 April 1972.
Robert W. Pohl, Göttingen, 7 May 1971.
Otto Scherzer, Darmstadt, 14 July 1971.

D. DISSERTATIONS AND MANUSCRIPTS

Courant, Richard. "Reminiscences from Hilbert's Göttingen." Colloquium given in the Department of History of Science and Medicine, Yale University, 13 January 1964. Transcribed from a tape-recording, mimeographed.
Finkelnburg, Wolfgang. "Der Kampf gegen die Partei-Physik." Manuscript.
Forman, Paul. "The Environment and Practice of Atomic Physics in Weimar Germany: A Study in the History of Science." Ph.D. dissertation, University of California, Berkeley, 1967.
———. "The Helmholtz-Gesellschaft: Support of Academic Physical Research by German Industry after the First World War." Manuscript.
Gill, E. W. B. "German Academic Scientists and the War," Manuscript prepared for the Field Information Agency, Technical (F.I.A.T.) of the Allied Control Commission for Germany, 2 August 1945.
Kelly, Reece C. "National Socialism and German University Teachers: NSDAP's Efforts To Create a National Socialist Professoriate and Scholarship." Ph.D. dissertation, University of Washington, 1973.
Preston, David L. "Science, Society and the German Jews: 1870–1933." Ph.D. dissertation, University of Illinois, 1971.
Pyenson, Lewis. "The Göttingen Reception of Einstein's General Theory of Relativity." Ph.D. dissertation, Johns Hopkins University, 1973.

Rothfeder, Herbert. "A Study of Alfred Rosenberg's Organization for National Socialist Ideology." Ph.D. dissertation, University of Michigan, 1963.

Schröder-Gudehus, Brigitte. *Deutsche Wissenschaft und internationale Zusammenarbeit 1914–1928.* Ph.D. dissertation, University of Geneva, 1966. Geneva: Dumaret & Golay, 1966.

Wetzel, Charles J. "The American Rescue of Refugee Scholars and Scientists from Europe, 1933–45." Ph.D. dissertation, University of Wisconsin, 1964.

Zwerling, Craig. "The Influence of the Nazis on Physics in the German Universities." Senior thesis, Harvard University, 1966.

II.   BOOKS AND PAMPHLETS

(Works cited on one occasion in the notes are not included here or below unless they are of general significance for this study.)

Allen, William Sheridan. *The Nazi Seizure of Power: The Experience of of a Single German Town, 1930–1935.* Chicago: Quadrangle, 1965.

Becker, August, ed. *Naturforschung im Aufbruch: Reden und Voträge zur Einweihungsfeier des Philipp Lenard-Instituts der Universität Heidelberg am 13. und 14. Dezember 1935.* Munich: J. F. Lehmanns, 1936.

Ben-David, Joseph. *The Scientist's Role in Society: A Comparative Study.* Foundations of Modern Sociology Series, edited by Alex Inkeles. Englewood Cliffs, N.J.: Prentice-Hall, 1971.

Berlin, Freie Universität. *Nationalsozialismus und die deutsche Universität.* Berlin: W. de Gruyter, 1966.

Berstein, Jeremy. *Einstein.* Modern Masters Series, edited by Frank Kermode. New York: Viking Press, 1973.

Bollmus, Reinhard. *Das Amt Rosenberg und seine Gegner: Zum Machtkampf im nationalsozialistischen Herrschaftssystem.* Studien zur Zeitgeschichte, published by the Institut für Zeitgeschichte. Stuttgart: Deutsche Verlags-Anstalt, 1970.

Born, Max. *My Life and My Views.* New York: Charles Scribner's Sons, 1968.

———, ed. *Albert Einstein-Hedwig und Max Born: Briefwechsel 1916–1955.* Munich: Nymphenburger, 1969.

Bracher, Karl Dietrich. *The German Dictatorship: The Origins, Structure and Effect of National Socialism.* Translated by Jean Steinberg. New York and Washington: Praeger, 1970.

Bracher, Karl Dietrich; Sauer, Wolfgang; Schulz, Gerhard. *Die nationalsozialistische Machtergreifung: Studien zur Errichtung des totalitären Herrschaftssystems in Deutschland 1933/34.* Cologne: Westdeutscher Verlag, 1960.

Bullock, Alan. *Hitler: A Study in Tyranny*. Rev. ed. New York and Evanston: Harper & Row, 1962.

Busch, Alexander. *Die Geschichte des Privatdozenten*. Göttinger Abhandlungen zur Soziologie, vol. 5, edited by H. Plessner. Stuttgart: F. Enke, 1959.

Calic, Edouard, ed. *Ohne Maske: Hitler-Breiting Geheimgespräche 1931*. Frankfort on the Main: Societäts-Verlag, 1968.

Cecil Robert. *The Myth of the Master Race: Alfred Rosenberg and Nazi Ideology*. New York: Dodd Mead & Co. 1972.

Chamberlain, Houston Stewart. *Die Grundlagen des neunzehnten Jahrhunderts*. 2d ed. Munich: F. Bruckmann, 1900.

Clark, Ronald W. *Einstein. The Life and Times*. New York and Cleveland: World Publishing Co., 1971.

Dawidowicz, Lucy S. *The War against the Jews 1933–1945*. New York: Holt, Rinehart and Winston, 1975.

Diehl-Thiele, Peter. *Partei und Staat im Dritten Reich: Untersuchungen zum Verhältnis von NSDAP und allgemeiner innerer Staatsverwaltung 1933–1945*. Münchener Studien zur Politik, vol. 9, edited by Gottfried-Karl Kindermann, Nikolaus Lobkowicz, and Hans Maier. Munich: C. H. Beck, 1969.

Eilers, Rolf. *Die nationalsozialistische Schulpolitik: Eine Studie zur Funktion der Erziehung im totalitären Staat*. Staat und Politik, vol. 4, edited by Ernst Fraenkel et al. Cologne and Opladen: Westdeutscher Verlag, 1963.

Einstein, Albert. *Mein Weltbild*. Amsterdam: Querido Verlag, 1934.

Fest, Joachim. *The Face of the Third Reich: Portraits of the Nazi Leadership*. Translated by Michael Bullock. New York: Random House, 1970.

———. *Hitler*. Translated by Richard and Clara Winston. New York: Harcourt, Brace, Jovanovich, 1974.

Fleming, Donald, and Bailyn, Bernard, eds. *The Intellectual Migration: Europe and America 1930–1960*. Cambridge, Mass.: Harvard University Press, 1969.

Fraenkel, Abraham Adolf. *Lebenskrise: Aus den Erinnerungen eines jüdischen Mathematikers*. Stuttgart: Deutsche Verlags-Anstalt, 1967.

Frank, Philipp. *Einstein: Sein Leben und seine Zeit*. Munich, Leipzig, Freiburg i. Br.: Paul List, 1949.

Gasman, Daniel. *The Scientific Origins of National Socialism: Social Darwinism in Ernst Haeckel and the German Monist League*. History of Science Library, edited by Michael A. Hoskin. London: MacDonald, 1971.

Gay, Peter. *Weimar Culture: The Outsider as Insider*. New York and Evanston: Harper & Row, 1968.

Glum, Friedrich. *Zwischen Wissenschaft, Wirtschaft und Politik*. Bonn: Bouvier, 1964.

268SELECTED BIBLIOGRAPHY

Goebbels, Joseph. *The Goebbels Diaries, 1942–43.* Translated and edited by Louis P. Lochner. London: Hamilton, 1948.

Goran, Morris. *The Story of Fritz Haber.* Norman, Okla.: University of Oklahoma Press, 1967.

Goudsmit, Samuel A. *Alsos.* New York: Schuman, 1947.

Gumbel, Emil J., ed. *Freie Naturwissenschaft: Ein Sammelbuch der deutschen Emigration.* Strasbourg: Sebastian Brant Verlag, 1938.

Haberer, Joseph. *Politics and the Community of Science.* New York, etc.: Van Nostrand Reinhold, 1969.

Hahn, Otto. *My Life.* Translated by Ernst Kaiser and Eithne Wilkins. London: MacDonald, 1970.

Hartshorne, Edward Y. *The German Universities and National Socialism.* London: Allen & Unwin, 1937.

———. *The German Universities and the Government.* Philadelphia: privately printed, 1938.

Heiber, Helmut. *Walter Frank und sein Reichsinstitut für die Geschichte des neuen Deutschlands.* Quellen und Darstellungen zur Zeitgeschichte, vol. 13, Stuttgart: Deutsche Verlags-Anstalt, 1966.

Heisenberg, Werner. *Der Teil und das Ganze: Gespräche im Umkreis der Atomphysik.* Munich: R. Piper, 1969.

Hermann, Armin. *Max Planck in Selbstzeugnissen und Bilddokumenten.* Reinbek bei Hamburg: Rowohlt, 1973.

———, ed. *Albert Einstein/Arnold Sommerfeld, Briefwechsel: 60 Briefe aus dem goldenen Zeitalter der deutschen Physik.* Basel and Stuttgart: Schwabe, 1968.

Herneck, Friedrich. *Albert Einstein: Ein Leben für Wahrheit, Menschlichkeit und Frieden.* Berlin [East]: Buchverlag der Morgen, 1963.

Hilberg, Raul. *The Destruction of the European Jews.* Chicago: Quadrangle, 1967.

Hitler, Adolf. *Mein Kampf.* 352d–354th printing. Munich: Zentralverlag der NSDAP, Frz. Eher, Nachf., 1938.

Hofer, Walther, ed. *Der Nationalsozialismus Dokumente: 1933/1945.* Frankfort on the Main: Fischer-Bücherei, 1957.

Hoffman, Banesh. *Albert Einstein: Creator and Rebel.* Prepared with the collaboration of Helen Dukas. New York: Viking Press, 1972.

Irving, David. *The Virus House: Germany's Atomic Research and Allied Countermeasures.* London: W. Kimber, 1967.

Jammer, Max. *The Conceptual Development of Quantum Mechanics.* New York: McGraw-Hill, 1966.

Jordan, Pascual. *Die Physik des 20. Jahrhunderts: Einführung in den Gedankeninhalt der modernen Physik.* Brunswick: Friedrich Vieweg, 1936.

Jungk, Robert. *Brighter than a Thousand Suns: A Personal History of the Atomic Scientists.* Translated by James Cleugh. New York: Harcourt, Brace, 1958.

Kahle, Paul E. *Bonn University in Pre-Nazi and Nazi Times (1932–1939).* London: privately printed, 1945.

Kaufman, Louis, et al. *Moe Berg: Athlete, Scholar, Spy.* Boston and Toronto: Little, Brown, 1975.

Kuhn, Thomas S. *The Structure of Scientific Revolutions.* Chicago and London: University of Chicago Press, 1962.

Laue, Max von. *Gesammelte Schriften und Vorträge.* Vol. 3. Brunswick: Friedrich Vieweg & Sohn, 1961.

Lenard, Philipp. *Deutsche Physik.* 4 vols. Munich: J. F. Lenmanns, 1936–37.

———. *England und Deutschland zur Zeit des grossen Krieges.* Heidelberg: Carl Winter, 1914.

———. *Grosse Naturforscher: Eine Geschichte der Naturforschung in Lebensbeschreibungen.* 2d ed. Munich: J. F. Lehmanns, 1930.

———. *Ueber Aether und Uräther: Mit einem Mahnwort an detusche Naturforscher.* 2d ed. (expanded). Leipzig: S. Hirzel, 1922.

———. *Ueber Relativitätsprinzip, Aether, Gravitation: Mit einem Zusatz betreffend d. Nauheimer Diskussion.* 3d ed. Leipzig: S. Hirzel, 1921.

Ludwig, Karl-Heinz. *Technik und Ingenieure im Dritten Reich.* Düsseldorf: Droste Verlag, 1974.

Merkl, Peter. *Political Violence under the Swastika.* Princeton, N.J.: Princeton University Press, 1975.

Mommsen, Hans. *Beamtentum im Dritten Reich.* No. 12 of *Schriftenreihe der Vierteljahrshefte für Zeitgeschichte.* Stuttgart: Deutsche Verlagsanstalt, 1966.

Mosse, George L. *The Crisis of German Ideology: Intellectual Origins of the Third Reich.* The Universal Library. New York: Grosset & Dunlap, 1964.

———, ed. *Nazi Culture: Intellectual, Cultural and Social Life in the Third Reich.* Translated by Salvator Attanasio and others. New York: Grosset & Dunlap, 1966.

München, Universität. *Die deutsche Universität im Dritten Reich: Eine Vortragsreihe der Universität München.* Munich: R. Piper, 1966.

Nathan, Otto, and Norden, Heinz, eds. *Einstein on Peace.* New York: Simon and Schuster, 1960.

Nationalsozialistischer Lehrerbund Deutschland/Sachsen. *Bekenntnis der Professoren an den deutschen Universitäten und Hochschulen zu Adolf Hitler und dem nationalsozialistischen Staat.* Dresden: W. Limpert, 1933.

Nipperdey, Thomas, and Schmugge, Ludwig. *50 Jahre Forschungsförderung in Deutschland: Ein Abriss der Geschichte der Deutschen*

Forschungsgemeinschaft 1920–1970. Bad Godesberg: privately printed for the Deutsche Forschungsgemeinschaft, 1970.

Noakes, Jeremy. *The Nazi Party in Lower Saxony, 1921–1933.* London: Oxford University Press, 1971.

Nobel Foundation, ed. *Nobel Lectures. Physics, 1901–1921.* Amsterdam, London, New York: Elsevier, 1964.

Notgemeinschaft deutscher Wissenschaftler im Ausland. *List of Displaced Scholars.* London: privately printed, 1936.

Peterson, Edward N. *The Limits of Hitler's Power.* Princeton, N.J.: Princeton University Press, 1969.

Planck, Max, ed. *25 Jahre Kaiser Wilhelm-Gesellschaft zur Förderung der Wissenschaften.* Berlin: J. Springer, 1936.

Poliakov, Leon, and Wulf, Josef, eds. *Das Dritte und seine Denker: Dokumente.* Berlin-Grunewald: Arani, 1959.

———. *Das Dritte Reich und die Juden: Dokumente und Aufsätze.* Berlin–Grunewald: Arani, 1961.

Ramsauer, Carl. *Physik–Technik–Pädagogik: Erfahrungen und Erinnerungen.* Karlsruhe: Braun, 1949.

———. *Ueber Leistung und Organisation der angelsächsischen Physik: Mit Ausblicken auf die deutsche Physik.* Schriften der deutschen Akademie der Luftfahrtforschung. Berlin: Deutsche Akademie der Luftfahrtforschung, 1943.

Rauschning, Hermann. *Gespräche mit Hitler.* New York: Europa Verlag, 1940.

Reid, Constance. *Hilbert.* New York: Springer, 1970.

Relativitätstheorie und Weltanschauung: Zur philosophischen und wissenschaftspolitischen Wirkung Albert Einsteins. Berlin [East]: VEB Deutscher Verlag der Wissenschaften, 1967.

Remak, Joachim, ed. *The Nazi Years: A Documentary History.* Englewood Cliffs, N.J.: Prentice-Hall, 1969.

Richter, Steffen. *Forschungsförderung in Deutschland 1920–1936: Dargestellt am Beispiel der Notgemeinschaft der Deutschen Wissenschaft und ihrem Wirken für das Fach Physik.* No. 23 Technikgeschichte in Einzeldarstellungen. Düsseldorf: Verein Deutscher Ingenieure, 1972.

Ringer, Fritz. *The Decline of the German Mandarins: The German Academic Community, 1890–1933.* Cambridge, Mass.: Harvard University Press, 1969.

Rosenberg, Alfred. *Der Mythus des 20. Jahrhunderts: Eine Wertung der seelisch-geistigen Gestaltenkämpfe unserer Zeit.* 95th–98th printing. Munich: Hoheneichen, 1936.

Schaffner, Kenneth F. *Nineteenth-Century Aether Theories.* Selected Readings in Physics, edited by D. Ter Haar. Oxford, New York, etc.: Pergamon Press, 1972.

Schemm, Hans. *Hans Schemm spricht: Seine Reden und sein Werk.*

Edited by G. Kahl-Furthmann. Bayreuth: Gauleitung der Bayerischen Ostmark, 1936.

Schleunes, Karl A. *The Twisted Road to Auschwitz: Nazi Policy toward German Jews, 1933–1939*. Urbana, Chicago, London: University of Illinois Press, 1970.

Schmidt-Schönbeck, Charlotte. *300 Jahre Physik und Astronomie an der Kieler Universität*. Kiel: F. Hirt, 1965.

Schoenbaum, David. *Hitler's Social Revolution: Class and Status in Germany, 1933–1945*. Garden City, N.Y.: Doubleday, Anchor Books, 1967.

Speer, Albert. *Inside the Third Reich: Memoirs*. Translated by Richard and Clara Winston. New York: Macmillan, 1970.

Stark, Johannes. *Adolf Hitler und die deutsche Forschung*. Berlin: Pass & Garleb, 1934.

———. *Adolf Hitlers Ziele und Persönlichkeit*. Munich: Deutscher Volksverlag, 1930.

———. *Das alte und das neue Berufungsverfahren*. Greifswald: privately printed, 1919.

———. *Die gegenwärtige Krisis in der deutschen Physik*. Leipzig: J. A. Barth, 1922.

———. *Nationalsozialismus und Wissenschaft*. Munich: Frz. Eher, Nachf., 1934.

———. *Die Organisation der akademischen Kreise*. Greifswald: privately printed, 1919.

———. *Zur Abwehr ungerechtfertigter Angriffe*. Eppenstatt bei Traunstein, Upper Bavaria: privately printed, 1947.

———. *Zur Auseinandersetzung zwischen der pragmatischen und der dogmatischen Physik*. Eppenstatt bei Traunstein, Upper Bavaria: privately printed, 1949.

———, and Müller, Wilhelm. *Jüdische und deutsche Physik*. Leipzig: Helingsche Verlagsanstalt, 1941.

Stern, Fritz. *The Politics of Cultural Despair: A Study in the Rise of the Germanic Ideology*. Garden City, New York: Doubleday, Anchor Books, 1965.

Swenson, Loyd S. *The Ethereal Aether: A History of the Michelson-Morley-Miller Aether-Drift Experiments, 1880–1930*. Austin: University of Texas Press, 1972.

Tübingen, Universität. *Deutsches Geistesleben und Nationalsozialismus*. Tübingen: Rainer Wunderlich, 1965.

Von Ferber, Christian. *Die Entwicklung des Lehrkörpers der deutschen Universitäten und Hochschulen, 1864–1954*. Volume 3 of Untersuchungen zur Lage der deutschen Hochschullehrer. Göttingen: Vandenhoeck & Ruprecht, 1956.

Weinreich, Max. *Hitler's Professors: The Part of Scholarship in Ger-

many's Crimes against the Jewish People. New York: Yiddish Scientific Institute, 1946.

Whittaker, Edmund T. *A History of the Theories of Aether and Electricity.* 2 vols. New York: Philosophical Library, 1951–54.

Willstätter, Richard. *From My Life.* Translated by Lilli S. Hornig. New York, Amsterdam: W. A. Benjamin, 1965.

Wulf, Josef, ed *Literatur und Dichtung im Dritten Reich: Eine Dokumentation.* Gütersloh: S. Mohn, 1963.

Zierold, Kurt. *Forschungsförderung in drei Epochen. Deutsche Forschungsgemeinschaft. Geschichte, Arbeitsweise, Kommentar.* Wiesbaden: Franz Steiner, 1968.

III. Journals and Articles

Born, Max. "Arnold Johannes Wilhelm Sommerfeld." *Obituary Notices of the Royal Society* 8 (1952) : 275–96.

———. "Max K. E. L. Planck." *Obituary Notices of the Royal Society* 6 (1948) : 161–88.

———. "Sommerfeld als Begründer einer Schule." *Die Naturwissenschaften* 16 (7 December 1928) : 1035–36.

"Boycott of Jews." *The Times,* London, 3 April 1933, p. 14.

Brüche, Ernst. " 'Deutsche Physik' und die deutschen Physiker." *Physikalische Blatter,* 2 (1946) : 232–36.

Brüche, Ernst, and Marx, Hugo. "Der Fall Philipp Lenard—Mensch und 'Politiker.' " *Physikalische Blätter,* 23 (1967), 262–67.

Bühl, Alfons. "Naturwissenschaft und Weltanschauung." *Deutsche Mathematik* 2 (April 1937) : 3–5.

Deubner, Alexander. "Die Physik an der Berliner Universität von 1910 bis 1960." In *Wissenschaftliche Zeitschrift der Humboldt Universität zu Berlin* (1959–60), Beiheft 14, pp. 85–89.

Deutsche Mathematik. vols. 1–7, 1936–44.

Dingler, Hugo. "Ueber den Kern einer fruchtbaren Diskussion über die 'moderne theoretische Physik.' " *Zeitschrift für die gesamte Naturwissenschaft* 9 (October/December 1943) : 212–21.

———. "Zur Entstehung der sogenannten modernen theoretischen Physik." *Zeitschrift für die gesamte Naturwissenschaft* 4 (December 1938/January 1939) : 329–41.

Ewald, P. P. "Max von Laue." *Biographical Memoirs of Fellows of the Royal Society* 6 (1960) : 135–56.

———. "Max von Laue, 1879–1960." *Acta Crystallographia* 13 (July 1960) : 513–15.

Forman, Paul. "The Financial Support and Political Alignment of

Physicists in Weimar Germany." *Minerva,* 12 (January 1974) : 39–66.

——. "Scientific Internationalism and the Weimar Physicists: The Ideology and Its Manipulation in Germany after the First World War." *Isis* 64 (June 1973) : 151–80.

——. "Weimar Culture, Causality, and the Quantum Theory, 1918–1927: Adaptation by German Physicists and Mathematicians to a Hostile Intellectual Environment." *Historical Studies in the Physical Sciences* 3 (1971) : 1–115.

Goldberg, Stanley. "In Defense of Ether: The British Response to Einstein's Special Theory of Relativity 1905–11." *Historical Studies in the Physical Sciences* 2 (1970) : 88–125.

Goran, Morris. "Swastika Science." *The Nation,* 148 (3 June 39), 641–43.

Haberditzl, Werner, "Der Widerstand deutscher Naturwissenschaftler gegen die 'Deutsche Physik' und andere faschistische Zerrbilder der Wissenschaft." In *Naturwissenschaft, Tradition, Fortschritt.* Beiheft zur Zeitschrift NTM, pp. 320–26. Berlin [East]: VEB Deutscher Verlag der Wissenschaften, 1963.

Hahn, Otto. "Eine persönliche Erinnerung an Max Planck." *Mitteilungen der Max Planck-Gesellschaft zur Förderung der Wissenschaften* (1957), 243–46.

——. "Zur Erinnerung an die Haber-Gedächtnisfeier vor 25 Jahren, am 29. Januar 1935, im Harnack-Haus in Berlin-Dahlem." *Mitteilungen der Max Planck-Gesellschaft zur Förderung der Wissenschaften* (1960), 3–13.

Hartshorne, Edward Y. "Numerical Changes in the German Student Body." *Nature* 142 (23 July 1938) : 175–76.

Heisenberg, Werner. "Die Bewertung der 'modernen theoretischen Physik.'" *Zeitschrift für die gesamte Naturwissenschaft* 9 (October/December 1943) : 201–12.

——. "Zum Artikel 'Deutsche und Jüdische Physik.'" *Völkischer Beobachter,* Berlin, 28 February 1936, p. 6.

Hermann, Armin. "Albert Einstein und Johannes Stark: Briefwechsel und Verhältnis der beiden Nobelpreisträger." *Sudhoffs Archiv* 50 (1966) : 267–85.

——. "Die frühe Diskussion zwischen Stark und Sommerfeld über die Quantenhypothese." *Centaurus* 12 (1967) : 38–59.

Herneck, Friedrich. "Der 'Fall Einstein' und die Ehre der deutschen Nation." *Wissenschaftliche Zeitschrift der Humboldt Universität zu Berlin: Geschichtlich-Sprachwissenschaftliche Reihe* 12 (1963) : 329–33.

Holton, Gerald. "Einstein, Michelson and the 'Crucial' Experiment." *Isis* 60 (Summer 1969) : 133–97.

——. "Mach, Einstein, and the Search for Reality." *Daedalus* 97 (Spring 1968) : 636–73.

Hund, Friedrich. "Höhepunkte der Göttinger Physik I." *Physikalische Blätter* 25 (1969) : 145–53.
———. "Höhepunkte der Göttinger Physik II." *Physikalische Blätter* 25 (1969) : 210–15.
Köhler, Fritz. "Zur Vertreibung humanistischer Gelehrter 1933/34." *Blätter für deutsche und internationale Politik* 11 (July 1966) : 696–707.
Kubach, Fritz. "Geheimrat Lenards 75. Geburtstag." *Zeitschrift für die gesamte Naturwissenschaft* 3 (August 1937) : 164–65.
———. "Review of *Deutsche Physik*, vol. I, by Philipp Lenard." *Deutsche Mathematik* 1 (April 1936) : 256–58.
———. "Studenten, in Front!" *Deutsche Mathematik* 1 (January 1936) : 5–8.
Kuhn, Heinrich G. "James Franck." *Biographical Memoirs of Fellows of the Royal Society* 11 (1965) : 53–74.
Laue, Max von. "Ansprache bei Eröffnung der Physikertagung in Würzburg am 18. September 1933." *Physikalische Zeitschrift* 34 (15 December 1933) : 889–90.
———. "Arnold Berliner." *Die Naturwissenschaften* 33 (15 November 1946) : 257–58.
———. "Bemerkungen zu 'J. Stark, Zu den Kämpfen in der Physik während der Hitler-Zeit.'" *Physikalische Blätter* 3 (1947) : 272–73.
———. "Fritz Haber." *Die Naturwissenschaften* 22 (16 February 1934) : 97.
———. "Die Kriegstätigkeit der deutschen Physiker." *Physikalische Blätter* 3 (1947) : 424–25.
Lenard, Philipp. "Ein grosser Tag für die Naturforschung." *Völkischer Beobachter*, 13 May 1933, zweites Beiblatt.
———. "Gedanken zu deutscher Naturwissenschaft." *Volk im Werden* 4 (1936) : 381–83.
———. "Johannes Stark zum 70. Geburtstag." *Völkischer Beobachter*, Munich, 15 April 1944, p. 4.
———. "Wilhelm Wien." *Völkischer Beobachter*, Munich, 12 September 1928, p. 2.
Lenard, Philipp, and Stark, Johannes. "Hitlergeist und Wissenschaft." *Grossdeutsche Zeitung*, 8 May 1924, p. 1.
Mentzel, Rudolf. "Deutsche Forschung im Kriege." *Physikalische Blätter* 1 (August 1944) : 103–06.
Menzel, Willi. "Deutsche Physik und jüdische Physik." *Völkischer Beobachter*, 29 January 1936, p. 5.
Mitteilungen der Gesellschaft Deutscher Naturforscher und Aerzte, 1931–39.
Müller, "Jüdischer Geist in der Physik." *Zeitschrift für die gesamte Naturwissenschaft* 5 (August 1939) : 162–75.

————. "Die Lage der theoretischen Physik an den Universitäten." *Zeitschrift für die gesamte Naturwissenschaft* 6 (November/December 1940) : 281–98.

Die Naturwissenschaften. Annual reports of the Kaiser Wilhelm-Gesellschaft zur Förderung der Wissenschaften, 1929–40.

"Nazi 'Purge' of the Universities: A Long List of Dismissals." *The Manchester Guardian Weekly,* 19 May 1933, p. 399.

Nolte, Ernst. "Zur Typologie des Verhaltens der Hochschullehrer im Dritten Reich." In *Aus Politik und Geschichte.* Supplement to *Das Parlament* 46 (17 November 1965) : 3–14.

"Parole: Wissenschaft." *Frankfurter Zeitung,* 10 November 1936, p. 3.

Peierls, Rudolf. "Atomic Germans." Review of W. Heisenberg, *Physics and Beyond. The New York Review of Books* 16 (1 July 1971) : 23–24.

Pinl, Max, and Furtmüller, Lux. "Mathematicians under Hitler." *Yearbook of the Leo Baeck Institute* 18 (1973) : 129–82.

Planck, Max. "Mein Besuch bei Hitler." *Physikalische Blätter* 3 (1947) : 143.

Ramsauer, Carl. "Eingabe an Rust." *Physikalische Blätter* 3 (1947) : 43–46.

————. "Zur Geschichte der Deutschen Physikalischen Gesellschaft in der Hitlerzeit." *Physikalische Blätter* 3 (1947) : 110–14.

Seier, Hellmut. "Der Rektor als Führer: Zur Hochschulpolitik des Reichserziehungsministeriums 1934–1945." *Vierteljahrshefte für Zeitgeschichte* 12 (1964) : 105–46.

Sitzungsberichte der Preussischen Akademie der Wissenschaften, 1932–38.

Stark, Johannes. "The Attitude of the German Government toward Science." *Nature* 133 (21 April 1934) : 614.

————. "Experimentelle Fortschritte der Atomforschung." *Zeitschrift für die gesamte Naturwissenschaft* 4 (November 1938) : 289–313.

————. "International Status and Obligations of Science." *Nature* 133 (24 February 1934) : 290.

————. "Organisation der physikalischen Forschung." *Zeitschrift für technische Physik* 14 (1933) : 433–35.

————. "Philipp Lenard als deutscher Naturforscher." *Nationalsozialistische Monatshefte,* Heft 71 (February 1936) : 106–12.

————. "Physikalische Wirklichkeit und dogmatische Atomtheorien." *Physikalische Zeitschrift* 39 (1 March 1938) : 189–92.

————. "Stellungnahme von Prof. Dr. J. Stark." *Völkischer Beobachter,* Berlin, 28 February 1936, p. 6.

————. "Zu den Kämpfen in der Physik während der Hitler-Zeit." *Physikalische Blätter* 3 (1947) : 271–72.

————. "Zur Kritik der Bohrschen Theorie der Lichtemission." *Jahrbuch der Radioaktivität und Elektronik* 17 (23 December 1920) : 161–73.

Stark, Johannes, et al. " 'Weisse Juden' in der Wissenschaft," *Das Schwarze Korps,* 15 July 1937, p. 6.

Strätz, Hans-Wolfgang. "Die studentische 'Aktion wider den undeutschen Geist' im Frühjahr 1933." *Vierteljahrshefte für Zeitgeschichte* 6 (1968) : 347–72.

Thüring, Bruno. "Albert Einsteins Umsturzversuch in der Physik und seine inneren Möglichkeiten und Ursachen." *Forschungen zur Judenfrage* 4 (1940) : 134–62.

———. "Physik und Astronomie in jüdischen Händen.' *Zeitschrift für die gesamte Naturwissenschaft* 3 (May/June 1937) : 55–70.

Tolischus, Otto D. "Nazis Would Junk Theoretic Physics." *The New York Times,* 9 March 1936, p. 19.

Verhandlungen der Deutschen Physikalischen Gesellschaft. Reports of the autumn physicists' convention (Physikertagung) held biannually 1921–29 and annually 1930–40 (no convention in 1939).

———. Membership list published at the beginning of each year, 1920–36. Published separately under title *Mitgliederliste der Deutschen Physikalischen Gesellschaft,* 1937 onward.

"Vorträge und Diskussionen von der 86. Naturforscherversammlung in Nauheim vom 19.–25. September 1920." *Physikalische Zeitschrift* 21 (1/15 December 1920) : 649–99.

Wesch, Ludwig. "Lenards Werk—Vorbild zukünftiger Forschung." *Zeitschrift für die gesamte Naturwissenschaft* 8 (May/June 1942) : 101–14.

———. "Philipp Lenard—Vorbild und Verpflichtung." *Zeitschrift für die gesamte Naturwissenschaft* 3 (May/June 1937) : 42–45.

Westphal, Wilhelm H. "Das Physikalische Institut der TU Berlin." *Physikalische Blätter* 11 (1955) : 554–58.

Weyl, Hermann. "Emmy Noether." In *Gesammelte Abhandlungen,* edited by K. Chandrasekharan. Berlin, New York: Springer, 3 (1968): 425–44.

Zeitschrift für die gesamte Naturwissenschaft. Vols. 1–10, 1935/36–44.

Zeitschrift für technische Physik. Annual reports of the Deutsche Gesellschaft für technische Physik, 1920, 1930–40.

Index